Melville's

Evermoving

Dawn

Melville's

CENTENNIAL ESSAYS

Evermoving

EDITED BY JOHN BRYANT AND ROBERT MILDER

Dawn

THE KENT STATE UNIVERSITY PRESS

KENT, OHIO & LONDON, ENGLAND

Library of Congress Catalog Card Number 96-42483
ISBN 0-87338-562-4
Manufactured in the United States of America

04 03 02 01 00 99 98 97   5 4 3 2 1

Library of Congress Cataloging-in-Publication Data
Melville's evermoving dawn : centennial essays / edited by John Bryant
and Robert Milder.
p.   cm.
Includes bibliographical references (p.) and index.
ISBN 0-87338-562-4 (cloth : alk. paper) ∞
1. Melville, Herman, 1819–1891—Criticism and interpretation—
Congresses.   I. Bryant, John, 1949–   .   II. Milder, Robert.
PS2387.M425   1997
813'.3—DC20   96-42483

British Library Cataloging-in-Publication data are available.

Dedicated to the memory of

Hennig Cohen

1920–1996

For spite of all the Indian-summery sunlight on the hither side of Hawthorne's soul, the other side—like the dark half of the physical sphere—is shrouded in a blackness, ten times black. But this darkness but gives more effect to the ever-moving dawn, that forever advances through it, and circumnavigates his world.

—Herman Melville, "Hawthorne and His *Mosses*"

Contents

Preface

ROBERT MILDER

The essays in this volume are the partial fruit of three separate celebrations arranged by The Melville Society in honor of the 1991 centennial of Melville's death and organized and overseen by the chair of the Centennial Committee, Thomas F. Heffernan, along with Ruth Degenhardt of the Berkshire Athenaeum (Pittsfield), John Bryant, and Mary K. Bercaw Edwards. The first conference, held on May 16–18 in Pittsfield, Massachusetts, not far from Melville's Arrowhead home, was organized by Ms. Degenhardt and hosted by the Athenaeum; Program Chair Robert Milder defined the topics and assembled the panels of speakers. The second commemoration, a series of activities and programs organized by Professors Heffernan and Bryant, took place in New York City during "Melville Week" (September 22–28) as proclaimed by Mayor David Dinkins; it featured sessions on scholarly and textual problems, on Melville and race, and on Melville's *Pierre* and Pierre's New York. Participating institutions included the American Museum of Natural History, the New York Public Library, the Schomburg Center for Research in African American Culture, and the New-York Historical Society. The final conference, arranged by Professor Heffernan and staged in the theater of the National Archives in Washington, D.C., on October 7, focused on Melville as a sailor in 1840s America and as a customs officer after the Civil War. Other centennial programs, unrelated to The Melville Society's, were sponsored by groups at Siena College, at the Fairhaven (Massachusetts) Public Library, at UCLA, and in Madison, Wisconsin.

Held in mid-May amidst a Berkshire world as "green and golden" as Pierre's Saddle Meadows, the Pittsfield Conference was a festival of Melvillean geniality and fine talk. Yet one could hardly help wondering how Melville, should he return, would have looked on his admirers as they analyzed and psychoanalyzed him, constructed and deconstructed his texts. One hopes we would have fared better under his eye than those commentators on Homer and Aristotle in *Gulliver's Travels,* forced to keep their distance in the afterworld "through a Consciousness of Shame and Guilt, because they had so horribly represented the Meaning of those Authors to Posterity." Melville descendants at the Athenaeum and later on the grounds of Arrowhead itself were universally gracious to us, as was actor Jack Putnam, a Melville look-alike who read from "Loomings," "The Lightening-Rod Man," and Father Mapple's sermon and kept us happily abashed as he strolled the lawn and eavesdropped on our chat with an air of benign privilege. One could almost imagine Melville himself, who once feared immortalization "as a 'man who had lived among the cannibals,'" gazing down on us with a quizzical Whitmanesque smile, "Who knows but I am enjoying this? / Who knows but I am as good as looking at you now, for all you cannot see me?"

In lieu of such a hovering authorial presence to remind us of the purposes of the day—not adulation (which Melville would have scorned) but homage to the intensity of a life and the nuanced complexity of its literary record—we had only one another, bound together by our participation in an enterprise grown astoundingly diverse and by a common debt to the first great generation of Melvilleans, represented at Pittsfield by Harrison Hayford and Walter E. Bezanson. Along with F. O. Matthiessen, whose *American Renaissance* was enjoying its half-centennial, the scholar-critics of the early 1940s—Hayford, Bezanson, Sealts, Gilman, Davis, Foster, Wright; Leyda and Howard would join them a few years later; Henry A. Murray anteceded all—had established Melville studies on the basis of a respect for evidence and a sympathetic but cautious willingness to speculate that distinguished them at once from the literalness of resolutely empirical scholarship and the irresponsibility of loose conjecture and self-serving critical ingenuity. And yet "each age," as Emerson said, "must write its own books; or rather, each generation for the next succeeding." How would our books, we had to wonder, look during the Melville sesquicentennial of 2041?

   In selecting essays for the present collection, the editors have tried to offer a broad and multivocal assessment of what, after fifty years of academic study, Melville scholarship and criticism have achieved and where they seemed to be heading. Challenges to the canon and new directions in critical theory and practice have made literary commemorations an occasion for stock-taking as much as a celebration of origins. Those who came to Pittsfield, New York, and Washington did so to honor Melville but also, as Melville would have understood, to take their bearings anew in an unusually centrifugal intellectual age. Like all centennials, but more self-consciously, perhaps, than most, the Melville centennial of 1991 was a Janus-faced event of retrospect and prospect, an effort to preserve the organic continuity of Melville studies even as scholar-critics moved ahead from the long valued and the authoritatively known to the terra incognita of the critical future.

Abbreviations

The following short titles and abbreviations have been used in parenthetical documentation throughout the volume's essays.

Log	Jay Leyda, ed. *The Melville Log: A Documentary Life of Herman Melville, 1819–1891.* New York: Harcourt, Brace, 1951; rpt. with supplement, New York: Gordian, 1969.
NN *Clarel*	*Clarel: A Poem and Pilgrimage in the Holy Land.* By Herman Melville. Ed. Walter E. Bezanson, Harrison Hayford, Alma A. MacDougall, Hershel Parker, and G. Thomas Tanselle. Evanston and Chicago: Northwestern UP and the Newberry Library, 1991.
NN *Correspondence*	*Correspondence.* By Herman Melville. Ed. Lynn Horth, Harrison Hayford, Hershel Parker, and G. Thomas Tanselle. Evanston and Chicago: Northwestern UP and the Newberry Library, 1993.

NN *Journals*   *Journals.* By Herman Melville. Ed. Howard Horsford, Harrison Hayford, Hershel Parker, and G. Thomas Tanselle. Evanston and Chicago: Northwestern UP and the Newberry Library, 1989.

NN *Mardi*   *Mardi; And a Voyage Thither.* By Herman Melville. Ed. Harrison Hayford, Hershel Parker, and G. Thomas Tanselle. Evanston and Chicago: Northwestern UP and the Newberry Library, 1970.

NN *MD*   *Moby-Dick.* By Herman Melville. Ed. Harrison Hayford, Hershel Parker, and G. Thomas Tanselle. Evanston and Chicago: Northwestern UP and the Newberry Library, 1988.

NN *Pierre*   *Pierre: or, the Ambiguities.* By Herman Melville. Ed. Harrison Hayford, Hershel Parker, and G. Thomas Tanselle. Evanston and Chicago: Northwestern UP and the Newberry Library, 1971.

NN *PT*   *The Piazza Tales, and Other Prose Pieces (1839–1860).* By Herman Melville. Ed. Harrison Hayford, Hershel Parker, and G. Thomas Tanselle. Evanston and Chicago: Northwestern UP and the Newberry Library, 1987.

NN *Typee*   *Typee, or a Peep at Polynesian Life.* By Herman Melville. Ed. Harrison Hayford, Hershel Parker, and G. Thomas Tanselle. Evanston and Chicago: Northwestern UP and the Newberry Library, 1967.

NN *WJ*   *White-Jacket.* By Herman Melville. Ed. Harrison Hayford, Hershel Parker, and G. Thomas Tanselle. Evanston and Chicago: Northwestern UP and the Newberry Library, 1970.

Introduction

1

The Persistence of Melville:
Representative Writer for a Multicultural Age

JOHN BRYANT

I

Melville's Evermoving Dawn brings together twenty essays on the life, creativity, and impact of Herman Melville. Occasioned by the 1991 observation of the centennial of Melville's death, the collection is diverse, and yet its diversity signifies a deeper coherency. This volume represents some of the best critical studies being written today on one of America's representative artists.

Of course, the claim that Melville, or any particular author, is "representative" is bound to draw fire, for as the nation's canon wars have reminded us, we take a perilous step when we surrender our cultural identity to a set of representative "classics." Indeed, the very notion of representation challenges the possibility of democracy even as it enacts democracy. In a culture that has always been diverse and always on the brink of disunity, the question of what part shall represent the whole of us has been a continual, in fact biennial, reminder of the fragile status of our political being in what is essentially a perpetually revolutionary society. Who will stand for me? Who *can* speak for me? These anxious interrogatives remind us of the startling fact that in a representative democracy we make synecdoche, a mere fictive trope, into a serious social obligation, one that becomes for any minority an equally serious threat. Parts can never speak for wholes, no more than a thumb or even a heart or head can stand for the body. For that matter, in a culture as diverse as our own, there is a significant doubt that a body itself, a single coherent political corpus, is at all real. Thus, the synecdochal foundation of representative democracy seems at best a myth: There are no responsive parts; there is no whole. But myths have their utility. And despite it all, we send our representatives to Congress every other year, and we seek to redefine America along some larger coherency that may allow partisans to become participants.

As with politics, so too with literary history. No single artist, like Melville, can ever represent an entire culture. The resistance to synecdoche is healthy. While there is nothing particularly wrong with reading the works of a singularly talented "dead white male" such as Melville, there is no profit in insisting that we read him because he is "America's Shakespeare," or even a "saint" in the pantheon of American literature. Such hero worship denies us the critical distancing that allows us a chance to discover the kinds of unanticipated flexibilities in a writer that would make him or her truly representative of the kind of humanity that gives meaning to culture. If a volume such as this is to achieve credibility in its claim for Melville's representativeness, it too must achieve a strong degree of coverage. Indeed, the contributors to this volume come not merely to praise Melville but to probe the meaning of his fictive acts, the phenomenon of his presence, the mysteries of his creativity, his uses of history and mind, and the inescapable factors of gender, race, and ideology in his work. Above all, this volume announces through its diversity of approaches the variety of ways that we may use Melville to understand ourselves, and to this degree it may be said that it is a representative sample of today's view of Melville and our culture.

To be sure, the collection does not exhaust all possible critical approaches available over the past two decades; it is necessarily selective. But our principles of selection were broad. And if the volume embraces the particular problems of historicism, race, psychology, biography, reading, and manuscript and edition, and these problems only, it is because in casting our net to find the best that might be offered during one year—the centennial of Melville's death—these are the species of loose fish ensnared. High in yield from that year were the kinds of historicist and rhetorical approaches found in these pages; nonexistent were poststructural and deconstructionist readings. Their absence may be a sign of the sample; their vogue is waning as the New Historicism grows.

Whatever our collection has to offer, our willingness to accept Melville as a "representative artist" in an age that has so urgently called cultural and artistic representation into question rests upon a readiness to grow beyond certain critical presumptions. The concept of a representative artist seems doomed to fail in this postmodern age in which form and language are seen to operate independently of the conditions of their creation and creator, where an artist can represent (as Foucault tells us) only a limited and idiosyncratic version of meaning. Better that we look for a representative unconsciousness in our culture (if such a thing can be), or a representative reader, or no representative at all. There seems, after all, to be little support in today's critical community for the notion that a Melville can speak for the culture any more than a Wheatley or Jacobs or Hurston, a Douglass or DuBois or Wright, a Dickinson or Stowe or Cather. Melville's consciousness represents one consciousness and only that. And this, too, is the fate of consciousness.

But it is time to take stock of this limiting view, for without returning to an uncritically sexist, Emersonian presumption of a culture of "Representative Men," and without rejecting recent advances in reader-response approaches, we can entertain the following possibilities: that some writers have a consciousness which in speaking *of* the Other can speak *for* others; that such writers may speak in diverse voices and through multiple forms, and that by dint of this diversity these artists reflect the conflicts in language, culture, and self and thereby speak representatively for us all. Melville is one such diversity.

Consider the roles he played: traveler, ethnographer, allegorist, humorist, tragedian, philosopher, closet dramatist, psychologist, biographer, novelist, talespinner, and poet. He was, like his confidence man, a cosmopolitan artist, not only because he experimented with so many fictive forms but because he explored so fully the range of his voice. He could speak volumes. And most compelling, he could speak the forbidden—not just the blasphemous plunges into nihilism but the secret voicings of his pansexuality, from his dalliances with Toby, Fayaway, and Marnoo in *Typee* to the exuberant celebration of homosexual longing and heterosexual gestation in *Moby-Dick* to the frank sexual "alarms" of Pierre to the loss, denial, and attack in *Clarel* and *Billy Budd*. Few writers of his time made so much love. That these varied acts are often deeply submerged in a form of dramatized symbolism, ambivalence, circumlocution, and even silence makes his writings all the more alluring.

Melville was white, but he knew the Other. This seemed to be part of his initiating impulse to write in the first place. He saw in Typee the gaze of the native, longed for acceptance and yet sensed his own intrusion. He pierced (one of his favorite words) to the heart of such alien encounters, thus making them—the silent incommunicable stares between the savage and civilized—a touchstone for America's postcolonial racial interactions and interdependencies. His essaying of Darkness and Whiteness in *Moby-Dick* clinches Melville's genius for Nobel laureate Toni Morrison who has marveled over the writer's lonely and singular confrontation with American racism. Indeed, few white writers of the nineteenth century drew black characters against the stereotype as well as Melville's rendering of the castaway Pip, that little black seed of salvation offered up to Ahab and all white readers—and yet allegorical Pip seems real not so much because of any inscrutable black consciousness but because of his quite rational madness that penetrates to the core of our humanity and urges all readers, white and black, toward a transracial commonality.

Laid out before us, these facts of Melville's range and diversity are astonishing. Add to them the facts of his life and literary career. Spanning most of the nineteenth century, the seventy-two-year-old author witnessed the very upheavals and devolutions of the "American Experiment"—Civil War, capitalist expansion, and empire—that were the seeds of conflict for our present cultural condition. And contrary to the general assumption, Melville wrote continuously throughout his life. Failing to publish for the masses, he somehow forgot to perish. The silent decades after the failure of *Battle-Pieces* (1866) are full of production—poetry mostly, including the magisterial *Clarel* (a record of Victorian thought set in the Holy Land), but also *Billy Budd*. Melville's perseverance is a part of his diversity. He wrote for an audience even when they were not listening, and he continued to experiment and evolve. The creative act called *Billy Budd* began as a nostalgic poem with a small headnote and grew with incremental prose additions of one character and another past tale to a short novel with an appended poem at the end, "Billy in the Darbies," the artifact seed that started the whole process rolling. Both Melville's career—novelist turned poet turned novelist-poet—and the unique evolution of his creative process within the literary marketplace serve as fascinating allegories of the conflicts between artist and society and between the artist and himself. Small wonder, then, that we may call this always changing creator a "representative artist."

Melville is representative because he is a diversity; because his literary cosmopolitanism extended beyond the mercantilism of his father and the Calvinism of his mother to a belief that his art could speak both regionally and universally; and because he suffered the doubts of his mother, the common-enough loss of his father at an early age, but also the uncommon loss of his suicide son Malcolm. What is remarkable is that Melville was able to live with the stunning pain, mystery, doubt, and self-recriminations associated with "self-slaying" Malcolm and to convert it years later into certain poems and *Billy Budd*. The family side of Melville—his role as a son, husband, and father—remains one of the most fascinating, still-unexhausted wellsprings of Melville biography.

And there is Melville's relation to his reader, always a problematic matter. Like Shakespeare, Wordsworth, Longfellow, or Hawthorne, Melville adopted an amiable line designed for popular consumption and immediate accessibility. But his designs never fully worked. Perhaps the anger and anguish in his life offset the geniality; or maybe the pressurized fusion of anguish and humor in his writing, a sort of tense repose, simply threw readers off balance. If writing gave Melville great release, reading him rarely gave readers great comfort. For all his desire to sell and to clarify social commitment, his personal narratives—even the popular *Typee*—lack the gore and horror of Mary Rowlandson's captivity narrative or Frederick Douglass's slave narrative. When Harriet Beecher Stowe strove forthrightly to warn Americans of the disasters of slavery, and addressed her readers in 1851 (the year of *Moby-Dick's* publication) directly without irony or seemingly any care for unity of voice, her sentiment and sincerity (richly conceived and effective in their own ways) won her the kind of best-seller acclaim Melville could only dream of. This style and form—the popular "*other* way," as he called it—were not his way, try as he might. Rather than write an *Uncle Tom's Cabin*, he worked his own experiences of whaling into a psychological and social drama so deeply textured and exuberant in its private discovery of symbol that readers failed to see his own clear warnings of demagoguery and impending civil war. The book did not sell.

The fact that Melville was not popular with readers in his day is enough to discount for some the author's cultural centrality. But since most writers fail to find markets (perhaps some more justly so than others), failure in the marketplace can surely be taken as a legitimate sign of an author's representationality. The success of a Longfellow, Susan Warner, or Twain (and they had their failures, too) can tell us a great deal about what a reading culture wants to hear and how they like to hear it, but only the colossal failures of a Melville will give us insight into what a culture most deeply fears and the styles it will not accept. Melville's swaggering remark in his review of Hawthorne that "Failure is the true test of greatness" (NN *PT* 248) was a convenient bit of proleptic posturing anticipating the publication of *Moby-Dick*, but it also acknowledges the struggle to find voice and audience that goes to the heart of any rhetorical enterprise. For Melville each new book was a renewed attempt to shape a reader to fit his roving, continually "essaying" mind. *Typee* is anxious to please us and yet sting; *Mardi* preaches politics in a metaphysical line; *Moby-Dick* pits Ishmaelian lyricism against Ahab's dramaturgy, leaving us stunned; *Pierre* batters us with the voicelessness of god and art; *The Confidence-Man* deserts us; *Billy Budd* hurts us. There is always some challenge for us as readers to catch up. We are participants in the creation of meaning; we are victims of narrative cons.

It is not that Melville is for the thoughtful reader only. He is for those who think they have nothing but who in reading discover they have much. The pleasure of Melville's texts is that in reading them we participate in discovery. Melville lets us find hidden meaning but also hidden selves, and we rejoice in the uncovering as if we created the meanings and selves on our own. At least this is what Melville felt in response to Sophia Hawthorne's description of her reading of *Moby-Dick*. And in works like *The Confidence-Man*, which give up symbolism for voiceless and detached narration, we swim in Melville's silences, feeling the palpable, drenching weight of his sea of doubt and never fully comprehending the dimension of that sea itself. We come in this reading experience to enact the struggle for awareness that the writer himself—any writer and hence any reader—may feel. Most writers will feel the failure to engage language and audience, and many modern writers have made it the subject of their work, but few like Melville invite the reader to fail along with him. It is an odd embrace—Come fail with me. And this rhetorical aspect of his diversity makes him representative too.

A final facet is the relevance of Melville's reputation. The issue is not *that* he is a Famous Writer but *how* he got to be famous. The derogation that Melville is the white-est and male-est and dead-est of dead white male writers persists in certain corners of academia like a tiresome dustball that refuses to be swept away. (One critic, Paul Lauter, has argued cogently but somewhat narrowly that Melville was resurrected by 1920s academics in order to "masculinize" American literature.[1]) And perhaps this is understandable. Melville was not popular in his day. His success came immediately with *Typee* and petered out with each successive work—each brilliant and readable in its own way, each capable of success with some later audience, and yet each less than remunerative in the 1840s and 1850s. After his turn to poetry in the 1860s proved to be a career, if not artistic, error, he enjoyed an occasional lift only when one or two generally radical readers rediscovered him through a particular book that he had long since worked beyond; they wrote to tell him how great he *had been* not to ask what he was writing *now*. He was on the verge of a small revival of interest in his work when he died in 1891, still ignored and virtually unknown.

The Melville we know today was resurrected thirty years later when other white male academics, now dead, "revived" him and assigned him to students. Melville caught on first in the University. But from the 1890s on, discrete readerships—socialists, artists, gays, castaways and renegades like C. L. R. James, and various nonacademics (some decidedly female)—kept a flame for Melville burning (NN *MD* 732–54). D. H. Lawrence's inclusion of Melville in his *Classic American Literature* (1919), Raymond Weaver's biography (1921), and the discovery of *Billy Budd* in 1924 brought Melville into the limelight. *Moby-Dick* became a successful movie three times in the following thirty years, and now you cannot peruse a backwater restaurant guide without finding a Melville Pub or Moby Dick seafood eatery. Everyone recognizes Moby Dick as a menacing white whale; Ahab or some angry man with one leg is the cartoonist's archetype; "Call me Fred," or Irving, or Joe, is a perennial gagline. Few pieces of writing have ever had such an impact on the popular imagination (Inge). But few read the novel unless it is assigned, and herein lies that dust-ball of resentment. The once-obscure and ignored Herman Melville has become a canonized saint, and his writings are "classic" when they are, in fact, quite idiosyncratic and perhaps justly deserving in the nineteenth century of their obscurity. If Melville is so representative, what and whom does he represent?

But the bankruptcy of this objection lies in its blindness to the fact that Melville's startling revival was itself a canon-busting event and that Melville's modern champions insisted upon his inclusion not necessarily to exclude others (although I fear that Longfellow, Irving, Stowe, Whittier, and others may have suffered at his expense) but to expand the field of relevant writers to include Melville's radicalism, his attacks upon conservatism, authority, and imperialism. Melville was the ideal Jeffersonian artist for modern radicals willing to settle for a New Deal. And while it is the dialectical nature of radicalism to cast off forefathers and precursors, today's revisioning of the American canon would do well to resurrect Melville, once again, but in new terms. It may be (although I hope not) that Melville has passed his mid-twentieth-century utility as a hero of liberal democracy. But by dint of his diversity Melville contains a variety of radicalisms, and each makes him still relevant, still useful for today's readers intent upon a deeper inspection of the workings of a democratic culture. If politics was the initiating factor for Melville's revival, it was a politics of inclusion at work (to include the commoner, the abused, the isolato of all sexual orientations, races, beliefs, or nonbeliefs), one that today's historicists should emulate.

Why, then, is Melville "representative"? The diversity of his mind and rhetorical skill would seem to be enough to justify the term. The fact of his astonishing revival epitomizes the inevitability of revolution inherent in democratic culture: what was kept down so long shall rise. And this, too, would seem enough. But finally, Melville is and shall persist in being a representative artist simply because he continues to be useful to us. Here is the solid ineluctability of critical pragmatism. Writers and readers (students and teachers) will sustain Melville because they can use him to articulate a deeper and clearer sense of ourselves in the context of our culture. His work has become and shall continue to be a catalyst for the discussion of what America is, how one creates in the democracy, and what constitutes "greatness" in a canon. Melville's diversity, his experimentation, his cosmopolitanism, the odd turns and shape of his career—all these have lasting relevance because they expose the perpetual needs, conflicts, and nature of self, art, and democracy in our lives. This is the key to the persistence of Melville.

It is a lugubrious, even ironic, thought that this volume is meant to observe the hundredth anniversary of the death of an author. Such observances are often utterly gratuitous, and I suppose at this point one could mark the centennial of just about any event in Melville's life or reputation. (The government of French Polynesia, for instance, sponsored the sesquicentennial celebration of Melville's 1842 ship-jumping on Nukuhiva with the 1992 dedication of the only monument to Melville in the world.) But it is the notion of Melville's persistence through his diversity that allows us to convert our 1991 obituary observation into an all-embracing celebration. Melville's death did not put a period to his influence or utility. Indeed, he offers a kind of perpetual intellectual and artistic luster to our culture. Thus, our title, *Melville's Evermoving Dawn,* is particularly apt. The image, drawn from Melville's fulsome review of Hawthorne's *Mosses from an Old Manse,* was conceived to body forth the marginal and liminal condition of Hawthorne's art (NN *PT* 243). It is neither complete darkness nor complete sunlight, but that in-between state of mind always moving out of despair and toward redemption, always giving "equal eye" to the diverse topography of our existence. Somewhere on earth and at all times there is this condition of dawn; and in its ever-western movement it circumnavigates the globe touching all cultures. In speaking of Hawthorne,

Melville was in fact speaking of himself. For him, that evermoving crescive moment was the essence of art. It is, as well, the essence of Melville.

II

The essays that open this volume are a complementary pair. Written by two of the most highly regarded scholar-critics in the field of Melville studies, they provide an overview of Melville from two elemental points of view: writer and reader. Walter Bezanson's "Uncommon Common Sailor" converts the familiar ground of Melville's sailing years into a moving study of the young sailor's compulsion to write. Based on his keynote speech to the Pittsfield Centennial Conference, Bezanson investigates the familial, social, and experimental forces that shaped the writer and his work culminating in *Moby-Dick*. Focusing exclusively on *Moby-Dick* but from a different perspective, Merton M. Sealts poses the question "Whose Book Is *Moby-Dick*?" and artfully responds as a means of gauging decades of divergent readings. The shift from Bezanson's writer to Sealts's reader demonstrates the dynamism of Melville's text: it is the fusion of creative process and reader response. Both share in the making of "Melville," and the essays that complete our volume are designed in their individual ways to take the pulse of that fusion.

The remaining essays fall into six distinct categories. The first three sections—on History, Race, and Personality—address larger social contexts of successively narrowed focus. The second three—on Biography, Creative Process and Texts, and Reading—turn our attention to an even narrower but dynamic double focus. Here the organizing principle involves the problem of how a writer creates for family and self and how readers may transform those creations (in particular the problematic novel *Pierre*). Taken as a whole, these two sections of the collection explore Contexts and Texts of the fusions of Melville's creativity and audience response.

Melville in Context

First is the historicist's problem of Melville's relation to the culture of his day, and with Lawrence Buell and Wai Chee Dimock we have representative examples of two historicist approaches—the traditional and the new—which in coming together establish a discourse on how we may *read historically*. Actually, Buell and Dimock are not far apart in sensibility; both attempt to locate

Melville not so much in specific historical events but in the larger historical conflicts that shape a culture. Buell's Melville confronts the culture's "post-colonial anxiety" by shaping texts to address both American (nationalist) and European (cosmopolitan) audiences. This new internationalism allows us to find even more (socioeconomic) complexities in Melville's famously indeterminate rhetoric. Dimock focuses more closely on a single work ("The Paradise of Bachelors and Tartarus of Maids"), a single mansion in Melville's mind (greater awareness), and a single manifestation of culture (the woman worker). For her, Melville's micromanagement of words reveals a breakdown in language that in turn signals the inability of art to "encapsulate" history. Both Buell and Dimock remark upon a certain "muddiness" in Melville's ironies and indirections, and the degrees to which both critics find a revealing pathology in this linguistic mud indicates both the potentials and limits of art as a rhetorical extension of historicized experience. In this regard, Buell with his "transnational" approach is perhaps more "new" than "traditional," and Dimock goes beyond "new" altogether to argue for the "incompleteness" of historicism. Such historicist constructions and implied deconstructions of Melville epitomize the volatility of the historicist debate in today's critical discourse.

In turning to the issue of race, we take the problems of historicism to "a little lower layer" where "self" and "other" reside in both anticipation and denial of a merge. Here we see Melville not only as an artist in the context of his time but as a consciousness rooted in the conditions of being and the structures of mind. We can only know a thing by its opposite, Ishmael asserts; self is defined by other. Thus, ontology impinges directly upon historicity, for self and other are necessarily coordinates of time and emanations of the past. They are occasioned by movements of power, the taking of colonies and of slaves, the migration and mingling of cultures, the hyphenation of ethnic identity. If we are to read Melville historically, then we must read him as well in terms of race, and this simple imperative was the organizing principle behind the 1991 Centennial Conference on Melville and Race at the New York Public Library's Schomburg Center.

More than any other issue, race is the crucial defining element of the American democratic experiment because it has us ask questions that probe the foundations of being, freedom, and equality. How do we define ourselves—as products of a given ethnicity or as individuals in a larger unifying culture that transcends region and ethnicity? Are we ever free to "escape" our ethnicity, and what are the consequences of a cosmopolitan freedom that grasps at the one by an embracing of the many? If true equality comes only when we begin to see that our sense of being is shaped by a consciousness of the other, and yet if the distribution of power invariably detaches one from another, then can the races ever find a mutual interdependency? What astonishes us about Melville is not his refreshingly frank grasp of the problems of race but his penetration toward the other mind and indeed his articulate frustration in not being able to pierce to its root. There is in Melville always the warm spark and hug of Queequeg but always, too, the impenetrable stare of the Typees and Babo.

Those in search of the "political Melville" have existed since the beginning of the Melville revival, but scholarship has been slow to probe directly into the matter of race. To be sure, scholars as early as Matthiessen have touched on the author's involvement with slavery as it impinged upon liberal democracy. In misreading some of Melville's more deeply ironic texts, scholars as perceptive as Stanley Williams were frankly misguided in their embarrassment over Melville's presumed lapses into racism. But not until the 1960s with the work of Sidney Kaplan, and later in 1980 with Carolyn Karcher's *Shadow Over Promised Land,* did critics begin a more systematic assessment of Melville's cagier strategies, especially his unusual tale of a slave revolt, "Benito Cereno." If literary scholars were slow to acknowledge Melville's subtle unpinning of racism, other writers caught up in the immediacy of racialism in their own lives were not. As panel moderator Henry Louis Gates, Jr., noted in his introductory comments at the Schomburg program, novelist D. H. Lawrence sensed the deeper connection to race, and social critic C. L. R. James used Melville during his McCarthy-era incarceration as a touchstone for the spiritual survival of all minorities.

Certainly one of the most striking aspects of *Moby-Dick* is the way that racial consciousness becomes the crucial point on which the tragedy turns; it shapes our response to Ahab's alienation and Ishmael's comic integrations. At the center is black cabin boy Pip, who, temporarily cast away at sea, witnesses the emptiness of existence, goes mad, and yet becomes the thread tying mad Ahab back to humanity. In describing him, Melville begins in stereotype but builds through, around, and finally away from his audience's vile assumptions about black consciousness. Compared "in outer aspect" to his white counterpart, Dough-Boy, Pip is "like a black pony," but beneath the animalism, he is "over tender-hearted, . . . very bright, with that pleasant, genial, jolly brightness peculiar to his tribe" (NN *MD* 411–12). Once introducing this "tribal" stereotype, Melville turns on his readers. Listen to his special appeal: "Nor smile so, while I write that this little black was brilliant, for even blackness has its brilliancy; behold yon lustrous ebony, paneled in king's cabinets. But Pip loved life, and all life's peaceable securities; so that the panic-striking business in which he had somehow unaccountably become entrapped, had most sadly blurred his brightness" (412). Melville's rhetorical strategy hinges upon three words—"Nor smile so"—that signal his attempt to transform his white audience's denial of anything "brilliant" about African Americans. Each subsequent phrasing is a measured step dissolving racist assumptions: the elevation of blackness to the less pernicious but equally stereotypical monarchist associations (king's cabinets), the lowering to a commoner's geniality (love and peace), and the plunge into the panic-striking horrors of his "entrapment" (slavery) that erase the brightness we would have initially denied. Thus, by a remarkable prestidigitation, Melville has white readers accepting Pip's humanity at the very moment of its annihilation. We come to feel the Other most deeply just as he is gone. Such "ungraspable phantoms," like the phantom tingling of life Ahab thinks he feels in his lost leg, are what drive Ahab mad. The dramatic irony is that Pip is the mechanism Melville chooses to lure Ahab back to sanity. Pip (like a son to the orphaned captain) even offers to be Ahab's new leg.

In "Our Crowd, Their Crowd," novelist David Bradley acknowledges his strong debt to Melville in his own richly creative life, and in particular in his award-winning novel *The Chaneysville Incident*. But his critical observations on "Our Crowd" writers (i.e., the minority "out" group) trying to reach "Their Crowd" audiences (the established "in" group) provide a succinct description of any writer's condition when he or she sets out to "explain" him or herself. Moreover, it is a rhetorical and aesthetic condition that parallels the social condition of any minority group seeking to gain a voice in an alien society, seeking to inform, manage, and manipulate readers into a deeper understanding of the Other and one's self. Bradley's insights into creativity and ethnicity offer an important avenue of transracial unity amid today's disturbing polarizations.

H. Bruce Franklin's concise and comprehensive analysis of Melville's narrative strategy in "Benito Cereno" reaches similar conclusions but through the social and political context of Melville's rhetorical condition. He pulls together abundant evidence of America's perilous venturing into imperialism and slavocracy at the very moment of the tale's publication. In modifying the original source for his tale of a slave revolt (the bland travel journals of the tale's flawed central consciousness Amasa Delano), Melville left his own abhorrence of slavery unvoiced by purposefully creating a racist narrator whose errors in judgment play out with puzzling consequences the fatal errors of the audience's own stereotyping. As with Pip, Melville plays upon and against the white reader's expectations. The final effect, to borrow Bradley's language, is of an "out" crowd writer (Melville) teasing "in" readers toward a deeper inspection of their precarious antebellum world.

Bradley and Franklin show how two of Melville's most racially involved texts (*Moby-Dick* and "Benito Cereno") enable a single consciousness—Bradley stresses the apoliticized creator, Franklin the politicized—to manipulate the seemingly intractable consciousness of a white reader. Arnold Rampersad turns our attention to Melville's impact upon the modern black consciousness. In calling the writer "one of the principal interpreters of the American obsession with race," he seconds Toni Morrison's praise and calls upon today's critics to search more deeply into the issue of Melville and race, to acknowledge white sources along with black genius. Linking together Stowe, Wright, C. L. R. James, Baldwin, and Baraka, Rampersad traces the subtle but cable-strength connections of the black writer's condition to Melville's life and prose. The central figure, however, is the late Ralph Waldo Ellison, whose *Invisible Man*, like Melville's "Benito Cereno," places a "veil" between text and white audience, a device that separates, but only partially obscures, one consciousness from another, bidding readers to merge the two.

If Melville's deep engagement with the Other and the newly assessed confrontation with race is both startling and inspiring, his legendary encounter with selfhood—philosophically, psychologically, socially—remains the salient rock upon which our ongoing critique of American identity may be based. Of course, Melville's psychological investigations are so fraught with the anxiety, doubt, and instability of his white-hot sense of being that "molten lava" rather than "salient rock" seems the better metaphor. And yet the persistence of his art—fragile, tense, but calm—in placing a control over his essayings of (him)self has given his various writings, rooted in time, a unique transcendence and therefore a unique utility.

The inclusion of "Personality" beside "History and Race" seems obligatory, then, in any collection of essays on Melville, and yet this section's inclusion has an additional imperative. To know the self means coming to terms with knowing the author. In Melville's day this was a given; people read in order, as one of Melville's contemporaries put it, to know the person behind the text (O'Brien). Today, the force of criticism has so devalued the relevance of authorial presence in a text that one must make a special plea for a return to a writer's role in those transactions between mind and text and reader, and additional pleas for renewed study of the creative process. But how Melville conceived of the self is a vital, defining contextual concern: What are the dimensions of Melville's creative personality and how was that sense of self shaped by his society, sexuality, and family? For Richard Brodhead that personality relates to Melville's maleness; and in turning to the patterns of aggression in Melville's writing, he proposes a larger reorientation of our understanding of the formation of male identity vis-à-vis recent and highly cogent studies of the feminine self. Unlike Dimock, who finds a breakdown in Melville's approach to gender, Brodhead discovers a complex "psychological logic" at work wherein the failure at self-sovereignty is an unconsciously perceived insufficiency that ignites a violence that only feeds upon a fuller sense of inadequacy. Such is the fate of that organism hieroglyphically denominated XY.

Shirley Dettlaff's more aesthetic and yet no less probing assessment of Melville's sense of personality converts Brodhead's focus on male and female to the traditional mental faculties of head and heart: the Hellenic and Hebraic. These Arnoldian categories are familiar, but in Dettlaff's hands they become contrapuntal themes in a long Melvillean figure that achieves its highest tonality in the little-read and yet essential poem *Clarel*. Although this definitive study of classical and romantic conceptions of self finally presents Melville favoring the darker Hebraic view, Dettlaff carefully observes that Melville has designed his poem to leave readers perpetually weighing the balance of the two counternatures. Hence, Melville's sense of self is shaped as much by an anticipated reader response as by the writer's own self-projection—it is as much rhetoric as ontology.

Melville as Text

History, race, personality—the degree to which these ways of using Melville to achieve critical legitimacy is measured by the degree to which each enterprise is grounded in biography, or rather "what it meant to be Herman Melville." This fact is not always openly acknowledged—in fact, it is frequently denied—for critics (whether textual or contextual) invariably focus their attentions on generalized cultural forces and rarely upon the living agent—the life—that felt the forces and wrote the words. And yet, no critic, not even the antibiographical new critic, operates without some conception of the author's life. Unfortunately, those conceptions tend to be the broadest of legends, grossly stereotypical, even cartoonish in nature. There is Melville the orphan, the abusive husband and father, the embittered alcoholic, the manic depressive, the rejected homosexual. Each panel in the Ahabian cartoon has a grain of truth, of course, but there are also the Ishmaelian sides of Melville too mundane to caricature: the sane survivor, the inveterate reviser, the hot-gentle lover, the genial humorist.

Generally speaking, these snapshots are more the by-products of anxious critical transformations than of biography. And it may be that Melville's critical resiliency lies precisely in that his work so often serves as fertile ground for the projections of our culture's deepest anxieties. He has, for instance, drawn the scorn of one or two radical feminists who resent his putatively womanless fiction as well as various gay critics who deeply admire his closeted eroticism. Both angles are necessary for any legitimate study of Melville as man and text. Even so, as we look forward to a new era of Melville biography, let us hope for growth beyond reductive critical projections and toward a more dynamic engagement with the problem of how we construct biography, how we know Melville, and how Melville might stimulate us to rethink gender, sexuality, and being.

If the relevant use of biography in criticism—the building of analysis upon "life facts" in relation to "text facts"—is to be fully achieved, it will require at least three things: a renewed respect for the biographical enterprise, a better sense of what biography can and cannot do to illuminate texts, and, quite simply, more biographical facts. The general devaluation of biography in literary theory has effectively allowed critics to rest too confidently upon their more cherished generalizations about an author when in fact they should be mulling over the idiosyncratic specifics that do not fit past assumptions, or easy flag-waving characterizations. In looking at the erratic or unexpectedly broken patterns in any given life, we become more receptive to the more realistic, unanticipated ways in which a writer forges ideas and images out of experience. Moreover, like any intellectual endeavor, biography is most useful when its practitioners are alive to the varied interpretations of facts, when the focus of attention is placed not on self-assured speculations but on the debate over the meaning of our speculations. And since biography also thrives on the discovery of new facts (as well as the rethinking of the old), it will grow in respect and subtlety only when critics engage themselves more in the scholarly hunt for detail.

All of this is by way of saying that Melville biography is on the verge of a renaissance.

Up until recently there has been an odd dearth in Melville biography. Except for Edwin Haviland Miller's 1975 Freudian study, no major biography has appeared since Leon Howard's now-dated, but still standard, biography of

1951. The most likely cause of this forty-year silence is the simple fact that little new archival material has come to light. And yet we are now experiencing a new dawn. In 1984 the discovery of the *Typee* manuscript fragment and the Augusta Melville family papers provided an avalanche of new details. And the 1993 publication of Melville's *Correspondence* by Lynn Horth of the Northwestern-Newberry (NN) project ballooned the number of Melville letters to over three hundred. One letter by Melville to his brother announcing the birth of his first son, Malcolm, has inspired a volume-length analysis by Hennig Cohen and Donald Yannella on the mixture of authoritarianism and liberality in the Melville family. Also, Stanton Garner's recent *Civil War World of Herman Melville* (1993) immeasurably deepens our understanding of Melville experiences as the writer of *Battle-Pieces*. As of this writing, volume 2 of Hershel Parker's life of Melville (1996) is in press, as is Robert Ryan's Northwestern-Newberry edition of Melville's poetic manuscripts. Also in the works is a massive new edition of Jay Leyda's remarkable compilation *The Melville Log*. This wealth of new writing is a welcome compensation for the preceding dry decades since Howard. Thus, it was only fitting that the Melville Society asked Donald Yannella, former editor and president of the Melville Society, to assemble himself and the aforementioned new biographers into a panel to discuss the peculiar facts of Melville's life and the peculiarities of Melville biography. The transcribed discussion printed here is valuable not only for the new facts disclosed and the taste it gives us of the new vision scholars are constructing but also as a reminder that biography is a discourse. Here we find individuals agreeing and disagreeing, modifying each other, and clarifying new characterizations as they deconstruct old, and, most importantly, as they critique their own defining roles as biographers.

Biography is no less interpretive than criticism. Like history, it is a fiction. But it is a useful fiction. In confronting any serious biographical work, we must not be snowed by any presumptions of full objectivity. Each biographer shapes and selects the facts molding them into something more than just a record of personal events. These products are a transformation, a reconstruction of a life, a double reflecting mirror of themselves as biographers and of Melville. The more attuned we become to the nature of a biographical work, the more we shall be able to incorporate its form of discourse into the broader discourse of critical thought. Thus, we offer here two examples of the biographical art. Hershel Parker's study of Melville's earliest ambition to publish as a poet and Stanton Garner's assessment of Melville's customs house experience. In placing these essays after the discussion panel, we give the reader the rare opportunity to compare two scholars' discussion of their craft to their actual performance of it.

Hershel Parker's "The Lost *Poems* (1860)" is a succinct example of what Parker does best as a biographer: he invents. For some this would be a violation of the scholar's obligation to objectivity; for others, invention is all that any biographer can do. For the Melville biographer, invention is perhaps even more of a necessity simply because there are so many gaps in the record. Of course, the problem with "filling in the gaps" is to make it credible. Parker achieves credibility not through rhetorical sleights of hand but by the careful "teasing out" of data. We have known for some time that Melville had planned a book of poems in 1860 and that he had left the details of their publication to family and friends while he set sail with his brother Tom for a journey around the world. We know the book was not accepted and that Melville cut short his trip in San Francisco, returning home by steamer. By rubbing these facts together with marginalia in the books Melville read on board his brother's ship, Parker is able to elaborate upon Melville's expectations of success and further plans as an epic poet, giving us a mixture of what must and might have happened. This kind of extension beyond the dry facts is crucial to the biographical art; but like the restorers of old paintings who call attention to their "fillings in," the biographer must invent and yet remind the readers that what they invent is necessarily educated guessing. Here, Parker's guessing is cogent, convincing, and readable.

Stanton Garner's talent for teasing out new information from old facts are equally credible, equally enticing. His focus encompasses the twenty-year period when Melville was constrained to enter for good the World of Work. Melville spent much of his life laboring in some daily capacity either as a seaman or farmer, and while he was spared the dreariness of the occupations of merchant, surveyor, and lawyer that his family probably expected him to adopt, he was forced as he reached the age of forty-eight to become a customs inspector. The legends in scholarship concerning Melville's life are legion, but the one most cherished—perhaps because it satisfies our assumptions of the failure of art in the marketplace—is the belief that these years on the docks were bitter and degrading. In fact, Garner reveals that Melville's service, although never free of the anxieties associated with a patronage job, afforded him a fair income, abundant free time, and none of the baggage and weights one might expect. The customs years also encompassed most of Melville's years as a poet. It was the failure of the Civil War poems, *Battle-Pieces* (1866), that initiated Melville's demoralizing "career shift." This, too, was Melville's darkest time—his midlife crisis—occasioned by severe marital tensions and culminating in the suicide of his teenage son Malcolm. Settling into these personal failures and tragedies, Melville reinvented himself and produced some of our culture's most striking protomodern poetry, including the epic *Clarel* and the poem-become-novel *Billy Budd*. In a way, this period was no less productive than Melville's more famous ten years as a novelist. One can only speculate along with Garner how the odd moments of freedom and constraint incumbent upon his offices contributed to the tight lines and yet wide-ranging ideas of *Clarel*, the nostalgia of *John Marr,* the artful sensuality of *Timoleon* and the Rose Poems in *Weeds and Wildings,* and the reflections upon "form" and "law" in *Billy Budd*.

If in recent decades biography has grown out of favor among both textualists and historicists, so, too, have the equally central concerns of the creative process and textual editing suffered neglect. Both enterprises have their roots in the venerable discipline of philology, and there is no doubt that their time was up when the New Criticism declared intentionality a fallacy and texts verbal icons. Perhaps the virtual demise of traditional philological scholarship was in part the consequence of a kind of academic elitism based not so much upon any aristocratic pretensions of its practitioners but rather upon the inaccessibility of their materials: letters, papers, journals, manuscripts, and rare books. Today, these materials are far more accessible to those unable to travel to major resource depositories, and with the current debates over the meaning and use of textual editing serving as a spark to ignite new interest in things philological, one eagerly awaits a resurgence.

In shifting the focus of literary analysis from the creation and publication of texts (social causes and authorial intentions) to unities and structures of a text (its internal effects and reader responses), the New Criticism "democratized" literary studies. Scholarship designed to establish an author's creative process became a trivial pursuit—mere speculation rather than objective analysis of a text; and that text might be any text given that it was reasonably readable and uncorrupt. The good news of New Criticism was the movement away from belletrism, but the revolution came at the expense of modern philology. Not even John Nichol's amusing discovery that F. O. Matthiessen had based his reading of *White-Jacket* on the typographical error "soiled fish" rather than Melville's intended "coiled fish"—not even this reminder that interpretation must begin with reliable authoritative textual facts—could avert the general disregard for the "antiquated" pursuit of philology (Nichol).

As a critic I have profited as much as anyone from the democratization of literary analysis, and yet as a scholar I see much work to be done to rectify the sins of that necessary critical revolution. Of course, the rejection of philology was never total; various partisans and advocates of textual scholarship and even of the creative process have endured the long winter of ahistoricism. And several indicators suggest that we may be seeing the dawning of a New Philology, or rather a New Bibliography. The recent discourse over the relative merits of the eclectic (or "critical") and social editions, generally supported by G. Thomas Tanselle and Jerome McGann, respectively, has invigorated new interest in old problems: how authors and audiences collaborate throughout time to shape the texts we read. Also, as with biography, unanticipated discoveries of new material often excite new interest in once seemingly or putatively moribund scholarship. The recovery, for instance, of the first half of the *Huckleberry Finn* manuscript, lost throughout this century, has ignited new fires for Twain's creativity. Dickinson scholars, both radical and traditional, are beginning to look seriously at how to reedit the poet so as to rectify past errors and inspire new, critical readerships. The publication of *Writing the American Classics* by editors James Barbour and Tom Quirk refocuses attention on the creative process. And the establishment in 1986 of the American Literature Association has provided a yearly forum for textual scholars and exegetical critics to begin to forge new and healthy alliances.

These are only a few random examples of the growing interest in the new philology, and since the 1950s the development of Melville studies has been part and parcel of the attempt to accommodate scholarship and criticism (if in fact those two can ever be separated). The Northwestern-Newberry edition of *The Writings of Herman Melville* spearheaded by Harrison Hayford, Hershel Parker, and G. Thomas Tanselle has, since the publication of its first volume in 1967, provided the academic community with not only a full set of reliable Melville texts but a model for others of what the modern critical edition can be. The apparatus for each volume records textual facts that reveal Melville's often precarious interactions with editors, publishers, and audiences. What these volumes offer as well is a clear sense that "antiquated philology" is an interpretive art in which objective findings are always positioned in the context of the editors' necessary judgments. If the new philology is to have a valid impact, it will be to show readers that what we read is the product of many judgments, a cultural collaboration, if you will, and that the process of reading begins with the process of retrieving the text itself and reconstructing the creative process.

In many ways the fifth section in our collection, "Creation and Revision," illuminates some of the problems in reading that come with the new philology. In my contribution on the newly discovered *Typee* manuscript fragment, I try to show how our understanding of Melville's first book is enhanced by reading "trifocally," that is by giving "equal eye" to the phases of creativity represented in the book's manuscript, first edition, and expurgated edition. My assumption is that we can fully appreciate a text only when we absorb the various phases it endured in its creation: the first writings and revisions found in the working draft, the "final" intentions frozen into the lead type of the first printed edition, and the alterations Melville endured, sanctioned, and even initiated in the subsequent edition designed to accommodate his audience. These all contribute to the "rhetorical conditions of Melville's creativity," which is an all-the-more fascinating focus when we realize just how much Melville was learning as he wrote: how to write, how to tell a story, how to forge ideology, indeed, how to be himself. And from an opposing angle of vision—that of the audience's demands—we also see beyond the initial creative process and final polishings into the decision making of a young professional writer trying to succeed, perhaps despite himself, in the marketplace. Thus, with the trifocal approach I propose, we are able to reenvision what a text is: rather than a frozen verbal icon, it is the fluid totality of its many stages of conception, revision, and reception. Robert Ryan's closely focused study of Melville's famous poem "Art" offers us a vivid series of snapshots that together outline certain stages of Melville's creativity in the later phases of his life. If the *Typee* fragment shows us the freshman writer of prose, the "Art" manuscripts reveal the exciting microscopic circuitry of an (as yet still) unacknowledged master of American poetry.

The second two essays in this section shift away from the strictly textual problems related to Melville's creativity to creative proposals for the displaying of Melville's texts. It is a shift from manuscript to edition. Jean Ashton's idea is to resurrect the now-forgotten nineteenth-century book-collecting phenomenon of the "extra-illustrated edition" as a critical tool for animating the context of Melville's only urban novel, *Pierre*. In creating such an edition, the collector essentially assembles various physical materials (engravings, mementos, found objects) associated with any and all allusions found in the verbal text. Such a book collector's item is in effect a personal scrapbook recording a single (and often singular) reader's necessarily idiosyncratic interaction with a text. As such, it is too large for practical distribution; indeed, original, nineteenth-century extra-illustrated editions are invariably immured in private collections with no hopes of being reproduced. Of what practical value is this book-collecting oddity to us who might want to read Melville historically? At the very least, Ashton's proposed assemblage of cultural artifacts (the material culture surrounding the event we call *Pierre*) gives palpable substance and immediacy to the invisible word-images Melville gives us on his pages. It is not a contextualizing through mere annotation (i.e., more words in annotation written to "explain" the author's words); it is essentially a museum constructed around the author's text, an embodiment of Melville's world. Moreover, the proposal for an extra-illustrated *Pierre* reminds us that in annotating we never really "explain" a text; we only add to it. Thus, in matching visual versions of the urban conditions Melville experienced to Melville's fiction, Ashton supplies a collocation of word and artifact that creates, even as it stylizes, a new reader experience, one that, in its attempt to contextualize, involves the reader in more immediate ways.

G. Thomas Tanselle's proposal for the twenty-first-century reader is more familiar and yet no less engaging. As one of the nation's preeminent textual scholars and the textual editor for the NN edition of Melville's writings, Tanselle is generally presumed to be a "champion" of the critical or eclectic edition. But Tanselle would be the first to eschew such a label as it implies a battle between warring sides that need not exist. The presumed battle is between intentionalists and contextualists, those who would make an edition that reflects the author's lasting intentions and those who would make a edition that represents the social contingencies that shaped a particular version of a text at a particular moment in time. The reason there is no real split here is that both kinds of editors are historicists. The one would take *Typee*, let's say, and restore it to its first-edition status with judicious emendations of that copy text to correct any corruptions that might have crept in through the printing process or barged in because of social pressures. The other might consider reprinting the first edition of *Typee* alongside the expurgated edition, or printing the two separately so as to emphasize for modern readers the very social pressures that the intentionalist argues the author would have wanted to ignore. There is merit to both approaches, or rather as Tanselle writes, each approach has its own benefits and drawbacks; each packages the same information differently to emphasize different aspects of the creative process and reading experience. While some critics will surely insist on the irreconcilability of these two, the new philologist welcomes each on its own terms. Tanselle's argument in this vein is that while the NN edition has succeeded admirably in offering reliable eclectic editions of Melville, readers will surely benefit from facsimile reproductions of a specific printing, for they give readers a more direct sense of what it was like to read Melville as Melville's first readers read him.

In all, whether the focus is on manuscript, first edition, illustrated edition, emended copy text, or facsimile, readers will find in this section on creativity and editing a true, Melvillean taste for the new philology and, perhaps more to the point, an exciting discourse upon the varied ways of reading Melville.

The final section of essays extends the issue of reading Melville beyond the philological to the exegetical, with one of Melville's more problematic fictions, *Pierre,* as our principal example. Why *Pierre*? The question is fair, and fairly answered by the circumstances of the centennial conferences held at Pittsfield and New York City that generated the three essays included here. *Pierre* is a divided book. It is about the divided self; it is about Melville's personally felt division from his family; it is a dividing point in his career, the beginning of the end of his popularity. And it is about a divided America: half pastoral, half urban. In setting our conferences in two of Melville's most familiar landscapes—the Berkshires and Manhattan—we hoped to encompass most of the terrain Melville inhabited. (We were not able to find a venue at sea.) And in the process we necessarily emphasized the divisions inherent in Melville's country/city novel. Thus, *Pierre* is a natural focal text, and one over which readers also find themselves divided.

The principal division addressed in the three essays that constitute "Reading Melville: The Example of *Pierre*" is between the almost rigidly dualized pastoral and urban halves of the novel. Samuel Otter's and Wyn Kelley's essays focus exclusively on the separated landscapes, the pastoral and urban, respectively. These are admirable studies by two gifted, younger critics whose individual focuses deepen our understanding of Melville's radical departures from contemporary renderings of country and town. Situated between them and linking the two is John Seelye's deeply textured and wittily composed analysis focusing on the aesthetic and rhetorical contexts for the problem of why Melville moves from pastoral to urban settings instead of the other way around. All three essays attempt, as Seelye puts it, to "contextualize," to read Melville as he may have been read by his contemporaries in terms of the varying and complex conventions of the picturesque (Otter); Melville's literary associates Longfellow, Hawthorne, Dana, et al. (Seelye); or the popular urban novel of early-nineteenth-century America (Kelley).

In treating Pierre's vision of Saddle Meadows, his American Eden, Otter explores the aesthetic and political forces at work in the American picturesque. He finds different "eyes" at work in painter Thomas Cole, litterateur N. P. Willis, and transcendentalist Ralph Waldo Emerson. But against this is Pierre's own almost absurdly excessive vision, the outpourings of which derive not from a loving, hungry, or quiescent eye but one infected by sexual, racial, and political anxiety. The well-known and disastrous excesses in *Pierre* stem, according to Otter, from Melville's struggle with his own aristocratic (racial) past and the anti-rent fracas of upstate New York. As with Wai Chee Dimock's treatment of Melville and the female laborers of Lowell, Massachusetts, Melville's struggle with ideology is manifested in the pathology of his style.

Pierre is not John Seelye's favorite book. And yet like others before him, he wonders how or why the novel went wrong. He does not declare *Pierre* to be "a bad book," as did one early critic; nor does he pursue Hershel Parker and Brian Higgins's line that Melville's anger "wrecked" the book in its final compositional stages. Rather, he ponders a curious retrogression: Melville's transportation of Pierre and Isabel (and later Lucy) from Saddle Meadows to the city. It is an urban retreat rather than the pastoral one in vogue during the first half of the century. Why this inversion? The question takes us to the heart of Melville's always-strained relationship to his literary contemporaries and mentors, in particular Longfellow and Hawthorne. *Kavanagh,* Longfellow's little-known but popular enough novel (it outsold *Typee* by the tens of thousands), contains enough parallels to *Pierre* that it was surely an analogue if not source for Melville. And yet its conventional and Christianized pastoralism, like Hawthorne's in *The Scarlet Letter,* suggests by way of contrast that Melville's urban inversion is a critique of the Unitarian optimism inherent in Longfellow. One has to return to the late-eighteenth-century works of Charles Brockden Brown to find urban depictions as intense as *Pierre.*

Seelye's compelling thesis is all the more convincing given the carefully exposed interconnections between Melville, Longfellow, and Hawthorne—all of whom ended their lives in big cities. But Wyn Kelley argues that Melville's inversion of the pastoral retreat was not so unconventional. Numerous popular novels of the period, including the works of Ned Buntline and George Lippard, can be said to constitute a significant literary tradition focusing in particular upon a young country dweller's entry into the bewildering city. But like Seelye, Kelley also finds Melville departing from the tradition of what she calls the "labyrinth literature of New York." Contrary to the established pattern (co-opted by Walt Whitman), *Pierre* depicts an urban maze that is not so much a physical world to surmount and control but a mental construct as well, far more in the Cretan mode of the Minotaur myth than in the myth of Christian redemption found in the newly emergent sentimental mode of America's popular fiction. One other significant point of agreement is that both Seelye and Kelley see Pierre as being drawn to the city because of an inner compulsion; thus, the city becomes for them a form of fate: modern, urban, and democratic.

"Reading Melville" offers three ways to "textualize" *Pierre*. Although the shifting focuses provide a clear coherence with respect to the tensions in the novel's landscapes and Melville's divided self, these essays do not presume to offer a comprehensive assessment of Melville's fiction. These are selected essays on a selected work.

They do, however, demonstrate (beyond their individual findings) that criticism, indeed reading itself, is not so much a set of mechanistic "approaches" as it is the colorations emitted from specific critical sensibilities, individuals who have read and thought deeply, articulate people striving to give palpable shape to their ideas, to transform vision into communicable words. One reader reads *Pierre* and hears the clamor of renters, another hears Longfellow, another the strains of Cretan myth. What odd particularity this is. How odd, too, that one writer like Herman Melville could, on the centennial of his death, inspire so many other "odd particularities" to discourse upon historicism, race, gender, biography, and philology, as well as *Pierre*. And yet as I have already urged, this collocation of singularities is, by dint of its focus on the diversity of Melville, a representative sample of current work on a representative writer. If Melville has in our day achieved the rank of greatness, he is "great" largely because of his diversity: the diverse responses he continually inspires and the diverse uses to which he may be put. But "greatness" is a justly outmoded concept. It smacks of enforced canonization, authoritarian preachment, and an ideological insistence upon the elevation of a single mind above all others. Melville, then, is not so much great as he is full. He is not a cultural icon to worship or inflict upon the disempowered but a historical person and a body of texts—a person-text—whose fullness fills us. His diversity triggers in us a diversity of responses and, more, a deeper sense of cultural fluidity. It is in this way that we may claim for him not a particularizing exclusivity but a critically useful representationality.

Melville is a representative diversity because he is himself an "evermoving dawn," a constantly growing light transversing a world of ideas and feeling, illuminating with his palette of crepuscular colors what he calls in *Billy Budd* the "ragged edges" of truth. And yet there is a lower layer in the appeal of the life and works of this writer, and that is this: he turns us, too, into searchers, questioners, discoverers, and evermoving dawns.

NOTE

1. Various modern readers lionized Melville for various reasons. Gay readerships from the late nineteenth to mid-twentieth centuries, as well as a range of leftists and African Americanists, have contributed significantly to Melville's modern popularity. Reducing an aesthetic and political movement such as the reinvention of Melville in the twentieth century to one vaguely masculinizing impulse not only flattens out all complexities but reinforces the unfounded stereotype that Melville hated and never wrote about women. Melville's "use" of women in his life and writings is rich and surprisingly progressive. The challenge for feminists and all critics today is to return to Melville's fictive women (Fayaway, Lucy, Isabel, the Cholla widow, "The Tartarus of Maids," *Clarel*'s Ruth, and even Ishmael's "Madame Leviathan") as well as the women with whom he lived (mother, sisters, wife, and daughters) and map out his complex relation to both genders.

WORKS CITED

Barbour, James, and Tom Quirk, eds. *Writing the American Classics.* Chapel Hill: U of North Carolina P, 1990.

Bryant, John. *Melville and Repose: The Rhetoric of Humor in the American Renaissance.* New York: Oxford UP, 1993.

————, ed. *A Companion to Melville Studies.* Westport, CT: Greenwood, 1986.

Cohen, Hennig, and Donald Yannella. *Herman Melville's Malcolm Letter: Man's Final Lore.* New York: Fordham UP, 1992.

Foucault, Michel. "What Is an Author?" In *Modern Criticism and Theory.* Ed. David Lodge. London: Longman, 1988. 197–210.

Garner, Stanton. *The Civil War World of Herman Melville.* Lawrence: UP of Kansas, 1993.

Higgins, Brian, and Hershel Parker. "The Flawed Grandeur of Melville's *Pierre.*" In *New Perspectives on Melville.* Ed. Faith Pullin. Kent, Ohio: Kent State UP, 1978.

Howard, Leon. *Herman Melville: A Biography.* Berkeley: U of California P, 1951.

Inge, M. Thomas. "Melville in Popular Culture." In *A Companion to Melville Studies.* Ed. John Bryant. Westport, CT: Greenwood, 1986. 695–740.

James, C. L. R. *Mariners, Renegades and Castaways: The Story of Herman Melville and the World We Live in.* London: Allison and Busby, 1953.

Kaplan, Sidney. *American Studies in Black and White.* Amherst: U of Massachusetts P, 1991.

Karcher, Carolyn L. *Shadow Over Promised Land: Slavery, Race, and Violence in Melville's America.* Baton Rouge: Louisiana State UP, 1980.

Lauter, Paul. "Melville Climbs the Canon." *American Literature* 66 (March 1994): 1–24.

Lawrence, D. H. *Studies in Classic American Literature*. New York: Thomas Seltzer, 1923.

McGann, Jerome. *The Textual Condition*. Princeton: Princeton UP, 1991.

Miller, Edwin H. *Herman Melville: A Biography*. New York: Braziller, 1975.

Morrison, Toni. "Unspeakable Things Unspoken: The Afro-American Presence in American Literature." *Michigan Quarterly Review* (Winter 1989): 1–18.

Nichol, John W. "Melville's '"Soiled" Fish of the Sea.'" *American Literature* 21 (November 1949): 338–39.

O'Brien, Fitz-James. "Our Authors and Authorship: Melville and Curtis." *Putnam's Monthly Magazine* 9 (April 1857): 384–93.

Tanselle, G. Thomas. *A Rationale of Textual Criticism*. Philadelphia: U of Pennsylvania P, 1989.

Weaver, Raymond M. *Herman Melville: Mariner and Mystic*. New York: George H. Doran, 1921.

Loomings and Legacies

2

Herman Melville:
Uncommon Common Sailor

WALTER E. BEZANSON

Incredible as it now seems, the obituaries of 1891 had to instruct the new generation that the man who had just died at the age of seventy-two "was once one of the most popular writers in the United States." Under the heading "DEATH OF A ONCE POPULAR AUTHOR," the same reporter recalled that Melville had "reached the height of his fame about 1852, his first novel having been printed about 1847," adding that "his books are now little known" (*Log* 836). With few exceptions, this and other obituaries were marked less by surprise at Melville's death than astonishment that he had been alive all this time.

The "recovery" of Melville's life and works over the past one hundred years since his death is indeed one of the more remarkable events in America's somewhat mottled cultural history, matched only by Emily Dickinson's ascent from total anonymity to the role of major American poet. How two such great writers could have been in the one case "forgotten" and in the other smothered (until she had wheeled away into eternity) is a haunting question. Perhaps the role of some writers may not be to civilize their contemporaries but, by risking disturbing ranges of style or inquiry, to decivilize them. The price can be either fame or exile. For Melville, fortune's wheel stopped first at celebrity, moved on to exile, and then at last reached renown.

Melville was a hot number for the first five years of his writing career (1846–51) and a cool success for five more. Then his reputation, chilled by the risks he had taken in *Pierre* and the perplexities presented in *The Confidence-Man,* simply froze. Almost willfully, as the years passed, he moved into exile. It has taken two generations of critics, readers, and scholars to bring him home and thaw out his life and works. But for some time now his genius has again become available. Melville is among us, alive and well, an almost mythic hero back from oblivion with messages for new generations.

In celebration of his genius, I want first to recall the almost explosive force with which young Melville, still in his twenties, burst on the Anglo-American literary scene, offering himself as a half-savage explorer of islands in the unknown waters of the far Pacific and simultaneously raising serious questions for himself about the kind of writer he meant to become. Then I want to recall the nature and range of these early adventures, the actual experiences that preceded writing, to consider whether his Atlantic initiation and his Pacific escapades not only provided endless things to write about but could have been themselves mind-shaping forces that energized and shaped his talents toward *Moby-Dick* as he determinedly made his way up the slopes of genius. At midpoint I will discuss a series of episodes on climbing the mast as an example of the way a specific sea experience entered his writing and his later life. Along the way we will keep an eye open for glimpses of the uncommon, for hints of genius germinating.

CHALLENGED BY SUCCESS, 1846

"Narrative of a Four Months' Residence Among the Natives of a Valley of the Marquesas Islands; or, A Peep at Polynesian Life." So read the title of Melville's first book, thereafter known as *Typee*. What a stir it made in the 1840s, at home and abroad. Was it true? Were there really cannibals in the Marquesas? Had Melville actually been there, or was this the kind of hoax Poe had perpetrated a decade earlier in his wild Antarctic tale, *The Narrative of Arthur Gordon Pym*?

England published *Typee* first, and its appearance there in Murray's Home and Colonial Library, along with such sober travelers' accounts as Darwin's *Naturalist's Voyage Around the World,* Bishop Heber's *Journal in India,* and Borrow's *Bible in Spain,* suggests that John Murray, notably wary of fictions and freethinking, found Melville's narrative believable. But everyone didn't think so, and the English reviewers, most of whom were quite enchanted by the book, played games with the problem of authenticity. For a rich sampling of their reactions to *Typee* we turn to the "Publishers' Advertisement," eight pages of reviews bound into the back of the 1847 American revised edition of *Typee.*

One reviewer imagined a literary trial: "An individual, who gave the name of Herman Melville, was brought up on a charge of having forged several valuable documents relative to the Marquesas"; he concluded that no decision was possible except that Melville's talent and ingenuity were such that every member of the court "should read the whole of the alleged forgeries, without missing a word" (*Typee* xx). The prestigious *London Times* critic, although he thought Melville's narrative one of the best in Murray's Library, prided himself on seeing through the deception: "a very clever production . . . introduced to the English public as authentic, which we by no means think it to be." The sailor narrator, he complained, cites learned works and Flemish paintings, and the style is not only "lifelike and vigorous," it is "sometimes masterly." How absurd to think *Typee* was written by "a poor outcast working seaman" on board a South Sea whaler; it is the production of "an educated literary man." His sly conclusion: "We have called Mr. Melville a common sailor; but he is a very uncommon common sailor" (*Typee* xvii).

Two aspects of the authenticity problem are significant. One of these is Melville's own problem with truth-telling. *Typee* was meant to inform, of course, but at the cost of Melville's irrepressible need to entertain and impress, or even to seduce and then subvert the reader. Whether or not by temperament he was prone to exaggerate, his nearly five years at sea was a training course in yarn spinning, with vast personal rewards for the sailor who could amusingly interpret daily events, making a story out of random happenings and building a canon of tales about the frequent life-and-death encounters. The need to dramatize could easily slide into duplicity. Thus we have the notable instance in *Typee,* as modern scholarship has shown, of Melville's exactly-one-month stay on the island of Nukuhiva (July 9–August 9, 1842) being blithely quadrupled, the deception brazenly displayed in the title itself! This is what Mark Twain, that master of the tall tale, would lovingly call a "stretcher." Sailors at sea, like miners in their camps, easily found more truth in a good story than in facts.

Although Melville, from *Typee* on, felt increasingly the attractions of fiction, he was also reluctant to relinquish his authoritative role as the man who had been there. His sea books up through *Moby-Dick,* with one exception, reflect a struggle to keep his feet on the deck, not to get washed overboard by waves of rhetoric or his love for digression. Dana's severity with facts in *Two Years Before the Mast* (1840) was a model he admired, but Cooper's manufactured fictions were even older favorites. Shortly Melville would become impatient with all mentors, but in *Typee* and *Omoo* he wisely held, if not to accuracy, to the air of accuracy, well aware that his trump card up to now was simply that he really had experienced wild events, places, and people.

Two years later his mind was bursting with ideas and possibilities piling up from his voracious reading and the excitements of cultural life in New York City. Midway through *Mardi* he simply abandoned authenticity for a fantastic voyage through archipelagoes of mind, in the process experimenting wildly with styles. Hostile critics and an instinct for survival drove him back to two solid fictional narratives, *Redburn* and *White-Jacket*, but not for long. Exhilarated by his memorable trip to Europe in 1849 and driven by a mounting sense of his own genius, Melville began his immense encounter with the White Whale; he knew for sure that the beast would be both real and mythic. *Typee* problems of authenticity gave way to a complex quest for large meanings, whatever that might do to surface realities. He was now a long distance from *Typee*, where the game had been to satisfy a publisher and please a crowd.

A second significance of the authenticity problem, like the first, began simply enough. As we have seen, the *London Times* was confident that a common sailor could not be a literary fellow. If this amused Melville at first, it eventually exasperated him and soon became a cause. When John Murray in the spring of 1848 persisted in asking for "documentary evidences" that he had actually been in the South Seas, Melville lost patience: "Bless my soul, Sir, will you Britons not credit that an American can be a gentleman, & . . . have been in the tar-bucket?—You make miracles of what are common-places to us.—I will give no evidence.—Truth is mighty & will prevail—& shall & must" (Davis and Gilman, eds. 72). Unlike Irving and Hawthorne, who successfully strove to become "authors" in the English mold, Melville belonged to a newer generation of writers and thinkers for whom Emerson spoke when in 1836, in the opening lines of "Nature," he demanded: "Why should not we also enjoy an original relation to the universe?" Emerson's protest against "the fathers" (and by implication against the "mother country") paralleled the surge of self-assurance Melville was feeling as a heroic adventurer winning applause in a young society transformed by Jacksonian democracy. He was greedy for success to the point of accepting revisions for *Typee*, revisions meant to placate moralists and the defenders of missionaries. Yet his book had an arrogant innocence and an emergent colloquialism that distinguished it from other books in Murray's Home and Colonial Library. Trying to define that difference, the English reviewers called it fresh, vigorous, colorful, energetic. At least one English critic from the beginning understood the cultural differences and spelled them out:

> Had this work [*Typee*] been put forward as the production of an English common sailor, we should have had some doubts of its authenticity in the absence of distinct proof. But in the United States it is different. There social opinion does not invest any employment with discredit; and it seems customary with young men of respectability to serve as common seamen, either as a probationership to the navy or as a mode of seeing life. Cooper and Dana are examples of this practice. (*London Spectator; Typee* xxii)

The *London Athenaeum* was simpler and more to the point: "Mr. Melville's manner is New World all over" (*Typee* xxi). The remark speaks succinctly to Melville's intentions in the first decade of his career. Like Emerson and Whitman, Melville, once on his way, wanted to be a new voice from a new world.

One of the attractions of *Typee* to the English was its offer of escape from the new industrial society. Douglas Jerrold's *Shilling Magazine,* listing the cares that drag Englishmen down, longed for a world where "one need not fear . . . the letter of the impatient dun or threatening attorney; nor butchers' nor bakers' bills; nor quarter-days with griping landlord and brutal brokers; nor tax-gatherers; nor income tax collectors gauging with greedy exactness the drops that have fallen from his brow" (*Typee* xviii). In contrast to this Dickensian world, *Typee* offered, at least to the imagination, exotic escape and hints of Eros: "Enviable Herman! A happier dog it is impossible to imagine than Herman in the Typee Valley. To describe a day's existence would be to tell of the promised joys of the Mohamedan's paradise. Nothing but pure physical delight; sunny days, bright skies, absence of care, presence of lovely woman Fayaway" (*Typee* xvi). Melville had encouraged such day dreaming and mild sexual fantasies in his narrative, right from the start promising in his title a "Peep" at Polynesian life. In a nifty bit of genre crossing he had given his Pacific island narrative some of the trappings of the Oriental romance, as the envious reviewer testifies by his reference to "the Mohamedan's paradise."

New World readers may have been less in need of escape than their depressed English cousins, but Wiley and Putnam, the American publishers, nevertheless promised plenty of excitement: "cannibal banquets, groves of cocoanuts, coral reefs, tattooed chiefs and bamboo temples; sunny valleys, planted with bread-fruit trees, carved canoes dancing on the flashing blue waters, savage woodlands guarded by horrible idols, *heathenish rites and human sacrifices*" (*Typee* xv). This splendid example of Early American Hype captivated American readers and established a popular audience that gave Melville his public reputation and then, when he deviated from their expectations (*Mardi, Pierre, The Confidence-Man*), denounced or deserted him. They were drawn to his robust and often comic presentation of outlandish adventures. Most of what was known about "savage tribes" one hundred fifty years ago was buried in sober, often multivolume works not easily available. Melville, plundering several of these as he wrote, artfully weaving memory, fact, and fiction, had made *his* travel narrative exciting. That's what his readers wanted. And shortly, that's what Melville wanted to transcend.

ATLANTIC INITIATION, 1839

Thousands of young Americans had gone to sea before Melville, coiling lines and climbing riggings on merchant ships that crossed the Atlantic, as Herman did aboard the *St. Lawrence*. Hundreds more shipped out on whalers like the *Acushnet* and began to learn the lesson that Starbuck, first mate aboard the *Pequod*, taught the crew: "I will have no man in my boat . . . who is not afraid of a whale" (ch. 26). Hundreds of other young men, to avoid the tedium of the merchant service, the stench of whaleships, and the low reputations of their crews, signed up as midshipmen with the United States Navy, attracted by uniforms, youthful patriotism, and perhaps a chance for fame and glory; for more pragmatic reasons, Melville, stranded in Honolulu, signed for a single cruise. He needed a ride home.

Thus the range of Melville's sea experiences—merchant service, whaling industry, and U.S. Navy—was indeed exceptional. His background was both wider in variety and longer in time—some four years—than that of either James Fenimore Cooper, famous in Melville's youth for his sea romances (*The Pilot, The Red Rover,* and *The Water Witch*), or R. H. Dana, Jr., whose documentary-type record of rounding the Horn to California and back, *Two Years Before the Mast,* set a new standard of literacy for the genre. Capping these shipboard adventures and giving Melville his special cachet to a broad public, as we have seen, was his reckless sojourn among an island tribe of savages, possibly cannibals, followed by rash wanderings as an island beach-

comber. Each of these five sequences of adventure—the three maritime services, island captivity, and beachcombing—gave Melville one of his first six
books, *Mardi* being the important illegitimate child.[1] Our inquiry into these
adventures, after asking why Melville went to sea in the first place, looks for
moments and circumstances in his adventures that may have affected the kind
of writer and the kind of person he became.

When Melville signed aboard the *St. Lawrence* in June 1839, bound for
Liverpool and return, he may not himself have understood the mixture of
motives and forces that were taking him to sea for the next four months. A
few weeks before sailing he had published in his local newspaper two floridly
literary pieces that he named "Fragments from a Writing Desk" (*Log* 83–84).
The titles as well as the contents suggest a budding talent in search of something worth writing about. We do not know that he went to sea consciously
looking for tales to bring to his writing desk, since other factors were at
work. As second son in a fatherless family of eight children, he was expected,
and had tried, to help his mother. But after clerking in a bank and in his
older brother's fur cap store, stints of teaching in country schools, and a half-
hearted try at a career in engineering, he was out of work and up against the
havoc caused by the Panic of 1837. The fall from fortune for a distinguished
family—grandfathers Peter Gansevoort (heroic general at Fort Stanwix) and
Major Thomas Melvill (veteran of the Boston Tea Party)—was harsh. A
second tradition was in the making, however. Captain John D'Wolf, an uncle
who visited the family on occasion, had made famous voyages and crossed
Siberia; and an older cousin, Thomas Melvill, had made Pacific cruises with
the navy, visiting Tahiti and the same Typee valley that Herman would make
famous; and in June 1839 cousin Tom was about to ship out on his third Pacific
whaling cruise. Hard times had already sent three Gansevoort cousins to sea as
midshipmen; one, Leonard, a schoolmate of Herman's at Albany Academy,
had already been whaling for two years and in 1837 had made the same Liverpool run that Melville was about to make (Gilman).

It is clear that Melville went to sea out of necessity and within a growing
family tradition. It is also likely that this rambunctious young man was happy
indeed to escape family misfortunes, the tangle of his unsuccessful efforts at a
career, and the dominance of the very brother who seems to have arranged
Herman's Liverpool adventure. Of course he went to sea to see, and perhaps
hoping to write about what he saw. But first of all it was a job.

The *St. Lawrence* provided Melville a relatively placid way to break into
the often violent world of sea-going. She was a slow trader, three masted and
square rigged, 120 feet long; she sailed when cargo could be obtained and

offered passage to a few cabin passengers and cheaper rates in steerage (especially to emigrants on the return voyage). The *St. Lawrence* was but half the size of the prize packets—those fast-sailing passenger ships that Charles Dickens thought "the finest in the world"; packet officers drove the crews hard to keep on schedule. Captain Oliver P. Brown, Swedish born, had fifteen years at sea. The two mates, aged thirty-eight and twenty-eight, were natives of New York and Massachusetts, respectively, and like the other fourteen members of the crew had common English-American names. As was the custom, the cook and steward were African Americans. The only non-native Americans were an Irish citizen of Great Britain and a Greenlander named Peter Brown (Gilman 333). The *St. Lawrence* made a slow four-week crossing and a sluggish seven-week voyage home. Melville's first contact with Old World culture was a grimy encounter with its underbelly—filthy dockside Liverpool, where he was stranded aboard ship for six weeks. If Melville was tale hunting, he had found nothing very romantic thus far.

It could not have been easy for Melville, two months from his twentieth birthday, to have to sign up as a "boy," the only option for new hands in the merchant service whatever their age or status. Ships company consisted of captain, mates, able seamen, ordinary seamen, cook, steward, and—at the very bottom and everyone's prey—a "boy." He was immediately faced with a vast confusion of rigging, ropes, stays and shrouds going in different directions, enormous masts, yards, booms and gaffs, twenty-five or more sails overhead—each thing with a name of its own and all governed by an unfamiliar language of coded shouts and bells. A "boy" learned simply by doing it, with coarse rebuffs or punishments for ineptitude. Just how complex a machine the nineteenth-century square-rigged sailing vessel had become is attested by *The Seaman's Friend* (1841), a no-nonsense guide dedicated "especially to those commencing the sea life." The text was compiled by New England's most famous young sailor, who became a Cambridge lawyer and later a friend of Melville's, R. H. Dana, Jr. One section of the book is a "Dictionary of Sea Terms" (some nine hundred of them) and five drawings keyed to more than two hundred terms (see Plates I and II).[2] The book would have been available to Melville only after he returned from the Pacific (1844); by that time, if he had had Dana's methodical mind, he could have compiled it himself.

The *St. Lawrence* experience did several things for Melville. The three-month apprenticeship enabled him to get rid of the rating "boy"; should he ever go to sea again, he was qualified as ordinary seaman. At a deeper level the experience gave him a secure sense of having proved his manhood, of becoming, one might say, his own older brother. And in turn this would begin shaping the devil-may-care style that would make his first two books so popular.

On returning from Liverpool in 1839, Melville could see that there wasn't sufficient "story," if he had hoped for it, in an Atlantic crossing. Only after man-size adventures in the Pacific would he be able to step back and be amused by his boyish venture. Ten years later he wrote such a book, making a game of teasing the innocence of his fifteen-year-old narrator: *Redburn: His First Voyage. Being the Sailor-Boy Confessions and Reminiscences of the Son-of-a-Gentleman, in the Merchant Service.* By then he had the distance, the skill and confidence, to mock the plight of greenhorns and to add bits of melodrama to his own fairly humdrum voyage. *Redburn* was Melville's fourth book; by then he was an artful fabricator of pseudo-real events. The thirty-two steerage emigrants on the *St. Lawrence,* all of whom reached New York safely, become five hundred aboard the fictional *Highlander* (a true Melville stretcher), and thirty corpses are pitched overboard when pestilence sweeps through the hold (ch. 58). Of two impressed sailors dragged aboard drunk on leaving Liverpool, one gets delirium tremens and rushes overboard; the other, after stinking up the forecastle, is discovered dead of "animal combustion" and is partly consumed by "curls of soft blue flame." Jackson, a vicious tyrant of the forecastle and one of Melville's most vivid sea characters, makes his memorable plunge from the main-topsail-yard to his death (chs. 10, 48, 59). These lurid demises are best understood, I should think, as a melding of the Poe-esque, popular in the 1840s, and the kind of yarns sailors have told each other ever since Noah. They are used in *Redburn* to give the sense of fear experienced by a boy newly among men.

MONKEYSHINES ALOFT

Before pursuing Melville into the Pacific, I want to call attention to a particular shipboard experience that is central in *Redburn,* his book on the merchant service, and that reappears in *White-Jacket* and *Moby-Dick,* the navy and whaling books: climbing the mast. It was the most common daily event of every nineteenth-century sailor's life the world over.

It was a big moment for a "boy" the first time he was sent aloft. Melville, at his writing desk ten years after his own initiation, decided to give Redburn's

Plate I.

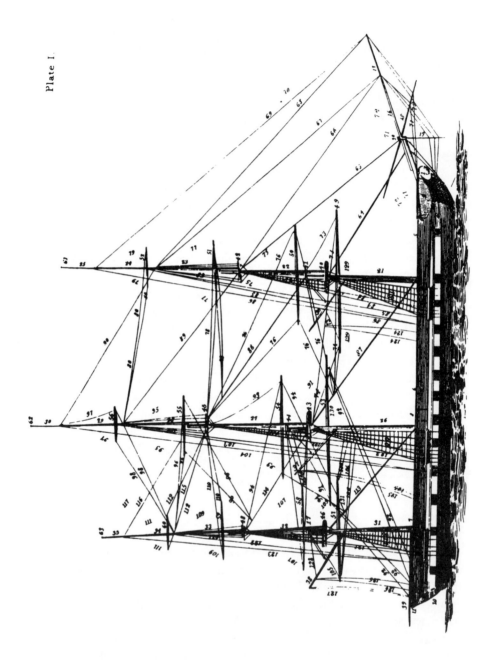

PLATE I.

THE SPARS AND RIGGING OF A SHIP.

INDEX OF REFERENCES.

1 Head.
2 Head-boards.
3 Stem.
4 Bows.
5 Forecastle.
6 Waist.
7 Quarter-deck.
8 Gangway.
9 Counter.
10 Stern.
11 Tafferel.
12 Fore chains.
13 Main chains.
14 Mizzen chains.
15 Bowsprit.
16 Jib-boom.
17 Flying jib-boom.
18 Spritsail yard.
19 Martingale.
20 Bowsprit cap.
21 Foremast.
22 Fore topmast.
23 Fore topgallant mast.
24 Fore royal mast.
25 Fore skysail mast.
26 Main mast.
27 Main topmast.
28 Main topgallant mast.
29 Main royal mast.
30 Main skysail mast.
31 Mizzen mast.
32 Mizzen topmast.
33 Mizzen topgallant mast.
34 Mizzen royal mast.
35 Mizzen skysail mast.
36 Fore spencer gaff.
37 Main spencer gaff.
38 Spanker gaff.
39 Spanker boom.
40 Fore top.
41 Foremast cap.
42 Fore topmast cross-trees.
43 Main top.
44 Mainmast cap.
45 Main topmast cross-trees.

46 Mizzen top.
47 Mizzenmast cap.
48 Mizzen topmast cross-trees.
49 Fore yard.
50 Fore topsail yard.
51 Fore topgallant yard.
52 Fore royal yard.
53 Main yard.
54 Main topsail yard.
55 Main topgallant yard.
56 Main royal yard.
57 Cross-jack yard.
58 Mizzen topsail yard.
59 Mizzen topgallant yard.
60 Mizzen royal yard.
61 Fore truck.
62 Main truck.
63 Mizzen truck.
64 Fore stay.
65 Fore topmast stay.
66 Jib stay.
67 Fore topgallant stay.
70 Fore skysail stay.
71 Jib guys.
72 Flying-jib guys.
73 Fore lifts.
74 Fore braces.
75 Fore topsail lifts.
76 Fore topsail braces.
77 Fore topgallant lifts.
78 Fore topgallant braces.
79 Fore royal lifts.
80 Fore royal braces.
81 Fore rigging.
82 Fore topmast rigging.
83 Fore topgallant shrouds.
84 Fore topmast backstays.
85 Fore topgallant backstays.
86 Fore royal backstays.
87 Main stay.
88 Main topmast stay.
89 Main topgallant stay.
90 Main royal stay.
91 Main lifts.
68 Flying-jib stay.
69 Fore royal stay.

92 Main braces.
93 Main topsail lifts.
94 Main topsail braces.
95 Main topgallant lifts.
96 Main topgallant braces.
97 Main royal lifts.
98 Main royal braces.
99 Main rigging.
100 Main topmast rigging.
101 Main topgallant rigging.
102 Main topmast backstays.
103 Main topgallant backstays.
104 Main royal backstays.
105 Cross-jack lifts.
106 Cross-jack braces.
107 Mizzen topsail lifts.
108 Mizzen topsail braces.
109 Mizzen topgallant lifts.
110 Mizzen topgal't braces.
111 Mizzen royal lifts.
112 Mizzen royal braces.
113 Mizzen stay.
114 Mizzen topmast stay.
115 Mizzen topgallant stay.
116 Mizzen royal stay.
117 Mizzen skysail stay.
118 Mizzen rigging.
119 Mizzen topmast rigging.
120 Mizzen topgal. shrouds.
121 Mizzen topmast backstays.
122 Mizzen topgal'nt backstays.
123 Mizzen royal backstays.
124 Fore spencer vangs.
125 Main spencer vangs.
126 Spanker vangs.
127 Ensign halyards.
128 Spanker peak halyards.
129 Foot-rope to fore yard.
130 Foot-rope to main yard.
131 Foot-rope to cross-jack yard.

42

Plate·II.

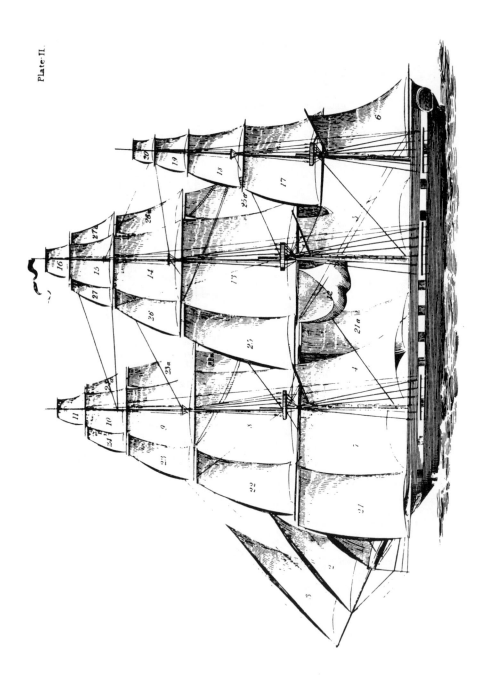

PLATE II.

A SHIP'S SAILS.

INDEX OF REFERENCES.

1 Fore topmast staysail.
2 Jib.
3 Flying jib.
4 Fore spencer.
5 Main spencer.
6 Spanker.
7 Foresail.
8 Fore topsail.
9 Fore topgallant sail.
10 Fore royal.
11 Fore skysail.
12 Mainsail.
13 Main topsail.
14 Main topgallant sail.
15 Main royal.
16 Main skysail.
17 Mizzen topsail.

18 Mizzen topgallant sail.
19 Mizzen royal.
20 Mizzen skysail.
21 Lower studdingsail.
21a Lee ditto.
22 Fore topmast studdingsail.
22a Lee ditto.
23 Fore topgallant studdingsail.
23a Lee ditto.
24 Fore royal studdingsail.
24a Lee ditto.
25 Main topmast studdingsail.
25a Lee ditto.
26 Main topgallant studdingsail.
26a Lee ditto.
27 Main royal studdingsail.
27a Lee ditto.

first ascent a whole chapter. Although the event had occurred the second night out of port, Redburn waits until one quarter through his tale, to give it weight, before announcing: "At Dead of Night He Is Sent Up to Loose the Main-Skysail" (ch. 16).

The skysail is "the fifth and highest sail from the deck," he tells us, and all but out of sight (see Plate II, no. 16). As charmingly pointed out to Redburn by the old Dutch sailor (a fiction: there was no Dutch sailor on the *St. Lawrence*), "Now, d'ye see dat leetle fellow way up dare? *dare*, just behind dem stars dare . . . ." Once aloft Redburn is "awe-stricken and mute . . . the sea looked like a great, black gulf," and he begins the sensation of "falling—falling—falling, as I have felt when the nightmare has been on me." We must tread warily here: the fear is Redburn's, but in spite of its Poe-like echoes, it has the odor of authenticity, especially in the light of what follows.

Redburn gets safely down, but Melville returns to the fear of mast climbing on the voyage home (ch. 50). A new hand, Harry Bolton, a "girlish youth" that Redburn has befriended, insists *"he could not go aloft; his nerves would not hear of it,"* and later, *"his nerves could not stand it"* (Melville's emphasis). The context of this scene is not comic; the power of the fear of falling Melville assigns to Harry Bolton is unmistakable.

This fear reappears when Melville chooses as climax for Redburn's voyage the death of Jackson. The already half-dead Jackson appears on deck "from his dark tomb in the forecastle." Melville sends him aloft in a gale, placing him "at the extreme weather-end of the topsail-yard" (see Plate I, no. 54). From there he meets his end. With a "blasphemous cry" (anticipating Ahab's final curse), Jackson goes to his death in the most memorable *action* in *Redburn*: "his hands dropped to his side, and the bellying sail was splattered with a torrent of blood from his lungs. As the man next to him stretched out his arm to save him, Jackson fell headlong from the yard, and with a long seethe, plunged like a diver into the sea" (ch. 59).

Once past the skysail nightmare that he was falling, Redburn discovers the thrill of not falling. The new self is announced in a chapter entitled "He Begins to Hop About in the Rigging Like a Saint Jago's Monkey" (ch. 24). Now he can claim "great delight in furling the top-gallant sails and royals [see Plate II, nos. 14, 15] in a hard blow"—that last phrase having just a touch of the Davy Crockett boast. In deliberate contrast, the sad fate of Harry Bolton dramatizes the cost of failure. Having been forced aloft once, Harry refused ever again to climb the rigging. For this he was mercilessly harrassed: "the crew now reckoned him fair play for their worst jibes and jeers," says Redburn, "and [Harry] led a miserable life indeed" (ch. 50). Meanwhile, Redburn moves from fear to frolic to ecstasy. The first time he reefed topsails at night in heavy weather, "hanging over the yard with eleven others, the ship lunging and rearing like a mad horse," he thought he would surely lose his hold and so "hung on with tooth and nail." But surprisingly soon, he says, "my nerves became as steady as the earth's diameter, and I felt as fearless on the royal yard [see Plate I, no. 56], as Sam Patch on the cliff of Niagara." The sailor's rule aloft is one hand for the ship and one for yourself, but in his excitement Redburn abandons himself to the night: "There was a wild delirium about it; a fine rushing of the blood about the heart; and a glad thrilling and throbbing of the whole system, to find yourself tossed up at every pitch into the clouds of a stormy sky, and hovering like a judgment angel between heaven and earth; both hands free, with one foot in the rigging, and one somewhere behind you in the air" (ch. 24). The moment is epiphanic. An event has become an *action:* the narrator alive to danger, the text made alive through danger. The presence of Melville, in an act of sharp recall, is felt.

In *White-Jacket,* his next book, there are two significant mast-climbing episodes; both are dangerous accidents, and each carries a thematic burden. In a book in which the value system of the naval hierarchy is constantly being challenged, the first fall is offered as a case of unjust authority. The little Scot "Baldy," a captain of the mizzen-top (see Plate II, no. 17), is put under extreme pressure from the bullying of an officer on the deck. "'You, Baldy! are you afraid of falling?'" the First Lieutenant cries. Baldy, frenzied, loses his hold: "the *bunt-gasket* parted; and a dark form dropped through the air . . . with a horrid crash of all his bones, Baldy came, like a thunder-bolt, upon the deck." Baldy survives, but he is maimed for life. The event leads Melville's narrator to catalog falls: on a neighboring English line-of-battle ship in the same harbor, "a seaman fell from the main-royal-yard [see Plate I, no. 56] . . . and buried his ankle-bones in the deck, leaving two indentations there." Sometimes, says White-Jacket, men fall from an upper yard, taking down a shipmate on a lower yard, and killing both of them. A man-of-war rarely completes a cruise, he says, "without the loss of some of her crew from aloft" (ch. 46).[3]

Baldy's calamity is preparation for the narrator's own fall, a few pages from the end of *White-Jacket,* the climactic *action* of the book (ch. 59). The event is more complex than Redburn's imagined nightmare fall (of which it is an extension) in that the fall through the air is matched by a descent into the sea, followed by the deeply symbolic destruction of the cherished and hated jacket. White-Jacket falls from the top-gallant-yard (see Plate I, no. 55). First comes "the rush of the air . . . all else was a nightmare . . . I fell—down, down, with lungs collapsed as in death . . . into the speechless profound of the sea. . . . I fell, soul becalmed, through the eddying whirl and swirl of the Maelstrom air." Then comes the descent: "there I hung, vibrating in the mid-deep. . . . The life-and-death poise soon passed." He ascends, dangerously encumbered by his water-soaked jacket; with a knife "I ripped my jacket straight up and down, as if I were ripping open myself." Now at last he is "free," he says—free, that is, of the enigmatic constraints of the jacket, which he had himself made, and leaving the reader free to think about what the jacket meant. White-Jacket's fall from the mast is a powerful episode. Scholars have discovered that in writing it Melville borrowed heavily from another sailor-writer, who had in fact fallen from the mast, as Melville had not. To survive such a fall was extraordinary. Melville eagerly melded the sensations of Nathaniel Ames, who years later claimed to remember exactly what they were, with his own precisely remembered fears (Vincent ch. 17). Melville's ability to recollect sensations from his sea experiences, and turn those sensations into dramatic action, may be exactly the attribute of his work that led Hawthorne to write Duyckinck: "No writer ever put the reality before his reader more unflinchingly than he does in 'Redburn' and 'White-Jacket'" (*Log* 391).

Some four months after commending young Redburn for hopping about the rigging like a Santiago (San Jago's) monkey, Melville, aged thirty and now famous, was on the way to England aboard the packet *Southampton;* after a storm that had made all the other passengers seasick, he put on a show: "They seem to regard me as a hero," he wrote in his journal, "proof against wind and weather. My occasional feats in the rigging are regarded as a species of tight-rope dancing." Twelve days later: "Ran about aloft a good deal." During good weather Melville spent much of his time in the rigging with his newfound friend, George Adler, a scholar of German who turned out to be "full of the German metaphysics"; Melville set out to empty him. It is one of the great scenes of Melville's double life: aloft in the maintop, simultaneously renewing the enchantments of the sea world and passionately absorbing "the German metaphysics" (NN *Journals* 4–9). Four months later he began *Moby-Dick.*

It was while he was writing *Moby-Dick* that the famous picnic on Monument Mountain occurred, August 5, 1850. Among those enjoying this summer frolic in the Berkshires were Melville's neighbor, Nathaniel Hawthorne (the first meeting of the two); his New York mentor, Evert Duyckinck; James T. Fields, the Boston publisher; and Oliver Wendell Holmes, Mr. Boston himself. While the champagne was going round, Melville resurrected his monkey-shines. "We scattered over the cliffs," Duyckinck wrote home to his wife,

"Herman Melville to seat himself, the boldest of all, astride a projecting bow sprit of rock." And Fields recalled much later, "We scrambled to the top with great spirit, and when we arrived, Melville, I remember, bestrode a peaked rock, which ran out like a bowsprit, and pulled and hauled imaginary ropes for our delectation" (*Log* 384). The daring may have been further emphasized when one member of the party read aloud Bryant's poem "Monument Mountain," at the end of which the Indian maiden, lovelorn, climbed to that spot at dusk: "she threw herself / From that steep rock and perished" (Bryant 102–07).

A similar personal episode occurred one year later. A party of Melville's friends had struggled up Mt. Greylock and become separated in the process. They heard distant shouts; whereupon "one of our party," Sarah Morewood recalled, "with the agility of a well trained sailor (as he was) soon ascends the trunk of a tall tree, and from a seat which appears to us dangerously insecure, echoes shout for shout, till the remaining few of our party . . . make their appearance" (*Log* 423ff). For the moment, Melville is again *as he was*—a common sailor—reenacting the life of danger.

The central actions in *Moby-Dick,* published that fall, are certainly the nerve-tingling moments when the men lower boats following cries from the mastheads. It is therefore a fine moment, at the end of one of Ishmael's jovial and indulgent chapters, "The Mast-Head" (35), when we hear him in his prophetic mode, calling out from aloft his priestly warning, as if he were Jonathan Edwards. Ishmael's precarious pulpit is at the cross-trees of the main topmast (see Plate I, no. 45), from where he is supposed to cry out the sighting of a whale. But "the serenity of those seductive seas" is too much for "a dreamy meditative man" like Ishmael, and he is lulled into "an opium-like listlessness of vacant, unconscious reverie." This of course is the moment of utmost danger: "But while this sleep, this dream is on ye, move your foot or hand an inch, slip your hold at all; and your identity comes back in horror. Over Descartian vortices you hover. And perhaps, at mid-day, in the fairest weather, with one half-throttled shriek you drop through that transparent air into the summer sea, no more to rise for ever. Heed it well, ye Pantheists!" Edwards revisted—Pantheists in the Hands of an Angry God.[4] To Ishmael's first-chapter promise that "meditation and water are wedded forever" some corollaries might be added: the wedding could be dangerous; safe may not be safe; and above all—*for God's sake hold on tight!* The "Descartian vortices" may prove more mortal than White-Jacket's "Maelstrom air."[5]

A final nonfictional event remained for Melville, as if to validate the memory of Redburn and Harry Bolton, Jackson, White-Jacket, and Ishmael. On a last sea voyage, 1860, aboard the clipper ship *Meteor,* captained by his young brother Tom (he was thirty, Herman forty-one), Melville again faced the archetypal tragedy of the common sailor. From his brief journal:

> Ray, a Nantucketer, about 25 years old, a good honest fellow . . . fell this morning about day-break from the main topsail yard [the same yard from which Jackson plunged to his death] to the deck, & striking head-foremost upon one of the spars was instantly killed. . . . It was in vain to wash the blood from the head—the body bled incessantly & up to the moment of burying; which was about one o'clock, and from the poop, in the interval between blinding squalls of sharp sleet. Tom read some lines from the prayer-book—the plank was sloped, and—God help his mother.

The setting itself was Melvillean: the *Meteor* was dead off the Horn in midwinter (August 9); the day before, "Just before sunset, in a squall, the mist lifted & showed, within 12 or fifteen miles the horrid sight of Cape Horn—(the Cape proper)—a black, bare steep cliff, the face of it facing the South Pole;—within some miles were other awful islands and rocks—an infernal group." And then, the day after, like a caution in an Ishmael chapter: "Calm: blue sky, sun out, dry deck. Calm lasting all day—almost pleasant enough to atone for the gales, but not for Ray's fate, which belongs to that order of human events, which staggers those whom the Primal Philosophy hath not confirmed" (NN *Journals* 134). The life that Melville had known, now imitating the fiction that he had written.

PACIFIC ESCAPADE

Even a quick summary of the Pacific years (1841–44) reminds us of the layers of action and excitement Melville compounded for future exploitation. Teaching school and a trip to Illinois had been feckless ventures, so here he was in New Bedford shipping out on the whaler *Acushnet* (Captain Valentine Pease, Jr., of Edgartown, master) presumably for the entire cruise. His actual itinerary was quite different: eighteen months in the forecastle of the *Acushnet*; overboard with a shipmate in the Marquesas, leading to a month living among the Typee tribe, island of Nukuhiva; escape to the Australian whaler *Lucy Ann*, an old ship with a sick master, leading to mutiny of the crew and temporary imprisonment ashore on Tahiti; a month of roving about the neighboring island of Eimeo; six months as boat steerer on the Nantucket whaler *Charles and Henry*; and a summer of odd jobs in the Hawaiian Islands. Then, in August 1843, he signed aboard the navy frigate *United States* for the last half of her Pacific cruise, visiting South American ports, making the violent return passage around Cape Horn, and so home at last, entering Boston Harbor in October 1844. If we ask why Melville went whaling rather than take a second round on a merchant ship, the answer seems evident: he wanted not a career but adventure. Events came too fast to absorb them; he would spend the next seven years (1845–51) reimagining them in six books.

If danger was the magnet, the whaling industry was the right place to find it. Of several perils, the first, always, was the sea itself. Melville wrote that more than seven hundred American whalers and twenty thousand seamen were roaming the South Seas and the far Pacific in the 1840s (*MD*, Hayford and Parker, eds., 529ff), venturing often into uncharted waters, at risk from shoals, reefs, and treacherous currents often first recorded in whaleship logs. Storms, gales, and the dreaded typhoon took their toll on these tough, small, bluff-bowed sailing ships, often worn down by months or even years at sea.[6] The *Acushnet* was wrecked in the Bering Sea, on St. Lawrence Island on August 16, 1851, just as Melville was finishing *Moby-Dick;* her crew and some barrels of oil were saved, but the ship was a total loss. Four days later the *Ann Alexander,* out of New Bedford, was rammed and sunk by a whale, the second such recorded attack since the famous 1820 sinking of the whaler *Essex* by an enraged sperm whale. Melville's third whaler, the *Charles and Henry,* was wrecked on the island of Corvo in the Azores on August 17, 1845, two years after his tour aboard it (*Log* 426, 198; also McElderry). No one said it better than Ishmael: "however baby man may brag of his science and skill, and however much, in a flattering future, that science and skill may augment; yet for ever and for ever, to the crack of doom, the sea will insult and murder him, and pulverize the stateliest, stiffest frigate he can make . . . ." Here, as when addressing the risks of mast sitting, we see Ishmael in his "for ever" mood, signaling his passion to celebrate the life of danger. Not a day passes, Ishmael continues, but "the live sea swallows up ships and crews" (ch. 58). That claim is supported by endless tales and records of whalers disabled, wrecked, or simply never seen again. That death at sea and by the sea and sea burials are a running theme of the Melville tales is not a sign of moribund temperament or fictional enthusiasm; it is a rendering of what he himself had seen, buttressed by what he had heard and read about from others with comparable experiences.

The special peril of the industry, of course, was the war against the whales. The frequent comparisons between war and whaling in *Moby-Dick* are legitimate. Melville was in much greater danger when aboard each of three whalers than during his fourteen months in the United States Navy. Whales were the enemy and whalemen were mercenaries, hired to engage, kill, and process as many of these giant beasts as possible. The modern sensibility, happily, has been formed by whale-watching trips during summer vacations, by tapes of their extraordinary "songs," and by the literature of Save-the-Whale movements. It is necessary, therefore, to recall four precise terrors facing six men in a light boat when they moved in for the kill: the smashing power of the whale's flukes, the crunching power of the sperm whale's mighty jaws, able to cut the boat in two and mangle the men; the sheer bulk of the body rising under the boat and throwing the men into the sea; and the incredible strength of the largest animal on earth when "in a flurry," his death agony. These dangers were the subject of endless yarns by all whalemen and the focus of powerful paintings (such as "Pêche du Cachalot" by Garneray, Ishmael's favorite) and sensational lithographs hawked in the streets (such as the Currier and Ives's "The Sperm Whale 'in a Flurry'").[7] In *Moby-Dick* the seven or so pursuits and killings, culminating in Ahab's three-day chase, are dramatic *actions* presenting the book's premise of life at risk. Harpoons and lances were the required tools, but skill and courage were the necessary weapons. Once within what Ishmael calls "the charmed, churned circle of the hunted sperm whale" (ch. 48), the six men in the whaleboat catch a whiff of eternity that will last a lifetime.

"Believe me," Melville wrote in his March 1847 review of J. Ross Browne's book on whaling, "it's quite as terrible as going into battle to a raw recruit." *Moby-Dick* was still three years away, but in that review Melville, after clowning around, could not resist writing three paragraphs of his own version of the chase scene, as if in rehearsal for the inevitable whaling book that lay ahead. When *Moby-Dick* was done, there again was the "raw recruit, marching . . . into the fever heat of his first battle" (ch. 48). No wonder the child Pip, hired as ship-keeper not as boat-crew, twice jumped from Stubb's whaleboat (ch. 93). No wonder most whalers carried two spare boats amidships as well as the four in the davits. Twelve days before Melville came aboard the navy frigate *United States* in Honolulu, the following random entry was recorded in her log: "August 5th [1843]. American barque Elizabeth came in, having lost her Captain & a boats crew of 5 in taking a whale" (Anderson 74). No comparable disaster occurred to the frigate.

Killings brought another series of dangers. The sixty-ton corpse of a sixty-foot whale had to be towed alongside, cut into and the case bailed, the giant strips of blubber hauled aboard, cut up, tried out in the deck furnaces, and the precious oil—the whole point of the voyage—barreled and stowed below. The ship became a floating factory, the jobs not unlike those in a Chicago slaughterhouse a half-century later. The work was hard and dirty as well as dangerous. Though forced to acknowledge that whaling is "a butchering sort of business," Ishmael maintains it is no worse than war: "The disordered slippery decks of a whale-ship are comparable to the unspeakable carrion of . . . battlefields" (ch. 24). A man who has been whaling has the right to claim his role as war veteran.

Like soldiers, whalers deserve memorials, and thus the black-bordered marble tablets in Ishmael's "Whaleman's Chapel" naming three mortal dangers of the trade. He acknowledges fictionalizing his three inscriptions: John Talbot, 18, "lost overboard . . . off Patagonia"; the six men of a whaleboat "towed out of sight by a Whale, On the Off-shore Ground in the PACIFIC"; and a captain "killed by a Sperm Whale" while "in the bows of his boat" (ch. 7). Two things come through in the Chapel chapters: Ishmael's insistence on the danger theme—both physical and, in Mapple's sermon, spiritual—and Ishmael's determination to keep his visionary and mythical tale firmly bottomed on reality. Thus, the Chapel is the Seamen's Bethel, still standing in New Bedford, its walls even now lined with tragic cenotaphs. Thus, Father Mapple is a recreation of the famous nautical preacher Father Taylor at the Boston Bethel, heard by Emerson and Dickens as well as by Dana and Melville (*MD*, Mansfield and Vincent, eds., 612–15). Whether or not Melville ever saw the Bethel tablet for Captain William Swain is not known, but it reads in part, "carried overboard by the line, and drowned, May 19th 1844, in the 49th year of his age," thus validating the manner of fictional Captain Ahab's death, as the sinking of the *Essex* by a whale validates the destruction of the mythical *Pequod*. Ishmael keeps his dream and danger narrative "something like"— as he says of his invented inscriptions—the realities of Melville's own experiences. The old problem of authenticity evoked "The Affidavit" chapter in *Moby-Dick* (ch. 45), lest his tale be taken "as a monstrous fable" (which it was), "or still worse and more detestable, a hideous and intolerable allegory" (which, obviously, he feared and knew it was, admitting this to the Hawthornes). Within fable and allegory, reality; inside the blubber, poetry.[8]

Melville's response to the dangers of sea, whales, and butchering is double in his writings. Although his narrators strive almost fiercely to involve the reader in the fear, even the terror, of some events—mast-climbing, battling the whales, surviving the sea, avoiding the sharks—the narratives bristle with jokes and hilarities uncommon in sea tales. Dana seems such an earnest young undergraduate, too admirably anxious—to prove his manhood and redefine the romance of the sea—for joking. And Cooper's wooden shoes simply wouldn't let him dance. Conrad, greatest of the European sea writers, entranced with his own kind of deep moral issues, was impatient with Melville's game playing, if that's what he meant by his curious rejection of *Moby-Dick* as "not having a single sincere line in the three volumes" (Parker and Hayford, eds., 122–23). Melville's comic flare no doubt began with temperament, nourished by youth and good health. But the nub of its style came right out of the fisheries, especially the sort of hangman's humor not unlike the black comedy bred by modern wars.

Ishmael argues in fact that the disastrous events of the first lowering led directly to his fabrication of a "genial, desperado philosophy." The only way he can accept the terrors of the chase is to consider them "a part of the general joke. There is nothing like the perils of whaling," he claims, "to breed this free and easy sort of genial, desperado philosophy; and with it I now regarded this whole voyage of the Pequod, and the great White Whale its object" (ch. 49). Though Ishmael is joking about joking here—going below to draft his will—he quite seriously indicates later in "The Line" (ch. 60) exactly when and where the desperado philosophy got its start. The occasion is whaling's most dangerous moment—when "the six men composing the crew pull into the jaws of death, with a halter around every neck, as you may say." The crew are facing the stern, where the mate, chanting his rhythmic obscenities (Ishmael has sanitized them, you can be sure), is steering his cockleshell right onto the back of Leviathan, whom they can't see; in seconds the harpoon will strike, the whale will run, or sound, or thrash, and the deadly line will whiz through the boat. And the Men? They "shudder," they "quiver," they turn to "shaken jelly." Now comes the incredible truth: "Yet habit—strange thing! what cannot habit accomplish?" asks Ishmael; "Gayer sallies, more merry mirth, better jokes, and brighter repartees, you never heard over your mahogany, than you will hear over the half-inch white cedar of the whale-boat, when thus hung in hangman's nooses. . . ." Given a temperamental bent toward humor (merely struggling for existence in the pre-Pacific writings), Melville found right here in the whaleboat the perfect incubator for his hyena laugh. It erupts in the sea books; it declines, or perhaps ascends, into subtler ironies in the later years.

Comedy in the face of danger was not the only thing Melville learned from the habits of whalemen. The evidence is everywhere, scattered through the log books and the histories of the industry, that they were mainly an unsavory lot (by middle-class terms), drifters and desperadoes living at the edge of a social world they had abandoned. In the usual crew of some twenty-five men (plus the mates, captain, cook, steward, blacksmith, and cooper) there might be an ambitious young New Englander or two, heading toward a mate-captain-merchant sequence as a career. At the opposite end there might be escaped criminals, vicious types like Jackson in *Redburn,* sick in body and mind, yet with a flair for seamanship. The majority of the crew were simply random re-peaters, dreaming of someday making a life ashore but inevitably ending up on another cruise for lack of actual alternatives or because they were carried aboard by the professional crimps, who for a price dragged them out of the boarding houses, brothels, and grog shops into which they fell on reaching port. As Melville acknowledged in his "Preface" to *Omoo,* "the Sperm Whale Fishery . . . is not only peculiarly fitted to attract the most reckless seamen of all nations, but in various ways, is calculated to foster in them a spirit of the utmost license."

Both ship and shore involved Melville in daily contacts and conflicts be-tween classes and cultures. As did Cooper and Dana, he experienced the class conflict inherent in his patrician upbringing. The narrator of *Mardi* is forth-right: contact among forecastle sailors is "too near and constant to favor deceit." It is useless "to assume qualities not yours; or to conceal those you possess. Incognitos, however desirable, are out of the question." There was no hiding, he says, his upper-class vocabulary, his interest in literature, even his style of eating (ch. 3). The pattern of his writings suggests that Melville made his way by finding an agreeable companion or two and winning respect, at least, from others by doing his share of the work. Aboard the *Acushnet,* Toby Greene, with whom he deserted ship at Nukuhiva, was a good friend; Toby later named a son Herman Melville Greene and made a small literary career out of their association (*Log* xxvii). Melville's domineering brother, Ganse-voort, wrote that Herman, after seven months at sea, was satisfied: "being one of a crew so much superior in morale and early advantages to the ordinary run of whaling crews affords him constant gratification" (*Log* 119). But it is possible that Herman's lost letter to his brother was telling him what Ganse-voort wanted to hear, and certain that Gansevoort, a rising young lawyer re-laying this information to an old family friend who was also chief justice of the Massachusetts courts, is advocating his own high moral stance, as was his wont. In any case the notes Melville jotted down in 1850, "What became of the ship's crew," according to a shipmate who visited him, suggest a somewhat grimmer forecastle scene. A Portuguese boatsteerer "either ran away or [was] killed" in the Marquesas; the carpenter "went ashore at Mowee [Maui] half dead with disreputable disease," as did "Tom Johnson, black"; three crewmen ran away—Columbia coast, Rio, and to a Sydney ship—and a fourth made "various attempts at running away" but came home; the blacksmith ran away in San Francisco; another crewman "went ashore half dead at the Marquesas," and a "young fellow—went ashore half dead, spitting blood, at Oahu." A second boatsteerer deserted in Peru. The first mate "had a fight with the captain & went ashore at Payta [Peru]"; the third mate did the same. Captain Valentine Pease, Jr., "retired & lives ashore at the Vineyard" (*Log* 399–400). So much for Gansevoort's "superior" crew.

Melville's life on three whaleships was both complicated and enriched, as *Moby-Dick* shows, by the mixture of races in the industry. Ishmael claims that less than half the men on American whalers are American born, though most officers are. Captain and mates, as on the *Pequod,* were Yankees from New England coastal towns, Cape Cod, or the Islands (Martha's Vineyard and Nantucket). The choice of harpooners for the *Pequod*—a South Sea Islander, a Gay Head Native American (from the Vineyard), and a giant African—is an unusual but possible combination, suggesting that Melville wants Ishmael's story to make a statement about geography and racial values, in this case Ahab's enlistment of a worldwide primitivism for his wild quest. The crew is so racially mixed that Ishmael calls it "an Anacharsis Clootz deputation"—that is, a collection of revolutionaries "from all the isles of the sea, and all the ends of the earth" (ch. 27). The name *Pequod,* primarily chosen to mark the ship as doomed, recalls the annihilation of an Indian village in the Pequot War of 1637 by savage Puritans; it also suggests the tribal quality of Ahab's crew. The great ballet in "Midnight, Forecastle" (ch. 40) begins as a parade of some twenty different nations and races, full of song and dance in celebration of the quest; but the ballet ends ominously with a knife fight between Daggoo and the Spanish sailor over a racial slur. The brawl on deck is broken up only by a violent squall overhead and the mate's frantic orders to reef topsails. Little Pip's final monologue begs the "big white God aloft somewhere in yon darkness" to have mercy on a small black boy and "preserve him from all men that have no bowels to feel fear!" Race conflict runs deep.

The heroic and altogether admirable Queequeg, and the bosom friendship that develops between him and Ishmael, is a counterargument for racial harmony. At first Ishmael is terrified of this "wild cannibal" with the tomahawk pipe: "what a sight! Such a face! It was of a dark, purplish, yellow color, here and there stuck over with large, blackish looking squares." Beneath the comedy of their misunderstandings of one another lies a useful sense that if people take the trouble, accommodation is possible; "What's all this fuss I have been making about, thought I to myself—the man's a human being just as I am: he has just as much reason to fear me, as I have to be afraid of him" (ch. 3).

The secret of Ishmael's willingness to try to understand Queequeg, of course, was learned by Melville during his month among the natives of Typee Valley. According to the log-keeper on the *United States,* "The view of this steep and lofty Island is truly sublime and beautiful. . . . The inhabitants are cannibals and are tattooed from head to foot and go entirely in a state of nudity. . . . Their weapons consist of spears set with sharks teeth and clubs made of a very heavy wood" (Anderson 57–58). These were the realities that Melville experienced, the Valley almost untouched by outside culture. His captivity was a version of anthropological field work almost unavailable in our time, anywhere. Today the tribes are likely to give information about themselves that they learned from previous field workers. Cannibalism or not, Melville's experience was intense and mind shaping. He learned all he could about working one's way through racial barriers. And time and again he watched social action—governed by religious rules, tradition, and especially the system of "taboo" (as invisible and as powerful as an electric current)— whose meanings he repeatedly acknowledged he could not penetrate. Thus the island experience lasted long after the writing of *Typee; Moby-Dick* is alive with primitivism, and the powerful sense of impenetrable human actions is a central quality in such later writings as "Bartleby, the Scrivener," "Benito Cereno," and *Billy Budd, Sailor.*

The Pacific turned out to be as dangerous as Melville had hoped. He climbed to the yardarms a thousand times, fair weather and foul, without a serious fall. He deserted ship without being recaptured. He lived through and escaped from savage captivity that seemed to be life-threatening. He withstood two years in the cramped and fetid forecastles of three whalers without losing his mind. He joined in a mutiny that resulted only in ritual imprisonment. He endured fourteen months among five hundred sailors jammed into a navy frigate without dying of boredom or being flogged. The capacity of common sailors for self-destruction was unlimited. But, said the *London Critic* in its review of *Typee,* "The author is no common man" (*Typee* xxii). It was uncommon, we can conclude, that Melville escaped the whale fisheries alive, unmutilated, and without disease. Moreover it was quite wonderful that he came home bearded and vigorous, his memory and imagination brimful. But the great thing was that with the hyena laugh ringing in his ears—a common sailor's only sufficient retort to danger and death—he was ready to explore his nascent genius, driven by the need to reimagine his life thus far. For "I only am escaped alone to tell thee."

NOTES

1. Melville's remarkable performance in seven years: *Typee* (1846), island captivity; *Omoo* (1847), beachcombing; *Mardi* (1849), Pacific allegory; *Redburn* (1849), merchant service; *White-Jacket* (1850), U.S. Navy; *Moby-Dick* (1851), whaling.

2. Plates I and II are from Dana.

3. In her two-year cruise, the *United States* had no such accident. However, in "Deaths During the Cruise," the log lists thirteen men and the captain; all but one died of "Disease" (Anderson 77). Five of the six deaths recorded while Melville was aboard led to sea burials, which he must have witnessed.

4. "Sinners in the Hands of an Angry God," Edwards's famous Enfield sermon, took as text "Their foot shall slide in due time" (Deut. 32:35).

5. Descartes's elaborate drawing of the Vortices in his *Principles of Philosophy* is startling; falling through them would be quite an experience. Melville must have seen the drawing (reproduced in Andrade 41).

6. Two readable and reliable histories of the whaling industry are by Hohman and by Stackpole.

7. Ishmael discusses whaling images in chapters 55, 56, 57; for commentary see Frank.

8. Melville set up the blubber poetry conflict in his important May 1, 1850, letter to Dana and wrote of his afterthoughts on allegory in a letter to Sophia Hawthorne (Davis and Gilman, eds., 106–08, 145–47).

WORKS CITED

Anderson, Charles Roberts, ed. *Journal of a Cruise to the Pacific Ocean, 1842–1849, in the Frigate "United States."* Durham, NC: Duke UP, 1937.

Andrade, E. N. *Isaac Newton.* New York: Chanticleer, 1950.

Bryant, William Cullen. *Poems.* Philadelphia: A. Hart, 1852.

Dana, R. H., Jr. *The Seaman's Friend.* 13th rev. ed. Boston: Thomas Groom, 1873.

Davis, Merrell R., and William H. Gilman, eds. *The Letters of Herman Melville.* New Haven: Yale UP, 1960.

Frank, Stuart M. *Herman Melville's Picture Gallery.* Fairhaven, MA: Lefkowicz, 1986.

Gilman, William H. *Melville's Early Life and "Redburn."* New York: New York UP, 1951.

Hohman, Elmo Paul. *The American Whaleman: A Study of Life and Labor in the Whaling Industry.* New York: Longmans, 1928.

McElderry, B. R., ed. *Narrative of the Most Extraordinary and Distressing Shipwreck of the Whaleship Essex by Owen Chase. With . . . Herman Melville's Notes.* New York: Corinth, 1963.

Melville, Herman. *Moby-Dick.* Ed. Harrison Hayford and Hershel Parker. New York: Norton, 1967.

————. *Moby-Dick.* Ed. Luther S. Mansfield and Howard P. Vincent. New York: Hendricks House, 1952.

————. *Redburn.* Ed. Harrison Hayford, Hershel Parker, and G. Thomas Tanselle. Evanston and Chicago: Northwestern UP and the Newberry Library, 1969.

————. *Typee: A Peep at Polynesian Life.* Rev. ed. ("Publishers' Advertisement" [pp. xv–xxii] bound into back.) New York: Wiley and Putnam, 1847.

Parker, Hershel, and Harrison Hayford, eds. *Moby-Dick as Doubloon.* New York: Norton, 1970.

Stackpole, Edward. *The Sea Hunters: The New England Whalemen During Two Centuries, 1635–1835.* Philadelphia: Lippincott, 1953.

Vincent, Howard. *The Tailoring of Melville's White-Jacket.* Evanston: Northwestern UP, 1970.

3

Whose Book Is *Moby-Dick*?

MERTON M. SEALTS, JR.

During the early years of the Melville revival, which began in this country in the aftermath of World War I, roughly a hundred years after Melville's birth in 1819, there was much discussion of *Moby-Dick* as a rediscovered masterpiece. But then as now, many people merely talked about the book instead of actually reading it. When Harold Ross founded *The New Yorker* magazine in 1925, according to the late James Thurber in *The Years with Ross* (1959), he was "unembarrassed by his ignorance of the great novels of any country," including his own. One day, Thurber reports, "he stuck his head into the checking department of the magazine . . . to ask 'Is Moby Dick the whale or the man?'" (77). But whether or not they've ever read the book, most literate Americans today know that it was Ahab who pursued the White Whale and are also well aware of still another character in *Moby-Dick:* the one who speaks that memorable opening line, "Call me Ishmael."

Whose book, then, is *Moby-Dick*? Should we award it to the title character, the invincible whale himself? Or to Captain Ahab, who dooms his ship and

From Merton M. Sealts, Jr., *Beyond the Classroom: Essays on American Authors,* University of Missouri Press. © 1996 by The Curators of the University of Missouri. Reprinted with permission of the author and the publisher.

crew in his desperate quest to slay the monster who had reaped away his leg? Or to narrator Ishmael, the one human survivor of the inevitable catastrophe, who alone escapes to tell the story? Since the book was first published in 1851, the question has been posed repeatedly, but the answers to it, as we shall see, have been various indeed. For the entire book is like that gold doubloon, the coin of great value that Ahab nailed to his ship's mainmast, promising it as a reward to the first man who should sight the White Whale. Witness these words of Ahab himself: "'this round gold is but the image of the rounder globe, which, like a magician's glass, to each and every man in turn but mirrors back his own mysterious self'" (NN *MD* 431). So with the book—and so too with its principal characters. All of them mirror back the reader and whatever he or she has brought to the experience of reading.

But Melville's own contemporaries saw little of themselves in either the characters or the book, despite all that he himself had put into it for those possessing eyes to see. Like two other innovative literary works of the 1850s in America, Thoreau's *Walden* and Whitman's "Song of Myself," Herman Melville's *Moby-Dick* had to wait the better part of a century for the readership that we now think it deserves. What each of the three writers had to say in these works and the unique way in which he said it seemed somehow foreign to their contemporaries, who had other ideas about what literary productions should be and do. We see a similar divergence in our own day between popular taste and the ground-breaking work of new artists in various media, not only in poetry and prose but also in music and painting or in architecture and interior design. Indeed, every creative artist, if he is "great and at the same time *original,* has had the task of *creating* the taste by which he is to be enjoyed." So Wordsworth, speaking from experience, put it as long ago as 1815, for he and Coleridge as innovators in poetry had faced the same problem in England since publishing their *Lyrical Ballads* in 1798.[1]

Different as they are in both subject matter and form from the poetry of Wordsworth and from one another, *Walden,* "Song of Myself," and *Moby-Dick* as innovative works have much in common with the pervasive Romantic spirit that had animated European art and literature long before its influence was felt on this side of the Atlantic, but they also draw on experience that we recognize immediately as uniquely American. Like much Romantic art, moreover, they are intensely subjective in character. Each of the three employs what Wayne Booth has called a "dramatized narrator," an "I" who not only tells the reader about events of the past but also addresses him directly in the narrative present, as in the opening paragraphs of *Walden:*

> In most books, the *I*, or first person, is omitted; in this it will be retained; that, in respect to egotism, is the main difference. . . . I should not talk so much about myself if there were any body else whom I knew as well.

Here are the first three lines of "Song of Myself":

> I celebrate myself,
> And what I assume you shall assume,
> For every atom belonging to me as good belongs to you. (25)

And here too are the familiar opening lines of chapter 1 of *Moby-Dick,* also addressed directly to the reader—to "you":

> Call me Ishmael. Some years ago—never mind how long precisely—having little or no money in my purse, and nothing in particular to interest me on shore, I thought I would sail about a little and see the watery part of the world. It is a way I have of driving off the spleen, and regulating the circulation. (3)

Again in Romantic fashion, each of the three works proceeds to take both the "I" and the reader into nature and the open air: with Thoreau to "the shore of Walden Pond, in Concord, Massachusetts," there to transact what he calls some private business; with Whitman "to the bank by the wood," there to "loafe and invite my soul"; with Melville's Ishmael, again "waterward"— since "as every one knows, meditation and water are wedded for ever" (NN *MD* 4)—and ultimately to sea, motivated chiefly by "the overwhelming idea of the great whale himself" (7), for "only on the profound unbounded sea, can the fully invested whale be truly and livingly found out" (454).

To speak now about Melville's book in particular, are we to read it as a story both by and about its narrator, like *Walden,* or is it about what Ishmael calls "the fully invested whale"—specifically the title character, though Moby Dick himself does not appear until the third chapter from the end? Or is it really about still another character, one linked both to Moby Dick and to Ishmael—Captain Ahab? Ahab, that "grand, ungodly, god-like man," as Captain Peleg describes him to Ishmael (79), makes his entrance only after Melville has given us a hundred pages of Ishmael's story, but he seemingly dominates the action thereafter. Is it then Ahab's book, or the Whale's, or narrator Ishmael's? Contemporary reviewers first raised these questions; twentieth-century readers have raised them again.

On the evidence of the original titles, *The Whale* in the first English edition of 1851 and *Moby-Dick; or, The Whale* in the first American, a reader might well infer that Melville himself thought of whales and especially of one White Whale—Moby Dick—as central to the book. As a persuasive twentieth-century reader put it in 1966, Melville presents Moby Dick as "the crown and consummation of the imperial breed of whales"; moreover, "the logic of the book as a whole works to give whales in general, and him in particular, a mythic and heroic stature. He gains this stature only by having whalers and whaling share it; but because they do, he gains it more triumphantly. . . . Moby Dick *is,* in the most relevant sense, the book's protagonist" (Buckley 12).

Upon first reading you may be inclined to agree with this eloquent statement and say that the book is indeed Moby Dick's. But before you go that far, consider as well these differing opinions from three other twentieth-century essays, also by readers of the 1960s:

Second Reader: "I say 'Call me an Ishmaelite' because I assume that this is primarily Ishmael's book. The drama of Ahab and the whale is most significant when seen in relation to Ishmael experiencing that drama. . . . Ahab never would (nor could) have written this book; Ishmael does (and must)." (Roper 2, 3)

Third Reader: "But this is not Ishmael's story. He is a delightful narrator in the beginning, and for a time at sea plays the role admirably, but when Melville becomes truly engrossed in telling the story of Ahab, he pushes Ishmael aside and gives insights denied his first-person narrator." (Braswell 16–17)

Fourth Reader: "But is Ahab then the 'hero' of *Moby Dick?* To answer with an unqualified affirmative is to neglect just half of the book. For if it is the tragedy of Captain Ahab, it is also the novel of Ishmael." (Halverson 444)

On a purely literal level, one must grant, Ahab certainly couldn't have written such a book, if only because it describes his own death, and Ishmael does indeed disappear from our view in later chapters when Ahab comes to the fore and at last encounters Moby Dick. The narrative as we have it gives readers not only "insights" but also basic information that sailor Ishmael could not conceivably have obtained aboard the *Pequod:* for example, what Ahab said either in his private soliloquies or in exchanges with Stubb, Starbuck, and Pip that no other member of the crew would have easily overheard. To the question

"Whose book is *Moby-Dick*?" there is still no generally accepted answer among those who variously name the White Whale, Ishmael, and Ahab as its principal figure. Moreover, there has been further disagreement over the genre and form of *Moby-Dick:* can a book be considered aesthetically unified if it is at once "the tragedy of Captain Ahab," "the novel of Ishmael," and, what one early reviewer called it, a "Whaliad,"[2] meaning a prose epic treating learnedly and exhaustively, or exhaustingly, of whales and whaling?

I

For an indication of how and when these associated questions first arose, let us begin with a glance at aspects of the nineteenth-century response to *Moby-Dick.* Neither Ishmael, Ahab, nor the White Whale attracted many readers to the book during Melville's lifetime—to his deep disappointment, as we know, for he had composed *Moby-Dick* with the sense that a literary masterwork might well be taking form under his hand. The initial reviews had been mixed. Even those British critics who had high praise for some attributes of the book were troubled nevertheless by what they considered its faults of style and structure: for example, they noted that Melville did not consistently maintain Ishmael's first-person point of view and, since the London edition did not include the Epilogue, they complained that the book offered no explanation of Ishmael's survival after the sinking of the *Pequod;* how, then, could he be alive to tell his story?

The first American reviewers were less concerned with such technical matters, partly because the first New York edition not only provided the Epilogue but also carried the Etymology and the Extracts on whales and whaling at the beginning of the narrative rather than at the end, where they had appeared in the earlier London edition. But Americans too were uncertain about how to classify the new work, and several of them objected to its general tone. One leading journal, the *New York Literary World,* published by Melville's friends Evert and George Duyckinck, dealt with it as "two if not three books . . . rolled into one." Their two-part review praised Melville's "brilliantly illustrated" account of the great Sperm Whale and identified Moby Dick as his "hero," going on to express reservations about both the characterization of Ahab and the prominence given Ishmael and his inveterate philosophizing.[3] To the Duyckincks, Ahab's story seemed melodramatic rather than tragic; and with other American critics of the 1850s, they considered Ishmael's speculations to be shockingly irreverent. Melville himself, wrote a representative critic in 1857, should give over his "metaphysical and morbid meditations" and return to the vein of *Typee* and *Omoo,* the books of adventure that had so pleased the public a decade earlier (O'Brien 390).

With the decline of the whaling industry in later years of the century, when petroleum, natural gas, and electricity in turn replaced whale oil in American and European households, interest in books about whales and whaling declined as well. But a small band of admirers in England kept Melville's name alive there, and with the conclusion of World War I a new generation of American readers found that *Moby-Dick,* along with *Walden* and "Song of Myself," was speaking to them in a way that most nineteenth-century readers had simply failed to understand and enjoy. By 1951, the book's centennial year, *Moby-Dick* had become a standard work on American college reading lists and a subject for proliferating critical and scholarly study.

II

The one twentieth-century work that in effect legitimated an aesthetic approach to Melville and his American contemporaries was F. O. Matthiessen's *American Renaissance: Art and Expression in the Age of Emerson and Whitman,* first published in 1941. Other scholars writing during the 1950s and 1960s significantly broadened the context of both research and teaching by relating the work of our nineteenth-century authors to the Romantic and symbolist movements in both America and Europe. One example is Morse Peckham, a theorist of Romanticism who dealt with Melville and *Moby-Dick* in terms of the perennial Romantic themes;[4] another is Charles Feidelson, whose *Symbolism and American Literature* (1953) traced the affiliations of American writers not only with their European predecessors but with their modern heirs and successors as well.[5]

These studies and others like them had a remarkable effect on ways of reading *Moby-Dick.* Where some commentators since the 1850s had seen the book as a structural hybrid, an uneasy juxtaposition of epic and essay, or novel and tragedy, that failed to conform to the accepted rules of any one literary genre, others writing in the spirit of Matthiessen and Peckham were now praising it as a highly successful example of Romantic art, creating its own form not mechanically, after some existing model, but organically—again like *Walden* and "Song of Myself." As Ishmael puts it at the beginning of chapter 63,

"Out of the trunk, the branches grow; out of them, the twigs. So, in productive subjects, grow the chapters" (289). And as Walter Bezanson remarked in his "*Moby-Dick:* Work of Art," a landmark essay first read as a lecture in the centennial year of 1951, "Organic form is not a particular form but a structural principle. In *Moby-Dick* this principle would seem to be a peculiar quality of making and unmaking itself as it goes. . . . Ishmael's narrative is always in process and in all but the most literal sense remains unfinished. For the good reader the experience of *Moby-Dick* is a participation in the act of creation" (56).[6]

The approach to *Moby-Dick* represented by Bezanson's essay brought with it a reconsideration of two of the interrelated issues under discussion here: does the book have a unified structure, and whom does it identify as its central character? During the early stages of the Melville revival, the usual emphasis of both readers and critics was clearly on Ahab and his struggle with the Whale, with lesser regard for Ishmael and what were often objected to as his philosophical "digressions." Interpreters as late as the 1940s tended to see the opposition between Ahab and Moby Dick in allegorical terms, praising Ahab as a self-reliant, Promethean individual confronting in Moby Dick the embodiment of all the forces of evil—physical or metaphysical—that beset oppressed humanity. For Melville, wrote one representative commentator, "the essence of the world is a dualism between good and evil," and man's appointed role is "to fight evil without compromise and without respite." So Ahab is fated "to spend his life pursuing Moby Dick, knowing that the master of the *Pequod* could never conquer the whale. In the end Ahab saved his soul, maintained inviolate his personal integrity by going down in unconquered defeat while Moby Dick swam on for other Ahabs to pursue. Ahab was the personification of Melville's philosophy of individualism."[7]

Much can be said for such a reading, as for most serious approaches to any complex book, but there are also other factors to be considered. What, for instance, are we to make of a monomaniac captain, repeatedly denominated as "crazy" or "mad," and his willful dedication of his ship and her crew to the fulfillment of his private quest for what his chief mate calls "vengeance on a dumb brute" (NN *MD* 163)? Isn't Melville offering an implied *criticism* of self-reliant individualism—perhaps of capitalist entrepreneurs generally—rather than an endorsement? Even so, Ishmael's admiration of the man informs the portrait he is essaying. As a "tragic dramatist who would depict mortal indomitableness in its fullest sweep and direst swing," he must acknowledge that Ahab lacks "all outward majestical trappings and housings." Therefore, "what shall be grand" in the resulting portrait "must needs be plucked at from the skies, and dived for in the deep, and featured in the unbodied air!" (148).

Melville's presentation of Ahab through Ishmael's words shows him as a commanding figure of tragic stature, flawed by "fatal pride" (519) yet not incapable of compassion, as we see in his treatment of Pip and even of Starbuck; he is no mere cardboard "personification." As Leon Howard wrote as long ago as 1950, when critics were beginning to deal with the book in a more searching and understanding way, "It was the author's emotional sympathy" for Ahab as "a character of whom he intellectually disapproved which gave *Moby Dick* much of its ambiguity and dramatic intensity" (xiii).

In the newer readings of *Moby-Dick*, the White Whale emerges as more than that fixed allegorical embodiment of pure evil that Ahab persisted in seeing; instead, critics after the 1950s write of the Whale's function in the overall structure of the book as that of a dynamic and ever-changing symbol, a cynosure that gradually accumulates not only meaning but multiple significance. From Etymology and Extracts through what Howard Vincent called its "cetological center" (*Trying Out* 119–367) to its concluding Epilogue, the book is filled with the lore of whales and whaling, showing how whales have figured in time and place over the centuries, how they appear not only to artists and scientists but to men actually risking their lives in the whale fishery. As a former whaleman, Melville well knew that "the only mode in which you can derive even a tolerable idea of [the whale's] living contour, is by going a whaling yourself; but by so doing, you run no small risk of being eternally stove and sunk by him" (NN *MD* 264).

As Ishmael revealed at the outset, "the overwhelming idea of the great whale" had been a leading motive for his own decision to go a whaling. But as his narrative progresses, we learn with him how Captain Ahab had projected his rage and hate upon one particular White Whale, and we begin to understand as well how Ishmael came first to share and later to distance himself from Ahab's obsession. And in due course, as initiated readers we are at last prepared to confront Moby Dick himself, in all his magnitude and surpassing beauty:

> Not the white bull Jupiter swimming away with ravished Europa clinging to his graceful horns . . . ; not Jove, not that great majesty Supreme! did surpass the glorified White Whale as he so divinely swam. . . . No wonder there had been some among the hunters who namelessly transported and allured by all that serenity, had ventured to assail it; but had

fatally found that quietude but the vesture of tornadoes. Yet calm, enticing calm, oh whale! thou glidest on, to all who for the first time eye thee, no matter how many in that same way thou may'st have bejuggled and destroyed before. (548)

However any one critic may view Moby Dick—as "the deepest blood-being of the white race," in the words of D. H. Lawrence, or the Freudian Superego, as Henry A. Murray suggested,[8] or Deity, or Death, or Nature, or the universe itself, to cite some other interpretations—there is likely to be no more agreement about his ultimate meaning than there was among the crews aboard the various ships we as readers encounter in the nine gams of the *Pequod.* "Shall we ever identify Moby Dick?" Harry Levin once asked. "Yes," he answered, "when we have sprinkled salt on the tail of the Absolute; but not before" (265).

III

During the 1950s, while critics were still thinking of Ahab as Melville's protagonist confronting his antagonist in Moby Dick, Bezanson and other scholars had also begun to write of Ishmael and his point of view as the unifying center of the story. Although there was minimal reference to *Moby-Dick* in Wayne Booth's influential book of 1961, *The Rhetoric of Fiction,* Booth's work inspired others to undertake a close examination of the technical aspects of Melville's fiction—notably his use of narrative point of view and his employment of dramatized narrators.[9] With *Moby-Dick* in particular, this approach of course involved a reappraisal of Ishmael's role.

Bezanson had already distinguished between the younger Ishmael who had once sailed aboard the *Pequod* and the older Ishmael who is now telling his story; in 1962 Warner Berthoff, in *The Example of Melville*—the best book to date on Melville as a literary craftsman—demonstrated how artfully Melville used Ishmael first to set the nautical scene and then to prepare us for both Ahab and the Whale. As Berthoff explained, Ishmael conducts us as readers through "four distinct 'worlds.'" We meet him first in the world of "the dry land, or at least the thronged edges of it: New York, New Bedford, Nantucket." Next, Melville and Ishmael take us aboard the *Pequod,* herself "a virtual city of the races and talents of men," and there, through a great opening-out, into "the non-human world of the sea and the indifferent elements." Then at last we are prepared to enter "the final, furthest 'world' set out in *Moby Dick,*" one that "communicates to men only in signs, portents, and equivocal omens, and seems intelligible only to madmen like Ahab and Pip" (Berthoff 79–86).

Into the fourth of these worlds, the realm beyond physical nature, it is fair to add that Melville himself could never have conducted us directly. Instead, speaking by indirection—first through Ishmael's voice and later through that of Ahab himself—he "craftily says, or sometimes insinuates," what would be "all but madness" for an author to utter or even to hint to us "in his own proper character." So Melville himself had once written of Shakespeare, at the very time when *Moby-Dick* was taking form; so Emily Dickinson would enjoin us to "Tell all the Truth but tell it slant— / Success in Circuit lies."[10] Even as truth-teller Ishmael is leading us out of our everyday world into the world of ships and the sea, where at last we meet Ahab and ultimately Moby Dick, he is at the same time securing for Melville the needed aesthetic distance from those two antagonists that as their creator he had to establish and maintain.

When any writer becomes "identified with the objects of [his] horror or compassion," as in our own century Scott Fitzgerald would declare in *The Crack-Up,* the result, as Fitzgerald had learned to his own cost, is "the death of accomplishment" (81). An author who fails to guard against such identification risks artistic disaster, and perhaps a psychological crisis as well. Witness Melville himself in his next book, *Pierre, or the Ambiguities* (1852), where there is no Ishmael to stand between him and his title character: reviewers unanimously condemned *Pierre,* and some readers and critics even questioned its author's sanity. In *Moby-Dick,* by contrast, Ishmael as intervening narrator had provided Melville with essential insulation, as Nick Carraway would do for Fitzgerald in *The Great Gatsby* and Marlow for Joseph Conrad in *Heart of Darkness,* each narrator distancing the creator from his creation. Were there no Ishmael in *Moby-Dick,* Melville would never have been able to give us his protagonist and antagonist—or to purge himself of his own pity and terror by doing so. That is why he could say, with relief, to Hawthorne, "I have written a wicked book, and feel spotless as the lamb" (*Correspondence* 212).

IV

Ishmael's dual role as narrator and actor has been profitably explored by several critics since Bezanson distinguished between "the enfolding sensibility . . . , the hand that writes the tale, the imagination through which all matters of the book pass," and that "young man of whom, among others, narrator Ishmael tells us in his story." The older narrator looking back upon his younger self had been a feature of Melville's earlier works, the differences between the two growing sharper in *Redburn* (1849) and *White-Jacket* (1850), the immediate predecessors of *Moby-Dick*. Now in a fully dramatized Ishmael, we witness "the narrator's unfolding sensibility. Whereas forecastle Ishmael drops in and out of the narrative . . . , the Ishmael voice is there every moment" (Bezanson 36, 41).

The fullest exploration of "the Ishmael voice" is Paul Brodtkorb's book-length "phenomenological reading" of *Moby-Dick, Ishmael's White World* (1965), which presupposes that narrator Ishmael is not only "the vessel that contains the book," but "in a major sense he *is* the book" (4). In 1961 Glauco Cambon had written of Ishmael as "the artist in the act of telling us, and struggling to understand, his crucial experience" (523); in 1970 Barry A. Marks further pointed out that like other "retrospective narrators" in Thoreau and Whitman, Ishmael is in fact presenting two stories simultaneously. One, his "past-time story," is about his recollected experience that is now over and done; the other, his "writing-time story," is about experience still in progress—an ongoing story of "a narrator's *telling* about his past" (366–67).[11]

Like speakers in Thoreau and Whitman, Ishmael too addresses his reader directly; he frequently pauses in his narration to consider the larger implications for the narrative present of something in the past that he had just described or related. "Yes, there is death in this business of whaling," he remarks after telling of the memorial tablets in Father Mapple's chapel (NN *MD* 37). Again, in concluding his chapter on "The Line," he observes that "All men live enveloped in whale-lines. All are born with halters round their necks; but it is only when caught in the swift, sudden turn of death, that mortals realize the silent, subtle, ever-present perils of life" (281). And at the end of "The Try-Works" he specifically warns the reader: "Give not thyself up, then, to fire, lest it invert thee, deaden thee; as for the time it did me. There is a wisdom that is woe; but there is a woe that is madness" (425).

As for his ongoing story, Ishmael makes us fully aware of the challenge facing "a whale author like me" who is presently engaged in "writing of this Leviathan" and earnestly striving "to produce a mighty book" on such "a mighty theme" (456). So daunting an enterprise, he contends, demands "a careful disorderliness" as "the true method" (361). "I promise nothing complete," he tells us in his chapter "Cetology"; he holds the typical Romantic view that "any human thing supposed to be complete, must for that very reason infallibly be faulty. . . . God keep me from ever completing anything. This whole book is but a draught—nay, but the draught of a draught" (136, 145).

Concerning Ishmael's several departures from his original first-person point of view, that unconventional practice that so troubled nineteenth-century reviewers and twentieth-century formalist critics as well, and other instances of what have been called "formal discontinuities" in *Moby-Dick*, Cambon has argued that Ishmael's supposed disappearance from the story is a legitimate rhetorical device that has its parallels both in the classical poets and historians and in twentieth-century fiction. Thus Ishmael's "imaginative reconstruction" of the other characters anticipates what Quentin Compson was to do in Faulkner's *Absalom, Absalom!,* where "memory modulates into imagination" and where once again the reader "share[s] the experience of creation in progress" (Cambon 523).

v

Emphasis on Ishmael as narrator rather than actor—and on Ishmael-like observers in contemporary American criticism, fiction, and intellectual life generally—has dismayed other commentators. "Ahab and the whale do not appear in our novels," one of them complained in 1959; "we write only about Ishmael."[12] A decade later, in the midst of the campus activism of the late sixties, an angry black contributor to *Partisan Review* blasted narrator Ishmael as "the precursor of the modern white liberal-intellectual" that he found infesting American universities. If Ishmael were really an active "character" in the story, according to Cecil Brown, he "would have repelled Ahab!" (459, 457).[13]

More recently, historicist and contextualist critics of *Moby-Dick* have indeed been shifting their focus from Ishmael back to Ahab, at the same time exploring what they see as the book's political implications rather than the cetological, metaphysical, and literary elements that variously engaged their predecessors. Meanwhile, scholars investigating the origins and textual development of the book have once again cast doubt on its artistic unity, citing a panoply of minor inconsistencies in Melville's text and even suggesting "unnecessary duplicates" among his characters.[14] Such instances of apparent disunity in the book can of course be cited against Bezanson and other champions of organic form—a concept that its opponents in an age of deconstruction dismiss as a convenient mask for hiding both minor and major artistic failings.[15]

To the degree that the Ishmaels of this world overshadow its Ahabs and White Whales, the anti-Ishmaelites do indeed have a point. But it also seems fair to say that in the final analysis the book is not the story of any one or even two of its characters. The only feasible way *to* Ahab and at last to the White Whale is *through* Ishmael, Melville's necessary surrogate and the reader's veritable guide, philosopher, and friend; and *all three figures* are equally indispensable to the author, to his book, and to its readers. As for the question of unity or disunity, the real test comes in the very act of responsive reading. In Brodtkorb's words, "literary unity is in the mental set of the reader as much as in the literary work" (4), and in the case of *Moby-Dick* that "mental set" is powerfully influenced and shaped by Ishmael—favorably so, as for Bezanson and his followers, or unfavorably, as for Cecil Brown.

For further guidance from Ishmael himself, consider his distinctions in chapter 89 between Fast-Fish and Loose-Fish, based on "the laws and regulations of the whale fishery" with respect to harpooned whales:

> I. A Fast-Fish belongs to the party fast to it.
> II. A Loose-Fish is fair game for anybody who can soonest catch it. (395–96)

Whose book, then, *is* this much-hunted Loose-Fish? It cannot be just Ahab's or the Whale's or Ishmael's; nor is it entirely Melville's, since you and I as individual readers have genuine claims of our own as well. "There is then creative reading, as well as creative writing," as Emerson long ago observed (58), and modern critics such as Bezanson and Cambon have applied his idea to *Moby-Dick*. "For the good reader," Bezanson told us, "the experience of *Moby-Dick* is a participation in the act of creation." In Cambon's phrasing, such a reader "will share the experience of creation in progress"—the same experience that Barry Marks has illustrated for us in Melville along with Thoreau and Whitman.

Once you as reader share that experience, then you have indeed made fast to *Moby-Dick*, and in a real sense it has become *your* book—*your* Fast-Fish, as I feel it to be very much mine. But if this comment sounds like an endorsement of what is now called reader-response criticism, we must nevertheless remember that there is a reciprocal corollary: Melville, reaching out through Ishmael as his surrogate, has at the same time figuratively harpooned *us* as his readers, making us fast to his book and therefore belonging to it. As narrator Ishmael, once again turning directly to each of us, pointedly asks, "What are you, reader, but a Loose-Fish, and a Fast Fish, too?" (398).

At the conclusion of *Moby-Dick*, the fated *Pequod* has been lost—lost with all her crew save one. Protagonist Ahab has met his lonely death on lonely life, while the White Whale, his invincible antagonist, swims on victorious. It is Ishmael, survivor of the *Pequod*'s wreck, who escapes alone to tell their story.

And by addressing us indirectly through Ishmael's omnipresent voice, Melville himself persuades us, like the authors of *Walden* and "Song of Myself," to assume what he has assumed in this mighty book and to celebrate, with him and with Ishmael, its mighty theme.

NOTES

1. William Wordsworth, "Essay Supplementary to Preface (1815)," 195. Wordsworth credited the idea to Coleridge.

2. *New York Daily Tribune,* quoted in Parker and Hayford, eds., 47. *Moby-Dick as Doubloon,* as its editors remark, "contains most of the best and some of the worst that has been written about *Moby-Dick*" through 1970 (xv). A full listing of reviews and criticism through 1960 will be found in Brian Higgins's *Annotated Bibliography, 1846-1930* and *Reference Guide, 1931–1960.* See also Hayes and Parker's *Checklist* and periodic updates of newfound reviews in *Melville Society Extracts.*

3. See Parker and Hayford, eds., 50–51, 35; or the Norton Edition of *Moby-Dick* 613–15. For other contemporary identifications of the Whale as "hero," see Parker and Hayford, eds., 24, 39, 56, 61. Another reviewer chose Ahab (11) and still others named Ishmael—or Melville (4, 53, 85, 87); for Ishmael, see also Parker 183.

4. See in particular Peckham, "Toward a Theory of Romanticism" 5–23; Adams 419–32; and Peckham, "Hawthorne and Melville as European Authors," 42–62. In the last essay cited, Peckham surveyed "the great Romantic themes" as they appear in *Moby-Dick,* suggesting that by 1851 "Melville had absorbed . . . all stages of Romanticism up to his own time, and had presented them in *Moby-Dick* in inextricable confusion." This is the reason, he speculated, that "the interpretation of *Moby-Dick* is so difficult and why in all probability it will never be understood with clarity or agreement" (58–59).

5. Charles Feidelson, Jr., *Symbolism and American Literature* (Chicago: University of Chicago Press, 1953). Feidelson observed that mid-nineteenth-century American writers "inherited the basic problem of romanticism: the vindication of imaginative thought in a world grown abstract and material . . . ; their solution . . . is closer to modern notions of symbolic reality than to romantic egoism" (4). He credited Edmund Wilson as the first critic to note their affinity with "the symbolist aesthetic that produced modern literature."

6. Bezanson's essay is reprinted in part in the Norton Edition of *Moby-Dick* (651–71) and in Vincent, *Merrill Studies* 87–103.

7. Gabriel 74. For other representative comments that take Moby Dick as symbolizing evil, see Winters 201, "the chief symbol and spirit of evil"; and Myers 77, "the white whale of evil."

8. Lawrence and Murray as reprinted in Vincent, *Merrill Studies* 50, 61.

9. Booth's book was immediately influential, especially among younger scholars. John Bryant singled out "the shift to rhetorical criticism, narrative, and point of view" as perhaps the most significant trend among dissertators of the 1960s (xvii).

10. Melville in "Hawthorne and His *Mosses*" (1850), as reprinted in NN *PT* 244; Dickinson 506 (#1129).

11. This neglected essay, which is especially valuable for classroom teachers and is well worth the attention of literary critics as well, contains a provocative analysis of the "two stories" that Ishmael tells in *Moby-Dick.* According to Marks,

The shape, and finally the meaning also, . . . stems from the fact that Ishmael's changing manner of narration is more than mere aimlessness; rather it is a significantly patterned search for efficacious speech. . . . The writing-time story of the retrospective narrative parallels the essential shape and meaning of its related past-time story. The narrative present is a metaphoric or mimetic version of the narrative past. . . . The writing-time story is a means of showing directly and immediately meanings which the author despairs of being able to communicate by conventional language and literary forms. (374)

12. Robert Hazel, speaking in 1959 at the December meeting of the Modern Language Association of America in New York City.

13. "The white whale" in Brown's view "is none other than you, Ishmael—the white, disembodied, overliterate, boring, snobbish, insipid, jew-bastard, nigger-lover, effete, mediocre, assistant-professor type, liberal" (454).

14. See Harrison Hayford, "Unnecessary Duplicates" 128–61 and "Discussions of Adopted Readings" in the NN *MD* 809–906, passim. Melville himself, after beginning *Moby-Dick* with high hopes for its success, finished writing it only under great difficulties, complaining to Hawthorne of his "ditcher's work" with the book and his fear that all his books were "botches" (*Correspondence* 212, 191). Although some present-day critics profess to discuss *Moby-Dick* as a virtually seamless narrative web, Paul Brodtkorb going so far as to charge Ishmael rather than Melville himself with the "mistakes and inconsistencies" observable in the narrative (4–5, 7), others such as Hayford have taken such occurrences as possible clues to the compositional history of the book. For a succinct review of various theories concerning its genesis and development, see section 5 of the Historical Note to the NN *MD* 648–59.

15. In 1951, the centennial year of *Moby-Dick*, when Walter Bezanson first described the book as a work of organic art, James Benziger remarked that "modern organic critics use their theory to check the pretensions of the biographical and historical critics," adding that *any* theory must be "applied with judgment" (48). His caution is applicable today, now that successive generations of historically minded critics have reacted in turn against the organicists.

WORKS CITED

Adams, R. P. "Romanticism and the American Renaissance." *American Literature* 23 (January 1952): 419–32.

Benziger, James. "Organic Unity: Leibniz to Coleridge." *PMLA* 66 (March 1951): 24–48.

Berthoff, Warner. *The Example of Melville.* Princeton: Princeton UP, 1962.

Bezanson, Walter E. "*Moby-Dick:* Work of Art." In Hillway and Mansfield, eds., 30–58.

Booth, Wayne C. *The Rhetoric of Fiction.* Chicago: U of Chicago P, 1961.

Braswell, William. "The Main Theme of *Moby-Dick.*" *Emerson Society Quarterly* no. 28, part 3: Melville Supplement (1962): 15–17.

Brodtkorb, Paul, Jr. *Ishmael's White World: A Phenomenological Reading of "Moby Dick."* New Haven: Yale UP, 1965.

Brown, Cecil M. "The White Whale." *Partisan Review* 36 (1969): 453–59.

Bryant, John. *Melville Dissertations, 1924–1980: An Annotated Bibliography and Subject Index.* Westport, CT: Greenwood, 1983.

Buckley, Vincent. "The White Whale as Hero." *Critical Review* (Melbourne) no. 9 (1966): 1–21.

Cambon, Glauco. "Ishmael and the Problem of Formal Discontinuities in *Moby Dick*." *Modern Language Notes* 76 (June 1961): 516–23.

Dickinson, Emily. *Complete Poems*. Ed. Thomas H. Johnson. Boston: Little, Brown, 1960.

Emerson, Ralph Waldo. "The American Scholar." 1837. In *Nature, Addresses, and Lectures*. Ed. Alfred R. Ferguson and Robert E. Spiller. Cambridge, MA: Harvard UP, 1971. 7–45.

Feidelson, Charles, Jr. *Symbolism and American Literature*. Chicago: U of Chicago P, 1953.

Fitzgerald, F. Scott. "Pasting It Together." 1936. In *The Crack-Up*. 1945. Ed. Edmund Wilson. New York: New Directions, 1956. 80–84.

Gabriel, Ralph H. *The Course of American Democratic Thought: An Intellectual History since 1815*. New York: Ronald Press Co., 1940.

Halverson, John. "The Shadow in *Moby-Dick*." *American Quarterly* 15 (Fall 1963): 436–46.

Hayes, Kevin J., and Hershel Parker. *Checklist of Melville Reviews*. Evanston: Northwestern UP, 1991.

Hayford, Harrison. "Unnecessary Duplicates: A Key to the Writing of *Moby-Dick*." In Pullin, ed., 128–61.

Higgins, Brian. *Herman Melville: An Annotated Bibliography, 1846–1930*. Boston: G. K. Hall, 1979.

————. *Herman Melville: A Reference Guide, 1931–1960*. Boston: G. K. Hall, 1987.

Hillway, Tyrus, and Luther S. Mansfield, eds. *Moby-Dick: Centennial Essays*. Dallas: Southern Methodist UP, 1953.

Howard, Leon. Introduction. *Moby Dick or, The Whale*. By Herman Melville. New York: Modern Library, 1950. v–xvi.

Lawrence, D. H. "Herman Melville's 'Moby Dick.'" 1923. Reprinted in Vincent, *Merrill Studies* 44–50.

Levin, Harry. *Symbolism and Fiction*. 1956. Extracted in Parker and Hayford, eds., 264–65.

Marks, Barry A. "Retrospective Narrative in Nineteenth Century American Literature." *College English* 31 (January 1970): 366–75.

Matthiessen, F. O. *American Renaissance: Art and Expression in the Age of Emerson and Whitman*. New York: Oxford UP, 1941.

Melville, Herman. *Moby-Dick*. Ed. Harrison Hayford and Hershel Parker. Norton Critical Edition. New York: W. W. Norton, 1967.

Murray, Henry A. "In Nomine Diaboli." 1951. Reprinted in Hillway and Mansfield, eds., 3–21; and in Vincent, *Merrill Studies* 52–66.

Myers, Henry Alonzo. "Captain Ahab's Discovery: The Meaning of *Moby Dick*." *Tragedy: A View of Life*. Ithaca: Cornell UP, 1956. 57–77.

O'Brien, Fitz-James. "Our Authors and Authorship: Melville and Curtis." *Putnam's Monthly Magazine* 9 (April 1857): 384–93.

Parker, Hershel. "Five Reviews Not in *Moby-Dick as Doubloon*." *English Language Notes* 9 (March 1972): 182–85.

Parker, Hershel, and Harrison Hayford, eds. *Moby-Dick as Doubloon: Essays and Extracts (1851–1970)*. New York: W. W. Norton, 1970.

Peckham, Morse. "Hawthorne and Melville as European Authors." In Vincent, *Melville and Hawthorne* 42–62.

———. "Toward a Theory of Romanticism." *PMLA* 66 (March 1951): 5–23.

Pullin, Faith, ed. *New Perspectives on Melville*. Kent, OH: Kent State UP, 1978.

Roper, Gordon. "On Teaching *Moby-Dick*." *Emerson Society Quarterly* no. 28, part 3: Melville Supplement (1962): 2–4.

Thoreau, Henry David. *Walden*. Ed. J. Lyndon Shanley. Princeton: Princeton UP, 1971.

Thurber, James. *The Years with Ross*. Boston: Little, Brown, 1959.

Vincent, Howard P. *The Trying-Out of Moby-Dick*. Boston: Houghton Mifflin, 1949.

———, comp. *The Merrill Studies in Moby-Dick*. Columbus, OH: Charles E. Merrill, 1969.

———, ed. *Melville and Hawthorne in the Berkshires*. Kent, OH: Kent State UP, 1968.

Whitman, Walt. *Leaves of Grass: The First (1855) Edition*. Ed. Malcolm Cowley. New York: Viking, 1959.

Winters, Yvor. "Herman Melville and the Problems of Moral Navigation." 1938. Reprinted in *In Defense of Reason*. New York: Swallow Press and Morrow, 1947. 200–233.

Wordsworth, William. "Essay Supplementary to Preface." 1815. In *Wordsworth's Literary Criticism*. Ed. Nowell C. Smith. London: Humphrey Milford, 1905. 168–202.

The Uses of the Present:
Melville and History

4

Melville and the Question of American Decolonization

LAWRENCE BUELL

It is striking that the last great work of the so-called American Renaissance should have been a tale about the consequences of impressment, a tale that portrays the forcible absorption into an imperial or old world order of a protagonist who, as R. W. B. Lewis long ago pointed out, is transparently a kind of republican or new world representative, although nominally British (146–52). Melville's *Billy Budd* thus opens by obliquely reopening one of the greatest grievances that postrevolutionary America harbored against Britain, a grievance that helped precipitate the War of 1812, our "second war of independence." Billy's impressment story goes on to become an ambiguous parable of the rite of passage to cultural maturity, from a comparatively egalitarian "state-of-nature" community aboard the *Rights of Man* to the *Bellipotent*'s more hierarchical and "advanced" society, dominated by a rule of law. Through the figure of Billy Budd, the notion of American difference is insinuated only to be preempted and repressed except as a kind of nostalgic afterglow.

The symbolic polarity between the two ships also hints at coming of age in a literary sense: Billy is translated from something like an oral culture, in

Lawrence Buell, "Melville and the Problem of American Decolonization," *American Literature* 64:2 (May 1992), 215–37. © 1992 by Duke University Press. Reprinted with permission.

which disputes get resolved through the wisdom of untutored virtue ostensibly acting without restraint by written codes of law, to the stage of print culture, where orality is forced underground (persisting in gossip and balladry) and disputes get resolved through discourse and by appeal to codified rules—a culture, furthermore, in which the presiding figure of Captain Vere is directly aligned with a canonical text from the British poetic tradition, Andrew Marvell's "Upon Appleton House," which Melville quotes as follows:

> This 'tis to have been from the first
> In a domestic heaven nursed,
> Under the discipline severe
> Of Fairfax and the starry Vere.[1]

The "this" of the quatrain refers in the broadest sense to the whole Appleton estate but more specifically to Mary Fairfax's genteelly constructed upbringing, which Marvell praises, although (as Melville perhaps knew) her prospects were almost as ominous as Billy Budd's—her marriage, as Raymond Williams puts it, being "that kind of political deal in which property and title were reconstituted" (57). Mary and Billy, then, were each young innocents whose nurture within the pseudo-Eden of Vere's patriarchy proved baleful, not auspicious. Melville would doubtless also have noticed that the poet himself was in a position akin to theirs—less naive but still an inhabitant of that same domestic heaven, working within the patronage system both as tutor and as bard of the local manor.

With the hint supplied by this poem in mind, we can imagine the polarity of *Billy Budd*'s two shipboard microcosms as reflecting not only upon issues of personal maturation, moral philosophy, and political values, but also upon the issue of American expression in the age of literary emergence. More specifically, it invites us to read Melville's last literary will and testament as a reminiscence about what happens when an American autodidact (as the young ex-sailor Melville liked to picture himself) enters the arena of cosmopolitan culture. The young writer—like the young sailor—quickly finds that free expression is regulated and constrained by Vere's world of "measured forms." This ultimately leads, in the mature writer, to a style of insinuation rather than direct statement.

Coming so near the end of the nineteenth century, and Melville's life, *Billy Budd* is a dramatic instance of American literature dwelling upon the idea of transition to personal and cultural maturity long after personal and cultural maturity have supposedly been reached. As such it provides an image of American postcolonial anxiety. But it is only one of many such images in Melville's work, which differ mutually and to some extent clash. For example, in *Redburn,* the protagonist's innocence takes the form not of unlettered Adamism but of an internalization of his father's genteel Anglophilia. In *Israel Potter* it takes the form of Israel's never grasping that the republican establishment is just as self-interested, in its own way, as the imperial. In *White-Jacket* and *Moby-Dick* innocence takes the form of not realizing at first how imperial forms persist in American enterprise. These and other such scenarios have to do with the theme of intellectual coming of age within contexts that either literally or metaphorically contrast America and Europe, but these individual contrasts and (even more) the totality of them become ironized and complicated to the point that the predictable opposition of republican virtue and imperial decadence becomes even more muddied than in Henry James. It is not so much the employment of the scenario, or even its repetition, as the inconsistency and muddying of it that is the definitive mark of what I'm calling postcolonial anxiety.[2] This essay explores its sources and unfolding in Melville's life and work.

* * *

One obvious place to begin would be with the signs of Melvillean Anglophilia in the biographical record: for example, the pleasure Melville took during his 1849 trip to Britain in buying and reading English authors like DeQuincey, or his thawing out the frigidity of one London publisher, Edward Moxon, by conversing enthusiastically about Charles Lamb.[3] These are two small indicators among many that it did not come naturally for Melville to think of himself simply and cleanly as an American man of letters, that he sought from the first to align himself with the larger Anglophone literary tradition rather than to classify himself (as Americanists do today) as an exclusively American writer—notwithstanding the famous dedication of *Moby-Dick* to Hawthorne and certain jingoistic remarks made in "Hawthorne and His *Mosses*" about supporting native authors for the sake of cultural nationalism.[4] "Bartleby the Scrivener" is more Dickensian than Poe-esque, *Moby-Dick* at least as Shakespearean as Hawthornian; and *The Confidence-Man* owes at least as much to Swift, Fielding, and Sterne as it does to the American vernacular conning tradition.

Such biographical and intertextual evidence looks all the more important given the exigencies of Melville's position as literary professional during the formative years of his career. Recent scholarship on postcolonial writing in the various European languages has directed attention to what might be called the "two audiences" phenomenon: namely, the issue of how postcolonial authors negotiate the problem of writing both for their countrymen and for the Western world audience, on which commercial success in good part also depends. In a study of African writers' consciousness of audience based on personal interviews, the West African critic Phanuel Egejuru claims that Africans writing in European languages have been caught in the dilemma of having to serve as agents of cultural independence while remaining "dependent on the ex-masters' literary tradition, taste, and approval" (9).[5] Egejuru presses her point too judgmentally, overgeneralizing from her interviewees' responses and sometimes assuming the ideological co-optation she is supposedly trying to prove; but in her excess of zeal she identifies an important creative irritant, pertinent to the American as well as the African case.

Take for example this passage from one of the already canonical African Anglophone novels, Ngugi wa Thiong'o's *Petals of Blood,* an anatomy of neo-colonial corruption and popular resistance in Kenya:

> [T]here are many questions about our history which remain unanswered. Our present day historians, following on similar theories yarned out by defenders of imperialism, insist we only arrived here yesterday. Where went all the Kenyan people who used to trade with China, India, Arabia, long before Vasco da Gama came to the scene and on the strength of gunpowder ushered in an era of blood and terror and instability—an era that climaxed in the reign of imperialism over Kenya? . . . The story of this heroic resistance: who will sing it? Their struggles to defend their land, their wealth, their lives: who'll tell of it? (67)

This passage clearly tries to address two constituencies, each with its own interest: the audience for whom darkest Africa has no history (the position characterized and refuted in the second and third sentences) and the compatriot for whom the historicity is self-evident but needs an articulation that the passage seeks to encourage ("who'll tell of it?"). The first audience is "European," the second "native"—categories, however, that refer more to attitudes than literal citizenship, since some Kenyan readers will have colonized minds and Ngugi does not wish to be trapped into localizing the honorable position of cultural insidership too much. So the passage creates a studiously amphibious "we": the "our" of "our history" means "Kenyan" or "African," but "our historians" could mean "Europeans"; the community of readers appealed to by the rhetorical questions might be as specific as "those leftist writers of Kenya who might undertake such a revisionist task" or as inclusive as "potentially sympathetic world opinion." For present purposes, it is less important to speculate further on what referent is intended when than simply to see the passage as an instance of rhetorical complexity forced upon the postcolonial writer by reason of the two audiences phenomenon, an enforcement that an able writer like Ngugi will turn into an aesthetic opportunity.

Students of nineteenth-century American literature tend to assume that American Renaissance texts were written for American readers[6]; yet on reflection we know that that is no more accurate than the assumption that American authors read only American books. Clearly, the dream of reaching a bicontinental audience strongly influenced American writers, for reasons both of economics and prestige, from the dawn of national literary emergence with Washington Irving's *Sketch Book* until well after the American book market had surpassed the British in the 1850s. The rhetoric of American Renaissance literature reflects this. Irving's essay on "English Writers on America" garnered praise on both sides of the Atlantic for the diplomatic suavity with which it mediated gently between British condescension and American hypersensitivity. While continuing to underscore his own position as American, and by implication the perceptual gap between the two audiences (Americans are always "we," the English "they"), Irving promotes a rapprochement by a conciliatory citizen-of-the-world urbanity, diagnosing both partisans as self-victimized by silly prejudices that inhibit the recognition of their common bonds. This strategy wards off the intellectual oppressor at the cost (also, however, a potential benefit) of having to grant the provincialism of one's own cultural camp (Irving 786–94).

Melville, thirty-five years younger than Irving, has been justly seen as carrying the cause of American literary independence further; yet he too was baptized into authorship in such a way as to be made equally conscious of the two audiences phenomenon, and he was at least as shrewd in developing a rhetorical repertoire to accommodate himself to it and exploit it. Not by mere chance was Irving one of the young Melville's backers among the publishers of London. *Typee* was a self-styled American narrative got up, however, in a special effort to ingratiate itself with a British publisher and public and then remade so as to address a different problem of reception back home. The Preface, purporting to speak the "unvarnished truth," seems to have been designed to help market the book in Britain by appeasing both the publisher's and the public's demand for a factual narrative. In other words, if we read this great American author in chronological order, we start with an essay that wasn't written for "us" but for British readers. *Typee* in fact remains throughout strongly Anglophilic; and the Appendix (on Hawaiian politics) is so egregiously pro-British (and as a consequence anti–American missionary) as to make Charles Anderson suppose it to have been written at least partly "to promote the sale of *Typee* in England" (336). In America, this very accommodationism ran Melville into trouble. Leon Howard points out in the Historical Note to the Northwestern-Newberry Edition that whereas for British reviewers the vexing issue was veracity, for American reviewers the issue was Melville's censure of missionaries, which in combination with the mild eroticism of his Polynesian sketchery drove one evangelical reviewer to charge him with truckling to decadent European taste: "the work was made, not for America, but for a circle, and that not the highest, in London, where theatres, opera-dancers, and voluptuous prints have made such unblushing walks along the edge of modesty as are . . . rather more admired than we hope they are among us" (Howard 293–94; Hetherington, 47).

Melville responded to criticism of his impiety and salaciousness by both bowdlerizing *Typee* in a revised American edition (deleting the offensive Appendix, for instance) and persisting in his offense thereafter by developing in subsequent books a more murky, innuendo-laden style. I like to imagine Melville, even when dutifully applying the razor to the text of *Typee,* trying at the same time to bump the limit of what he could get away with. For instance, from the chapter on "Religion in Polynesia" he cut the last paragraph, which pretends to view the Typees "as a back-slidden generation" that "require a spiritual revival"—I trust because he thought that the sudden donning of the evangelical persona would be considered a too-transparent reductio ad absurdum. But he let stand a slightly more oblique earlier passage on the practice of ritualistic idol-mocking, which portrays, tongue-in-cheek, the Typees as a species of Yankee Congregational rabble:

> The "independent electors" of the valley were not to be brow-beaten by chiefs, priests, idols, or devils. As for the luckless idols, they received more hard knocks than supplications. I do not wonder that some of them looked so grim, and stood so bolt upright as if fearful of looking to the right or the left lest they should give any one offense. The fact is, they had to carry themselves *"pretty straight,"* or suffer the consequences. Their worshippers were such a precious set of fickle-minded and irreverent heathens that there was no telling when they might topple one of them over. (NN *Typee* 177–78)[7]

Perhaps Melville thought the passage had enough protective coloring to obscure the parallel that his Yankeeisms drive home: that this could almost as
easily be a satire on religious and social anarchy in the burned-over district of
upper New York State—where evangelical ferment was at its height in Melville's youth—as a wide-eyed account of barbarous practices in the South Seas.
Considering the book as directed at a British readership, we can imagine this
stylization as designed to promote the illusion of the authenticity of the
Yankee persona; in an American context, especially that of the revised edition,
it makes equal sense to read Melville as trying to insinuate something about
the absurdity of religious excess.

* * *

The publication history of *Typee,* then, shows Melville actively seeking to con-
ciliate his respective British and American audiences while maintaining a kind
of independence via obliquity or insinuation. In the long run, his binocular
vision of the two audiences was clearly one source, though of course hardly
the only one, of the nuanced convolution that marks his later fiction. Take,
for instance, this footnote from *White-Jacket* on the subject of (interestingly)
impressment. In the American edition, the note climaxes with a patriotic outburst: "These things should be known; for in case the English government . . .
should again resort to indiscriminate impressment . . . it is well that both Englishmen and Americans, that all the world be prepared to put down an iniquity outrageous and insulting to God and man," (NN *WJ* 381). But in the
English edition this is prefixed by one disclaimer ("It is not intended to revive
old feuds") and suffixed by another ("It is hardly to be anticipated" that an institution would ever be revived that "must surely seem iniquitous to the great
body of Englishmen"). The result is an intricate piece of have-your-cake-and-
eat-it-tooism, a warmup for the rhetorical tackings in *Moby-Dick, Pierre,* and
The Confidence-Man.

   A more significant instance is the plot of *Redburn,* the novel immediately
preceding *White-Jacket.* The dual audience phenomenon provides us with
a key to achieving a juster respect for the complexity of thinking that underlay
this pot-boiler—if not for the finished product. One of *Redburn's* obvious
"failures," yet a very provocative one, is the introduction in the last third of
the book of Harry Bolton, the young English gentleman who becomes friends
with Redburn and ships back to America with him after they take their abor-
tive trip to London. Bolton has often been thought of as a flimsy, anticlimactic
piece of cardboard. And so he is. Yet he is important as Redburn's double—

another gentry-class nautical greenhorn who has to have the good breeding beaten out of him in order to make it as a sailor and ultimately also as an American. As such, Bolton reruns the initiation theme in British guise and thus becomes the protagonist in a subplot that might answer to the vicarious needs of the British implied reader as Redburn does to the American.

From this standpoint, the problem with the Bolton subplot is not that it is a belated tack-on, but rather that it is not developed enough to become symmetrical with the main plot. Bolton remains an outsized episode in Redburn's series of experiences. Yet that too is important, indeed much more deeply so, in that the affair with Bolton both reenacts and displays the quixoticism of Redburn's attempt to decolonize himself, to shake off his own inbred genteel Anglophilia that initially makes him a maladroit sailor and leads to a pathetically naive pilgrimage in his father's footsteps through Liverpool with the aid of an ancient guidebook brought from home. The familiar guidebook episode is itself one of Melville's most inventive portrayals of intellectual colonization, in both familial and national senses. The map's gross inaccuracy and Redburn's brush with the urban slums begin to awaken him mentally, but Harry Bolton matures him further, first by proving an initially attractive but then disillusioning image of English gentlemanliness and second through Redburn's sense of the contrast between Bolton's utter incompetence at sea and his own comparative seasoning. Yet Redburn is never emancipated. The narrative is about a decolonization *process* that never ends. The book concludes by focusing on Bolton more than on Redburn. It is by no means clear that Redburn has exorcised the Bolton within himself; on the contrary, it proves easier for him to exorcise the fearful Jackson (Bolton's opposite, the demotic tyrant) than the friendlier but more persistently demanding Bolton. Even as the presumably older and wiser narrator, Redburn continues to play the sentimental naïf, albeit on a slightly more enlightened plane of cognizance.[8]

* * *

The putative double audience awareness in *Redburn*, assuming I am right in inferring it, is surely connected with the pursuit of the decolonization narrative in *Redburn*, given that the motif of partial but incomplete disengagement from Anglocentrism operates at both rhetorical levels (the level of address to readers and the level of narrative point of view). But to explain the latter solely in terms of the former, to attribute Melville's tailoring of plot and character solely to his strategic accommodation to a bicontinental readership, would be thickheaded. Melville's life experiences as world traveler and amateur comparative anthropologist might in themselves have been enough to make him deeply skeptical of, if not downright hostile to (despite his occasional Young America–style setpieces), any attempt at descrying a clean distinction between old and new worlds. It is notable in this regard that Melville's most acidulous deflations of American claims of sociocultural difference and superiority occurred in magazine pieces of the 1850s directed at a cisatlantic rather than international market. In "Benito Cereno," for example, Melville arranged the antithesis between Delano and Benito as a pseudo-polarity so that the Yankee captain could not be exculpated from the racism, authoritarianism, and moral imbecility of his Hispanic (and by implication also Southern) counterparts. As in *Moby-Dick,* Melville tried to puncture democratic complacency by establishing a continuum between European imperialism and Yankee enterprise. But the Melville work most explicitly about postcolonialism is *Israel Potter,* whose protagonist finds himself ironically trapped in Britain for forty years after American independence.

The Treaty of Paris certainly did not free *this* American Israel, who languished in the captivity of London impoverishment until after the second war of independence (1812–15). *Israel Potter* raises the question of whether American independence means anything for the average American. To the extent that Israel is symbolically a kind of everyman, the answer is clearly no. For him, at any rate, republican institutions prove dysfunctional, and his errand into the wilderness of the London slums (a metaphor developed with grim gusto) leads to a greater privation than that from which his forefathers came, despite all his Yankee ingenuity. In this reading of the text, England isn't literally England—not *just* England anyhow—but alternatively or in addition a displaced version of the laissez-faire economics on which America itself is built.

Melville helps establish this equivalence by a series of revisions of his source text, *The Life and Remarkable Adventures of Israel Potter* (1826). He doctors his portraits of John Paul Jones and Benjamin Franklin to emphasize the megalomania and decadence of Jones (who at one point wishes he were a czar) and the courtierish duplicity of Franklin. The original Israel insists that if "that great and good man" Benjamin Franklin were still alive, "I should not have petitioned my country in vain" (NN *IP* 337). In Melville, it immediately becomes clear that bland, calculating Franklin would have made no effort to help Israel; in fact he intimidates him into giving back the quarter he starts to lend him. Here and throughout, Melville makes light of the original narrative's dogged patriotism. The process starts with Melville's first use of his source, in chapter 2: "It appears," says the narrator, that Israel "began his wanderings very early; moreover, that ere, on just principles throwing off the yoke of his king, Israel, on equally excusable grounds, emancipated himself from his sire"—who had forbidden his love-match (7). Linking these two items together as "equally excusable" rebellions reduces patriotism to parody. Later on, after reporting Israel's encounter with King George, the narrator laughs at Israel for being so impressed by royal magnanimity: "had it not been for the peculiar disinterested fidelity of our adventurer's patriotism, he would have soon sported the red coat" (32). This rather dampens the impression of Israel's Yankee staunchness. In the next episode, when Israel meets up with the pro-American underground, Melville replaces the original scene of high patriotic drama with a scene in which three wily bantering gentlemen ply Israel with drink to soften him up for an errand he does not understand. And so on. The cumulative effect of these alterations is to turn Israel into a comic-pathetic shuttlecock bounding back and forth between Tweedledum and Tweedledee—with the main line of division between good and bad being not ideological but economic—and to replace a narrative that loudly declares allegiance to America with an ironic meditation on the pseudo-polarity between republican freedom and the imperial yoke, exposing the quixotic, delusional character of the cultural nationalism that the historic Israel and his editor employ as a strategy of justification. This isn't to say that the Melvillean narrator lacks sympathy for Israel any more than the narrator of *Billy Budd* lacks sympathy for Billy Budd, only that in each case Melville sees to it that vernacular republicanism gets upstaged by a skeptical, detached narrative voice.

Melville's astringency toward republican economic and political institutions in the work of the 1850s that followed the overheated intensity and unsuccess of *Pierre* (1851) expresses another characteristic postcolonial motif: disillusionment at the incompletion of the social changes that ought to have followed from the political revolution. Indeed, the English-language inventor of this motif was the first major Anglophone writer to witness a revolution "completing" itself—John Milton, whose ironic sonnet "On the new forces of Conscience under the Long Parliament" charged that "*new Presbyter* is but *Old Priest* writ large" (439). Ngugi's *Petals of Blood* pursues this theme on a grander scale, anatomizing the reinvention of structures of domination by postindependence entrepreneurialism. From the standpoint of Melville and many other Northern liberal writers appalled by the Compromise of 1850, the American regime at midcentury looked, at worst, as retrograde as Kenya today under the presidency of Daniel arap Moi does to Ngugi. Not that the disaffection of Melville's later fiction can be traced to any specific political event. The sectional crises of the 1840s and 1850s may suffice to explain the political disaffections of Stowe's *Uncle Tom's Cabin,* Emerson's addresses on the Fugitive Slave Law, or Thoreau's "Slavery in Massachusetts," but the disaffections of *Moby-Dick,* "Bartleby," "Benito," and *Israel Potter* express a more comprehensive disillusionment with republican premises reflective on the one hand of a vision of human corruptibility at once more broadly Euroamerican and more idiosyncratically personal and on the other of the entrapment of the individual within oppressive political and/or economic orders by no means peculiar to America. A closer African parallel than Ngugi, closer because more abstract, would be the satire of neocolonial royalism in Wole Soyinka's writings about African strongmen, such as *Death and the King's Horseman* (1975), *Opera Wonosi* (1981), and *A Play of Giants* (1984). In these works particular instances are treated as type cases with a stylized intensity that seem to have their origins not just in the immediate contexts but in a magisterial vision of historical and even cosmic irony, surcharged by classical, Brechtian, and absurdist intertextuality. Soyinka's repeated exposures of the abuse of power recalls Melville's repeated commentary on the incongruity of monarchical codes of shipboard discipline persisting in a republic. *White-Jacket* is especially eloquent on this score, indicting the American Articles of War as "an importation from abroad, even from Britain, whose laws we Americans hurled off as tyrannical, and yet retained the most tyrannical of all" (NN *WJ* 297).

No less significant for Melville than the bare injustice of shipboard imperialism were the psychological consequences thereof, the venality, emasculation, and cruelty that it can mask and produce. Yet equally compelling for us as readers is how, notwithstanding, Melville's texts reproduce a version of that very hierarchicalism at the level of narrative consciousness. In *White-Jacket,* the idealized "ordinary" seaman is Jack Chase, a Briton whose suavity and command of literary quotations make him a persuasive intercessor with the captain and (given that he is also a darned good fellow) the cynosure of the crew as well. The combination of these traits is what makes him a fit friend for the antiauthoritarian but also fastidious and effete *White-Jacket*. One quickly infers from this that the text has sought to create as a counterpoint to the titled officers not a direct opposite but a "natural aristocrat" who in fact functions as more of an aristocrat than the text intends. A similar ambiguity invests Ishmael's bond with Ahab in *Moby-Dick*. More like Starbuck than he acknowledges, Ishmael obeys, rebelling, alternately critical of and fascinated by Ahab.

Ishmael's notorious "disappearance" in the latter stages of the text could be read as a consequence of the text's investment in Ishmael's fascination in that it permits—just as Ishmael has previously permitted—Ahabian power to dominate for the while over Ishmaelish reserve. The vision of Captain Ahab as a latter-day Lear or Macbeth—or, for that matter, as a latter-day Old Testament Ahab, a grand ungodly neobiblical hero-villain—threatens to eclipse the "democratic" critique of Ahab as an abuser of authority.

Melville's practice of muddying the moral polarity of the monarchy/ democracy antithesis arises from a combination of usurpation by his literary models (here one recalls Whitman's deduction from Shakespeare's greatness— that his imagination was tied to the feudal system) and conscious intent to rise to some metaposition from which "opposite" alternatives appear as mirror images of insufficiency. Melville seems to have been consciously reaching after this latter intention, which regulates the narrative voice in *Billy Budd,* as early as *Mardi,* his third novel and the first work to anticipate closely his mature style. The primary sign of this is *Mardi*'s appropriation of the convention of reverse orientalism originally pioneered in the eighteenth century by Montesquieu's *Persian Letters*—which turns on the device of imagining how Western society would look to an Oriental traveler. In Melville's version, the narrator-protagonist Taji is escorted by the "oriental" King Media and several of his courtiers through all the realms of Mardi. During the latter stages of this tour, the voyagers visit England (Dominora) and the United States (Vivenza), passing by Europe (Porpheero), which is caught in the Revolutions of 1848. Melville's American perspective is evident from such signs as the decision to give Vivenza more than equal time, but the narrative form of this progress establishes an equivalence between the cultures of imperialist Britain and bumptious postcolonial America as social pathologies witnessed from an Olympian point of view. Indeed, the text suggests specific parallels between imperialism and American-style democracy in its satire on American slavery and expansionist designs on Mexico and Cuba. That Melville was well aware of the scandalousness of this analogizing is clear from the fact it is broached most explicitly in a mysterious scroll read by the infuriated Vivenzans that the text strongly hints was surreptitiously posted by one of the voyagers, perhaps either Media or the sage Babbalanja (NN *Mardi* 524–30). This is the only portion of the whole vast, sprawling novel that cannot be attributed to any specific personal voice.

Melville did not always feel it necessary to handle the subject so delicately. In the sixty-fourth chapter of *White-Jacket,* the *Neversink* prepares to race a

British frigate. The narrator disingenuously fans the fires of partisan enthusiasm by informing us that nearby lay a "British" ship that had been captured from the U.S. Navy in the War of 1812. "Think of it, my gallant countrymen, one and all, down the seacoast and along the endless banks of the Ohio and Columbia—think of the twinges we sea-patriots must have felt to behold the live-oak of the Floridas and the pines of green Maine built into the oaken walls of Old England!" (NN *WJ* 266). But he abruptly deflates his mounting drama of cross-national rivalry with an aside about a Sioux Indian he once saw "exhibiting on the back of his blanket a crowd of human hands," the record of his trophies. The moral is obvious: "what is the American frigate Macedonian, or the English frigate President [each captured in the past war by the other side], but as two bloody red hands painted on this poor savage's blanket?" (267). The ensuing race is chronicled with an odd mixture of narrative gusto and ironic detachment from the event as a ludicrous exercise in patriotic overcompensation.

* * *

Altogether, what is perhaps most characteristic of Melville's use of literal and symbolic contrasts between "English" or "European" and "American" positions is their instability—their shiftingness, their discontinuities, and at times their sheer adventitiousness and fortuity. (The Dominora-Vivenza sequence in *Mardi* reads suspiciously like a belated tack-on, for example.) As we try to understand what to make of all this, it is well to bear in mind an important controversy in (post)colonial studies, brought into focus by the much-publicized mid-1980s exchange between Fredric Jameson and Aijaz Ahmad concerning the characteristic preoccupations of Third World literature. Jameson claimed that "all third-world texts are necessarily, I want to argue, allegorical, and in a very specific way: they are to be read as what I will call *national allegories*" (69). Ahmad objected to this as an intolerably totalizing diagnosis, denying heterogeneity of all antecedence, purpose, and result, trapping "us" in "the same allegory, the nationalist farce, re-written, over and over again, until the end of time." Instancing the case of Urdu, his own literary culture, Ahmad went on to state that before Pakistan's independence, "the theme of anti-colonialism is woven into" Urdu fiction "but never in an exclusive or even dominant emphasis" (9, 21) and that the subsequent prominence of nationality as a theme has to do with the peculiar circumstances of Pakistani independence (involving partition, traumatic mass migration, and a bloodbath that still continues). The controversy sheds analogical light on the American case. Jameson here might stand for the practice, long in-grained among Americanists, of imagining American literary development in terms of cultural differentiation: the discovery of a native poetic language and form (e.g., Whitmanian catalogs), the development of a repertoire of native or adopted genres (e.g., the captivity, the slave narrative, the jeremiad, the wild-erness romance), the invention of an American mythography (e.g., American Adamism). Ahmad stands for the insufficiency of any theory of a national-ist agenda. Both oversimplify (Jameson must homogenize the Third World; Ahmad must minimize the extent to which his case study provides qualified evidence supporting Jameson); both are, up to a point, right. My essay on the whole is more Jamesonian than not, even though it runs counter to the main drift of Americanist work in stressing the impossibility of making a clean break from Europe in literary practice. To make this case, however, it risks reducing American letters to still another "main theme." So the Ahmadian countertruth ought now be insisted upon with full force: the "main theme" (the preoccupation with Anglo-American imbrication and / or juxtaposition at any level) tells us only a limited amount about Melville's work, although what it does say is helpful, indeed decisive in its own way.

An example that will help bring this point into sharper focus is an amusing episode near the end of Melville's second novel, *Omoo,* just before the narra-tor's departure from Tahiti on the American whaler *Leviathan.* The narrator takes great pains to convince the captain that he is, in fact, a Yankee. This he must do in order to get the suspicious skipper to agree to sign him on as a member of the crew. But when first he approaches the captain, together with his Australian shipmate and traveling companion Doctor Long Ghost, the captain insists that our hero is himself Australian, a species "in excessively bad odor" throughout the Pacific (NN *Omoo* 313). This comical episode, show-ing that you sometimes need to put on an act in order to convince people that you are what you are, suggests at once the author-narrator's deracination and his early awareness of the theatricality of any discourse of national identity. Although the episode describes the persona only *qua* experiencer, the lesson is clearly also one that Melville had to relearn in his capacity as author, for at least two purposes: first in order to create a beachcomber persona that would negotiate the borderland between "civilization" and "savagery" in a way both cogent and pleasing to Anglo-American readers, and second in order to respond to the pressure upon him to engraft the unvarnished narrative of an ordinary Yankee upon what one Melvillean has called "the complex psy-chology of a failed patrician" (Herbert 155; see also Arvin 23). Thus Melville's renditions of cultural nationalism are typically short run, qualified, and self-conscious. No better example can be found than the peroration to the first "Knights and Squires" chapter of *Moby-Dick,* where Ishmael calls upon the "great democratic God" to bear him out as he seeks to "ascribe high qualities" "to meanest mariners, and renegades and castaways" (117). F. O. Matthiessen made this passage canonical when, in *American Renaissance,* he held it up as the example par excellence of Melville's democratization of Shakespearean rhetoric, characterizing it as a "full-voiced affirmation of democratic dignity" (444–45). Matthiessen was right in asserting that the passage masterfully interweaves colloquial and high cultural rhetoric, but he erred in overlooking its studiously bombastical nature, which telegraphs to the urbane reader that this noisy apotheosis of the common man is a playful extravagance, a mask for the occasion.

Matthiessen, like Jameson, and like most of us who are Matthiessen's Americanist successors today, strives to identify distinctively national subtexts and national styles of expression in our "classic" authors. The New Historicist practice of identifying American slavery in general and the Compromise of 1850 in particular as master-referents of classic American literature (equally important in their absence as well as their presence) is the most striking recent case of the quest for the national subtext.[9] I certainly do not want to discredit this project (and others like it) but merely worry about the blindness that seems inevitably to accompany its insight: namely, the taking for granted that the American 1850 is a more important litmus test of the social themes of mid-nineteenth-century American literature than, say, the growth of the international market economy, the impact of European socialist thinking, or the European revolutions of 1848.[10] My view is that the 1850 test is a test that Melville, for one, cannot be expected to pass without very significant qualifications, any more than Urdu literature can pass the national allegory test imposed by Jameson. In *Mardi,* for example, Melville indeed wishes to address the problem of American slavery as a national scandal but not as "an exclusive or even dominant emphasis." This preoccupation with the great national evil, as we have seen, is contained within an internationalist framework of vision whereby Vivenza and Dominora look like counterparts; and this whole section of the text is a relatively brief island in the vast ocean of quest romance whose most salient literary pretext is Shelley's *Alastor.*

To be sure, some of Melville's later writings fit much better into a theory of his career as developing some kind of American project. Taken in isolation from the rest of his canon, works like "Bartleby," *Pierre,* and especially *The*

Confidence-Man can be invoked to make the case that Melville's attention turned increasingly toward anatomies of American social issues and toward the question of what sort of expression, artistic or otherwise, is possible within the context of American institutions. *White-Jacket* and *Moby-Dick,* read as critiques of the American navy and the whaling industry respectively, might be seen as transitional works leading Melville toward predominantly cisatlantic preoccupations in the later works just mentioned. The insufficiency of this view of Melville, however, if it is not already clear from the foregoing, becomes immediately so when we consider his last monumental work—*Clarel* (1876), Melville's five-hundred-page, four-part autobiographically based narrative poem focusing on the impressions of a group of more-or-less pilgrims as they visit and reflect upon holy sites of Palestine.

This is the great white elephant, the great unread—not only among the ambitious works of the Melville canon but among all the major works of all the canonical nineteenth-century English-language authors. Melville's achievement is often generalized without reference to it. Yet this religious epic—which, despite its repellently relentless iambic tetrameter couplet prosody, deserves honor as the second-most-learned, intricate, and profoundly intellected work Melville wrote—helps greatly to put into perspective his achievement as an American writer. Its basic plot device, which *Clarel* helps us to recognize was Melville's staple device almost from start to finish, is to juxtapose a medley of culturally disparate individuals within a closed setting, suggesting a world in microcosm. America is disproportionately represented, most of the featured pilgrims being American expatriates or wanderers, and American history (e.g., the Civil War) is often brought up, but seemingly neither in a spirit of postcolonial anxiety nor of nationalist assertion. These have yielded to a detachedly anthropological perspective from which vantage point it looks, as the Redburnly most Melvillean character puts it, as if

> . . . Our New World bold
> Had fain improved upon the Old;
> But the hemispheres are counterparts. (NN *Clarel* 4.5.62–64)

America has "come of age"; it no longer worries about the shadow of Europe; but its maturity is nothing to be proud of, for it merely establishes America on the same footing. In one exchange, surrounded by a knot of irresolute skeptics and malcontents from the Americas, the one European character (a doggedly optimistic Anglican priest) points out the irony that "I of the Old World, all alone" maintain "hope and ground for cheer / 'Gainst ye, the offspring of the

New" (4.19.103–05). A thrice-marginalized Civil War veteran (Confederate, Catholic, part-Indian) retorts:

> *Old* World? If age's test
> Be this—advanced experience,
> Then in the truer moral sense,
> *Ours* is the Old World. You, at best,
> In dreams of your advanced Reform,
> Adopt the cast skin of our worm. (2.108–13)

This might easily have been a nationalist statement—as in later years it was for Gertrude Stein. Instead, it reflects a perspective from which particular pilgrims' points of national origin are much less material than their philosophical standpoints. Even Melville's rhetoric and prosody do this: he avoids vernacularization to the extent possible and stiffens his verse into a rough archaic dignity not identifiably American or even modern. *Clarel*'s presumption concerning the national project—not the American alone but all forms of modern nationalism—seems to be that the riddle of identity, in all the ways that term can be construed, leads back to the ancient world, which supplies a venue for examining the wreckage of latter-day Levantine and Euro-American civilization as interchangeable symptoms of the bankruptcy of nineteenth-century thought. Thus the case of Nathan, the Illinoisan of Puritan stock who converts to Judaism and becomes a Zionist, is almost interchangeable with that of the Swede Mortmain, whose disillusionment with the revolution of 1848 turns his utopianism into cosmic pessimism. Thus the motif of expatriation, which virtually all the pilgrims share, does not have the same social valence that it had for Redburn or Israel Potter, or even for the noted American literary expatriates from Irving to Henry James or Gertrude Stein. Expatriation is neither an instrument of cultural awakening nor a means of comparing national difference so much as a symptom of the pathology of national identity as such.

Clarel prepares us to return to our starting point—Melville's next and final masterpiece, *Billy Budd*. The obliquity with which *Billy Budd* invokes one of the most vexing stigmata of postcolonial America would not have been possible without the detached vision of which Melville shows himself to be capable in *Clarel*, which develops the theme of interchangeable national narratives more fully than any other Melvillean work. The story of the consequences of impressment, for all Melville cares, can just as easily play itself out in the form of a British episode in the aftermath of the French Revolution as in the form of an Anglo-American confrontation during the early national period. The name of Billy Budd's first ship, the *Rights of Man,* can just as easily refer to the French avatar of Thomas Paine as to the American.

I must therefore refine my initial statement about *Billy Budd* as a postcolonial text in light of the path we have traversed. Reviewing Melville's career, we can see his voyage-plots from *Typee* to *Clarel* as manifesting a prolonged struggle over the business of writing an American narrative in any or all these senses—over whom he was writing for, what his subjects would be, what his models would be, where his social values lay. Out of this struggle Melville constructed personae that were at most self-consciously and fitfully American. Any visions or aspirations he harbored to become an *American* author or forge an *American* literature were held in check at the start by his pragmatic accommodation to international marketplace constraints. When he began to assert himself as an independent, "serious" artist in *Mardi,* the American project generally remained subordinate to comparative anthropology and metaphysical questing; modern political history took precedence over American history, world religion over Puritanism. The origins of this cosmopolitanism lay in his postcolonial anxiety to think transcontinentally, but it fully matured only after, and partially as a result of, going through a comparatively "American" phase at midcareer, during which Melville more directly confronted the parochialism of national narratives and of national styles of expression. The way *Billy Budd* engages the subject of impressment shows that. Melville perhaps never arrived at the zero degree of intellectual colonization (who ever does?), but he achieved a degree of magisterial casualness about an American subject that bespoke a security of conviction that it belonged not alone to the province of American literature but to world literature.

In conclusion, several broader inferences seem to follow from this account of Melville's career. My myth of Melville's trajectory suggests the need for Americanists to think about the history of "American" writing in more complexly transnational terms: to reflect on how other cases of postcolonial literary emergence might bear on the American; to foreground an awareness that the whole notion of emerging national literary autonomy is a totalizing fiction, a critical construct potentially as provincial in its own way as the state of intellectual colonization from which the supposed autonomy emerged; and to presume that "American" authors will be fitful and inconsistent in the degree to which they embrace "native" aesthetic norms, themes, subjects. Now that the dream of nationalism has been thoroughly demystified by Benedict Anderson and others who have revealed its status as a species of social fiction,[11] the approach to American literature as a species of distinctive national narrative ought also to be interrogated more strenuously as a myth that American authors broached and American critics formalized in a much more complicated transnational historical matrix that included contrary evidence and competing possibilities. This by no means denies all evidential basis to the myth, nor its psychohistorical necessity. (Since language does not really differentiate American literature, the need to assert cultural autonomy becomes all the greater—another common ground with other postcolonial literatures written in European languages.) But at least we also need to become more cognizant of the degree to which our instruments for measuring the Americanness of American literature are instruments of our desire.

NOTES

1. Marvell 105. These first four lines of stanza 91 italicize "Domestic Heaven," "Discipline," "Fairfax," and "Vere," with other orthographical changes indicated here; otherwise, Melville's quotation in section 6 of *Billy Budd* is identical (61).

2. The subject of American literature's slow and conflicted movement toward cultural autonomy has long been a topic of research. Two excellent recent studies in this tradition are Rubin-Dorsky and Lawson-Peebles. The differences between this tradition of inquiry and mine in this article are chiefly that I see the literary nationalist project as a more fitful, incomplete, and ultimately secondary affair and that I am inclined to see it comparatively, in relation to other cases of literary emergence in former colonies. Hence my use of "postcolonial." I do not mean to imply a simple equation between, say, a settler culture like that of Anglo-America and an indigenous culture like those of Nigeria or the Indian subcontinent; nor do I mean to suggest that, say, the United States and Australia offer interchangeable literary histories. I would simply argue that such cases can be mutually illuminating. For a preliminary justification of this, see Ashcroft, Griffiths, and Tiffin; for a more sophisticated application to a single genre, see Bhabha.

3. NN *Journals* 46–47, 23. Here are some other examples. Remembering a ride about London: "Here the poet Thompson [sic] dwelt. I was on top of the coach. Pope lived near here, at Twickenham" (16). On dining at Elm Court, Temple: "A set of fine fellows indeed. It recalled poor Lamb's 'Old Benchers'" (44). Melville's perception of a Europe resonant with associations rendered familiar yet exotic through previous reading is very much in the mold of the nineteenth-century sentimental traveler.

4. See particularly the burst of literary nationalism following Melville's comparison of Hawthorne to Shakespeare in "Hawthorne and His *Mosses*," in which Melville exclaims, "let America first praise mediocrity even, in her own children, before she praises . . . the best excellence in the children of any other land" (*Moby-Dick* 544). I argue below that this kind of rhetoric is an occasional motif in Melville, not a dominant or unqualified note. For an important statement that takes the case against defining American literature in terms of its Americanness a bit too far in the right direction, see Spengemann.

5. See Timothy Brennan's more tempered observation, in a recent essay on Salman Rushdie, that the last several decades have witnessed "a trend of cosmopolitan commentators on the Third World, who offer an *inside* view of formerly submerged peoples for target reading publics in Europe and North America in novels that comply with metropolitan literary tastes" (Bhabha 63). The question of the audience of African literature is discussed in broader terms in Bishop 47–58. With regard to the analogy to American antebellum writing, see also my discussion of the two audience issue in "American Literary Emergence as a Postcolonial Phenomenon."

6. See, for example, Railton, whose Melville chapter represents him as exclusively preoccupied with his relations to the American reading public even as it shows cognizance of his international publishing ventures (152–89). This assumption works better for some works (e.g., *Pierre*) than for others (e.g., *Typee*). Our vision of Melville may become more usefully complicated if we impute to him a multiple and shifting notion of the implied reader.

7. My notion of Melville's approach to the author-reader relation is obviously somewhat at variance, although not so much as it might seem, with Dimock's eloquent "imperial" reading. With regard to Melville's pipe dream of an ideal understanding reader for *Mardi*, Dimock remarks that this was "a fiction created by an imperial self, a self that annihilates what it refuses to imagine and appropriates what it projects as its own" (75). I argue for a more receptive, pragmatic, accommodationist Melville on the basis of his acceptance of a degree of enforced obliquity and censorship (both in the composition and the copyediting stages) and on the basis of his willingness to alternate between "serious" and "light" work until nearly the end of his active professional career as a novelist. But Dimock is surely correct in positing a willful Melville, whose energy I see as driving the passage just discussed, whether or not this energy can be diagnosed as a phenomenon of the American expansionist moment (10).

8. In other words, I question the theory that there is a stable ironic distance between the narrative voice and the figure of the young Redburn, though I would agree that they are not the same. This means that I would posit another distinction between narrative voice and the implied author as well as between the imperfect visions of both Redburn as actor and Redburn as narrator.

9. For an example of this practice, see Arac, the essay that I would regard as the first work of important New Historicist exegesis in American Renaissance studies. For a penetrating discussion of the significance of this move, see Fisher.

10. For the impact of the latter on antebellum American writers, see especially Reynolds. Scholarly handling of international events of 1848 is a particularly interesting indicator of the relative weight given by Americanist scholarship to cisatlantic and transatlantic reference. For example, Rogin, a landmark study that helped redirect Melvilleans to the study of his political context, clearly recognized that this context has to be understood as transcontinental and that the Young America circle with which Melville was connected in the 1840s "borrowed its name from Mazzini's Young Italy" (71); but when it comes to textual analysis, it is "the American 1848" on which Rogin concentrates: e.g., "As the biblical Ahab seized Naboth's vineyard, so America engrossed half of Mexico" (126). For a recent Americanist reading of another major figure's career of the period that focuses more squarely on his bicontinental vision, particularly as regards the challenge of socialism, see Bercovitch. Rogin, Bercovitch, and Reynolds all exemplify, in increasing degrees, the attempt to reach beyond cisatlanticism and achieve an internationalized perspective on their American subjects commensurate with the subjects' intellectual reach; but in order to do this, they and all other Americanists must struggle, as Reynolds points out, against the "critical tradition in American studies" to emphasize "the national features of the literature it has treated, thus obscuring the substantial international influences" (xii).

11. Anderson (28–37) develops the idea of novelistic form as a prototype for and influence upon the development of nationalism. Bhabha (308–11) criticizes Anderson's model for being

based on the assumption of novelistic realism, but Bhabha's skepticism is aimed at unsettling a too-simple way of imagining national history as narrative: his collection actually furthers Anderson's goal of demystifying nationalism by recourse to the analogy of fiction.

WORKS CITED

Ahmad, Aijaz. "Jameson's Rhetoric of Otherness and the 'National Allegory.'" *Social Text* 17 (Fall 1987): 9, 21.

Anderson, Benedict. *Imagined Communities: Reflections on the Origin and Spread of Nationalism.* London: Verso, 1983.

Anderson, Charles Roberts. *Melville in the South Seas.* New York: Columbia UP, 1939.

Arac, Jonathan. "The Politics of *The Scarlet Letter.*" In *Ideology and Classic American Literature.* Ed. Sacvan Bercovitch and Myra Jehlen. New York: Cambridge UP, 1986. 247–66.

Arvin, Newton. *Herman Melville.* New York: Houghton, 1950.

Ashcroft, Bill, Gareth Griffiths, and Helen Tiffin. *The Empire Writes Back: Theory and Practice in Post-Colonial Literatures.* New York: Routledge, 1989.

Bercovitch, Sacvan. "Emerson, Individualism, and the Ambiguities of Dissent." *South Atlantic Quarterly* 89 (1990): 623–62.

Bhabha, Homi K., "DissemiNation." In *Nation and Narration.* Ed. Homi K. Bhabha. New York: Routledge, 1990.

Bishop, Rand. *African Literature, African Critics: The Forming of Critical Standards, 1947–1966.* New York: Greenwood, 1988.

Dimock, Wai Chee. *Empire for Liberty.* Princeton: Princeton UP, 1989.

Egejuru, Phanuel. *Towards African Literary Independence: A Dialogue with Contemporary African Writers.* Westport, CT: Greenwood, 1980.

Fisher, Philip. Introduction. *The New American Studies: Essays from "Representations."* Berkeley: U of California P, 1992. xv–xviii.

Herbert, T. Walter, Jr. *Marquesan Encounters.* Cambridge, MA: Harvard UP, 1980.

Hetherington, Hugh. *Melville's Reviewers.* Chapel Hill: U of North Carolina P, 1961.

Howard, Leon. *Herman Melville: A Biography.* Berkeley: U of California P, 1951.

Irving, Washington. "English Writers on America." *The Sketch Book.* In *History, Tales and Sketches.* Ed. James Tuttleton. New York: Library of America, 1983.

Jameson, Fredric. "Third-World Literature in the Era of Multinational Capitalism." *Social Text* 15 (Fall 1986): 69.

Lawson-Peebles, Robert. *Landscape and Written Expression in Revolutionary America.* New York: Cambridge UP, 1988.

Lewis, R. W. B. *The American Adam.* Chicago: U of Chicago P, 1955.

Marvell, Andrew. *The Poems of Andrew Marvell.* Ed. Hugh MacDonald. Cambridge, MA: Harvard UP, 1952.

Matthiessen, F. O. *American Renaissance.* New York: Oxford UP, 1941.

Melville, Herman. *Billy Budd, Sailor.* Ed. Harrison Hayford and Merton M. Sealts, Jr. Chicago: U of Chicago P, 1962.

————. *Moby-Dick.* Ed. Harrison Hayford and Hershel Parker. New York: Norton, 1967.

Milton, John. *The Poetical Works of John Milton.* Ed. Helen Darbishire. New York: Oxford UP, 1958.

Railton, Stephen. *Authorship and Audience: Literary Performance in the American Renaissance.* Princeton: Princeton UP, 1991.

Reynolds, Larry J. *European Revolutions and the American Literary Renaissance.* New Haven: Yale UP, 1988.

Rogin, Michael Paul. *Subversive Genealogy.* New York: Knopf, 1983.

Rubin-Dorsky, Jeffrey. *Adrift in the Old World: The Psychological Pilgrimage of Washington Irving.* Chicago: U of Chicago P, 1988.

Spengemann, William. *A Mirror for Americanist.* Hanover, NH: UP of New England, 1989.

Thiong'o, Ngugi wa. *Petals of Blood.* New York: Dutton, 1978.

Williams, Raymond. *The Country and the City.* New York: Oxford UP, 1973.

5

Reading the Incomplete

WAI CHEE DIMOCK

I want to begin with a sense of unease that, in the past few years, seems suddenly to have found its way into talks, panel discussions, even casual conversations—a sense, shared by many in the profession, that we have reached something of an impasse in our practice of reading. Since "transcendence" has now become a suspect term, the alternative has often been an attempt to make literature as context-bound as possible, an attempt to read it as a sign, an emblematic index, of a larger social reality. We "historicize," that is, in order to bring to light a part-and-whole relation between literature and other cultural forms. Literature, on this view, is not only occasioned by history but, in some deep sense, also metonymic of history. From within its confines, it is understood to enact the logic of a historical whole, a whole that dictates and limits its possibilities for meaning.

New Historicism, as its critics have often pointed out, is heavily invested in the notion of *containability*—and in more than one sense of the word. Just as, on the level of thematics, it depicts all opposition as containable opposition, so too, on the level of interpretation, it imagines all meaning to be localized

Previously published in Wai Chee Dimock, *Residues of Justice: Literature, Law, Philosophy,* University of California Press. © 1996 by the Regents of the University of California.

meaning: meaning determined and encompassed by its moment of inscription. History is seen, then, not only as the genetic circumstance for literature but also as its hermeneutic limits, its bounds of meaning. To study literature is thus to study the way a text is "embedded" in history, that embeddedness being understood to inscribe in it a determinate content. And the task of critic is to "unpack" that determinate content by locating the historicity "in" the text and locating the text "in" history.

New Historicism is a criticism governed by the concept "in," we might say, a concept that has "come to seem as fixed and ineradicable from reality as the preposition is from our lexicon," as Charles Taylor suggests (186). Since this prepositional regime is very close to the one I have myself elaborated not so long ago (*Empire for Liberty*), I think I can say, with some authority, that it is not a regime in which one can find intellectual sustenance for any length of time, or with any degree of comfort. After all, if the "literary" turns out to be just a metonym for the historical, if the horizon of meaning in literature turns out always to be encompassed by history and collapsible in history, what is the point of studying literature to begin with? Wouldn't it make more sense simply to turn to historical documents themselves, or to works of historical scholarship? Or are we drawn to literature, exercised by it and compelled by it, in a way that we are not exercised or compelled by court records, congressional debates, newspaper editorials? How can we account for the continual meaningfulness of a literary text, the sense that it still speaks to us, resonates for us, endures for us?

It is with these questions in mind that I want to enter into a critical dialogue with New Historicism, by proposing a mode of literary studies not premised on meaning as a containable category. The hermeneutic relation between history and literature is necessary but insufficient, I argue. Just as the meanings of history might not be fully generalizable from one particular work of literature, so the meanings of literature might not be fully derivable from one particular historical moment. Rather than limiting ourselves to a search for "historicity" (and rather than equating historicity strictly with determinacy and locatability), we might want to turn instead to a hermeneutics that is less spatially ascriptive, less discretely periodizing, and more alive, perhaps, to the continuing meaningfulness of a text, more willing to study that meaningfulness beyond any function it might conceivably have performed at one particular moment.

Engaging the text, then, not as a part of a *concluded* whole —not as a piece of cultural work that has already served its purpose, that has meaning only in reference to the past—we might want to think of it, instead, as an evolving cluster of resonances, its semantic universe unfolding in time rather than in space, unfolding in response to the new perceptual horizons that we continue to bring to bear upon it and that never cease to extend to it new possibilities of meaning. The accumulating resonances of a text, its subtle shifts in nuance and accent, are a tribute, then, to the socialness of language, to the unending conversations of humanity over time. Inflected by those conversations, inflected by the historical life of language—a life at once more ancient and more recent than any locatable circumstance—the very linguistic character of a text must make it permeable in time, polyphonic over time, its resonances activated and reactivated by each new relation, each mutating meaning.

To equate the text with any single explanatory context thus seems to me unduly reductive—unduly collapsing an immaterial order into a set of material circumstances and a semantic universe into a narrow grid of instances. Against the violence of that reduction, much might be said, I think, for a criticism that makes no attempt to construct a hermeneutic totality for a text, to impose a determinate boundary on its meaning. Such a criticism will perhaps not make us "historicists" in the current understanding of that term. All the same, we will remain historically minded, although we will imagine history not as a domain of full inscription, in which the meaning of literature is given once and for all, given because of its determinate place "in" its time. Indeed, with a healthier skepticism toward the preposition "in," perhaps we will turn to some other relational categories—"between," "beside," "residual to," "in spite of," "above and beyond"—categories that engage the text not as the predictable part of a historical whole but as a perpetual witness to a history perpetually incomplete.

What might a reading look like that has no desire to imagine a whole, no desire to construct for the text a hermeneutic totality? I want to pursue that question by way of a practical demonstration, by turning now to Melville's "The Paradise of Bachelors and the Tartarus of Maids," a story that, almost providentially, foregrounds the relation between part and whole both as a formal and as a thematic problem. As the title suggests, this is a diptych, made up of two contrasting, complementary parts discretely opposed and inversely unifying. On one side there is convivial ambience, culinary delight, and carefree association—a world occupied monotonously by men. On the other side there is a brutal environment, regimented labor, and physical misery—a world occupied monotonously by women.

Given this complementary structure—these matching scenes of privilege and oppression—it is not surprising that the men should happen to be bachelors. For bachelorhood, here and elsewhere in Melville, is a species of manhood singled out for its privilege and distinguished, in that privilege, from manhood of the more run-of-the-mill sort, exemplified by the "Bene-dick tradesmen," who, being married, must spend their lives attending to the "rise of bread and fall of babies" (NN *PT* 316). The bachelors, by contrast, are free from all obligations, marital and paternal, free, it might seem, even from the necessity of work. Of course, we know that the bachelors actually do work. They are practicing lawyers, hailing from such places as Grey's Inn and Lincoln's Inn. However, as they are here presented they are eminently at leisure. The bachelors are portrayed, that is, as if they were gentlemen of means banded together, first and last, by their pleasure in idleness. Reveling as they do in a unique gender privilege, they make up a class by themselves.

The mapping of an aristocratic identity upon a bachelor identity—the map-ping of class upon gender—is, of course, something of a convention itself. As Eve Kosofsky Sedgwick points out, the "aristocratic," as perceived (no doubt wishfully) by the bourgeoisie in the nineteenth century, was marked by a clus-ter of attributes, including effeminacy, unspecified homosexuality, connois-seurship, and dissipation, all of which were conveniently personified by the pleasure-loving, leisure-flaunting bachelor (*Between Men* 83–96). Sedgwick is speaking of nineteenth-century England, but her insight applies equally to nineteenth-century America, where an even keener suspicion of the "aristo-cratic" prompted the same indictment of class through gender, making the effete bachelor a metonym for the entire upper order, real or imagined. This is certainly the case with Ik Marvell's *Reveries of a Bachelor* (1850), which makes that most unmanly of luxuries, daydreaming, the essence of well-heeled bachelorhood. And it is the case as well with "The Paradise of Bachelors and the Tartarus of Maids," which, in making effete aristocrats out of effete bache-lors, would seem to be operating within a well-defined tradition of populist critique.

"The Paradise of Bachelors" is thus pervaded (ostentatious references to "paradise" notwithstanding) by an aura of the degenerate, an aura of de-clension from a heroic past to a feminized present: "the iron heel is changed to a boot of patent-leather; the long two-handed sword to a one-handed quill"; "the helmet is a wig." Instead of "carving out immortal fame in glori-ous battling for the Holy Land," as the Crusaders once did, the modern-day bachelor is now reduced "to the carving of roast-mutton at a dinner-board" (NN *PT* 317–18). There is a time-honored quality to this portrait of degenerate leisure—time-honored, but, it would seem, also endlessly repeated. Melville was hardly alone, then, in his dire intimations, for as Francis Grund observed in 1837, Americans as a rule "know but the *horrors* of idleness" (2:1–2). And so it was that, in 1843, when Henry Ward Beecher gave a series of Sunday evening lectures to his congregation (subsequently collected in his *Lectures to Young Men*), the first lecture should be devoted to the subject of idleness. Like Melville's story, this also featured a certain *seedsman:*

> When Satan would put ordinary men to a crop of mischief, like a wise husbandman, he clears the ground and prepares it for seed; but he finds the idle man already prepared, and he has scarcely the trouble of sowing, for vices, like weeds, ask little strewing, except what the wind gives their ripe and winged seeds, shaking and scattering them all abroad. Indeed, lazy men may fitly be likened to a tropical prairie, over which the wind of temptation perpetually blows, drifting every vagrant seed from hedge and hill, and which—without a moment's rest through all the year—waves its rank harvest of luxuriant weeds. (35–36)

Such harsh judgment (not to say such figurative extravagance) might seem surprising. It is especially surprising coming from Beecher, who happened, after all, also to be the author of a popular novel, *Norwood* (1868), whose idealized hero, Reuben Wentworth, was not only idle in his youth but actually contemplated a career in idleness. He discussed the matter with his Uncle Eb, who, when asked whether one could "be a gentleman in any respectable calling," had answered, "Oh, dear, no. My gentleman must take all his time to it, spend his time at it, be jealous of everything else." Wentworth ends up not being a gentleman—he becomes a doctor—but what Uncle Eb said about the gentleman might equally be said of him: "He [is] so fine that he accomplishes more while doing nothing than others do with all their bustle" (23–24).

Elsewhere in Beecher there are further examples of people who accomplish more while doing nothing than others do with all their bustle. In an essay entitled "Dream-Culture" (1854), for example, he went so far as to argue that "the chief use of a farm, if it be well selected, and of a proper soil, is, to lie down upon." He called this unusual kind of husbandry "industrious lying down" and contrasted it with the other, more usual, variety practiced by farmers, which involved "standing up and lazing about after the plow or behind his scythe." *That* kind of farming was ordinary enough. "Industrious lying down," on the other hand, produced crops that were far more extraordinary: "harvests of associations, fancies, and dreamy broodings." And, to those who objected that such "farming" was "a mere waste of precious time," Beecher replied that it was completely justified "if it gives great delight . . . if it brings one a little out of conceit with hard economies . . . and the sweat and dust of life among selfish, sordid men" (263–69).

Beecher certainly seemed to be having things both ways.[1] He was not alone, however, for there was in fact very little agreement in the mid–nineteenth century about the merit of leisure and recreation. The controversy attracted a good many commentators, especially clergymen, itself a significant fact. In a book called *The Christian Law of Amusement* (1859), for example, James Leonard Corning, pastor of the Westminster Presbyterian Church in Buffalo, described the battle as being waged between those who denounced amusement "with most dogmatic intolerance as if nothing could be said in its favor" and those who praised it to the skies, "as if the progress of civilization depended on it" (7). However, this did not prevent Corning himself from joining the fray, determined as he was to prove that the necessity for amusement was a "Christian law." As for Henry Ward Beecher, the battle seemed to be going on inside his head and among his various pieces of writing. But there was a pattern as well behind these seemingly contrary pronouncements.[2] In *Norwood,* for example, it was the gentlemanly Dr. Wentworth, who, alone of all the townspeople, could afford to be seen standing under a cherry tree, "watching with a kind of sober smile the workmen" laboring away at their tasks (16). Leisure clearly meant different things when it was enjoyed by different people. Cheap amusements—such as the popular theater and the circus—were sinks of iniquity: a "universal pestilence," an "infernal chemistry of ruin," indeed "hell's first welcome" (*Lectures* 249–51).[3] More genteel pastimes, however— such as visiting the Louvre and the National Art Gallery or summering in the country—actually turned out to be morally uplifting, and indeed were recounted by Beecher as fond episodes in his own life. *Star Papers,* his collection of occasional essays, offered a record of his tour of Europe as well as his "vacations of three summers."

Beecher is something of a pivotal figure, from this perspective, testifying not only to the fluidity of class attributes in the nineteenth century but also (perhaps more crucial for my argument here) to the contending valencies within the social field, its failure to exhibit anything like a rationalized totality. Leisure, once flung in accusation at the feet of the upper class, was now claimed by the middle class, gingerly but also quite openly, not just as a birthright but as something of a requisite, at once identity-imparting and identity-certifying (see Brodhead). The social meaning of leisure would thus seem to be more variously marked, more variously nuanced and accented, than might appear generalizable from any simple economic given. It is against this complex semantic history of leisure that we can begin to gauge the dissonances in Beecher's own writings, or the dissonances between him and Melville. And it is against this complex semantic history, as well, that we can begin to gesture toward a historical criticism that is nonetheless not bound by the preposition "in." For the great interest of the Melville story is surely not what is *in* it, not the fact that leisure is here linked with degeneracy but the fact that it is so linked in accordance with an earlier, more populist, faintly anachronistic conception of class. Unlike the blandly decorous leisure in *Norwood* or *Star Papers,* leisure in "The Paradise of Bachelors" remains overrich, too savory, too alluring.[4] And, unlike Henry Ward Beecher, who apparently has come to accept leisure by accepting a selective version of it—the version newly sanitized by its association with the middle class—Melville has kept alive an older dynamics of attraction and revulsion, or attraction as revulsion, so that the spectacle of gentlemen at leisure becomes not so much a presumption in favor of leisure as a presumption against the gentlemen themselves, who, as leisured men, are also shown to be lesser men.

From that perspective, it is difficult to speak of the story as a "social critique"—as if that critique were its resident identity—for the critique is hardly located "in" the story but is intelligible only in relation to Beecher and only in relation to an earlier conception of class that, in the mid–nineteenth century, was just about to be superseded. Furthermore, even with this expanded semantic horizon, the text does not seem to possess a meaning integral enough or binding enough to give it anything like a *concluded* identity. For the Melville story, in its very polemical energy, in its metonymic attack on the leisured gentleman as effete bachelor, also carries with it something like a polemical overload, with consequences unintended, unexpected, and quite possibly unwelcome. One such consequence is that, even though the story is probably not "meant" to be homophobic, homophobia is nonetheless more than a dim shape on the horizon.[5] The resonances of the story (and for us, in the 1990s, they are troubling resonances) must far exceed anything Melville himself might have imagined. Given this signifying surcharge, and given the continual evolution of that surcharge, any attempt to come up with a "complete" reading of the text is bound to fail—woefully, but perhaps also happily. For that failure is surely a tribute to the story's continuing vitality, its continuing ability to sustain new meanings, even troubling meanings, over time. The semantic horizon of the text is thus commensurate neither with the sum of its parts nor with the sum of any number of readings. Taking these

incommensurabilities as reminders of a nonintegral universe, we should perhaps also take to heart their intimations of shortfall, as well as intimations
of possibility, in order to rethink the very idea of a hermeneutic totality and of
the text as an index to that totality.

Hermeneutic totality is, of course, an idea gestured at by the Melville story
itself, for the woman worker here is very much an index to a totality, a
metonym for the sufferings of the entire working class. This is apparently a
deliberate invention on Melville's part; as Judith A. McGaw points out, even
though there were actually *both* male and female workers in the Dalton paper
mill that Melville visited, the story takes as its exhibit only the latter (335).
This metonymic focus on the woman worker is in turn doubled upon itself,
since the focus is hardly on her general well-being but on one particular
feature of her person. It is her sexualized body that is being dramatized here,
the oppressions and deprivations of that body serving as a metonym for the
full range of her oppressions and deprivations. Female sexuality, in short,
becomes the generalized sign for the injury of class. Beginning with the journey to the paper mill (a protracted affair, vividly rendered as a grotesque encounter with the female anatomy), economic injustice is equated throughout
with sexual violation, industrial capitalism being figured here as a mechanized
rape of the female body.

It is this metonymic logic that confers on female sexuality its signifying primacy. To the extent that this signifying relation is understood to be a
complete relation, however—to the extent that this "rape" is understood fully
to summarize the female operatives as well as the entire working class—the
women are also turned into naturalized signs, welded into and subsumed
by what they signify. There they stand, "like so many mares haltered to the
rack," tending machines that "vertically thrust up a long, glittering scythe . . .
look[ing] exactly like a sword" (NN *PT* 329). Not surprisingly, they give
birth not to babies but to industrial products. The narrator reports a "scissory
sound . . . as of some cord being snapped, and down dropped an unfolded
sheet of perfect foolscap . . . still moist and warm" (332). In short, the sights
and sounds of industrial production cruelly mimic the sights and sounds of
biological reproduction, underscoring, at every turn, the simple equation between perverted womanhood and industrial victimhood.

Melville was not the only one to have lighted on the denaturalized woman
as a metonym for the sufferings of the working class. Joan Wallach Scott,
studying the representation of women workers in France during the same
period, has come upon images strikingly similar, images of female sexual dis-

order metonymically equated with the problems of the entire industrial order. As Scott points out, this mode of cultural figuration—this deployment of a class critique upon the symbolic body of woman—is not altogether disinterested. Indeed, as she documents it, political economists such as Jules Simon (who wrote a book called *L'Ouvrière*) not only routinely lamented the sexual plight of the women workers but also proposed, as a remedy, "the return of the mother to the family," for, as he said, "it is necessary that women be able to marry and that married women be able to remain at home all day, there to be the providence and the personification of the family." Given this view of things, it is not surprising that, according to Michelet, "ouvrière" was an "impious, sordid word that no language has ever known." Jules Simon, meanwhile, went so far as to say that "the woman who becomes a worker is no longer a woman" (158, 155). There is, of course, nothing quite so outspoken in "The Paradise of Bachelors and the Tartarus of Maids," nor anything to hint of the Cult of True Womanhood, the American counterpart to those pronouncements offered by Michelet and Simon.[6] Still, given Melville's anxieties about his literary career in an environment dominated by "scribbling women," it is certainly possible to see, in this story about "blank-looking girls" working on "blank paper," a half-resentful, half-wishful, and not especially well-disguised fantasy about women who wrote too mechanically and too much. Such speculations aside, we might note, as well, that, in his metonymic logic—in the implied equation between industrial victimhood and perverted womanhood—Melville would seem to have begged the very question of justice his writing so powerfully brings into focus. In his case, injustice is both self-evident and beside the point, both naturalized and rendered moot by that naturalization. Its spectacle excites only an obligatory apostrophe—"Oh! Paradise of Bachelors! and oh! Tartarus of Maids!"—an apostrophe almost "equal" to its object, we might even say, not only in repeating the diptych form of the story but also in completing it, turning its metonymic conceit into a natural circumference, a natural totality.

Against this formal closure—this inscription of a figural reality as full reality—I want to counter with an avowedly "incomplete" reading, one designed, that is, to go against the grain of the story, and most certainly against the grain of metonymic thinking. I want to suggest a reading predicated, that is, on the improbable presence of a historical "whole" in the text, an improbability whose consequences I take to be pragmatic, rather than self-deprecatingly rhetorical. In other words, if we concede that the meaning of literature is not a containable category, we would have to concede, infinitely more, that the meaning of history is also not containable—not containable as a hermeneutic totality and especially not as a hermeneutic totality in a text. Taking this hermeneutic incompleteness as an energizing relation between history and literature, and as a tribute to the evolving vitality of both, we might want to focus on those moments in the text where its historicity seems most tenuous, most problematic, using these moments to question the very idea of a unified "whole," both as it bears on the determining ground of literature and as it bears on the determinate shape of history.

Reading "The Paradise of Bachelors and the Tartarus of Maids," then, not as a totality, I want to engage it obliquely, engage it by dwelling on what it does *not* represent, which, in this case, happens to be an alternative account of the woman worker. That alternative figure casts a new light not only on the presumptive totality of Melville's story, but also on the presumptive totality of the historical process itself. For that figure was nothing if not emblematic in the 1830s and 1840s. Gleefully adduced—by company officials and ecstatic foreign visitors—that the woman worker was considered the pride of America and was routinely contrasted with the debased operatives in Manchester, England (see Bender 21–93; Kasson 53–106). Charles Dickens, who admitted to having "visited many mills in Manchester and elsewhere," reported with much-dramatized surprise that the American women workers "were all well dressed. . . . They were healthy in appearance, many of them remarkably so, and had the manners and deportment of young women: not of degraded brutes of burden." Indeed, "from all the crowd I saw in the different factories that day, I cannot recall or separate one young face that gave me a painful impression; not one young girl whom, assuming it to be a matter of necessity that she should gain her daily bread by the labour of her hands, I would have removed from those works if I had had the power" (60–61).

For Dickens, the American woman worker cut a different figure for obvious reasons: in being so happily unrecognizable to the English reader, she showed up everything that was wrong with industrial England. This juxtaposing function was, in fact, the standard function assigned her by English visitors. The Reverend William Scoresby, who visited the "factory girls" expressly to report to his congregation in Bradford, England, devoted chapters of his book, *American Factories and Their Female Operatives* (1845), to "Their Literary Pursuits," "Their Leisure Employments," "Their Moral Condition," and "Causes of Their Superiority." Scoresby found that these women were "clothed in silks, and otherwise gaily adorned"; that it was "a common thing for one of these girls to have five hundred dollars (a hundred guineas, nearly) in deposit" at the Lowell Institution for Savings; that their literary publication, the *Lowell Offering,* was "fair and comely," quite "a phenomenon in literature"; and that, in short, though "having no possible motive for flattering our transatlantic sisters," he must nonetheless conclude that in "general moral character, or superior intelligence, or great respectability—these factory girls do greatly surprise and interest us" and that they must commend themselves to "those who feel an interest in the improvement of the condition of our working population" (51–88).

These glowing nineteenth-century accounts are echoed by some twentieth-century historians, who, reacting against mainstream labor history, have called attention instead to the benefits of factory work for women.[7] Thomas Dublin, in particular, emphasizes the importance of industrialization not only to women's individual well-being but also to their potential for collective action. Dublin finds that—contrary to our usual view—the New England factory girls had not been driven to work by dire necessity. Indeed, according to him, the property holdings of the fathers put them in the broad middle ranges of wealth in their hometowns; fully 86 percent of the fathers had property valued at a hundred dollars or more. These women came because they wanted to, he argues, because they wanted the freedom of urban living, away from their rural families, and what they gained along the way was a sense of solidarity born out of the social relations of production. Work-sharing at the mills and communal living at the company boarding houses socialized the women in a way that the household economy would not, and that experience led directly to the collective action exemplified by strikes of the 1830s and the Ten Hour Movement of the 1840s, which saw the growth of a permanent labor organization among women, the Lowell Female Labor Reform Association, founded in December 1844. Dublin concludes that the factory experience "placed the Lowell women squarely within the evolving labor movement and indicated that crafts traditions were not the only legitimating forces in labor protests of the period" (89).

Such arguments, striking in their own right, do not pose as severe a challenge to the Melville story as they do to our current habit of reading. Any attempt to read the story as a metonym—as a container of history, an index to history—is bound to flounder here, for what is most striking about the story is surely its oblique relation to the lives of nineteenth-century women workers, its nonencapsulation of anything that might be called a "totality," and its unavoidable slipperiness as the ground of historical generalizations. To acknowledge this is not, of course, to argue for a lack of connections between history and literature. It is, however, a call to rethink the *nature* of those connections, to set aside our current metonymic premise, in favor of concepts such as un-evenness, off-centeredness, nonalignment. Such concepts, with their emphasis on imperfect closure, imperfect correspondence, qualify not only the her-meneutic relation between history and literature but also the very idea of a whole, whether social or textual.

For the nineteenth-century women workers themselves, it was the non-existence of a whole that made their lives livable, bearable, and, in the end, not just a metonym for the oppressions of industrial capitalism. Their sto-ries and poems, letters and memoirs stubbornly refused to bear witness to a principle of full integration, full adequation, a refusal that, at the very least, should compel us to rethink the postulate of "totality," with its attendant con-structs of body and mind, part and whole, and with its attendant assump-tions about the likelihood of a "complete" reading. Almost without exception, these women, even those writing for house organs such as the *Lowell Offer-ing*, commented on the physical ordeal of work, the fatigue and often the disfigurations suffered by the body. In a series entitled "Letters from Susan," one author, Harriet Farley, complained that

> the hours seemed very long . . . and when I went out at night the sound of the mill was in my ears, as of crickets, frogs, and jewsharps, all mingled to-gether in strange discord. . . . It makes my feet ache and swell to stand so much, . . . they almost all say that when they have worked here a year or two they have to procure shoes a size or two larger than before they came. The right hand, which is the one used in stopping and starting the loom, becomes larger than the left. (52)

What is remarkable, however, is that, such bodily afflictions notwithstand-ing, Farley also went on to report in the same letter that, while the factory girls "scorn to say they were contented, if asked the question, for it would com-promise their Yankee spirit. . . . Yet, withal, they are cheerful. I never saw a happier set of beings. They appear blithe in the mill, and out of it" (53). From aching ears and swollen feet, it might seem a long way to cheerfulness, hap-piness, and blitheness. But it was just this strange transport—this improbable outcome given the point of departure—that structured the daily lives of the women workers. Harriet Hanson Robinson, who started working in the Lowell mills in 1834, at the age of ten, offered yet another account of this phenomenon in her memoir, *Loom and Spindle*, published in 1898 when she was seventy-three years old. From the distance of some sixty years, she could still remember the excitement of gainful employment, of having money in her pocket for the first time, and of the magical transformation the women underwent:

[A]fter the first pay-day came, and they felt the jingle of silver in their pockets, and had begun to feel its mercurial influence, their bowed heads were lifted, their necks seemed braced with steel, they looked you in the face, sang blithely among their looms or frames, and walked with elastic step to and from their work. And when Sunday came, homespun was no longer their only wear; and how sedately gay in their new attire they walked to church, and how proudly they dropped their silver four-pences into the contribution-box! It seemed as if a great hope impelled them,—the harbinger of the new era that was about to dawn for them and for all women-kind. (43)

For women not accustomed to having earnings of their own, not accustomed to the luxury of city clothes, or the luxury of church patronage, leaving home and working in a factory brought with it a psychological well-being that shone forth in full view of the physical ordeal of repetitive labor and long working hours. One was not reducible to the other, or generalizable from the other, and that was precisely the point. For what was most remarkable about these accounts of factory life was surely the persistent lack of fit—the lack of absolute determination or absolute entailment—between standards of discomfort and states of mind, between the generalized conditions of work and the specific affect reported by the women workers. The women workers were workers, to be sure; they were bodies bound to machines, bodies that became aching ears and swollen feet. But they were women as well, and, as women, they had a prehistory significantly different from that of the men and a capacity for transformation (not to say a capacity for benefit) that was also significantly different. The experience of industrialization, it would seem, was not at all an integral experience, not at all evenly registered or universally shared, but locally composed for each particular group, its composition being directly related to the antecedents out of which that group emerged.[8] In the case of the women workers, coming as they did from under the shadow of the patriarchal household, the emotional satisfaction they enjoyed as newly independent wage earners might turn out to be as nontrivial a benefit as the physical drudgery of labor was nontrivial an oppression. It is here, in the perpetual lack of adequation between these two registers, that we can speak of the "nontrivial" as a crucial evidentiary category, a crucial supplement to any model of presumptive totality and generalizability. And it is here, as well, that we can speak of gender as an exemplary instance of the nontrivial, both in the relays it multiplies between body and mind, and in the challenge it poses to their supposed integration.

What emerged, then, from these writings by women workers, was a set of determinations that, while acknowledged, were also carefully kept from being too seamless, too absolute. Between the body and the person, and between the person and the class, there was always the possibility for inconclusivenss, always the possibility for imperfect alignment and contrary articulation. The bodies of the women told one story, their letters told another, and their organized strikes, it would seem, told yet a third. Lucy Larcom was speaking only in one of the many possible voices of the woman worker when she wrote:

> One great advantage which came to these many stranger girls through being brought together, away from their own homes, was that it taught them to go out of themselves, and enter into the lives of others. Home-life, when one always stays at home, is necessarily narrowing. That is one reason why so many women are petty and unthoughtful of any except their own family's interests. . . . For me, it was an incalculable help to find myself among so many working-girls, all of us thrown upon our own resources, but thrown much more upon each others' sympathies. (178–79)

Speaking in a voice related but not exactly identical, Larcom also mentioned that she was "dazzled" by the thought of "Mount Holyoke Seminary . . . as a vision of hope" and that "Mary Lyon's name was honored nowhere more than among the Lowell mill-girls" (223). And it was in yet another related but not exactly identical voice that Sally Rice wrote the following letter, explaining why she did not want to leave the factory and go home to the "wilderness":

> I can never be happy in among so many mountains. . . . I feel as though I have worn out shoes and strength enough walking over the mountains . . . . and as for marrying and settling in that wilderness, I wont. If a person ever expects to take comfort it is while they are young. . . . I am most 19 years old. I must of course have something of my own before many more years have passed over my head. And where is that something coming from if I

go home and earn nothing. . . . You may think me unkind but how can you blame me for wanting to stay here. I have but one life to live and I want to enjoy myself as well as I can while I live. (Dublin 37)

We would be hard put to find a unified identity in these letters and memoirs by women workers. What confronts us instead are many *circumstances* for identities, identities imagined as well as lived, all rhetorically mediated, and only partially harmonized. The women were not speaking out of a singular body called the "working class." They were not even speaking out of a singular body called the "person." For the "person," in every respect, turned out to be less than a singularity but also more than a body. Like the human voice itself, at once rooted in the body that nourishes it but also miraculously unencompassed by that body, the "person" too is at once material and immaterial, at once a determinate presence and a field of incipience. In that determination and in that incipience—and in the destabilizing relation between the two— these women make it clear that no reading of their lives will ever be complete.

NOTES

1. Nor was this the only occasion he was known to do so. For Beecher's "massive inconsistency," see McLoughlin 30.

2. As Rodgers points out, "The sermons explicitly directed at the young, the poor, or the working class tended also to be those in which the gospel of work was most prominent; in thinking of the prosperous, overtaxed businessmen in his congregation he often chose the counsel of leisure" (98).

3. As Levine has pointed out, the theater was popular entertainment in the nineteenth century, quite different from the exclusive pastime it has become today (11–82).

4. The allure of such a world as found in "The Paradise of Bachelors" was personally experienced by Melville himself during his visit to London in December 1849, when he was wined and dined by the literary and legal community.

5. For an argument about Melville's homophobia, see Sedgwick, *Epistemology* (91–130). For a contrary account, see Martin.

6. For a pioneering and still useful account, see Welter. For a summary of recent scholarship, see Kerber.

7. Stansell, for example, has emphasized the benefits of factory work as opposed to the take-home "outwork," which not only paid less but also "bolstered up older forms of patriarchical supervision and curtailed the ways in which single women could turn manufacturing work to the uses of independence." See also Dublin. For qualifying views, see Blewett and McGaw. For a useful survey of the vast scholarship on the subject, see Baron, "Gender and Labor History."

8. Here I am giving voice to a position well articulated by women historians. See Alexander; Baron, "Women and the Making of the American Working Class"; Hicks; Rose; Scott.

WORKS CITED

Alexander, Sally. "Women, Class, and Sexual Difference." *History Workshop* 17 (1984): 125–49.

Baron, Eva. "Gender and Labor History." In *Work Engendered*. Ed. Eva Baron. Ithaca: Cornell UP, 1991. 1–46.

———. "Women and the Making of the American Working Class: A Study of the Proletarianization of Printers." *Review of Radical Political Economics* 14 (Fall 1982): 23–43.

Beecher, Henry Ward. *Lectures to Young Men.* 1844. New York: J. C. Derby, 1856.

———. *Norwood: or, Village Life in New England.* New York: Charles S. Scribner, 1868.

———. *Star Papers: Experiences of Art and Nature.* New York: J. C. Derby, 1855.

Bender, John. *Toward an Urban Vision: Ideas and Institutions in Nineteenth Century America.* Baltimore: Johns Hopkins UP, 1975.

Blewett, Mary. *Men, Women, and Work: A Study of Class, Gender, and Protest in the Nineteenth Century Shoe Industry.* Urbana: U of Illinois P, 1988.

Brodhead, Richard. *Cultures of Letters.* Chicago: U of Chicago Press, 1993.

Corning, James Leonard. *The Christian Law of Amusement.* Buffalo: Phinney, 1859.

Dickens, Charles. *American Notes.* 1842. New York: St. Martin's, 1985.

Dimock, Wai Chee. *Empire for Liberty: Melville and the Poetics of Individualism.* Princeton: Princeton UP, 1989.

———. *Residues of Justice: Literature, Law, Philosophy.* Berkeley: U of California P, 1996.

Dublin, Thomas. *Women at Work: The Transformation of Work and Community in Lowell, Massachusetts, 1826–1860.* New York: Columbia UP, 1979.

Grund, Francis. *The Americans in Their Moral, Social, and Political Relations.* 2 vols. London: Longman, 1837.

Hicks, Emily. "Cultural Marxism: Nonsynchrony and Feminist Practice." In *Women and Revolution.* Ed. Lydia Sargent. Boston: South End, 1981. 219–38.

Kasson, John. *Civilizing the Machine: Technology and Republican Values in America, 1776–1900.* New York: Penguin, 1977.

Kerber, Linda. "Separate Spheres, Female Worlds, Woman's Place: The Rhetoric of Women's History." *Journal of American History* 75 (1988): 9–39.

Larcom, Lucy. *A New England Girlhood.* 1899. Gloucester, MA: Peter Smith, 1973.

Levine, Lawrence. *Highbrow/Lowbrow: The Emergence of Cultural Hierarchy.* Cambridge, MA: Harvard UP, 1988.

The Lowell Offering: Writings by New England Mill Women (1840–1845). Ed. Benita Eisler. Philadelphia: Lippincott, 1977.

McGaw, Judith. *Most Wonderful Machine: Mechanization and Social Change in Berkshire Paper Making, 1801–1885.* Princeton: Princeton UP, 1987.

McLoughlin, William. *The Meaning of Henry Ward Beecher: An Essay on the Shifting Values of Mid-Victorian America, 1840–1870.* New York: Knopf, 1970.

Martin, Robert K. *Hero, Captain, and Stranger: Male Friendship, Social Critique, and Literary Form in the Sea Novels of Herman Melville.* Chapel Hill: North Carolina UP, 1986.

Robinson, Harriet Hanson. *Loom and Spindle, or Life among the Early Mill Girls.* 1898. Kailua, HI: Press Pacifica, 1976.

Rodgers, Daniel. *The Work Ethic in Industrial America, 1850–1920.* Chicago: U of Chicago P, 1978.

Rose, Sonya. "Gender at Work: Sex, Class, and Industrial Capitalism." *History Workshop* 21 (Spring 1986): 113–21.

Scoresby, William. *American Factories and Their Female Operatives.* 1845. New York: Burt Franklin, 1968.

Scott, Joan Wallach. *Gender and the Politics of History.* New York: Columbia UP, 1988.

Sedgwick, Eve Kosofsky. *Between Men: English Literature and Male Homosocial Desire.* New York: Columbia UP, 1985.

———. *Epistemology of the Closet.* Berkeley: U of California P, 1990.

Stansell, Christine. *City of Women: Sex and Class in New York, 1789–1860.* Urbana: U of Illinois P. 1987.

Taylor, Charles. *Sources of the Self: The Making of the Modern Identity.* Cambridge, MA: Harvard UP, 1989.

Welter, Barbara. "The Cult of True Womanhood, 1820–1860." *American Quarterly* 18 (1966): 151–74.

Melville and Race

6

Our Crowd, Their Crowd:
Race, Reader, and *Moby-Dick*

DAVID BRADLEY

I am like one of those seeds taken out of the Egyptian Pyramids, which, after three thousand years as a seed and nothing but a seed, being planted in English soil, it developed itself, grew to greenness, and then fell to mould. So I.

—*Moby-Dick*

On November 14, 1851, a major work by an established American writer was published for the first time in this country. The writer was Herman Melville, from whom readers had come to expect autobiographical first-person adventures set on the high seas or South Sea Islands. In abstract the new work fulfilled popular expectations, being a romance based on Melville's experience aboard the New Bedford whaler *Acushnet* and the Nantucket whaler *Charles and Henry* and featuring colorful savages, a monstrous adversary, even a compelling chase. But somehow the novel confounded expectations. Melville's supposed friend, Evert A. Duyckinck, called it "an intellectual chowder" (613); an anonymous reviewer in the *Southern Quarterly* called it "Cause for a Writ de Lunatico" (619). As Willy Loman would have said, *Moby-Dick* was liked . . . but not *well* liked.

Indeed, the looming of *Moby-Dick* marked the beginning of the end of Melville's career. Five years before it his first novel, *Typee* (1846), had been published with commercial success, as had his second, *Omoo* (1847). His third, *Mardi* (1849), was a commercial disappointment but would surely have done better had Melville not forbidden his publisher to advertise it as by "the author of *Typee* and *Omoo*." His next two, *Redburn* (1849) and *White-Jacket* (1850), had recovered financially—and made Melville one of the best-known American writers in the world. Then came *Moby-Dick*. Five years later Melville finished what would be his final novel, *The Confidence-Man* (1857), at such emotional cost that his father-in-law, Judge Lemuel Shaw, financed a trip abroad designed to adjust Melville's attitude but which, as Charles Feidelson put it in the early 1960s, marked "the virtual end of Melville's public career as a writer. . . . In 1863 he finally obtained an official position, as Deputy Director of Customs. This was his public occupation for almost twenty years . . . his private life was that of a quiet amateur of letters . . . . He had been almost entirely forgotten as a writer when he died on September 28, 1891" (xiv). Such was the decline. Melville's death was marked by but a single obituary.

Thirty years before Feidelson, Russell Blankenship, in *American Literature as an Expression of the National Mind,* tried to account for "the disfavor of the vast majority of American readers." Melville, said Blankenship, "so often and so bluntly stated his contempt of society and civilization that his offended public set him down as a misanthrope, a hater of mankind. . . . In book after book Melville overlooked no chance to repudiate society and to excoriate the fruits of its most revered institutions" (378). Blankenship insisted that Melville was a misanthrope in fact as well as in fiction; he was "not willing to hob-nob with the crowd and slap backs with the most vulgar" and "from the touch of man he shrank aghast" (378). And more than an American Coriolanus, Melville was an escapist who created "many impersonations . . . he appeared in *Moby-Dick* as Ishmael, the outcast, the wanderer," and who imagined a South Seas "dream-land from which all plagues of earthly life are banished" (379). His attitudes were the those of an embittered utopian; his fall a result of psychological disappointment: "All his life he was tortured by his recollections, hopes and aspirations; never could he find peace" (383). And that was just in the *first* place.

In the next place . . . Melville, like Hawthorne, was burdened with the problem of evil, its origins, its meaning, and its final destiny. Especially prominent was this question in the greatest of his books, *Moby Dick*. Unlike Hawthorne, who set his discussions of evil in the dim shadows of the past, Melville insisted upon talking about the question in terms of contemporary civilization, and more than a few times his hot satire seared some object of unquestioned respectability. Such a novelist is bound to be uncomfortable, and if there is anything that the American of the fifties wanted to find in his literature it was comfort. Sentimental readers can snivel agreeably over the misfortunes of a wayward youth or maiden, but such people can get no pleasure out of a realistic analysis of comforting hypocrisies . . . Melville's realism repelled many. (379)

Melville's third failing, according to Blankenship, was obscurity: "the full meaning of *Moby Dick* is not exactly crystal clear," and "the meaning of *Moby Dick* is no clearer than is the ultimate meaning of *Hamlet*." Blankenship allowed that these reasons "might not have been potent enough to account for all of Melville's lack of popularity" but insisted that they "would account for at least some of it" (379, 385).

In fact they account for none of it. The third reason is ridiculous. That the "full meaning of *Moby Dick* is not exactly crystal clear" could hardly have been impediment to an audience accustomed to the King James Bible. Nor has obscurity done lasting harm to *Hamlet* or the reputation of Shakespeare. Nor is most of *Moby-Dick* obscure; Blankenship himself admitted that "the plain story of *Moby Dick* is simple," and that, "despite its length, the meaning of the informative passages and the thread of the narrative need no explanation" (384–85).

The first reason ignores such fictional techniques as Keatsian negative capability and Socratic irony: like many modern critics, Blankenship confused the identity of the author with that of the characters, seeing "impersonations" instead of creations. Some readers may have done the same. The *Southern Quarterly's* anonymous reviewer confused Ahab's "ravings, and the ravings of some of the tributary characters, and the ravings of Mr. Melville himself" (619). But if they had found misanthropy in Melville's earlier novels, in *Moby-Dick* they found apology; Ishmael sets out a bitter fellow, but after but a short time at sea he is exhorting all to "Squeeze! squeeze! squeeze! . . . Come; let us squeeze hands all round; nay, let us all squeeze ourselves into each other; let us squeeze ourselves universally into the very milk and sperm of kindness" (*Moby-Dick* 348–49).

Though the whale ship may seem utopian, it is neither idealized nor inaccessible to "the most vulgar." As Blankenship himself notes, 1851 "was a good time to tell the story of the whale. Nantucket and New Bedford ships were nosing into every corner of the seven seas in search of their quarry, and the fame of the harpooners and boatmen was a magnet to attract thousands of New England boys away from the safe but monotonous hill farms" (385).

Nor is it clear that *Moby-Dick* dealt with actual evil. Ahab was mad, which is to say abnormal, perhaps even perverted. But evil? And sure the *Pequod* was not evil, unless Ahab made her so by subverting her true nature and purpose, which was to kill whales. Other whaling ships were not evil, nor were the whalemen—Queequeg, after all, the most fearsome in aspect, was willing to greet ridicule with gentleness and then save the life of his tormentor at no little risk to his own. Greater love hath no cannibal.

Certainly whaling itself was not presented as evil. It is hard to imagine what "hot satire" could have seared "some object of unquestioned respectability," or what repellent "comforting hypocrisies" Melville subjected to realistic analysis. For thus saith Ishmael:

> . . . at the present day not one in two of the many thousand men before the mast employed in the American whale fishery, are American born, though pretty near all the officers are. Herein it is the same with the American whale fishery as with the American army and military and merchant navies, and the engineering forces employed in the construction of the American Canals and Railroads. The same, I say, because in all these cases the native American liberally provides the brains, the rest of the world as generously supplying the muscles. (108)

In connecting the grand, worthy venture of whaling with American enterprises of exploration and development, Ishmael implicitly declares those enterprises grand and worthy.

All this makes the story of Herman Melville frightening to a writer—and it is as a writer that I speak. Here we have a well-established author working to a proven formula. Here we have a book laid on dramatic keel, constructed of classic conflicts, colorfully crewed and rigged with romance, even flying the ensign of American achievement and Manifest Destiny. How could a book so far from treason have failed to prosper? How could it have done its author so much *harm*? To a black American writer—as which I also speak—the case of Melville is cause for particular trepidation. To explain that I must consult with two physicians—one a doctor of philosophy, the other a professor of jazz.

The Ph.D. is E. D. Hirsch, professor of English, who coined the term "cultural literacy," defining it as the "background information and the linguistic conventions that are needed to read, write and speak effectively" (22). Hirsch's notion, first presented in 1981 at the Modern Language Association, evolved into a book, *Cultural Literacy,* which, when published in 1987, caused quite a stir, in part because it included a list of names, dates, places, phrases, artistic works, and intellectual concepts "intended to illustrate the character and range of the knowledge literate Americans tend to share" (ix, 146) and in part because the Reagan administration (in the person of Secretary of Education William Bennett) oversimplified and politically exploited it. Poor Hirsch was branded a reactionary, and his hypothesis jingoistic, racist, and reactionary. This was nonsense; Hirsch stated explicitly that "standard written English has no intrinsic superiority to other languages" (xiv, 3), and his basic hypothesis has no essential political content at all: "The chief function of literacy is to make us masters of this standard instrument of knowledge and communication, thereby enabling us to give and receive complex information orally and in writing over time and space" (3).

For Hirsch the virtue of standard English is not that it's English, but that it's *standard.* It is to be favored only because so many Americans already speak some dialect of it and so much of our national culture is already encoded in it. According to the hypothesis, Esperanto or Kiswahili would do as well, once we'd all learned it and translated everything into it.

Three specific portions of the Hirsch hypothesis are useful here. The first is simply the importance of communication: "The complex undertakings of modern life depend on the cooperation of many people with different specialties in different places. Where communications fail, so do the undertakings. (That is the moral story of the Tower of Babel)" (2). The second portion is the definition of cultural literacy, and the consequent definition of a culturally literate person: "To be culturally literate is to possess the basic information needed to thrive in the modern world. The breadth of that information is great, extending over the major domains of human activity from sports to science" (xiii). The third is the implication of two of Hirsch's statements. First: "To understand what somebody is saying, we must understand more than the surface meanings of the words; we have to understand the context as well. The need for background information applies all the more to reading and writing. To grasp the words on a page we have to know a lot of information that isn't set down on the page." And second: "If they can take a lot for granted, their communications can be short and efficient, subtle and complex. But if strangers share very little knowledge, their communications must be long and relatively rudimentary" (3–4). In other words, culture controls the form, speed, and ease of what literary theorists call "discourse," and in clear corollary, the probability of success of a communication is a function of the degree to which cultural knowledge is shared by the communicants.

Hirsch—with a little help from his friends—sailed into the shoals when he tried to extend his hypothesis to politics and culture. Politically, Hirsch declared that "Cultural literacy constitutes the only sure avenue of opportunity for disadvantaged children, the only reliable way of combating the social determinism that now condemns them to remain in the same social and educational condition as their parents" (xiii).

While it is true that—as Ramsey Lewis, professor of jazz, might phrase it— one way the Out Crowd gets in with the In Crowd is by learning what the In Crowd knows, it is not the only way; witness the French Revolution of 1848. Nor is it a sure way; witness the *Plessy v. Ferguson* decision of 1896. Politically Hirsch's theory depends on the Out Crowd's staying off the barricades and on the In Crowd's not passing laws to keep Out-Crowders out no matter what they know.

Hirsch also tried to use true statements about language in an argument about culture, but he failed to transform his terms; he didn't say "standard American culture has no intrinsic superiority to other national cultures and alternative American cultures," a failure that gives the unfortunate impression that he didn't believe that there *are* valid alternative American cultures.

Eventually Hirsch ran his hypothesis onto the hard rock of content, admitting that what was necessary was only a "superficiality" of cultural knowledge (15–16). Indeed, in generating that troublesome list Hirsch was not "advocating a list of great books that every child in the land should be forced to read" but a fundamental ignorance of those titles: "Very few specific titles appear on the list," he declared in a second-edition defense, "and they usually appear as words, not works, because they represent writings that culturally literate people have read about but haven't read" (xiv). I am reminded of Twain calling a classic "something everybody wants to have read and nobody wants to read."

But despite his errors, Hirsch was right—especially with respect to the complex communications we call literature. To, and only to, the extent that we share—or come to share—a cultural data base can we engage in subtleties, move from speech to figures of speech, from intention to double entendre, and tell tales that go beyond the journalistic Who, What, Where, When.

Four items of refinement and reemphasis are necessary to make the Hirsch hypothesis fully applicable to literature. The first is to depoliticize the concept of Crowd; for while surely there are In Crowds and Out Crowds, to alter or preserve their identities and existing relationships is not the business of the artist—although artistic efforts may help accomplish such ends. A Crowd is as apolitical as Hirsch would have it; a group defined by *knowledge* of beliefs, technologies, customs, and experiences, not by power, influence, genotype, phenotype, or socioeconomic status. While such factors may control who *tends* to have convenient access to given cultural data, there are always exceptions, always a Frederick Douglass who finds a way to teach himself to read, a Richard Wright who checks books out of a segregated library on a borrowed card, a Louis Armstrong raised by Jews—always, as Ralph Ellison's music teacher said, "a little man hiding behind the stove" ("Little Man").

The second item is to note that while each of us is born into some Crowd, each of us, in the course of life, gains membership in additional Crowds while, to the extent allowed by memory, desire, and opportunity, retaining membership in our "Birth Crowd." The third item is to assert that the purpose of literary expression is not to explain one Crowd to another; that is the task of anthropology. As Ellison put it in "On Initiation Rites and Power," "I don't think that . . . it is a function of writing, to tell the reader what it feels like to be a Negro, as critics say over and over again about plays and novels and poems by black writers."

The fourth item is to point out that, while Hirsch speaks of communication between only two Crowds—he doesn't use that term; "Ramsey Lewis" is not on his list—literary communication involves at least three Crowds: the Crowd of the author, the Crowd of the characters, and the Crowd of the audience. (If the plot involves cultural confrontation, even more may be involved.) It is important to note this because in America it is often assumed that a writer is a member in good standing of his Character Crowd. This makes some sense, because if a writer is serious he or she will be drawn into an understanding of the culture of the Character Crowd, even if he or she is already a member of it. Jean Toomer, for example, who declared "As for being a Negro, this of course I am not—neither biologically nor socially" (Benson and Dillard 41), nonetheless asserted elsewhere that "In so far as the old folk songs, syncopated rhythms, the rich sweet taste of dark-skinned life, in so far as these are Negro, then I am body and soul, Negroid" (33). Thus it is a reasonable simplification to speak, as I shall, of a writer trying to tell an Our Crowd tale to Their Crowd. But this is a result of artistic activity; the writer is a Crowd unto himself—which causes real members of the Character Crowd to complain about inaccuracies in the way "they" are depicted and to insist the writer is exploiting the culture and/or is not truly "one of us."

Inaccuracies are quite possible, and exploitations have occurred, especially when the writer is a member of the Audience Crowd. But there are excellent artistic reasons why a writer would want to tell an Our Crowd tale to Their Crowd; often the most useful cultures are those about which the audience knows little. This does not deny the importance of universal themes and symbols, but—with all due respect to Carl Jung and Joseph Campbell—what makes a myth a tale is the way cultural assumptions refigure archetypal plots and motivate archetypal characters.

Still, all writers do not wish to tell an Our Crowd tale to Their Crowd. Some writers find their own Crowd has a culture complex enough to support good art and a population affluent and literate enough to support the artist. I do not necessarily refer to "privileged" writers. In 1975 Gwendolyn Brooks, expressing the philosophy of the Black Arts Movement, wrote: "The prevailing understanding: black literature is BY blacks, ABOUT blacks, directed TO blacks" (Dudley). Though a similar attitude is and has been characteristic of many white American writers—there has been a white arts movement in America for a very long time—some American writers have found it artistically and commercially desirable, if not necessary, to tell an Our Crowd tale to Their Crowd; obviously this was true of Franklin, Crèvecoeur, and Irving. Melville, for this reason, altered at least one chapter of *Moby-Dick* for British publication.

Nor is it a simple problem of imparting information, for while Their Crowd is culturally illiterate with respect to Our Crowd, Their Crowd usually has some beliefs—possibly cherished—about Our Crowd culture and Our Crowd itself. To call them prejudices would be unnecessarily pejorative; suffice it that they are a problem for the writer, not because of social concerns but because they distort the meaning of the tale. And so the writer who would tell an Our Crowd tale to Their Crowd must both educate and *uneducate* in order to allow Their Crowders to understand exactly what the characters think they are doing and why they think they are doing it.

At a basic level this problem is faced by all writers, for the audience is always ignorant of some specific data—the private business of an extended family, the quirky customs of a small town, the secret rites of a religion, the horrific practices of a peculiar institution. Obviously this is true of fiction, where any and all of these things may be invented. But for writers, even fiction writers, content to tell a tale of Our Crowd to Our Crowd, the problem is restricted to specifics. These writers, to return to Hirsch's language, "can take a lot for granted, their communications can be short and efficient." Their settings can be sketched, their characters easily motivated, their plots quickly established; they can "cut to the chase." But writers who try to tell an Our Crowd tale to Their Crowd dare not cut to the chase; if they do, the audience will not understand what is being chased or why.

Melville, in *Moby-Dick,* obviously did not cut to the chase. What is not so obvious to nonwriters is that he could not, because of Their Crowd's cultural illiteracy. Much of *Moby-Dick*'s audience was prejudiced, first by the popular (and culturally questionable) sea-based romances of James Fenimore Cooper—*The Pilot* (1823) and *The Red Rover* (1827)—and then by Melville's own work. That Melville was aware of the prejudice is clear; in his 1847 review of J. Ross Browne's *Etchings of a Whaling Cruise,* he spoke somewhat ambiguously of the power of factual accounts like Browne's and Richard Henry Dana's *Two Years Before the Mast* to "impair the charm with which poesy and fiction have invested the sea" (*Moby-Dick* 529). What was more, the culture of *Moby-Dick* was not the relative commonplace of merchantmen and men-o'-war, but the extended hunting cruise of the whaler, a distinction Melville made in 1847—"What Mr. Dana has so admirably done in describing the vicissitudes of the merchant sailor's life, Mr. Browne has very creditably achieved with respect to that of the hardy whaleman's" (530)—and reiterated in 1851: "Marchant service be damned. Talk not that lingo to me. Dost see that leg?—I'll take that leg away from thy stern, if ever thou talkest of the marchant service to me again" (68–69).

Melville's review of Browne reveals much that would find its way into *Moby-Dick*—symbolism, action, and also an aesthetic: "The scenes presented are always graphically and truthfully sketched . . . doubtless, the author never dreamed of softening down or withholding anything with a view of rendering his sketches more attractive and pretty. The book is . . . written with the set purpose of accomplishing good by revealing the simple truth" (530). The simple truth was again at issue in May 1850, when Melville wrote to Dana that he was "half way in the work" of *Moby-Dick;* he declared that "to cook the thing up one must needs throw in a little fancy, which from the nature of the thing, must be ungainly as the gambols of the whales themselves. Yet I mean to give the truth of the thing, spite of this" (551–52).

Critics have made much of what happened after this—Melville first read the work of Nathaniel Hawthorne, penned an essay on *Mosses from an Old Manse,* and met Hawthorne at a picnic at which the august possibilities of American literature were discussed, events that took place in late July and early August 1850. Hawthorne, as Feidelson put it, became "an ally in the creation of an American literature that would not be popular entertainment, but 'the art of Telling the Truth'" (xiii). What that meant for Hawthorne may have been theoretical, but Melville was in the midst of writing a novel, and theory had immediate implications for application and action. The result, at a time when Duyckinck reported to friends that "Melville has a new book mostly done," was what Leon Howard referred to as the "second growth of *Moby-Dick*" (quoted in *Moby-Dick* 709).

Howard, in delineating the changes that Melville made, emphasizes the dramatic structures, but also shows that factual sources could not have had much influence on the text before this time. As Howard notes, "it seems most probable that he had been engaged upon a narrative which he expected to supplement in various places rather than upon the progressive composition of the sort of book he later published . . . when he took it up again after the departure of his friends he not only began to enlarge but substantially rewrite his book" (710).

Howard insists that "Nothing that had ever happened to Melville in his travels was more important than the activities of his mind between August, 1850 and August, 1851. . . . His mind was swirling with new ideas and old memories," emphasizing the philosophical impact of Melville's visits with Hawthorne. But he also recounts another event: "A shipmate from the *Acushnet*, Henry F. Hubbard, had stopped by to see him with a report of what had happened to the voyage and the crew after Melville's desertion. If either of the two old friends had heard reports from the second voyage of the *Acushnet*, they might have discussed another chapter in the history of that ill-fated ship: the loss of a boat from the attack of a furious whale and the rescue of one of its crew, picked up hours afterward and miles away, swimming through an empty ocean" (721).

In November of 1851, Duyckinck, while damning *Moby-Dick* with faint praise, observed that Melville's earlier work had "a double character . . . . In one light they are romantic fictions, in another statements of absolute fact . . . it becomes quite impossible to submit such books to a distinct classification as fact, fiction or essay" (*Moby-Dick* 613). And, as Howard also notes, "Melville, having tried without much satisfaction in *Mardi* the method of expressing a general conception in a specific image, had gradually slipped into the practice of letting his mind play around concrete details until they were made luminous with suggestive implications" (725).

Howard's statement is part of a discussion of the allegorical nature of *Moby-Dick*, and it is almost a critical given that *Moby-Dick* was allegorical. But what

I would argue is that in his reworking of *Moby-Dick,* Melville was trying to create what could be called an anti-allegory. In a pure allegory, a metaphysical essence is projected upon physical existence by symbolic expression—the tale. The elements of the expression—plot, characterization, motivation, setting, etc.—are controlled by the essence, which usually results in a tale that seems unreal, though this is largely concealed by the casting of the allegory in verse. *Moby-Dick,* by contrast, was conceived in prose and born of whales and whaling, of Mocha Dick and the *Essex,* of legal and economic apparatus and technological implements. It was these existences, "discovered" by Melville through experience and research, that controlled expression; if projection occurred it was of physical existence onto metaphysical essence. Melville himself, in his letter to Mrs. Hawthorne on January 8, 1852, claimed to have had only "some vague idea while writing it, that the whole book was susceptible of an allegorical construction, & also that *parts* of it were" (*Moby-Dick* 568), which means he had not been shaping the tale to the template of an a priori metaphysical essence. He had, however, gone to great lengths to shape the tale according to the template of facts, and, as Howard notes, had in *Moby-Dick* used those facts in a far more organic way than in his previous works. In *Typee, Omoo, Redburn,* and *White-Jacket* Melville had to ensure that his audience had sufficient cultural literacy of the seafaring culture to comprehend the background of the tale. In *Moby-Dick* the matter was more critical, for in *Moby-Dick* background became foreground.

Melville had not, as Howard demonstrates, done much or any of the necessary refiguring before July 1850, if only because much of the raw material was not available to him. But Melville's knowledge is not the issue—the audience's knowledge is. In order for either allegory or anti-allegory to "work," the audience must possess understanding of the nature of the controlling factor. In order for *Paradise Lost* to work the audience had to understand the metaphysical "realities" as Milton understood them. Fortunately for Milton, the audience did—until the Byronic shift. For *Moby-Dick* to work the audience had to understand the physical "realities." Unfortunately for Melville, the audience did not. To have both the basic action and higher meaning of *Moby-Dick* comprehended as he intended, Melville had to develop techniques to educate the audience.

Thus *Moby-Dick* became, by dint of its primacy in history and Melville's genius at solving literary problems, what I will call a "master text"—a text that, whatever it might do for the reader or the critic, offers to the artist a wide range of imaginative and effective solutions to a specific compositional problem and to which, therefore, a large number of writers can and do refer as a model for attacking that problem. For the American writer who would tell an Our Crowd tale to Their Crowd, *Moby-Dick* is the master text.

In *Moby-Dick* Melville employed five types of technical structure to educate the reader in the intricacies of the whaling culture. The first was thematic; in addition to the leitmotif of whaling, Melville, both in the content of the tale and structure of the text, early and often sounded the motif of education. The first element in the text, the Etymology, is "supplied by a late consumptive usher to a grammar school," and the first actual entry is the following quote from Richard Hakluyt's *Principal Navigations,* which both echoes the motif and announces an intention: "While you take in hand to school others, and to teach them by what name a whale-fish is to be called in our tongue, leaving out, through ignorance, the letter H, which almost alone maketh up the signification of the word, you deliver that which is not true."

The Etymology and Extracts, coupled with those portions of the text known, and often dismissed, as the whaling chapters, are manifestations of a second type of structure, one that directly imparts information. Critics have spun many theories about what these structures, the whaling chapters in particular, actually do. One thing they do is obvious: they inform the audience—assuming, of course, they are read. But even if they are not, they at least inform the audience that something is being skipped.

The third type of structure is something the audience cannot avoid reading: metaphor, in various forms and extensions. A metaphor is an implicit analogy that equates one object or action with another. When both elements of the metaphor are familiar, this is evocative. When either is unfamiliar, it is instructive. Such is often the case in *Moby-Dick.* "With anxious grapnels I had sounded my pocket, and only brought up a few pieces of silver" (17), says Ishmael, and the reader, who may not know what a grapnel is, or understand the nautical meaning of the verb "to sound," will, on the basis of familiar context, familiar emotion, and the terms ("pocket" and "pieces of silver") understand the appearance and function of the unfamiliar elements. Later, in a slightly different form of the same technique, Melville encodes instruction as correction. Ishmael, in telling Bildad and Peleg of Queequeg's native Christianity, uses the phrase "we all join hands." Peleg responds, "Splice, thou mean'st *splice* hands" (83).

Melville expanded such sentence-level metaphors to large actions—the verbs and nouns of the narrative. An example of the former is the large oil-painting in the entry of the Spouter-Inn. The obvious narrative strategy would be to describe the painting; Melville never does. Instead he has Ishmael describe the process of "diligent study and a series of systematic visits to it, and a careful inquiry of the neighbors . . . much and earnest contemplation, and oft repeated ponderings." This process, motivated by "a sort of indefinite, half-attained, unimaginable sublimity about it that fairly froze you to it, till you involuntarily took an oath with yourself to find out what that marvelous painting meant" (20), produces a series of trial hypotheses that are finally discarded in favor of a "final theory," which is not to say an objective description. While this passage does nothing to advance the plot, it does advance Melville's agenda; the reader is schooled as to how the whale—and the text—must be approached.

The same concept applied to narrative nouns is the hymn preceding Father Mapple's sermon. In 1955 Luther Mansfield asserted that "No original has been found for this hymn. It's aptness for Melville's artistic purposes and the imaginative freedom with which it was written . . . suggests that Melville himself was the author." Later, David H. Battenfeld discovered that an original model does exist: "The source is the rhymed version of the first part of Psalm 18, as found in the psalms and hymns of the Reformed Protestant Dutch Church . . . . Needing an appropriate hymn for his artistic purposes, Melville may have remembered this psalm from his youth, or he may simply have gone looking through the hymnal" (Battenfeld 607–08). Battenfeld notes two kinds of alterations. One is stylistic; the other changes "the generalized theme of the Psalm to attain specific correspondence to the story of Jonah." The question is, why did Melville go to all the trouble of finding and transforming an existing hymn instead of just writing one, as Mansfield assumed he did? One answer is that, given the intention of the anti-allegory, Melville had to find useful elements in reality. Another answer is that, in transforming an extant hymn, Melville infused a Their Crowd cultural artifact with Our Crowd cultural referents. Part of the audience would not only recognize the hymn form, but the hymn itself—would possibly have been able to sing it using Melville's altered lyrics.

The fourth structure used by Melville to educate is usually seen only as a narrative strategy: the character of Ishmael. Ishmael is, of course, a first-person narrator. With regard to educating the reader, there are numerous advantages in this, the most obvious ones being that his every utterance forces the reader to share his experience and that even when Ishmael "tells" the reader something, it is a dramatic, rather than a didactic, act. There are also numerous disadvantages, the obvious one being that the flow of information to the reader is restricted by the obviously limited point of view of the character; Ishmael's "telling" is a dramatic act, but the reader has a right to wonder how Ishmael knows what he knows. Melville turned this disadvantage to advantage.

In creating and introducing Ishmael, Melville reinforced the thematic structures by giving equal emphasis to the sea and the school. Ishmael implies that "just previous" to going to sea he has been "lording it as a country schoolmaster, making the tallest boys stand in awe" (Feidelson 34). Some critics have "explained" this allusion with a gloss, noting that Melville was at times a schoolteacher, which is true but beside the point; the point is, Ishmael is a teacher and therefore able to impart information to the audience without being out of character or destroying Melville's aesthetic distance. And, more than a schoolmaster, Ishmael is a scholar, at times a pedantic pain in the posterior. He collects books on whaling, referring to "an old writer—of whose works I possess the only copy extant." He has studied the painting in the Spouter-Inn as only a scholar would.

But as Walter Bezanson pointed out, the schoolmaster and the scholar are not the same Ishmael, for this is a tale-told-in-retrospect; Melville begins with Ishmael saying "Some years ago—never mind how long precisely." Charles Feidelson, repeating Blankenship's misunderstanding of Socratic irony, wrote that "Ishmael . . . is not merely a surrogate for an absentee author. Behind him, always present as a kind of Doppelgänger, stands Herman Melville" (23). In fact, behind Ishmael stands Ishmael. The construct exists in two modes, Ishmael-as-character and Ishmael-as-narrator. Each mode carries a different cultural load. Ishmael-as-character, schoolmaster and merchant sailor, who sets off into the unknown on an adventure, is a culturally literate member of Their Crowd, but culturally illiterate with respect to Our Crowd—the whaling culture. Ishmael-as-narrator, the scholar and whaler, who knows now what he didn't know then, is a culturally literate member of both Crowds. He is able to speak knowledgeably about the whaling culture and what he says cannot be dismissed by Their Crowd, because, as Hirsch would say, he has mastered "the basic information needed to thrive" in Their Crowd's world.

The technical effects of such a bimodal first-person narrator are numerous. One effect is a major disadvantage: a loss of dramatic tension. The reader knows that Ishmael must survive to tell the tale. Outweighing this are numerous advantages, one being a loophole in the rules of point of view. Although it might not appear that way on first reading, Melville scrupulously maintains point of view—all immediate and sensory data comes through Ishmael-as-character, and there are few concrete references to the physical circumstances

of Ishmael-as-narrator. We hear his voice, but the corporal presence belongs to Ishmael-as-character. But we are also presented with events, information, and interpretations to which Ishmael-as-character does not have access,
often presented in stylized dramatic forms out of character for Ishmael-as-
character. These are impositions from Ishmael-as-narrator who, given larger
education and time for rumination, research, and artistic expression, is able
to dramatize what he believes or calculates happened, in the same way he
theorizes about the painting. Such impositions are educational—obviously so
in the whaling chapters, more subtly in smaller sequences, as when Ishmael
observes Queequeg shaving with the harpoon: "Thinks I, Queequeg, this is
using Rogers's best cutlery with a vengeance. Afterwards I wondered the less at
this operation when I came to know of what fine steel the head of a harpoon is
made, and how exceedingly sharp it is kept." The first portion gives the observation of Ishmael-as-character based on his Their Crowd cultural literacy.
The portion introduced by the preposition "afterwards" corrects the observation using the Our Crowd cultural literacy of Ishmael-as-narrator. The reader
sees both and realizes that what seems insane given only Their Crowd understanding is in fact perfectly reasonable. This pattern recurs in larger fractals,
with the alternation announced, with larger preposition-like sequences: "As
Queequeg and I are now fairly embarked in this business of whaling; and as
this business of whaling has somehow come to be regarded among landsmen
as a rather unpoetical and disreputable pursuit; therefore, I am all anxiety to
convince ye, ye landsmen, of the injustice hereby done to us hunters of the
whale."

The alternation makes Our Crowd information available to the audience
even though at the outset Ishmael-as-character is a bit ignorant. He does not
remain so, and the process of his education is the fifth structure. Though
Ishmael-as-character is a sailor as well as schoolmaster, Melville makes him
more the oil painting; it is only after this that Melville allows him to look at
the other wall, on which are hung the implements of whaling.

This sequence is a fractal of a larger movement. Before education can
take place, Ishmael's assumption that he knows what is to be learned must be
broken down. This is done through his gulling by Peter Coffin. Coffin tells him
the harpooner is "selling his head." Ishmael responds: "stop spinning that yarn
to me—I'm not green." But he is green, and at the end of the sequence has the
point pounded home. "Why didn't you tell me that infernal harpooneer was
a cannibal?" he demands. To which Coffin responds, "I thought ye know'd
it;—didn't I tell ye, he was peddlin' heads around town?" In fact, Coffin did
tell Ishmael—there are clues other than the head—but Melville also told the

reader. Ishmael missed those clues, and perhaps so did the reader. In any case, that reader is alerted that he is to be schooled by signs and must be an active student.

The student motif is recapitulated when Ishmael describes Queequeg: "But Queequeg, do you see, was a creature in the transition state . . . just enough civilized to show off his outlandishness in the strangest possible manner. His education was not yet completed. He was an undergraduate."

This statement comes from Ishmael-as-character and is exactly what a tolerant landsman, a member of Their Crowd, would think. It is both condescending and incorrect, for Queequeg, an experienced traveler, far from adapting, is doing what they do in Rome in order not to upset the Romans. To allow Ishmael-as-character to begin to see this, Melville puts him through a careful socialization process with Queequeg. Seeing Queequeg looking at a book, Ishmael

> endeavored to explain to him the purpose of the printing, and the meaning of the few pictures that were in it . . . and from that we went to jabbering the best we could about the various outer sights to be seen in this famous town. Soon I proposed a social smoke; and, producing his pouch and toma-hawk, he quietly offered me a puff. And then we sat exchanging puffs from that wild pipe of his, and keeping it regularly passing between us.

In a single paragraph Melville moves Ishmael from an intellectually superior position (he explains his Crowd artifact to a member of another Crowd) to an intellectually inferior position in which he, a stranger to New Bedford, questions Queequeg, a returning visitor, about the town. The process continues with the sharing of a practice (smoking) common to both his Crowd and Queequeg's but which is enjoyed using an implement of Queequeg's Crowd. Eventually Ishmael will be so much a member of Our Crowd that he will not only lie or stand beside Queequeg, or declare that Queequeg is a member of "the same ancient Catholic Church to which you and I . . . and all of us, and every mother's son and soul of us belong," but he will also take unto himself the student status he once assigned to Queequeg: "if, at my death, my executors, or more properly my creditors, find any precious MSS. in my desk, then here I prospectively ascribe all the honor and the glory to whaling; for a whale-ship was my Yale College and my Harvard."

The fifth structure is the beginning of the novel's journey. Obviously the sea voyage is a journey, but there is a land journey as well, and that part of the text is described as a process of education. Ishmael quits "the good city of old Manhatto," an island presented as being the center of Their Crowd culture, bound for Nantucket, "because there was a fine boisterous something about everything connected with that famous old island." The "fine boisterous something" is profoundly cultural. Though "New Bedford has of late been gradually monopolizing the business of whaling," and "poor old Nantucket is now much behind her," Nantucket remains "her great original—the Tyre of this Carthage." The journey from island to island is a journey from the cultural center of Their Crowd to the cultural center of Our Crowd.

But before reaching the center of the whaling culture Ishmael does stop in New Bedford. There he receives the bulk of his education at the Spouter-Inn and the Chapel. But before he is allowed to reach the Spouter, he has to journey to it. Some critics have described this journey as a descent into hell, but the hellishness comes from Ishmael's diction rather than from the nature of what he sees. In fact, where Ishmael goes is through the ghetto, where, through common Their Crowd misperception, he stumbles into the Negro church. Unwelcomed, he exits hastily, but not before perceiving a great deal: "It seemed the great Black Parliament sitting in Tophet. A hundred black faces turned round in their rows to peer; and beyond, the black Angel of Doom was beating a book in a pulpit. It was a negro church; and the preacher's text was about the blackness of darkness, and the weeping and wailing and teeth-gnashing there."

This odd side trip is significant. For Ishmael, leaving Their Crowd's world, encounters in the church what at the time was unmistakably a different Crowd (albeit not Our Crowd), a segregated church yet a creation of Their Crowd political and social culture. It is merely at the fringe. It is only after reaching and being rejected from Their Crowd's cultural fringe that he can approach the Spouter-Inn, the center of Our Crowd whaling culture.

The Spouter-Inn is a venue of instruction for Ishmael. But Melville also uses its physical description to educate the reader about the implements and tools of whaling and about the idea that whaling has a culture. The Spouter-Inn is in essence a museum of whaling, exhibiting not only implements but art and "storied weapons."

By the time Ishmael embarks for Nantucket, the reader is prepared to understand the first bit of seaborne action, the sequence aboard the schooner *Moss* in which Queequeg first puts paid to the "greenhorn" ringleader of the "lubber-like assembly, who marveled that two fellow-beings should be so companionable," then is falsely accused and summarily convicted of assault, and then saves both the ship and the greenhorn. Hirsch's point about efficiency is made manifest here, for though the entire sequence is played out in only slightly more space than is devoted to the oil painting, the action is clear and the attitude of the reader—who is by definition "lubber-like"—is sympathetic to Queequeg, hostile to the greenhorn.

That Melville was one of the first, if not *the* first, writers in English to try to tell a tale of Our Crowd to Their Crowd is a matter of historical timing. Certainly he was not the last to make the attempt, nor are his techniques the only ones available. Nor is any of this a matter of race. William Faulkner, for example, in order to write about the characters he found interesting and to tell the tales he found important, had to explain the South to a Northern audience that was bigoted against the South and unaware of many Southern cultural complications. In essence, Faulkner faced the same problem as his character Quentin Compson who in *Absalom, Absalom!* is confronted by a demand to "Tell about the South. What's it like there. What do they do there. Why do they live there. Why do they live at all." The demand is made not by a Yankee but a Canadian, because at this time, 1936, Northerners were not open-minded enough to ask the questions. While the opinion of *Absalom, Absalom!* put forth by Clifton Fadiman was extreme in its denigration—"the final blowup of what was once a remarkable, if minor, talent" (Henderson 41)—it was not untypical in its essence; meanwhile, the most popular novel of the year and the eventual winner of the Pulitzer Prize was Margaret Mitchell's *Gone With the Wind*. Faulkner's eventual fame owed much to academics who were not only heirs to Southern culture—which is to say members of Faulkner's Crowd—but acquainted with the difficulties of explaining that culture to a Northern audience that was certain it had been informed by Margaret Mitchell, and eventually Clark Gable and Vivian Leigh. These academics understood the artistic necessity behind such rococo Faulknerian structures as the not-but clause string: not that, not that, not even that, but this.

Given the bias of American society, there is inevitably a racial tinge to the business of Our Crowd and Their Crowd—Melville, in sending Ishmael to a Negro church, knew what he was signifying, and the modern American reader understands as perfectly as did Blankenship's American of the 1850s. But race aside, the problem faced by Melville and Faulkner was formally identical to that faced by Richard Wright—an audience as culturally illiterate as Mary Dalton, a socially concerned young woman who yet could say to a black person: "You know, Bigger, I've long wanted to go into those houses . . . and just see how you people live. You know what I mean? I've been to England, France and Mexico, but I don't know how people live ten blocks from me. We know so little about each other. I just want to see. I want to know these people. Never in my life have I been inside of a Negro home" (*Native Son* 70).

Wright, who early in his career received far more support from the Northern literary establishment than did Faulkner, had to deal with the expectations and beliefs of those supportive persons who tended to romanticize the oppressed in general and blacks in particular. Those expectations and beliefs caused Wright to have an ironic response to favorable reviews of his first book, *Uncle Tom's Children:*

> When the reviews of that book began to appear, I realized that I had made an awfully naïve mistake. I found that I had written a book which even bankers' daughters could read and weep over and feel good about. I swore to myself that if I ever wrote another book, no one would weep over it; that it would be so hard and deep that they would have to face it without the consolation of tears. ("How Bigger")

One of the most telling passages in the final scene of *Native Son*—which was, of course, not only another book but Wright's next—is this: "Max did not even know! Bigger felt that he had been slapped. Oh, what a fool he had been to build upon such shifting sand! But he had to make him know!" (387).

While I have not the time to discuss every text written by a black American since 1941, I would like to focus on several that make use of Melvillean techniques to educate the audience. The first is Ralph Waldo Ellison's *Invisible Man,* which, like *Moby-Dick,* has often been read as an allegorical text. I will not argue that, but will point out that much of the novel is based on reality. The rendering of Tuskegee Institute, for example, which some readers who know only of Booker T. Washington find fanciful, seems deadly realistic to those who recognize the name Robert Russa Moton. And surely it was part of Ellison's point that, with respect to America-at-large, black Americans comprised a rich, varied, but unseen Crowd. To help make that point Ellison at times adopted Melvillean symbol structures (the whiteness in the paint factory contrasting the greenness of the lawn at the college) and used numerous Melvillean techniques to school the reader, the most notable being the combination of the bimodal narrator and the tale-told-in-retrospect.

John Edgar Wideman, in his third novel, *The Lynchers* (1973), makes extensive use of prefatory matter to educate the audience about the practice of lynching and the conditions that make it seem reasonable. The story presents a group of black men who decide it would be appropriate to kidnap and lynch a Philadelphia policeman. Most blacks and many whites who lived in Philadelphia in the 1960s and early 1970s would understand the object of the exercise; those persons constitute a Philadelphia Crowd that was painfully aware that "Philadelphia's Finest" were some of Philadelphia's worst. But many Philadelphians, black and white, were unaware of the place of lynching in American history. Therefore Wideman included twenty pages of "Matter Prefatory" that describe lynchings and comment on the history of the practice, placing not only violence but violence in bizarre form in context; without the "Matter Prefatory" readers might think that the protagonists, a group of serious, thoughtful men, were merely crazy.

Two other Melvillean techniques can been seen at work in Barbara Chase-Riboud's *Echo of Lions* (1889). The novel tells the tale of the rebellion aboard the slave ship *Amistad* and the legal maneuverings that followed its salvage off the American coast. Chase-Riboud faced a complex problem in Crowd control. To begin with, she was writing a historical novel, which means that her contemporary audience was probably culturally illiterate with respect to American society at the time of the events, 1839. In the action of the novel, that society was bifurcated into liberal Northerners and free Northern blacks. Both of these Crowds were culturally illiterate with respect to the nineteenth-century African Crowd from which the *Amistad* rebels came. And the rebels, of course, were culturally illiterate with respect to 1839 America—they did not, for example, comprehend the forms of slavery or the sailing of ships.

One technique Chase-Riboud uses to address this problem is the symbolic land journey. She begins the tale at the home of Sengbe Pieh, or Cinque, a prosperous rice planter and slave owner—a member of an old established family in the land, as it were—who becomes the rebel leader. She follows him to a tribal tribunal, a lengthy sequence that allows us to see the workings of his Crowd's justice, establishing a cultural equivalence with the American justice system, into the gears of which Cinque will fall. She continues with his capture and transportation to the coastal baracoons. At each station of the journey the readers are educated—as Cinque is educated—to the harsh realities of his new life.

Unlike Melville, Chase-Riboud could not use a single first-person narrator; she does create a character named James Covey who, like the bimodal Ishamael, overlaps the several Crowds. A free-born African who was enslaved, then rescued by a British man-o'-war, and is now a British citizen, Covey acts as the linguistic interpreter of the captured Africans and as a cultural interpreter, bringing into the text the consciousness of a black who is a full citizen of a nation—as American blacks are not.

An Ishmael-like narrator can be found, however, in Charles Johnson's *Middle Passage.* This is a first-person narrative recorded by a black man who finds himself gulled aboard a slaver bound for Guinea. On the return trip, the Middle Passage, the slaves rebel and insist on being returned to Africa. The comparisons of Johnson's narrator, Calhoun, with Ishmael are legion, albeit often negative: Calhoun, no lover of the sea, ships out only to escape marriage and becomes the ship's cook, one of the offices that Ishmael rejected. It is the lady he is avoiding who is the schoolteacher, but Calhoun is as culturally literate as Ishmael ever was:

> My master, Reverend Peleg Chandler, had noticed this stickiness of my fingers when I was a child, a tendency I had to tell preposterous lies for the hell of it; he was convinced I was born to be hanged and did his damnedest to reeducate said fingers in finer pursuits such as good penmanship and playing the grand piano in his parlor. A Biblical scholar, he endlessly preached Old Testament virtues to me, and to this very day I remember his tedious disquisitions on Neoplatonism, the evils of nominalism, the genius of Aquinas, and the work of such seers as Jakob Bühme. (Johnson 3)

Having, like Melville, accounted for high-toned language, Johnson liberally applies it. Although Calhoun, like Ishmael, writes in retrospect, he does not engage in the kind of formal address of the audience that is so striking in *Moby-Dick.* This technique, however, can be observed in another text, one with which I am quite familiar. Indeed I can attest, by affidavit, that the author read and reread *Moby-Dick* and utilized it as a master text. Although I cannot claim to "possess the only copy extant," I do have a depressing number of copies in my garage. The book is *The Chaneysville Incident,* published in 1981.

The basic story is that of thirteen slaves who were escaping on the Underground Railroad sometime between the passage of the Fugitive Slave Act and the outbreak of the Civil War. They reached a point a few miles north of the Mason-Dixon Line, near a town called Chaneysville, in southwestern Pennsylvania. There they were about to be recaptured, but rather than return to slavery, they killed themselves. I could, if I chose, demonstrate how in shaping the narrative I used every technique arising out of *Moby-Dick.* I will not, however, because I would prefer to pretend I could come up with *something* on my own. I will focus on two specifics.

The first is the first-person narrator, John Washington. *The Chaneysville Incident* is not a tale-told-in-retrospect—which means it is possible for the narrator *not* to survive the end of the tale—but the narrator is bimodal; Washington exists in the text both as a child, growing up in the region in which the action takes place and acquiring the cultural literacy of that Crowd, and as an adult, becoming a college history professor with membership in Their Crowd and proving to be every bit as pedantic as Ishmael. As Melville used Ishmael, I used Washington as a vehicle to deliver information to an audience ignorant not of the character's culture but of its own. Although an understanding of such things as the Fugitive Slave Act is essential to comprehending both American history and the motivations of the characters in the book, few readers have that information. And again, like Melville, I put Washington through a process of education that the reader can observe and in which the reader can participate. The difference, in this text, is that Washington is a character in both modes. He tells stories of himself, but he also experiences events before the eyes of the reader—it is as if the reader were to watch Ishmael, returned from his voyage aboard the *Pequod,* going back to the Spouter-Inn to cipher out the meaning of the painting.

The second technique is the personification of the audience. In *Moby-Dick* the existence of a listener is assumed, as it is in parts of *The Chaneysville Incident.* But for various reasons too complicated for explanation here, Washington needed a listener, a visible representative of Their Crowd. And so the last third of the novel employs a white female of elite education and aristocratic Southern heritage as the "ear" of Their Crowd and to symbolize the process by which Their Crowd may become inculcated into Our Crowd mysteries.

In June 1851, as he neared the second "completion" of *Moby-Dick,* Melville wrote a despairing and somewhat incoherent letter to Hawthorne. "Truth," he declared, "is the silliest thing under the sun. Try to get a living by the Truth—and go to the Soup Societies. . . . Truth is ridiculous to men" (*Moby-Dick* 557). And elsewhere: "What's the use of elaborating what, in its very essence, is so short-lived as a modern book? Though I wrote the Gospels in this century, I should die in the gutter." And still elsewhere: "I am like one of those seeds taken out of the Egyptian Pyramids, which, after three thousand years as a seed and nothing but a seed, being planted in English soil, it developed itself, grew to greenness, and then fell to mould. So I" (559). His statements, especially the last, seem prescient. For, as Blankenship described Melville's career post mortem:

A history of American literature published in 1901 gives him one sentence. Another of about ten years later fails to mention him in the body of the work but allots him three lines in the appendix and gives the names of five of his works. The four-volume *Cambridge History of American Literature* (1918) gives him three pages and a careful bibliography. The centenary of his birth awakened a considerable interest in the man, and in 1921 came the first biography. . . . Since that time Melville has been the subject of innumerable articles and of at least two excellent biographical and critical studies. . . . Thus in the short space of thirty years the reputation of Melville has risen from a complete obscurity to an equality with that of the greatest writers of all time. (377–78)

To a writer this seems a triumphant ending. But every writer knows that stories have three parts. Melville profited from the bright beginning and endured the tragic middle, but for him the happy ending came too late; many a critic has made a better living writing about Melville than Melville ever made writing. And just as a writer who seeks to tell an Our Crowd tale to Their Crowd can ill afford to ignore *Moby-Dick* as a master text, so can he or she ill afford to ignore the life of Melville as a cautionary tale.

For it should be clear by now that in *Moby-Dick* Melville, far from arrogantly dismissing or insulting his readers went to great lengths to involve them, and that, given the twentieth-century resurrection of both of Melville and *Moby-Dick,* whatever fault that caused Melville to die in the literary gutter lay not in either. Indeed, to account for both the middle and the end of the Melville story, we must look not to author or to work but to audience. And the key does lie with Blankenship. For although his isolation of the causal factors was in error, his belief that something in *Moby-Dick* was offensive to the antebellum American social mind was correct. Much in *Moby-Dick* can be construed as excoriating the fruits of a revered institution. Melville's satire did sear some object of respectability and made "the American of the fifties uncomfortable." To discern that, we must look not at Melville but at America.

Eighteen fifty-one was an exciting year in America, even if one considers only those events that would have been close to Melville's interest. The schooner *America* sped around the Isle of Wight, defeated the British, and brought the America's Cup to the United States. The *New York Times* was first published. In literature, Longfellow's "The Golden Legend" and Hawthorne's *The House of the Seven Gables* appeared. The previous year had not been so auspicious. True, Emerson's "Representative Men" and Hawthorne's *Scarlet*

Letter had been published, but public discourse had centered on politics; in 1850, the failure of the American Experiment was a distinct possibility.

The basic issue, of course, was slavery—in particular, the expansion of slavery into the Territories. Those who favored expansion, arguing that it was legal under the so-called Calhoun Doctrine, had scheduled a convention for June in Nashville, Tennessee, where a vote for secession might have been taken. But in January the "Grand Master of Compromise," Henry Clay, returned to the Senate. On January 29 he proposed a series of resolutions that, by May, developed into an omnibus of legislation designed to preserve the Union—at the price of principle. Part of that omnibus was the Second Fugitive Slave Act, which took effect on September 18. Put simply, the act not only made it illegal to assist a fugitive slave but required any person, if called upon, to assist with the recapture and detention of any fugitive. The effect of the act was to incense many who were indifferent to slavery itself. As Bruce Levine put it:

> So long as slavery seemed geographically contained and remote, free-state residents could despise it without feeling much direct personal involvement in its workings; slavery could thus remain the peculiar institution of the South, not a problem or responsibility of the North. By sending slave hunters into the free states and requiring even antislavery citizens to aid them, however, the new law made such rationalizations impossible. (189)

What effect all this had on Melville is hard to say. He began 1850 in England, not returning to America until February 1. He was surely preoccupied with the business of his career and life; *White-Jacket* was published in New York on March 21. The summer was that busy time during which he first read, wrote of, and then met Hawthorne. In the fall, with money borrowed from his father-in-law, Lemuel Shaw, he purchased a farm and thereon took up residence in Massachusetts. Given this activity and the unavoidable rhythms and isolations of rural life, it is possible Melville paid no great attention to political events. Yet, as Michael Rogin has stated "Melville began *Moby-Dick* when the fears of disunion were strongest" (107). It is hard to believe that some awareness of the state of the Union did not impinge upon his consciousness. Massachusetts was an abolitionist stronghold. Protests against Clay's Compromise were especially loud in New Hampshire, whose representative, Daniel Webster, had supported it (Levine 189). The death of President Zachary Taylor, a Southern sympathizer, in July 1850, gave the matter a national salience. And as Rogin points out, "as Melville was writing the climax of his tale, the crisis over slavery reached a climax as well. Lemuel Shaw was the cause. In April of 1851 Shaw declared the Fugitive Slave Law constitutional and, in an action whose reverberations were nationwide, returned the first fugitive slave, Thomas Sims, from Massachusetts" (107). Still, despite this family connection, it is possible that Melville, enmeshed in Ishmael, paid this little or no mind. In December of 1850 he described in a letter to Duyckinck a typical day, making mention of feeding his horse and his cow but no mention of reading a newspaper (*Moby-Dick* 552–53).

But Blankenship's "American of the fifties" did read newspapers. And the news in those papers would have given such Americans plenty of reason to seek comfort in more literary print. Not that they would have expected to find it, necessarily; in 1845, as Melville struggled to complete his first novel (Tanselle 1410), literate Americans had found themselves confronted by *The Narrative of the Life of Frederick Douglass, An American Slave.* And in 1850 those literate Americans found themselves confounded by the raging condemnation of Daniel Webster in Whittier's "Ichabod":

> The soul is fled;
> When faith is lost, when honor dies.
> The man is dead!

And in the months immediately preceding *Moby-Dick*'s appearance, literate Americans found reason to fear they could not avoid "realistic analysis of comforting hypocrisies" (Blankenship 379) even in fiction. For in May 1851, as Melville was completing *Moby-Dick*, the first installments of Harriet Beecher Stowe's *Uncle Tom's Cabin* appeared and condemned at least half the nation— the entire nation, by implication.

Rogin placed the center of the social vortex two years earlier than Blankenship, in what he called "the American 1848," a mind-set generated by "political romances in the late 1840s" (19) and defined by "the eruption and apparent pacification of the slavery crisis between 1846 and 1851" (21). The actuality of the Fugitive Slave Act, specifically the Sims case, revealed that pacification as apparent—and temporary.

Why by November 1851 American readers should have wanted a bit of relief is therefore not hard to understand. It is perhaps harder to understand why *Moby-Dick,* full of distant adventure and philosophical complexity, should not have provided some of that relief. Today, it is hard to see how a book about a capital ship and an ocean trip in search of fun and profit could have provided anything but pure escape from the political and moral seriousness of the day. But Blankenship's "American of the fifties" might have seen it differently. It is possible, as Rogin says, that "The American 1848 . . . politicized Melville's romances," including *Moby-Dick*. Literate Americans might have recalled that Melville, in previous fictions, had not been loathe to mention, even praise, black American seamen, and though today that might seem a small thing, it is no smaller than the black American aboard the *Pequod:* Pip is first introduced in chapter 27 as an "Alabama boy" and later in chapter 93 as hailing from "Tolland County in Connecticut"—which is to say he is a fugitive slave. Those things, in the autumn of 1851, may have grated nerves rubbed raw by fear.

Given raw nerves, other elements in *Moby-Dick,* whatever Melville intended them to symbolize—if, indeed, he intended them to symbolize anything— might have seemed obnoxiously allusive to the problems of the American state—a nonrealistic analysis of comforting hypocrisies, to subvert Blankenship's phrase. Ishmael's rhetorical question "Who ain't a slave?" may have seemed an accusation, rather than a rhetorical question, and his juxtaposition of "Grand Contested Election for the Presidency of the United States" with "Whaling Voyage by One Ishmael" in his "grand programme of Providence" might have seemed less a fantasy than a reminder of the troubles in the land. The reference to the Black Parliament, which effected separation of the Church of England from the Catholic Church, must have struck some as a reference to secession. The chapter on Fast-Fish and Loose-Fish might have seemed an elaborate and satirical reference to the Fugitive Slave Act itself, especially as Melville noted en passant "What are the sinews and souls of Russian serfs and Republican slaves but Fast-Fish, whereof possession is the whole of the law?" The extract regarding the retaking of the good ship *Hobomack*— "It was not till the boats returned from the pursuit of these whales that the whites saw their ship in bloody possession of the savages enrolled among the crew"—might have seemed to be an allusion to the *Amistad* or the *Creole.* The tale of the harpooner who left off whaling "to go in a trading ship on a voyage to Africa" might have seemed to connect the enterprise of whaling to that of slaving—as might the fact that Melville steers the *Pequod* to the Pacific not by the Cape Horn route that Ishmael anticipates, and that Melville followed on his own voyages, but by way of the Cape of Good Hope, thus causing the fictional vessel to follow the course that would have been steered by a Salem slaver bound for the Guinea Coast. The whiteness of the whale and the fact that white is, in a twist of conventional symbolism, associated with evil— indeed, with horror—might have made Melville, despite the brotherhood theme in *Moby-Dick,* seem more or less what Blankenship took him to be: if not a hater of mankind, then a hater of his own kind—a race traitor, as David Duke would have it. That Melville referred to "Southern whaling" and the "Southern Whale Fishery" might have seemed a veritable stick in the eye. Even the references to New Bedford and Nantucket might have reminded readers that it was at a black abolitionist meeting in the former city that Frederick Douglass came to the attention of abolitionists and at a white abolitionist convention in the latter that he made his triumphant debut.

This is not to say that Melville intended these connotations. Certainly it is not to say that *Moby-Dick* is an attack on slavery—at least, it is not to say that here. It is merely to suggest that the negative effect *Moby-Dick* had on Melville's career can be explained if one considers the possibility that it was too much a technical success. The synergistic relationship between elements in any novel and the cultural context of the readership can produce unpredictable results. Such results are most likely to occur given a novel that forces the reader to pay attention that encourages him or her to see things. Wrote Melville to Sophia Hawthorne:

> It really amazed me that you should find any satisfaction in that book. . . . But, then, since you, with your spiritualizing nature, see more things than other people, and . . . refine all you see so that they are not the same things that other people see, but things which while you think you humbly discover them, you do in fact create them for yourself. Therefore . . . I do not so much marvel at your expressions concerning Moby Dick. (568)

Given a novel that is not an expression of essence but existence, what is seen is likely to be not so pretty as some readers would prefer. But such a novel is uniquely suited to the test of time. For truth will out. And thus we—readers and writers and In-, Out-, Their-, and Our-Crowders—have ever before us *Moby-Dick.* All of us can look to it as a model of and for many things. And all of us can ever look to Melville . . . and hope to join his Crowd.

WORKS CITED

Battenfeld, David H. "The Source for the Hymn in *Moby-Dick.*" In *Moby-Dick,* ed. Hayford and Parker, 607–10.
Benson, Joseph Brian, and Mabel Mayle Dillard. *Jean Toomer.* New York: Twayne, 1981.

Bezanson, Walter E. "*Moby-Dick:* Work of Art." 1953. In *Moby-Dick,* ed. Hayford and Parker, 651–71.

Blankenship, Russell. *American Literature as an Expression of the National Mind.* New York: Henry Holt, 1931.

Brooks, Gwendolyn. *A Capsule Course in Black Poetry Writing.* Ed. Dudley Randall. N.p., 1975.

"Cause for a Writ *de Lunatico.*" January 1852. In *Moby-Dick,* ed. Hayford and Parker, 619.

Duyckinck, Evert A. "Melville's *Moby-Dick;* or, The Whale." November 22, 1851. In *Moby-Dick,* ed. Hayford and Parker, 613–16.

Ellison, Ralph. "The Little Man at Chehaw Station: The American Artist and His Audience." 1977. *Going into the Territory.* New York: Random House, 1986.

———. "On Initiation Rites and Power." 1969. *Going into the Territory.*

Faulkner, William. *Absalom, Absalom!* 1936. New York: Vintage, 1986.

Feidelson, Charles, ed. Introduction. *Moby-Dick; or, The Whale.* By Herman Melville. Indianapolis: Bobbs-Merrill, 1964.

———. "Symbolism and American Literature." 1953. In *Moby-Dick,* ed. Hayford and Parker, 671–76.

Henderson, Bill, ed. *Rotten Reviews: A Literary Companion.* New York: Viking-Penguin, 1987.

Hirsch, E. D., Jr. *Cultural Literacy: What Every American Needs to Know.* New York: Vintage, 1988.

Howard, Leon. *Herman Melville: A Biography.* 1951. In *Moby-Dick,* ed. Hayford and Parker, 709–27.

Johnson, Charles. *Middle Passage.* New York: Atheneum, 1991.

Levine, Bruce. *Half Slave and Half Free: The Roots of the Civil War.* New York: Hill and Wang, 1992.

Melville, Herman. *Moby-Dick.* Ed. Harrison Hayford and Hershel Parker. New York: Norton, 1967.

Rogin, Michael Paul. *Subversive Genealogy: The Politics and Art of Herman Melville.* Berkeley: U of California P, 1985.

Tanselle, G. Thomas. Chronology. In *Melville: Redburn, White-Jacket, Moby-Dick.* New York: Library of America, 1983.

Twain, Mark. *The Disappearance of Literature.*

Wright, Richard, "How Bigger Was Born." *New York Times,* March 7, 1941.

———. *Native Son.* 1941. New York: Harper, 1966.

7

Slavery and Empire:
Melville's "Benito Cereno"

H. BRUCE FRANKLIN

The history of African slavery in our hemisphere is summed up in the figure-head on the prow of the slave ship *San Dominick* in Herman Melville's "Benito Cereno." Originally an image of Christopher Columbus (NN *PT* 107),[1] it is re-placed by the shrouded bones of the slaves' owner. At the story's climax, the figurehead is exposed for what it is: the "canvas shroud" is "whipped away . . . suddenly revealing . . . death for the figure-head, in a human skeleton; chalky comment on the chalked words below, *'Follow your leader'*" (99). It is Babo, leader of the rebelling slaves, who explains that this figurehead is literally the leader of the slavers and what it means: "'Keep faith with the blacks from here to Senegal, or you shall in spirit, as now in body, "follow your leader,"' point-ing to the prow" (107).

Columbus's voyages and claims helped transform Spain into the first truly global empire, one based on ruthless colonization, slave labor wrung from millions of kidnapped Africans, and a transcendent belief in the empire's

Portions of this essay have appeared in "Past, Present, and Future Seemed One" by H. Bruce Franklin, and are used by permission of G. K. Hall & Co., an imprint of Simon & Schuster Macmillan, from *Critical Essays on Herman Melville's "Benito Cereno,"* edited by Robert E. Burk-holder, pp. 230–46. © 1992 by Robert E. Burkholder.

Christian mission. The ship's name, *San Dominick,* evokes the island of San Domingo, also known as Hispaniola, which, not long after its discovery by Columbus, became the seat of Spanish power in the New World. After the Spaniards had exterminated most of the natives of San Domingo, the island became the site of the first large-scale importation of African slaves into the Western Hemisphere, as authorized in a 1517 decree issued by Charles V, first ruler of this vast empire and the last Holy Roman Emperor to be crowned by a pope.

When he thus initiated the Atlantic slave trade, Charles, like most oppressors, evidently convinced himself that he was motivated by the very best intentions. After all, he was responding to the pleas of the priest Bartolomé de Las Casas, who argued that it would be more humane to kidnap Africans and enslave them in the New World than to continue working the "Indians" to death in the Spanish mines and plantations.[2]

Melville made only one change to the basic plot of his primary source, the actual Amasa Delano's narrative: he has Benito Cereno, the Spanish captain, retire to a monastery where he soon dies. Shortly after Cereno is introduced, he is compared to "Charles V, just previous to the anchoritish retirement of that monarch from the throne" (53). Charles, who in name held absolute rule over more of the planet's surface than any person in history, ended his life as an almost spectral emblem of impotence, a captive and prisoner of the church and faith he sought to impose upon the world.[3] So in his monastic retirement and death, Benito Cereno is a true follower of his imperial leader. Cereno's ship gives off an eerie image of the monastery in Spain to which Charles had retreated, even appearing to be a "monastery . . . among the Pyrenees":

> . . . it was no purely fanciful resemblance which . . . almost led Captain Delano to think that nothing less than a ship-load of monks was before him. Peering over the bulwarks were what really seemed . . . throngs of dark cowls; while, fitfully revealed through the port-holes, other dark moving figures were dimly descried, as of Black Friars pacing the cloisters. (48)

The Black Friars were the Dominicans, who, operating directly under orders of Charles V, became the main executors of the Spanish Inquisition, a key instrument of imperialism and racism. In ironic twists, the Black Friars of "Benito Cereno" are the mutinous African slaves who now command the ship that Melville has rechristened the *San Dominick,* patron saint of the Dominican order, while the enslaved captain of this monastic ship sleeps in a cabin where the bulkhead bears a "meager crucifix," some "melancholy old rigging" lies like "a heap of poor friars' girdles," the washstand looks like a "font," and the settees are as "uncomfortable to look at as inquisitors' racks" (82–83). Here, amid these emblems of monasticism and the Inquisition, Babo carries out his most audacious reversal of imperial power: he forces Cereno to be shaved, sitting in a "large, misshapen armchair" that "seemed some grotesque, middle-age engine of torment" (82–83) and sporting as a barber's apron the flag of the Spanish empire.

By the time the story opens, in the closing year of the eighteenth century, the Spanish empire was becoming a mere ghost of its former self, and Melville's tale is pervaded by the theme of rotting imperialism. By then, it was the New World that threatened the stability of the Old as the antimonarchist, anticolonial, republican, and, in some aspects, democratic revolution of thirteen of Britain's American colonies brought European visions of rationalism and liberty home with a vengeance. Waves of revolution seemed to swell as they swept back and forth across the Atlantic. The French Revolution openly proclaimed the egalitarianism that had been subordinated by the triumphant merchants and planters of the American Revolution. And San Domingo, that original site of New World slavery, now became the vanguard of world revolution as the black slaves interpreted the message of the American and French revolutions precisely in the way most dreaded by the plantation owners of the South and the French Caribbean colonies. Acting upon the belief that the Rights of Man, the declaration that "all men are created equal," and the slogan "liberté, egalité, et fraternité" should apply to them also, the slaves of San Domingo rose in a rebellion that was to haunt slave owners for decades. By placing the rebellion on the *San Dominick* in 1799, Melville makes it contemporaneous with the extension of Toussaint L'Ouverture's revolution over the entire island of San Domingo.

The contradictions central to the new American republic in 1799, which had announced its independence from the decaying monarchies of Europe with the declaration "We hold these truths to be self-evident, that all men are created equal, that they are endowed with their Creator with certain unalienable rights, that among these are life, liberty, and the pursuit of happiness," are acted out on the decks of the *San Dominick* by the Yankee captain. Captain Delano demonstrates how America's republican ideals operated in practice as he doles out the water and food brought from his ship for the emiserated sailors and slaves of the *San Dominick*. First, "with republican impartiality," he distributes the water, "this republican element, which always seeks one level," "serving the oldest white no better than the youngest black"—except for his fellow captain, Don Benito, to whom he gives an entire pitcher, since his "condition, if not rank, demanded an extra allowance" (80). As soon as this egalitarian show is over, Delano dishes out the food: "Two of the less wilted pumpkins being reserved for the cabin table, the residue were minced up on the spot for the general regalement. But the soft bread, sugar, and bottled cider, Captain Delano would have given the whites alone, and in chief Don Benito" (80). Delano fails to see the blatant disparity between his "republican impartiality" and his racist, hierarchical behavior for the same reason that the Founding Fathers could proclaim that all men are created equal and possess the inalienable right to liberty while institutionalizing black chattel slavery in the very Constitution of their new republic.

And when Delano learns that the blacks on the *San Dominick* have in fact rebelled against slavery, his horrified response represents the main reaction of that new republic's white citizens to the rebellion of the slaves of San Domingo. Indeed, the San Domingo revolt continued to terrorize the imagination of slave-owning America right on through the publication of "Benito Cereno" in 1855. This nightmare of black insurrection was transformed into powerful propaganda for the expansion into the Caribbean of U.S. slavery, presented as a force of order and stability capable of replacing impotent, decadent, and sinister Spanish rule. As James Buchanan wrote in the Ostend Manifesto of 1854, the official U.S. State Department document that was to help make him the victorious Democratic presidential candidate of 1856, the United States had the moral duty to seize Cuba from the incompetent Spain, if Spain would not sell us the island, for otherwise Cuba might "be Africanized and become a second St. Domingo, with all its attendant horrors to the white race" (Ostend Manifesto 335). When Delano considers "withdrawing the command" from Benito Cereno "on some benevolent plea" because the "dark Spaniard" "was not fit to be trusted with the ship" (69), he serves as a representative American of his own time, of Melville's time, and of the time on the eve of our own century when the United States would achieve its "manifest destiny" by seizing what was left of the collapsing Spanish empire, thus itself becoming a global empire.[4]

At the time of "Benito Cereno"'s publication, the crusade to seize Cuba and other Caribbean lands was part of a larger strategy to expand U.S. slavery and make it dominate the nation's economic and political structure. With the inspiring slogan "Manifest Destiny," the forces of slavery and its allies turned both west and south. Texas, which had been torn away from Mexico by American colonists enriched by the slave plantation economy they imported from the Southern states, was annexed as a slave state in 1845. Supporters of slavery had then instigated war with Mexico, allowing the United States to annex the northern half of Mexico in 1848. The possibility of turning this vast area into slave states, thus ending the balance between slave and free states arranged by the Missouri Compromise of 1820, was confirmed by the so-called Compromise of 1850. This fateful series of acts established the principle that Congress had no authority to prohibit slavery in any part of the territory seized from Mexico or in any state formed from that territory, gave full U.S. government legitimacy to slavery within the District of Columbia and to slave-trading in and between every other slave-holding state and territory, and made the recapture and reenslavement of fugitive slaves the legal duty of all citizens of the United States and of all governments and courts of states, territories, and the District of Columbia. A new land of opportunity now lay open for slavery.

The path to it was widened by the 1852 landslide election of expansionist and anti-abolitionist Franklin Pierce, whose campaign biography—written by Nathaniel Hawthorne—denounced all anti-slavery "agitation" as threatening "the ruin of two races which now dwelt together" in "peace and affection" (164). In 1854, Pierce signed the Kansas-Nebraska Act, which explicitly repealed the Missouri Compromise and established "the principle of nonintervention by Congress with slavery in the States and Territories" (Kansas-Nebraska Act 332). Several months before the publication of "Benito Cereno," the Kansas legislature (elected by gangs of proslavery men who swarmed across the border from Missouri) made it a capital offense to aid a fugitive slave and a felony even to question the legality of owning slaves.

To the south, Cuba, with its thriving sugar and tobacco fields worked by slaves, beckoned as a potential bastion from which the entire Caribbean could be transformed into a U.S. slave plantation. This American dream of annexing Cuba had begun as early as Delano's revolutionary, slave-owning contemporary Thomas Jefferson, who called it essential to extending our "empire for liberty."[5] It was at the very heart of the campaign for Manifest Destiny from 1848 through 1855 and was a prominent feature of Pierce's Inaugural Address, which declared that American imperial expansion was "essential for the preservation of the rights of commerce and the peace of the world" (Rauch 254, passim).

This bleak scene for all those who were, like Melville, horrified by slavery was "Benito Cereno"'s context, and it informs the whole story.[6] Just as U.S. voters had evidently ratified Hawthorne's view that the millions of black slaves felt great "affection" for their masters, Delano sees "affection" in Babo's view of his master Cereno (NN *PT* 51), believes that "the negro" serves his master with "affectionate zeal" (52), and even exclaims, "'Don Benito, I envy you such a friend; slave I cannot call him'" (57). Like Hawthorne and the other Americans who chose to misread the messages being communicated by slave rebellions, abolitionism, and the conflict already emerging in Kansas, Delano suppresses his growing sense of alarm by reminding himself that "the blacks" were "too stupid" to be plotting against him and by asking himself the reassuring question, "Besides, who ever heard of a white so far a renegade as to apostatize from his very species almost, by leaguing in against it with negroes?" (75). Later, in authorizing the use of brutal force to recapture and reenslave every man, woman, and child among the rebellious Africans, Delano is doing just what the Fugitive Slave Act of 1850 required of all law-abiding U.S. citizens.

Indeed, Delano is presented by the narrator as a model of justice and legality, sharply contrasted to the aura of piracy associated with the Spanish ship. Though appropriate to the story's 1799 setting, the theme of piracy that permeates the story might seem at first glance rather remote from the context of its 1855 publication. But piracy, at least in the discourse of the mid–nineteenth century, was inextricably interwoven with "Benito Cereno"'s principal themes of slavery and imperialism.

Through Captain Delano's telescope we get our first view of the Spanish ship, sailing without colors on seas then frequented by pirates. Could it be a "freebooter" (47)? Later trying to convince himself that the apparent helplessness of the *San Dominick* proves that she could not "be of a piratical character," Delano remembers tales of "pirates" who only feign helplessness in order to ambush other vessels (68). But Delano's suspicions about the "piratical character" of the Spanish captain and his ship apply more to the American captain and his ship.

Melville has renamed Delano's ship the *Bachelor's Delight*. The *Bachelor's Delight* was in fact an infamous pirate vessel, carrying "the choicest batch of cutthroats on the Main" (von Hagen xxi) and terrorizing the seas where Delano's ship now prowls. A familiar synonym for pirate was "rover." Delano's suspicions about Cereno's piracy are punctuated by his eager views of his approaching boat, "Rover by name" (NN *PT* 77). Speculating that the innocent appearance of the Spanish ship may conceal its treacherous potential, Delano conjures up a fantasy that the *San Dominick* might "suddenly let loose energies now hid" and overwhelm his own ship. This image reverses the actual events, for it is the supposedly innocent, helpless, peaceful *Bachelor's Delight* that

will unleash hidden energies and overwhelm the *San Dominick*. When he decides to seize the Spanish ship, reenslave the blacks, and thus add to his profits
on the voyage, Delano chooses his chief mate, who was reputed to have been "a
pirate—to head the party" (101). To incite the greed and battle lust of his crewmen, Delano tells them that if they seize the ship they will share the booty:
"Take her, and no small part would be theirs. The sailors replied with a shout."
So Delano's projection of the *San Dominick* as a "haunted pirate-ship" (77)
seems far more accurate as a vision of the true nature of his own vessel, the
reincarnated *Bachelor's Delight*.

Melville's story about a mutiny by the human cargo of a slave ship and
its bloody recapture by an apparently well-intentioned, innocent Yankee
obliquely asks, "Who are the real pirates?" For Melville's contemporaries, this
question would invoke the most recent case of a successful uprising on a
Spanish slave ship, the *Amistad* revolt of 1839. Carolyn Karcher has indicated
how the theme of piracy connects "Benito Cereno" to the *Amistad* case:

> The American brig of war *Washington,* whose officers hoped to claim the
> *Amistad's* cargo as salvage, took the rebels into custody, and the Africans
> remained in jail for two years until the Supreme Court freed them in 1841.
> Charges of piracy were central to the trial. The press had repeatedly de-
> scribed the *Amistad* as a pirate ship when it was sighted off the East coast,
> but the Africans' defense team, headed by former President John Quincy
> Adams, successfully argued that it was not piracy for persons to rise up
> against those who illegally held them captive . . . (Karcher, Notes 2465)

As Melville was writing "Benito Cereno," there were also actual pirates in
operation. These were the "filibusters," those American adventurers who were
attempting to "rescue" Cuba, Haiti, and Central America by organizing war
parties similar to those Delano dispatched to capture the Spanish ship. The
term "filibuster" was the Anglicized form of a Spanish corruption of the
Dutch *vrijbuiter,* whose more direct English version was "freebooter," the very
term used to introduce the theme of piracy (47). Just as Delano projects onto
Cereno piratical schemes that he himself will blithely—and with the best
intentions—actually perpetrate, so the United States in the mid–nineteenth
century was projecting onto the decaying Spanish empire images that would
legitimize its own piratical—but of course well-intentioned—expansionism.

The theme of piracy offers a view of Melville's authorial strategy in "Benito
Cereno" and of what—or at least how—the story "means." Why would Melville secrete the theme in the Yankee captain's fantasies and the names of his

ship and boat? Because this maneuver is part of a cryptic show of symbols staged to perplex, hoodwink, and even pillory at least some of its readers. To comprehend its oblique, involuted meanings, one must contextualize "Benito Cereno" not only in the history it probes, but also in the development of Melville's narrative art, which was forced upon him by this history. It was no mere coincidence that Melville's strange and estranged relationship with his audience evolved in the early 1850s, along with his rhetorical strategy "directly calculated to deceive—egregiously deceive, the superficial skimmer of pages" (NN *PT* 251).

Herman Melville's greatest creative period, the years between 1846 and 1857, when he produced all nine novels and all the short stories to be published in his lifetime, was a time when the hopes for liberty and equality aroused by the American revolution and revolutions inspired by it seemed about to be swamped by a global tidal wave of reaction. While American slavery, imperialism, and industrial capitalism were surging in the Mexican War and its aftermath, the European revolutions of 1848 were being crushed all across the Continent. Drawing ever-increasing military and economic powers from industrial capitalism, the European empires were now able to execute the most enormous expansion in history. In 1799, at the time of the action of "Benito Cereno," about one third of the earth's surface was ruled by Europeans and their descendants. By 1875, white nations would rule over two-thirds of the globe. Having seen first-hand the operations of white imperial power, Melville branded "the white civilized man" as "the most ferocious animal on the face of the earth" (NN *Typee* 125).

Herman Melville's moral vision centered on the oppressed, the exploited, the victims of American, British, and European society. This vision, which was shaped by his own labor amid some of the most oppressed people of his age, was in stark contradiction to the values dominant among those in the nineteenth century who had the education and leisure to read serious fiction—that is, the affluent gentlemen and ladies who constituted his audience.[7] At first, Melville chose to address his bourgeois readers as a lowly worker, a common sailor whose experiences, quite alien from their own, they might find instructive. His first five novels are not only narrated by this sailor who had fallen from the readers' social ranks, but contain explicit denunciations of imperialism, militarism, capital and corporal punishment, prisons, slavery, racism, and even capitalism itself.

Melville's forthright pleas for liberty and equality found few receptive ears in a class whose imperial ambitions were burgeoning so spectacularly in this very period. The anti-imperialist core of *Typee* was censored out of the American edition. *Pierre* was savaged by the critics, who charged that Melville "strikes . . . at the very foundations of society," and called upon readers, "as representatives of our own race," to "freeze him into silence" (Peck 316–17). Less than two years after "Benito Cereno," Melville was indeed silenced.

In his last years as a fiction writer, Melville no longer spoke as one who had experienced oppression. Instead of addressing his affluent readers from below, Melville creates narrators who assume their point of view. The victims of exploitation and oppression are now the objects perceived, with little comprehension, by observers from the readers' own social class. In "Benito Cereno" we see the action through the eyes of a third-person narrator who takes the Yankee captain's point of view and through legalistic documents submitted to a Spanish imperial court. In this fiction, the people whose misery is the basis for the comforts of Melville's readers have very little to say. After the reenslavement of the Africans, Babo "uttered no sound, and could not be forced to" (NN *PT* 116).

Yet this fiction is a terrifying revelation of the society Melville sees developing, a society based on the enslavement of human beings, who are imprisoned in ships, plantations, factories, and offices, forced to expend their human creativity to enrich those who convert everything of human value into money. And the beneficiary of this ruthless oppression is the social class that includes his polite audience.

In "Benito Cereno" Melville devises a gentlemanly narrator whose consciousness approximates that of much of this audience, thereby providing another angle of misinterpretation besides Delano's. For example, as Babo prepares to fashion Benito Cereno into a living display of the fate of empire by draping him in the flag of Spain, forcing him to sit in one of the malacca chairs "uncomfortable to look at as inquisitors' racks," and plying a finely-honed razor on his throat, the narrator expatiates on what this reveals about "the negro":

There is something in the negro which, in a peculiar way, fits him for avocations about one's person. Most negroes are natural valets and hairdressers; taking to the comb and brush congenially as to the castinets, and flourishing them with almost equal satisfaction. There is, too, a smooth tact about them in this employment, with a marvelous, noiseless, gliding briskness, not ungraceful in its way, singularly pleasing to behold, and still more so to be the manipulated subject of. And above all is the great gift of good humor. Not the mere grin or laugh is here meant. Those were unsuitable. But a certain easy cheerfulness, harmonious in every glance and gesture; as though God had set the whole negro to some pleasant tune. (83)

This profoundly racist misreading of Babo's actions and their significance comes not from Delano but directly from the narrator, who next goes on to explain that the negro's suitability for personal servitude is enhanced by "the docility arising from the unaspiring contentment of a limited mind" (84). Because of this trait and the negro's "susceptibility of blind attachment some-times inhering in indisputable inferiors, one readily perceives why those hypo-chondriacs, Johnson and Byron," he expounds, "took to their hearts . . . their serving men, the negroes" (84). The narrator is as blandly racist as Delano, who, "like most men of a good, blithe heart," "took to negroes, not philan-thropically, but genially, just as other men to Newfoundland dogs" (84). But he is more literary and more intellectual than Delano, even closer than the sea captain to the class outlook of the typical mid-nineteenth-century American reader of high literature. The narrator entices the reader into joining Delano's amusement "with an odd instance of the African love of bright colors and fine shows, in the black's informally taking from the flag-locker a great piece of bunting of all hues, and lavishly tucking it under his master's chin for an apron" (84). When this bunting loosens to reveal its true identity, unwary readers are lured into sharing *Delano's* amusement, while insightful readers may share *Babo's* amusement:

> "The castle and the lion," exclaimed Captain Delano— "why, Don Benito, this is the flag of Spain you use here. It's well it's only I, and not the King, that sees this," he added with a smile, "but"—turning towards the black,— "it's all one, I suppose, so the colors be gay"; which playful remark did not fail somewhat to tickle the negro. (85)

Readers who identify with Delano or the narrator here become objects of Babo's brilliantly ironic show—which is of course also Melville's show. For neither showman is motivated primarily by a desire to entertain the audience.

Readers of "Benito Cereno" have two surrogates: Amasa Delano, who tries to penetrate the meaning of the spectacle being staged for him, and the narrator, who bridges the responses of the sea captain and those of the read-ers, for whom the spectacle is also being staged. But neither Delano nor the narrator is the surrogate of the author, who understands full well what the show means, because he has staged it. In fact, most of the scenes and spectacles that Melville adds to Delano's narrative—including the shaving scene, the skeleton figurehead, the giant slave in chains, Cereno's costume, the oakum pickers, the hatchet polishers, the display of "naked nature" by the young slave woman—are scenes and spectacles created by the slaves as parts of their show. And show it is. The "theatrical aspect of Don Benito in his harlequin ensign" makes Delano wonder if the shaving scene could be some mere "play of the barber" (87). Confronted with the spectacle of the giant in chains, Delano responds, "'. . . this scene surprises me; what means it, pray?'" (62).

Thus the surrogates of the author are Babo and the other Africans, fellow artists and dramatists, designers of shows intended "to deceive—egregiously deceive" those members of the audience who think like Delano and the narrator.[8] Indeed, Melville expresses an intriguing self-image when, at the end of the story, he refers to Babo's impaled head as "that hive of subtlety" (116).[9] But the captain cannot fathom the meaning of the show, for, unlike both Babo and Melville, he is "incapable of satire or irony" (63).

He is also a prisoner of his own racist, imperialist, authoritarian, and even sexist consciousness. Unlike Melville, who must constantly put himself in the position of the slaves in order to conjure with them their deceptive shows, Delano can view all other people only from the vantage point of his own privileged class, race, and sex. All this is illustrated most revealingly in the side show arranged by one of the slave women.

Just after he tries to question one of the Spanish sailors, Delano's "attention" is "drawn to a slumbering negress, partly disclosed through the lacework of some rigging, lying, with youthful limbs carelessly disposed" (73). Whatever her spread legs permit the captain to see makes him quickly forget the previous suspicious scene. He continues to ogle her exposed body through the suggestively revealing "lace-work": "Sprawling at her lapped breasts was her wide-awake fawn, stark naked, its black little body half lifted from the deck, crosswise with its dam's; its hands, like two paws, clambering upon her; its mouth and nose ineffectually rooting to get at the mark; and meantime giving a vexatious half-grunt, blending with the composed snore of the negress" (73). Like all those twentieth-century readers given license to gawk at the bare breasts of non-European women fortuitously displayed in *National Geographic* (usually in one article per issue), Delano's primitivist fantasy allows him to savor a spectacle that he could not openly indulge in if this were a woman of his own race and class. Of course, he has no inkling that the woman's snore may be "composed" in a more sophisticated sense. When she seems to wake, "as if not at all concerned at the attitude in which she had been caught, delightedly she caught the child up, with maternal transports, covering it with kisses." Delano's response indicates how well the show has worked—and why: "There's naked nature, now; pure tenderness and love, thought Captain Delano, well pleased." Utterly incapable of comprehending that this African woman may have been consciously manipulating his own racism and sexism to deceive him, the American captain can only believe that her show was merely an unconscious opportunity for his delight and entertainment. After all, isn't he the master of the *Bachelor's Delight*?

The namesake of Delano's vessel was originally a Danish slave ship. The pirates who seized it and turned it into their own predatory craft left no record of what they did with "the sixty black girls they found on board their prize" (Lloyd 44). But the gang rapes customarily perpetrated on slave ships suggest an unpleasant source for the ship's name. They also suggest the source of the special rage of the slave women on the *San Dominick,* whose consciousness remains alien to all those who cannot fathom the horrors of slavery and imperialism.[10]

Both Delano and the narrator epitomize all those respectable, prosperous nineteenth-century Americans who remained oblivious not only to the human price paid by others for their own comfort and power, but also to the future implicit in the exploitation and oppression to which the American republic had become deeply committed. By conquering the vessel of the decaying Spanish empire and inheriting its cargo of slaves, Delano—that representative American—embodies the message scrawled above the skeleton figurehead: "Follow Your Leader." It took the urban rebellions of 1964–68, the Vietnam War, and the subsequent economic and moral decay of America during the period of its apparent global triumph to create an audience capable of comprehending the deadly message of "Benito Cereno."

NOTES

1. For Melville's possible use of Washington Irving's *The Life and Voyages of Christopher Columbus* as a source, see Hallab. My argument about the role of Columbus is closer to that developed by Horsley-Meachem.

2. For a detailed and perceptive discussion of the role of Las Casas, as well as Melville's contemporaneous sources, see Horsley-Meachem 262–64, 266.

3. Melville, who refers to Charles's abdication and "dotage" in other works (see, for example, *Mardi* ch. 97; *White-Jacket* ch. 46; and "I and My Chimney"), seems in "Benito Cereno" to have

drawn on a source that was frequently reprinted in the early 1850s, William Stirling's *The Cloister Life of the Emperor Charles the Fifth.* In *The Wake of the Gods* (136–50), I offer a detailed account of Melville's possible use of Stirling to create the strange monastic surroundings of Benito Cereno on the *San Dominick,* suggest the demonic powers of the Church, and dramatize the theme of rotting empires.

4. Emery provides a very useful discussion of Manifest Destiny as context for "Benito Cereno," though he tends to understate the role of slavery in both the imperialist movement and the novella. My own historical contextualization of Melville's tale owes much to the splendid essays of Zagarell and Sundquist.

5. In 1809 Jefferson wrote, "I candidly confess that I have ever looked upon Cuba as the most interesting addition that can be made to our system of States"; and he argued that "We should then have only to include the North [Canada] in our confederacy, which should be, of course, in the first war, and we should have such an empire for liberty as she has never surveyed since the creation" (12:277).

6. In the last few decades, there has been much fine work on Melville's vision of slavery in his fiction and specifically in "Benito Cereno," including Grejda, Fisher, and the leading authority on the subject, Karcher. Many of the most important essays are collected in Burkholder.

7. My argument about relations among Melville's work experience, his moral vision, and the form and content of his fiction is made in more detail in "Redburn's Wicked End," *Prison Literature in America,* "From Outsider to Insider," and "Past, Present, and Future Seemed One."

8. Joyce Adler indicates that Babo "has the qualities of mind of a master psychologist, strategist, general, playwright, impresario, and poet"; notes that "Melville endows him with his own poetic insight"; and argues that Melville is "doing in this tale what he has Babo do, create a work of great imagination with a surface appearance and a hidden reality" (104, 109).

9. Babo's role as trickster-showman also foreshadows that of Black Guinea, who entertains the passengers and readers of *The Confidence-Man* with an exhibition of possibly apocalyptic disguises. Black Guinea first appears in the place of the mute lamblike man, just as Babo immediately follows Bartleby in Melville's arrangement of *The Piazza Tales.*

10. The research about the original *Bachelor's Delight* was done by Carolyn Karcher, who explores the background of shipboard rape of slave women (see Karcher, *Shadow*). The suggestion that the pirates may have named the ship in celebration of acts they perpetrated on the slave women they captured was made by Jane Franklin. The most powerful section of Melville's *The Encantadas,* Sketch Eighth, "Norfolk Isle and the Chola Widow," centers on gang rapes carried out by sailors against a defenseless woman.

WORKS CITED

Adler, Joyce. *War in Melville's Imagination.* New York: New York UP, 1981.
Burkholder, Robert E., ed. *Critical Essays on Herman Melville's "Benito Cereno."* New York: G. K. Hall, 1992.
Delano, Amasa. *A Narrative of Voyages and Travels . . . .* Boston: E. G. House, 1817.
Emery, Allan Moore. "'Benito Cereno' and Manifest Destiny." *Nineteenth-Century Fiction* 39 (June 1984): 48–68.
Fisher, Marvin. *Going Under: Melville's Short Fiction and the American 1850s.* Baton Rouge: Louisiana State UP, 1977.

Franklin, H. Bruce. "'Apparent Symbol of Despotic Command': Melville's 'Benito Cereno.'" *New England Quarterly* 34 (December 1961): 462–77.

———. "From Outsider to Insider: Melville's Narrative Strategies." *Melville Society Extracts* 76 (February 1989): 3–6.

———. "Herman Melville: Artist of the Worker's World." *Weapons of Criticism.* Ed. Norman Rudich. Palo Alto, CA: Ramparts, 1976.

———. "Past, Present, and Future Seemed One." In Burkholder.

———. *Prison Literature in America: The Victim as Criminal and Artist.* 1978. Expanded ed. New York: Oxford UP, 1989.

———. "Redburn's Wicked End." *Nineteenth-Century Fiction* 20 (September 1965): 190–94.

———. *The Wake of the Gods: Melville's Mythology.* 1963. Stanford: Stanford UP, 1982.

Grejda, Edward S. *The Common Continent of Men: Racial Equality in the Writings of Herman Melville.* Port Washington, NY: Kennikat, 1974.

Hallab, Mary Y. "Victims of 'Malign Machinations': Irving's *Christopher Columbus* and Melville's 'Benito Cereno.'" *Journal of Narrative Technique* 9 (Fall 1979): 199–206.

Hawthorne, Nathaniel. *Life of Franklin Pierce.* Vol. 17: *The Complete Writings of Nathaniel Hawthorne.* Boston: Houghton, Mifflin, 1900. 75–193.

Horsley-Meachem, Gloria. "The Monastic Slaver: Images and Meaning in 'Benito Cereno.'" *New England Quarterly* 66 (June 1983): 261–66.

Jefferson, Thomas. *The Writings of Thomas Jefferson.* Ed. Andrew A. Lipscomb and Albert E. Bergh. 20 vols. Washington, DC: The Thomas Jefferson Memorial Association, 1904.

"Kansas-Nebraska Act of 1854." *Documents of American History.* Ed. Henry Steele Commager. 6th ed. New York: Appleton-Century-Crofts, 1958. 331–32.

Karcher, Carolyn. Notes to "Benito Cereno." *The Heath Anthology of American Literature.* Vol. 1. Lexington, MA: D. C. Heath, 1990. 2464–522.

———. "The Riddle of the Sphinx: Melville's 'Benito Cereno' and the *Amistad* Case." In Burkholder.

———. *Shadow over the Promised Land: Slavery, Race, and Violence in Melville's America.* Baton Rouge: Louisiana State UP, 1980.

Kavanaugh, James. "'That Hive of Subtlety': 'Benito Cereno' as Critique of Ideology." *Bucknell Review* 29, no. 1 (1984): 127–57.

Lloyd, Christopher. *William Dampier.* Hamden, CT: Archon, 1966.

Morison, Samuel Eliot. *The Maritime History of Massachusetts, 1783–1860.* Boston: Houghton Mifflin, 1941.

"Ostend Manifesto." 1854. *Documents of American History.* Ed. Henry Steele Commager. 6th ed. New York: Appleton-Century-Crofts, 1958. 333–34.

[Peck, George Washington?]. Review of *Pierre. American Whig Review* 16 (November 1852): 446–54. In Watson G. Branch. *Melville: The Critical Heritage.* London: Routledge, 1974.

Putzel, Max. "The Source and the Symbols of Melville's 'Benito Cereno.'" *American Literature* 34 (May 1962): 189–206.

Rauch, Basil. *American Interest in Cuba: 1848–1855.* New York: Columbia UP, 1948.

Sumner, William Graham. "The Conquest of the United States by Spain." 1898. *War and Other Essays*. New York: Yale UP, 1911.

Sundquist, Eric J. "*Benito Cereno* and New World Slavery." In *Reconstructing American Literary History*. Ed. Sacvan Bercovitch. Cambridge, MA: Harvard UP, 1986. 93–122.

von Hagen, Victor Wolfgang, ed. *The Encantadas, or, Enchanted Isles, by Herman Melville*. Burlingame, CA: William P. Wreden, 1940.

Zagarell, Sandra A. "Reenvisioning America: Melville's 'Benito Cereno.'" *ESQ* 30, no. 1 (1984): 245–59.

8

Shadow and Veil:
Melville and Modern Black Consciousness

ARNOLD RAMPERSAD

Herman Melville is slowly settling into our consciousness as one of the major commentators on race in the history of American literature, but the degree of his impact, like the precise nature of his meanings on the subject, is hard to ascertain. One useful way to measure both the impact of his ideas and his meanings on this subject might be to attempt to trace his influence on black American writers and intellectuals. Few Americans are more sensitive to race than black writers have been, and yet Melville has only recently begun to emerge as one of the more influential whites on this central question. Why has Melville failed to make an impact to rival that of Mark Twain or Faulkner, for example, especially when many readers consider him a more radical commentator on race?

In part, the answer has to do with the infamous obscuring of Melville's reputation in the 1880s and 1890s and down into the twentieth century. In part, the answer lies in the difficulty of ascertaining his general position on race. Here, blacks were not helped by the mainstream of literary criticism, which is to say white scholars, critics, and teachers. In her landmark study *Shadow over the Promised Land: Slavery, Race, and Violence in Melville's America* (1980), Carolyn Karcher reminds us that "until the mid-1960s, there was almost no interest in Melville's racial views, and very little recognition of the prominent place that social criticism occupies in his writings." Even those critics who had identified themselves with strongly liberal or even radical social attitudes "insisted that a work like 'Benito Cereno,' for example, was not about slave revolt, but about good and evil." Furthermore, in this reading of 'Benito Cereno,' the fact that Melville makes whites represent good and blacks represent evil was said to have "no racial implications." The few critics who pointed out the racism of such assignations of symbolic value "accused Melville himself of racism" (ix).

Resisting the temptation to be self-righteous by indulging in hindsight, one should face the difficulty posed by Melville's narratives on the question of race. Karcher herself, declaring that his views were not always consistent, called him "a refractory conformist and a reluctant rebel." She argues only that "criticism of slavery and racism" were "pressing concerns of his that he kept bringing up in his antebellum novels and tales." However, "in a few works—notably *Moby-Dick* and *The Confidence-Man,*" she boldly asserts, "slavery and race are crucial themes," the study of which "not only takes us to the heart of the text, but radically transforms our perceptions of its total meaning" (3). Aldon Lynn Nielsen has made a similar point (15). Sometimes Melville seems to have had dubious racial views, in keeping with the intellectual world in which he lived; "But just as often he can be found puzzling out the way in which race appears in our representations to ourselves" (xi).

Blacks intellectuals were hardly reluctant themselves to try to puzzle out the ways of racial representation; but there may have been other reasons for their relative blindness to Melville. For one thing, there are dominating elements in Melville's body of work that are at odds with the tradition of black fiction. The classic black fictional narrative was far more often than not a domestic tale, tied to racial and political ambitions but bound by middle-class proprieties, including strong elements of sentiment, love, and marriage. And while Melville has something to offer in this line, it was not enough to make much of an impression. The author of *Typee* and *Omoo* and even *Moby-Dick* and *Billy Budd* encourages a fiction based on a sense of the author as voyager, rover, roamer, or even bum; a mixture of the bohemian spirit with adventurism in the Third World—something that had interested few black writers (for example, Langston Hughes, as one might infer from his autobiographies *The Big Sea* and *I Wonder as I Wander*). But the most daunting challenge presented by Melville lies in his merging of something like bohemianism with disturbing ideas about race. These ideas intimidated the black writer almost as much as they have challenged the white world, which recoiled from them in the 1850s and has only slowly come around to engaging them fully.

Not everyone flinched, and black writers of a more independent cast might have responded in kind. In his typically wild and yet inspired way, D. H. Lawrence caught more than a glimpse of Melville's radicalism on the subject of race. Melville "was a modern Viking. There is something curious about real blue-eyed people. They are never quite human. . . . In blue eyes there is sun and rain and abstract, uncreate element, water, ice, air, space, but not humanity." Melville in the South Seas, in *Typee* and *Omoo*, finds the Noble Savage and the ignoble white man. "Here at last," in *Typee*, "is Rousseau's Child of Nature and Chateaubriand's Noble Savage called upon and found at home. Yes, Melville loves his savage hosts. He finds them gentle, laughing lambs compared to the ravening wolves of his white brothers, left behind in America and on an American whaleship. The ugliest beast on earth is a white man, says Melville" (1031, 1035).

According to Lawrence, Melville cannot rest there. Unable finally to identify with the black savage, he also hated the white "renegade" held by "a long thin chain" around his ankle connected to "America, to civilization, to democracy, to the ideal world. . . . It never broke. It pulled him back." At the same time, however, he saw clearly the end of civilization, which he recorded in *Moby-Dick.* "Doom! Doom! Doom!" Lawrence intones.

> Something seems to whisper it in the very dark trees of America. Doom! Doom of what?
> Doom of our white day. We are doomed, doomed. And the doom is in America. The doom of our white day.
> . . . Melville knew. He knew his race was doomed. His white soul, doomed. His great white epoch, doomed. Himself, doomed. The idealist, doomed. The spirit, doomed.
> . . . What then is Moby-Dick? He is the deepest blood-being of the white race; he is our deepest blood-nature. . . . The last phallic being of the white man. Hunted into the death of upper consciousness and the ideal will. (1041, 1060)

Early in this century, a few black writers, notably W. E. B. Du Bois in certain places, were intrigued by the idea of the death of the white race, the fall of white culture. Far more often, black writers have tiptoed around the subject, as for generations they tiptoed around the subject of hatred and violence as the achieved consequence of racism. Of course, all that timidity was to change, first with the publication of Richard Wright's *Native Son* in 1940, then more explosively with the black power and the black consciousness movement of the 1960s and later.

Until Wright's novel, the blueprint for black fiction was that originated by Harriet Beecher Stowe in *Uncle Tom's Cabin* in 1851. (The fact that behind Stowe's novel, by her own admission, was the slave narrative only reinforced the centrality of her novel.) The black writer, in a real sense, had Stowe to one side and, on the other, Melville. Blacks almost always chose Stowe and her world: domestic, familial, womanly, religious, moral, separatist but apparently integrationist. Just as often they shunned Melville: nomadic, lonely, masculine, satanic, amoral, and (in the end, though different in the beginning) separationist. Du Bois openly admired Stowe; Langston Hughes comfortably published an introduction to *Uncle Tom's Cabin*. And why not? Her social radicalism came garbed distinctly in a highly moral, highly religious fabric, ideally suited for characterizations that involved submission, stoicism, or heroic sacrifice, as in her most memorable creations—black Uncle Tom and white Little Eva—as well as plots that moved inexorably toward success and fulfillment.

Thus a real landmark in African American literary and intellectual history is the celebrated attack on Mrs. Stowe by young James Baldwin in his June 1949 essay "Everybody's Protest Novel." Did Baldwin understand exactly what he was doing in attacking Harriet Beecher Stowe? Probably not. His essay, an attack on the protest novel in general, has always seemed to me in some way misguided. *Uncle Tom's Cabin* is held to be "a very bad novel," one that is "activated by what might be called a theological terror, the terror of damnation; and the spirit that breathes in this book . . . is not different from that spirit of medieval times which sought to exorcize evil by burning witches." The essay closes with an attack on what might have been Baldwin's real target all along—ironically, *Native Son,* which is held to be another protest novel steeped in race that disfigures the humanity of its black characters in order to hew to the formula of protest. "Bigger is Uncle Tom's descendant, flesh of his flesh, so exactly opposite a portrait that, when the books are placed together, it seems that the contemporary Negro novelist and the dead New England woman are locked together in a deadly, timeless battle; the one uttering merciless exhortations, the other shouting curses" (14, 22).

Without quite knowing it, I believe, Baldwin recognized something crucial and yet debilitating in the relationship between Stowe's work and black American literature. Whether Wright is most accurately seen as the inverse of Stowe is another matter, for Wright may be seen as a Melvillean, with "Benito Cereno" forming a kind of prediction of *Native Son*—that is, with Babo predicting Bigger Thomas. Babo and Bigger are alike in one supremely important way. In spite of the consumerist elements in Bigger's make-up, both men are singularly without a sense of ambivalence about their attitude to the white world and the America they know. The big difference between them is that Bigger appears to have little that might be called mature, purposeful political consciousness, in which Babo excels. Babo's gaze is fixed on freedom and Africa, and militantly against the whites, America, and all its works and pomps.

In 1949 Baldwin was not ready—far from it—for racial radicalism of such extreme degree, for the displays of rage that would make him be received as a prophet; otherwise he might have seen that Wright and *Native Son* deserved to be linked to the American mid-nineteenth-century world from which Stowe had come, but in a different way. But clearly he knew that something was in the wind. Interestingly, Baldwin comes to mind crucially in Aldon Lynn Nielsen's discussion of Melville in *Reading Race: White American Poets and the Racial Discourse in the Twentieth Century* (1988). Of the beheaded Babo, Nielsen writes: "Babo's eyes gaze out from the text . . . in stark announcement, not only of the terror which the slavers must have anticipated, but of a terror which must be faced by white culture generally, that dread that culture must face of having the 'bad other' it has called into being suddenly break through the abstraction of white description. Melville has forced just such a rent in the veil of racial discourse." Here, in this rent, Nielsen sights and cites none other than Baldwin: "The real terror that engulfs the white world now is a visceral terror. . . . It's the terror of being described by those they've been describing so long" (20).

Within four years after Baldwin's essay, the matter of Melville and race as perceived by blacks would take a decisive turn in the work of two black intellectuals and writers. First came the young Ralph Ellison, who had by this point moved from orthodox Marxism toward his full realization as an artist with the publication in 1952 of his novel *Invisible Man*. Foregrounding his admiration for Melville—unprecedented in African American writing, as far as I know— Ellison chose as one of his two epigraphs the question of Amasa Delano to the morose Don Benito near the end of "Benito Cereno": "'You are saved,' cried Captain Delano, more and more astonished and pained; 'you are saved: what has cast such a shadow upon you?'"

A year later, in 1953, the Trinidad-born writer C. L. R. James, well known as the author of *Black Jacobins* (about the Haitian revolution) and a brilliant disciple of Leon Trotsky, published *Mariners, Renegades and Castaways: The Story of Herman Melville and the World We Live in.* This was the first book by someone steeped in the problems posed by race to attempt to take the measure of Herman Melville. Much of the work was written on Ellis Island, where James was detained by the Department of Immigration as an undesirable alien in spite of his militant anticommunism. To James, Melville is astonishingly prophetic of the world of the 1950s. Of *Moby-Dick* he writes: "The question of questions is: how could a book from the world of 1850 contain so much of the world of the 1950s?" (80). How did James see Melville on the question of race?

James had only a limited idea of exactly how much of the future world was prophesied by Melville. As a Trotskyite, he viewed race and nationalism, including black nationalism, as a kind of banality. His book is dedicated to his son, "who will be 21 years old in 1970 by which time I hope he and his generation will have left behind them forever all the problems of nationality." In his Marxist zeal, he failed to take Melville's full measure. James comes close, in linking *Moby-Dick* to twentieth-century history. After World War I, Germany "sought a theory of society and a program. . . . The national state *was* the one god without any hypocrisies or pretenses. The national race *was* the master race." When the Germans followed a totalitarian leader to their doom, Melville had foreseen it all. "That this is how the masses of men would sooner or later behave is what Melville was pointing out in 1851. Being a creative artist, he had seen it in terms of human personality and human relations, and therefore could only present it that way." Denouncing Stalin and communism, who triumphed over the Nazis along with the capitalists, James sees Ahab as the "embodiment of the totalitarian type . . . concerned with two things only: 1) science, the management of things; and 2) politics, the management of men" (11–13).

Certainly James is alive to the ways in which Melville's depictions of blacks is an improvement on what had come before in American and European literature. Effortlessly, he links Melville to Stowe. "Melville, with his usual scientific precision, does not write of Negro slaves," says James. "He writes of the Negro race, civilized and uncivilized alike. Harriet Beecher Stowe, who wrote a few years before, wrote about Negroes, about Uncle Tom and Eva, who mean nothing today." He compares *Moby-Dick* to Cooper's *The Last of the Mohicans* and the age-old invocation of the noble savage. Queequeg is drawn first according to the stereotype of the noble savage; then Melville takes him in certain directions "or takes them [his black characters] over into the world he saw ahead." Melville's vision of race is embodied in his narrator Ishmael's, and is founded on a view of whiteness and of civilization as being corrupt and insupportable. Ishmael is "as isolated and bitter as Ahab and as helpless. He cannot stand the narrow, cramped, limited existence which civilization offers him. He hates the greed, the lies, the hypocrisy. Thus shut out from the world outside, he cannot get out of himself" (133, 41).

So far, there is perhaps little remarkable about this analysis; little that is remarkable today, in any event. At "Benito Cereno," however, James balks. He appreciates the elements that make it a tour de force; in fact, he, like other critics, uses precisely these elements to give weight to his final dislike of the tale. He faithfully presents the general enterprise of the story. Through Amasa Delano, Melville had "itemized every single belief cherished by an advanced civilization . . . about a backward people and then one by one showed that they were not merely false but were the direct cause of his own blindness and stupidity." And James sees the heroic character of the blacks and especially of their leader, and thus the radicalism of Melville: "As is usual with him, his protest is uncompromising, absolute. The Negroes fight to a finish, Babo is the most heroic character in Melville's fiction. He is a man of unbending will, a natural leader, an organizer of large schemes but a master of detail, ruthless against his enemies but without personal weakness. . . . Melville purposely makes him physically small, a man of internal power with a brain that is a 'hive of subtlety'" (133–34).

And yet "Benito Cereno" illustrates "Melville's decline into the shallowness of modern literature. It is a propaganda story, a mystery, written to prove a particular social or political point." In execution it is excellent, but "propaganda stories are of necessity limited. Ahab, for example, is a new type of human being. Bartleby is not. Still less is Babo." Of the slaves' heroism, "history tells us ten thousand such stories. Melville had ceased to be creative, and he had lost his vision of the future. Without such vision no writer can describe existing reality, for without it he does not know what is important or what is not, what will endure and what will pass" (134).

All of this is debatable. What must be debated is whether or not Babo is a "new type of human being" and whether Melville "had lost his vision of the future." And, of course, whether Melville had "ceased to be creative." Clearly Babo was not quite as new a figure as Ahab was; but I am not sure what black historical or literary personages James is referring to when he declared Babo not new. And yet one might see in Babo's homicidal desire for freedom, and his uncompromising hatred of Cereno and the whites, a kind of new black man. This man sees the world of blacks and the world of whites as irreconcilably separate. His head, chopped off and stuck on a pole in a public square, presents only hostility to the passing whites—or, as Melville put it, "met, un-abashed, the gaze of the whites."

Here we have in James a collision between race analysis and class analysis, as well as a conflict between partisan racial feeling and James's essential sense of himself as an intellectual and a personality. By his own admission, he considered himself a "black European" and conceded that his "whole life was toward European literature, European sociology" (396). It is useful to re-member the division between the Trotskyites and the Communist party over the Black Nation question, with the Communists after 1928 advocating self-determination for American blacks and the Trotskyites advocating a similar degree of freedom—but only as a step toward the eventual goal of an inter-racial, international coalition. James is being faithful to his Trotskyite views in reading Melville in the way he does, and particularly so on the question of race. But it seems safe to say that he sacrificed prophesy in adhering to Trotskyite ideology, not to say dogma.

How did Ralph Ellison come to the point of citing "Benito Cereno" as an epigraph to *Invisible Man*? Surely the black writer engaging Melville, like any writer thoroughly engaging Melville, necessarily also engages what one might call the deep tradition of American literature. He or she must be happy in that engagement, which is to say that the black writer must bring respect and even a degree of reverence for long-dead white writers; and such respect and reverence has not always been possible for the young black writer facing the national past. To this writer, the reputation of abolitionism, which one takes to represent the ultimate radicalism on the question of race in the mid–nineteenth century, does not sufficiently glamorize or even illuminate the past to warrant such devotion. Taken for granted is the absence of an intellec-tual force for liberty based on premises beyond abolitionism. Occasionally, however, someone probes deeply enough and discovers connections where connections were not supposed to exist. Such a figure, among black Ameri-can writers facing the American mid–nineteenth century, was Ralph Waldo Ellison.

As early as 1945, in a review in *The New Republic* of the white writer Buck-lin Moon's *Primer for White Folks,* Ellison looked at Melville and Melville's contemporaries and saw a group of writers with whom he obviously believed he had something in common. Between 1776 and 1876, he writes, "there was a conception of democracy current in this country that allowed the writer to identify himself with the Negro." Among those identified were "Whitman, Emerson, Thoreau, Hawthorne, Melville and Mark Twain. For slavery (it was not called a 'Negro problem' then) was a vital issue in the American consciousness, symbolic of the condition of Man, and a valid aspect of the writer's reality." Only later was the question of blacks "pushed into the underground of the American conscience and ignored" (107–08).

The year after the appearance of *Invisible Man,* in his essay "Twentieth-Century Fiction and the Black Mask of Humanity," delivered at Harvard University, Ellison singled out Melville as representative of writers of the nineteenth century. The main difference between Melville and these writers, on the one hand, and the writers of Ellison's time, on the other, was "not in the latter's lack of personal rituals" but rather "in the social effect aroused within their respective readers." Melville's own ritual and rhetoric were based on "a blending of his personal myth with universal myths as traditional as any used by Shakespeare or the Bible." What is different is that "Melville's belief could still find a public object. Whatever else his works were 'about' they also managed to be about democracy. But by our day the democratic dream had become too shaky a structure to support the furious pressures of the artist's doubts. And as always when the belief which nurtures a great social myth declines, large sections of society become prey to superstition. For man without myth is Othello with Desdemona gone: chaos descends, faith vanishes and superstitions prowl in the mind" (56–57).

In his allusion to Othello and Desdemona, Ellison shows the extent to which the dilemma of the black writer facing the white American tradition is on his mind and the nostalgia he feels for a vanished era, when the writer and the audience were far more at one than in our time—and the American writer was far more concerned with democracy and race than he or she was in 1953. In linking himself to the past, ironically, he opened his way into the future both ideologically and formally, as he explored racial alienation and created a structure that went beyond naturalism.

In breaking with naturalism, Ellison appears to have found his major support not so much in writers more contemporary with him than Wright or Dreiser as in moving backward toward Melville. Charles T. Davis has described Ellison's style in *Invisible Man* as one that is "always eclectic, changing to reflect the psychological shifts within his unnamed narrator." The style may be eclectic, but Davis reminds us that Ellison himself has spoken (in his interview called "The Art of Fiction" in *Paris Review* in 1955) of the three major parts of the novel being dominated respectively by naturalism, impressionism, and surrealism. "Even in the more naturalistic pages of *Invisible Man,*" Davis wrote, "we find a Melvillian duality, a delight in playing with two equally valid but opposed physical realities" (276).

How did Melville facilitate Ellison's decisive modification of naturalism by impressionism and surrealism, and thus his self-liberation from both the "domestic" and bourgeois discourse of Harriet Beecher Stowe and the almost dogmatic naturalism of Wright and Dreiser? In the exchange between Amasa Delano and Don Benito Cereno in which Ellison found an epigraph to his novel, Melville revealed how much he understood of the vagaries of meaning inherent in the Africanist presence in the United States. When Delano asks Don Benito, "what has cast such a shadow upon you?" Don Benito's reply is "The negro." The "shadow" of the "negro" is death to Cereno, who gathers his mantle about him "as if it were a pall." Does Don Benito mean Babo, or all negroes? I think the latter. Unacknowledged perhaps by most writers (George Washington Cable in *The Grandissimes* is perhaps an exception), the death-dealing shadow of blacks on whites in Melville is a concept, an image, that in its singularity is at least as powerful as the concept or image that, as a modification of Stowe's imaging of race, helped to define black writing in this century—Du Bois's concept and image of the "veil" in *The Souls of Black Folk*. (The artistic power of the image of the "shadow," which is crucial to my argument, is demonstrated deliberately in "Benito Cereno," of course, where it is the central, all-pervading image. Less centrally, it is also a powerful presence in *Moby-Dick*.)

A veil, Du Bois writes at the start of that book, separates blacks from whites in America. "After the Egyptian and Indian, the Greek and Roman, the Teuton and Mongolian, the Negro is a sort of seventh son, born with a veil, and gifted with second-sight in this American world,—a world which yields him no true self-consciousness, but only lets him see himself through the revelation of the other world. It is a peculiar sensation, this double-consciousness." The black American has "two souls, two thoughts, two unreconciled strivings; two warring ideals in one dark body, whose dogged strength alone keeps it from being torn asunder" (3).[1]

Melville's shadow and Du Bois's veil are similar in one respect but paradoxical in other respects. From the point of view of blacks, the former (as personified in Babo, or even Bigger Thomas, for example) speaks of unitary consciousness, the latter of a divided consciousness, out of which comes intrinsic drama but—by definition—the probability of political and cultural indecisiveness. For whites, however, the shadow operates as the veil does for blacks, in that it destabilizes unitary consciousness as well as political and cultural power. In another twist, if for the black writer divided consciousness, or the veil, is intrinsically dramatic, the shadow, on the other hand, presents a dead end in art even as it may represent a victory over whites. Thus the black writer, or the white writer completely sympathetic to blacks, who is possessed by a sense of the authenticity of unitary consciousness (again, as represented by Babo or Bigger) may face an end to art. C. L. R. James certainly saw the death-dealing shadow of the negro as a dead end for Melville, one that signals the death of hope, of faith in humanity.

I would suggest that *Invisible Man* gains much of its power from Ellison's establishment of a working tension between the shadow and the veil, the death-dealing shadow and the ambivalent veil. Repudiating neither concept, Ellison instead lets them play off against one another, before coming down on the side of the veil, which is to say on the side of optimism, the party of hope, the promise of America. "For, like almost everyone else in our country," Invisible says at the end, "I started out with my share of optimism. I believed in hard work and progress and action, but now, after first being 'for' society and then 'against' it, I assign myself no rank or any limit. . . . My world has become one of infinite possibilities" (498). What expedites Ellison's fusion is his major borrowing from Melville—that is, the character of his narrator, who resembles no one else in previous fiction so much as he resembles Ishmael of *Moby-Dick.*

Invisible is black, Ishmael white, but both feel the shadow of "the negro," or of race. The shadow falls across Ishmael but does not kill him, as it kills Don Benito. Rather, it opens up the wellsprings of his humanitarian consciousness early in the novel, through Queequeg, whose coffin also saves him in the end. Ellison signals his debt to Melville when, in the prologue to *Invisible Man,* he reprises a moment in the second chapter of *Moby-Dick.* Looking for a place to sleep in New Bedford, Ishmael goes from one inn to another, finding them uncongenial and too expensive. In the darkness, he moves toward the inns near the water, knowing they would be cheapest. "Such dreary streets! blocks of blackness, not houses, on either hand, and here and there a candle, like a candle moving about in a tomb. At this hour of the night, of the last day of the week, that quarter of the town proved all but deserted." He comes to "a smoky light proceeding from a low, wide building, the door of which stood invitingly open." Entering, he stumbles over an ash box. "Ha! thought I, ha, as the flying articles almost choked me, are these ashes from that destroyed city, Gomorrah?" Ishmael decides, jokingly, that this must be an inn called "The Trap." However, he hears a voice inside and "pushed on and opened a second, interior door. "A hundred black faces turned round in their rows to peer; and beyond, a black Angel of Doom was beating a book in the pulpit. It was a negro church; and the preacher's text was about the blackness of darkness, and the weeping and wailing and teeth-gnashing there" (28).

In the prologue to *Invisible Man,* Invisible recalls a prime moment of truth when he smoked marijuana and entered the spirit of music as for the first time: "I not only entered the music but descended, like Dante, into its depths." He hears an old woman singing a spiritual "as full of Weltschmerz as fla-menco," and then a naked light-skinned black girl "pleading in a voice like my mother's" at her own auction. Then, at "a lower level" yet, he hears a shout: "Brothers and sisters, my text this morning is the 'Blackness of Blackness.'" And the congregation answers: "That blackness is most black, brother, most black . . ." (12).

Thus Invisible crosses Ishmael's path, and enters his text; and thus Ishmael enters Invisible's text. Both men are innocents puzzling out the question of the meaning of blackness and whiteness. Ishmael's education begins with his en-counter with Queequeg. The major steps in Ishmael's conversion may be seen in the following quotations. At first: "I felt a melting in me. . . . Wild he was; a very sight of sights to see; yet I began to feel myself mysteriously drawn to-wards him" (*Moby-Dick* 59). And then, as he and Queequeg walk together in public: "we did not notice the jeering glances of the passengers, a lubber-like assembly, who marveled that two fellow beings should be so companionable; as though a white man were anything more dignified than a white-washed negro" (65). And after Queequeg has shown himself to be far braver and far more competent than Ishmael could ever be: "From that hour I clove to Quee-queg like a barnacle; yea, till poor Queequeg took his long last dive" (66).

If Ishmael's education begins with his meeting with Queequeg, then it might be said that Invisible's education begins with his meeting with Ishmael and Queequeg. By representing the humanity of blacks and the complexity of race and racism so acutely and generously in his text, Melville empowered Ellison to insist on a place in the American literary tradition, no matter how racism tried to exclude him. It is good to remember where Invisible lives. He lives not in Harlem proper "but in a border area"; his building is rented strictly to whites, but "I live rent-free . . . in a section of the basement that was shut off and forgotten during the nineteenth century, which I discovered when I was trying to escape from Ras the Destroyer" (*Invisible Man* 9). Ras personifies the destructive excesses of cultural nationalism, from which Elli-son, through Invisible, escapes by clinging to a notion of cultural inheritance and tradition based on an appreciation of the relevance of nineteenth-century American writing to his own desires as a writer.

Invisible Man could not have been written by someone without such a sense, although the novel looks forward technically and ideologically as readily as it looks backward. In other words, Ellison's novel exemplifies the spirit of T. S. Eliot's essay "Tradition and the Individual Talent," in which Eliot stresses the interrelationship of the living and the dead. No wonder, then, that the other epigraph to *Invisible Man* is from Eliot (from *The Cocktail Party*). The special challenge, as I have said, was for a black writer to find part of his tradition among whites; Ellison must have had few illusions about how Eliot viewed blacks and black culture. Ellison himself made a distinction between family and ancestors. Langston Hughes and Richard Wright were family; Eliot and Hemingway and Melville, presumably, were ancestors. He was surely not the first person—and absolutely not the first artist—to exalt his ancestors over his family.

Ellison's sense of tradition was not shared by the next generation of black writers, those who matured—if that is the right word—in the 1960s. Breaking with the white past, with white people, was the hallmark of the black power and black arts movements, of which the major leader, as an artist and a theorist, was almost certainly LeRoi Jones, later Amiri Baraka. And yet Melville evidently meant something to Jones before he became Baraka but as he was trying to become him. In 1962, in a lecture entitled "The Myth of 'Negro Literature,'" Jones heaped scorn on most black writing as being little more than the effluence of bourgeois mentalities bent on aping mediocre white writers while avoiding the best. Only Toomer, Wright, Ellison, and Baldwin, he declared, had created any examples of writing "that could succeed in passing themselves off as 'serious' writing. . . . That is, serious, if one has never read Herman Melville or James Joyce" (107).

This is hardly evidence of influence, but it is clear that Baraka and the Black Power movement would have understood Babo in his murderous hatred of Don Benito, indeed, identified with him, and excoriated Amasa Delano as the embodiment of fantastic white liberal values (notably the famed American value called "innocence"). All of which Melville fairly anticipated. And yet C. L. R. James was surely right in seeing the bleakness of it all, how destructive of art such radicalism is—art, that is, that depends on America (black or white) for its audience. Generally without saying so, the African American literary tradition has recognized this problem and effected a compromise with the past—a stern compromise, but a compromise nevertheless. The work of the leading black writers since the 1960s reflects this carefully negotiated truce with the American literary tradition. The echoes of Melville himself are there in the work of John Edgar Wideman and Barbara Chase-Riboud and, of course, Charles Johnson. And Melville has figured prominently in the work by the preeminent black writer today, Toni Morrison, in her attempt as a cultural interpreter to affect our sense of the American literary tradition—that is, to amplify the insights and intuitions of Ralph Ellison and others on this question.

Although what one might call a deep nationalism—a commitment to the "ancient properties" of black peoples—is an indispensable feature of Morrison's work, it is a feature surrounded by her sense of the necessity of a broader, deeper view of tradition and responsibility. She has best articulated her thoughts on this question in her essay "Unspeakable Things Unspoken: The Afro-American Presence in American Literature" (1989). There, she proposes to engage the multiple debates concerning the canon in American literature "in order to suggest ways of addressing the Afro-American presence in American Literature that require neither slaughter nor reification—views that may spring the whole literature of an entire nation from the solitude into which it has been locked" (1). And Melville is central to her project.

Admiring Michael Rogin's *Subversive Geneology: The Politics and Art of Herman Melville* (1983), Morrison differs from him, however, in identifying not slavery but the fabrication and idealization of whiteness as ideology, as the cause of Melville's alienation in his lifetime.

> If the whale is more than blind, indifferent Nature unsubduable by masculine aggression, we can consider the possibility that Melville's "truth" was his recognition of the moment in America when whiteness became ideology. And if the white whale is the ideology of race, what Ahab has lost to it is personal dismemberment and family and society and his own place as a human in the world. The trauma of racism is, for the racist and the victim, the severe fragmentation of the self, and has always seemed to me a cause (not a symptom) of psychosis. . . .
>
> Ahab . . . is navigating between an idea of civilization that he renounces and an idea of savagery he must annihilate, because the two cannot co-exist. The former is based on the latter. What is terrible in its complexity is that the idea of savagery is not the missionary one: it is white racial ideology that is savage and if, indeed, a white, nineteenth-century, American male took on not abolition, not the amelioration of racist institutions or their laws, but the very concept of whiteness as an inhuman idea, he would be very alone, very desperate, and very doomed. Madness would be the only appropriate description of such audacity. . . . What I am suggesting is that he was overwhelmed by the philosophical and metaphysical idea that

had its fullest manifestation in his own time in his own country, and that that idea was the successful assertion of whiteness as ideology. (15–16)

Quoting liberally from the chapter "The Whiteness of the Whale," Morrison stresses that "Melville is not exploring white *people,* but whiteness idealized." He is neither "engaged in some simple and simple-minded black/white didacticism" nor was he "satanizing white people." Melville's final observation on whiteness "reverberates with personal trauma. 'This visible [colored] world seems formed in love, the invisible [white] spheres were formed in fright.' The necessity for whiteness as privileged 'natural' state, the invention of it, was indeed formed in fright" (16).

Finally, she uses Father Mapple's sermon to measure the radicalism of *Moby-Dick:*

> To question the very notion of white progress, the very idea of racial superiority, of whiteness as privileged place in the evolutionary ladder of humankind, and to meditate on the fraudulent, self-destroying philosophy of that superiority, to "pluck it out from under the robes of Senators and Judges," to drag the "judge himself to the bar,"—that was dangerous, solitary, radical work. Especially then. Especially now. To be 'only a patriot to heaven' is no mean aspiration in Young America for a writer—or the captain of a whaling ship.

Embracing both white and black writers, Morrison's tribute to Melville is unequivocal: "To this day no novelist has so wrestled with its subject" (18).

For a number of reasons, some of them almost inscrutable, Melville saw into the heart of America on the question of race. He saw how the concept of innate white superiority—of whiteness as absolute—had been constructed out of economic and political pressures and desires in a "new" world, in which Europeans had come up against a native population and an imported African presence and redefined themselves according to those pressures. He saw not only the complex psychological consequences for whites but the ways in which the newly constructed ideology of whiteness would shape and invade the entire apparatus of signification, from color of skin to color in art to standards of facial beauty and far beyond into virtually every aspect of culture.

And I think he also clearly saw something of the complex psychological consequences for blacks, and the ways in which they would become, or had already become, entangled in the apparatus of signification designed to keep them in perpetual servitude. For daring to put these ideas in fiction, Melville was punished with neglect, silence, and then misappropriation and misinterpretation. He instead should be seen as one of the principal interpreters of the American obsession with race and commitment to racism, an artist to whose work we should turn for a fair measure of illumination and guidance.

NOTE

1. Note that Aldon Lynn Nielsen (1–2) also discusses Du Bois's concept of the veil in the context of Melville and identifies an additional prefiguring of *Invisible Man* (the "Battle Royal" episode) in *White-Jacket*.

WORKS CITED

Baldwin, James. *Notes of a Native Son*. Boston: Beacon, 1990.

Davis, Charles T. "The Mixed Heritage of the Modern Black Novel." In *Speaking for You: The Vision of Ralph Ellison*. Ed. Kimberly W. Benston. Washington, DC: Howard UP, 1987.

Du Bois, W. E. B. *The Souls of Black Folk*. Chicago: A. C. McClurg, 1903.

Ellison, Ralph. *Invisible Man*. New York: Random House, 1952.

———. *Shadow and Act*. New York: Signet, 1966.

James, C. L. R. *Mariners, Renegades and Castaways: The Story of Herman Melville and the World We Live in*. New York: Privately published, 1953.

Jones, LeRoi. *Home: Social Essays*. New York: Morrow, 1966.

Karcher, Carolyn L. *Shadow over the Promised Land: Slavery, Race, and Violence in Melville's America*. Baton Rouge: Louisiana State UP, 1980.

Lawrence, D. H. *Studies in Classic American Literature*. In *The Shock of Recognition*. Ed. Edmund Wilson. New York: Random House, 1955.

Melville, Herman. *Moby-Dick*. Boston: Houghton Mifflin, 1956.

Morrison, Toni "Unspeakable Things Unspoken: The Afro-American Presence in American Literature." *Michigan Quarterly Review* (Winter 1989): 1–18.

Nielsen, Aldon Lynn. *Reading Race: White American Poets and the Racial Discourse in the Twentieth Century*. Athens: U of Georgia P, 1988.

Robinson, Cedric J. *Black Marxism: The Making of the Black Radical Tradition*. London: Zed, 1983.

Rogin, Michael Paul. *Subversive Geneology: The Politics and Art of Herman Melville*. New York: Knopf, 1983.

Person and Personality:
Melville's Varied Selves

9

Melville; or, Aggression

RICHARD H. BRODHEAD

Every form of emotional energy, we could venture, has its poet laureate, the author who has brought this drive to richest expression and so has opened it to our fullest understanding. The laureate of boredom-bred longing, of desire generated as a release from boredom that nevertheless leads always back to boredom, is Flaubert, or, if we prefer, Stendhal. Dreiser is the corresponding laureate of consumer longing, of the self's will to construct an adequate center for itself by appropriating an adequate display of possessions. Poe and his sometime pupil Dostoyevski are the literary authorities on what Poe christened the perverse, the urge to do wrong and self-destructive things for the reason that they are wrong and self-destructive. To know the workings of the will to enjoy passionate experience in the mediated form of vicarious spectacle, we turn to Hawthorne and Henry James.

If we ask who is the laureate of aggression, various names would suggest themselves—Hemingway, for instance, or Richard Wright—but Melville would have to be regarded as a chief contender. If aggression is a seldom-discussed issue in Melville's work, it can only be because its presence is so overwhelmingly obvious. What is Melvillean plot (we could ask in the manner of "Fast-Fish and Loose-Fish") but the path toward an eruption of aggression:

the assault with boathook by which Tommo fights free of Typeean hospitality; or Ahab's long-postponed harpoon thrust at Moby Dick; or the blow by which Billy Budd drops Claggart to his death? What is a Melvillean hero in Melville's hero-loving phase but a man mastered by aggressive drives and so reborn as pure antagonist—as Ahab, mastered by "general rage and hate," has become identical with the will to strike, or as Pierre reconceives himself as an attack weapon: "With myself I front thee?" What human right does the Melvillean self claim as fundamental but the right to aggression in self-defense: "the privilege, inborn and inalienable, that every man has, of dying himself, and inflicting death upon another," in the resonant language of *White-Jacket*? What is even the best-adjusted of us, in Melville's redaction, but a self similarly filled with aggression who has learned to deflect it into substitutes for pistol and ball? When Ishmael, Melville's *homme moyen malheureux*, wants to explain what has propelled his career, he tells us that he suffers from the urge either to pause before coffin warehouses or to step into the street and knock people's hats off. He suffers, in other words, from the low-grade, chronic aggressiveness of everyday life, an animus interchangeably against others or against himself. If Ishmael avoids the blow that is the hero's usual destructive, self-destructive end, it is because he has redirected such urges into the less deadly realms of writing, irony, and verbal play.

Aggression is everywhere in Melville's stories, then. But what makes this drive so central to him is that it is not only a featured subject in his fiction: in Melville's case writing itself is significantly allied with aggressive impulses. We do not do sufficient justice to the strength of the polemic or pugilistic side of Melville's work; but already in *Typee*, Melville's first outing, writing has linked itself to the energies of verbal assault, as seen in Melville's harangues against the West. ("He didn't really want Eden. He wanted to fight" is D. H. Lawrence's apt summary of this pugnacious pastoral.) *White-Jacket* too is less a novel than a tirade, its prose endlessly reenergized by the scenario of righteous opposition. (Melville himself described this book's affective mode in a letter to Dana: "This man-of-war book, My Dear Sir, is in some parts rathar man-of-*warish* in style—rathar aggressive I fear" [NN *Correspondence* 140].) Melville's English contemporaries commonly regarded the novel as a vehicle for empathy and community formation. In his preface to the 1848 *Dombey and Son,* Dickens expressed the hope that his readers would have been brought together into a real extended family through their shared grief over Paul Dombey's fictive death. But Melville much more characteristically envisions the novelist as an affronter, a self asserted over against collectivities and collective understandings—"the man who, like Russia or the British Empire, declares himself a sovereign nature (in himself) amid the powers of heaven, hell, and earth," as he writes in a letter of 1851 (186). No wonder his former admirers found his most ambitious work intolerably aggressive—as Evert Duyckinck did when he complained of *Moby-Dick*'s "piratical running down of creeds."

"I will lift my hand in fury, for am I not struck?" This biblically cadenced sentence from *Pierre; or, the Ambiguities* could be taken to be the motto of both the Melvillean agent, the enraged one who would strike a blow, and the Melvillean author, who lifts his hand to write out of energies not wholly unrelated. But once the insistence of the aggressive is acknowledged, the question presents itself of what aggression means for Melville: what is it about this drive that makes it the object of such insistent attention? No single answer will help much with this question. An adequate response will have to understand that many factors contribute to determining this meaning, factors converging and interacting in often-obscure proportions and combinations. This essay will survey only a few of the components of Melvillean aggression, and it will treat even those in a sketchy, (I hope) suggestive, but certainly not authoritative fashion. But with these disclaimers made, we can still say with Ishmael: "Let us try."

What is the imaginative attraction of aggression for Melville? What freight does this instinct carry to make him give it such pride of place? A first reply might be that aggression interests Melville as an elemental fact of life. Konrad Lorenz, for many years the premier interpreter of aggression for Western audiences, regarded it as a fundamental constituent of all animal life, and Melville, we could argue, shares his sense that this (in one way) scandalous phenomenon is in another sense the great given of natural existence. Some of the great scenes of aggression in Melville—the powerful chapter "Stubb Kills a Whale" in *Moby-Dick,* for instance—image bloodthirsty assault in terms of the primitive drama of the hunting instinct. The cook Fleece can preach to the sharks that "if you gobern de shark in you, why den you be angel; for all angel is not'ing more dan de shark well goberned" (NN *MD* 295), but his appeal to a higher civilization fails to halt their "woraciousness." Their violence is "natur, and can't be helped"—a "natur," Melville regularly suggests, that makes sharks paradigmatic of other animal species, humankind included. When severe self-transcendence does appear in Melville's pages, Melville is always attentive to the aggression that continues to shadow such virtue, if in displaced forms. Pacifists or renouncers of aggression in the human realm, Melville's Nantucket Quakers are therefore all the more aggressive in the whale hunt, the activity into which they have rechanneled this primitive impulse: "some of these same Quakers are the most sanguinary of all sailors and whale-hunters. They are fighting Quakers; they are quakers with a vengeance" (73). Pierre's assault on the worldly wise trimming of Reverend Falsgrave when he dedicates himself to taking guidance only from "God Himself" is known to this hero as an act of pure high-mindedness, but to Melville as an act of moral aggression: an "act of wanton aggression upon sentiments and opinions now forever left in the rear."

But if it has the interest of a primary force, however unsuccessfully dis-owned, the antagonistic as Melville envisions it also has more particularized contents built into it, contents with meanings more narrowly cultural in scope. For one thing, aggression is clearly connected in its Melvillean formu-lation with the energies of the prophetic. Prophecy, that self-inflated and de-nunciatory speech that bears witness to the Truth against the Truth's lapsed adherents, is in essence an antagonistic mode, a kind of meeting place of speaking and aggression. "Arise, go to Nineveh, that great city, and cry against it; for their wickedness has come up before me," the word of the Lord tells Jonah, Melville's favorite of biblical prophets. As I have argued elsewhere, the prophetic model of selfhood—strongly revived in the more radical strains of Protestantism and reasserted again in their legatee romanticism—offered a highly powerful plan of identity in antebellum American culture, where it served as the chief source of self-conception and self-empowerment for in-dividualists and originals of all sorts. Examples of real nineteenth-century American selves organized around the figure of the prophet include Melville's literary contemporaries Whitman and Jones Very (who thought he was the messiah); religious contemporaries like Joseph Smith, bearer of the revelation of the *Book of Mormon,* and Frank Lloyd Wright's emigrant Welsh grandfather, a fundamentalist preacher whose personal motto was "TRUTH AGAINST THE WORLD"; and political contemporaries like Captain John Brown, the divinely appointed assailant of slavery of whom Thoreau wrote "when a man stands up serenely against the condemnation and vengeance of mankind . . . even though he were of late the vilest murderer, who has settled that matter with himself,—the spectacle is a sublime one." Aggression as Melville conceives it is often informed by a specifically prophetic understanding of antagonism's meaning, and for Melville aggression has the attraction of this privileged mode of being. Melville's Ahab would strike through the mask; his Pierre vows, "From all idols I tear all veils"; his Lear "the frantic King tears off the mask and speaks the sane madness of vital truth": the violence they intend is the violence of apocalypse, that rending or violation of a surface that allows a hidden reality to appear. "Delight is to him—a far, far upward, and inward delight—who against the proud commodores of this earth, ever stands forth his own inexorable self. . . . Delight is to him, who gives no quarter in the truth, and kills, burns, and destroys all sin though he pluck it out from under the robes of Senators and Judges" (NN *MD* 48): Father Mapple's hero is what Carlyle called the hero as prophet, the man whose ruthless oppositional violence—like John Brown's—is the very enactment of his divine election.

But if aggression is involved with issues of prophecy in Melville, it is also linked to issues of gender, specifically to the problem of being a man. Aggression is always a man's impulse in Melville: his few women characters throw no harpoons and rend no veils. More radically, the aggression of Melville's characters is made virtually synonymous with their manhood, is what makes them men. The otherwise rather quiescent White-Jacket comes to murderous life in the moment when he feels Captain Claret threatening what he calls his "man's manhood." The offense of flogging the Captain would visit on him lies not in its physical pain or social humiliation but in its threat to this citadel of gender security, and White-Jacket's preemptive aggression—his plan to knock the Captain overboard—means to prove that this core "manhood" cannot be touched: "No, I felt my man's manhood so bottomless within me, that no word, no blow, no scourge of Captain Claret could cut me deep enough for that." Aggression here comes out of a man's manhood and in turn strives to establish that man's manhood as beyond threat. The same scenario is at work in *Moby-Dick*. Ahab is turned into a major or titanic aggressor by the loss of a "living member" that his early, more minor aggressions have provoked: having sought "with a six inch blade to reach the fathom-deep life of the whale," Ahab has undergone a symbolic (and oddly pastoral) castration—"then it was, that suddenly sweeping his sickle-shaped lower jaw beneath him, Moby Dick had reaped away Ahab's leg, as a mower a blade of grass in the field." (Moby Dick performs the "cut" Captain Claret only threatened.) This wound to his manhood generates the aggression that is then a means for manhood—or at least parity of manly power—to be restored. "I now prophesy that I will dismember my dismemberer," Ahab vows, baring the masculine competitiveness that impels his assault.

In one sense, Melville's association of aggression with masculinity expresses a commonplace now elevated to scientific "truth." Studies recently popularized in the United States claim that the same hormone that produces masculine properties in the unsexed fetus also produce aggressive self-assertion; and Ahab can now be diagnosed as an early victim—now that masculinity is discussed as a disease—of what the *New York Times* has taught us to call "testosterone poisoning." Melville's associations of manliness and aggression also of course look toward a Freudian model of the masculine self, built at the troubled junction of phallic self-assertion and the castration anxieties that attend it. But my impression is that manly aggression takes on its Melvillean prominence not because of some eternal biological or psychological linkage of the two terms but for reasons more specifically cultural and historical. Manly aggression's salience in Melville, as I read it, intimately reflects the way the term "man" is being constituted in the culture of Melville's time.

A digression will help here. The most revolutionizing work that has been done on mid-nineteenth-century American culture in the last ten or twelve years has been the study of the cultural construction of "woman's sphere." This history has taught us that the rise of a new middle-class social order based on the separation of a work now performed outside the home and a domestic life now freed from productive functions traveled together with the articulation of a new normative definition of "woman's" proper character, a definition that helped stabilize a larger social model on the basis of individually embraced gender roles. Within this ideological construction, a correctly formed "womanly" self is associated with leisure or exemption from physical labor, with privacy and domestic enclosure, with piety, and with the work of instilling appropriate values in children's minds, child rearing now becoming in a newly exclusive sense a *mother's* work. But to guarantee these outcomes, the middle-class domestic model of a "feminine" self prescribed a prior organization of that self's elemental energies, not least its energies of rage. The popular antebellum domestic texts that disseminated this ideal make clear that the "womanly" self is founded through a primal proscription of anger and aggression, whose energies are then rerouted into the authority systems that forbid them. Ellen Montgomery, the heroine of Susan Warner's best-selling novel *The Wide, Wide World* (a book exactly contemporaneous with *Moby-Dick*), begins like Ahab by experiencing an outrageous loss—because of her father's lost lawsuit, her mother and father are going to leave her and move to Europe. This trauma threatens to throw the child into that combination of grief and rage that Warner calls "temper." But the instant she begins to experience "temper," it is made clear to her that she must not have such feelings: if you do not compose yourself, Ellen's ailing mother tells her, I shall get sicker and die. Utterly forbidden to express her rage in the form of rage— Ellen's plight is that her life is always provoking and that she must never be provoked—Ellen learns to accept the authority of her forbidders and to re-direct her thwarted emotional energies into the psychic underwriting of their authority. As this conversion of rebelliousness into inwardly authoritative moral imperative becomes habitual, Ellen becomes "herself"—becomes the perfect sharer, that is, of her mother's pious beliefs and the perfect practitioner of approved housewifely ways. She becomes, we might say, aggressively well-behaved—the form of aggression proper for a girl. The Uncle Tom of Harriet Beecher Stowe's 1852 best-seller *Uncle Tom's Cabin,* a male only by biology, shows a self composed on identical terms. Under the brutal fist of this book's most manly character and chief aggressor, Simon Legree, Uncle Tom might be tempted to fight back, as Frederick Douglass would. But the very prospect of resistance leads him (like Ellen) to feel an authority in whose name he must deny himself such self-assertion: the Christian rule that one must love one's enemy and return good to his evil. By obeying this principle, by reinvesting his thwarted aggression in the affirmation of its law, he becomes a male incarna-tion of the ideal female self of mid-nineteenth-century domestic ideology: the self as true believer, self-denier, loving servant, and physical nonresister.

The construction of the term "woman" in mid-nineteenth-century middle-class ideology has now been extensively studied by historians and literary critics alike. But what has been much less studied—although David Leverenz's *Manhood and the American Renaissance* has opened the way—is the fact that the normalization of this definition of "woman" occurred not by itself but in conjunction with a parallel ideological reconstruction of the term "man"—the social dissemination of a complementary masculine ideal that would produce the entrepreneurial, economically competitive, achievement-oriented "man" that is nineteenth-century middle-class culture's counterpart for the pious do-mestic "woman." For this "man," self-assertion and the drive to realize self-erected goals are as proper as self-denial and service are to his complementary "woman"; and for the development of these traits a different founding plan of the self is required. All the social pedagogues of middle-class manhood of this time stress that manly character formation requires the tolerance, even encouragement, of the aggression forbidden to women: in its primal scene the manly self is taught that submission to authority is the great forbidden thing and is asked to find its identity in an aggressive resistance to authority's claims. "He who would be a man, must be a non-conformist," Emerson writes in "Self-Reliance"; manhood is not something one has or is but something one establishes, through self-assertion against authoritative communal ways. Lydia Sigourney's much-reprinted domestic manual *Letters to Mothers* (1838) gives clear advice on how mothers should "observe"—for which we can read "produce"—the difference between their boy and girl children:

> In the discipline of sons, mothers need a double portion of the wisdom that is from above. Let them ever keep in view the different spheres allotted to the sexes. What they blame as obstinacy, may be that firmness, and fixedness of purpose, which will hereafter be needed to overcome the obstacles of their adventurous course. . . . The mother, who in the infancy of her children, puts in the arms of the girl a doll, and patiently endures the noise from the hammer of the boy-baby, conforms to the difference and the destination which has been marked on them by Creating Wisdom.

Hammers are for boys what dolls are for girls: the tools that will train them for their respective careers by exercising the requisite emotional aptitudes—in her case, motherlove and the will to nurture; in his, self-assertion, obstinacy, and the will to pound. Frederick Douglass's *Narrative* (1845) shows a real historical self understanding itself on those culturally sponsored terms. In Douglass's account his slavery ends not so much when he escapes to the North (the technical end of his bondage) as at the earlier moment when he physically resists the tyrannical Mr. Covey. This "resistance," Douglass says, "revived within me a sense of my own manhood" and marks the point where "a slave was made a man." Here again manhood is not a given but something that must be established, and established through acts of aggression against whatever would command one to obey.

From even so sketchy an account it will be clear that Melvillean aggression has everything in common with this socially mandated model of masculinity: a figure like Ahab, the purest of Melvillean aggressors, shows the male self of mid-nineteenth-century ideology brought to something like apocalyptic expression. What Ahab is, in the ideal self he so strenuously strives to embody, is an achiever: a person who drives himself toward his goals with unswervingly directed energies, and who feels it his moral duty to tolerate no obstructions to these drives. "The path to my fixed purpose is laid with iron rails, whereon my soul is grooved to run. . . . Naught's an obstacle, naught's an angle to the iron way!" exclaims this prize pupil of the Lydia Signorney school of male obstinacy. The outrage that fuels this achieveristic overdrive is, really, less that he has been castrated than that something has tried to delimit this ideally infinite drive of will: "How can the prisoner reach outside except by thrusting through the wall? To me, the white whale is that wall, shoved near to me," Ahab wails in

"The Quarter-Deck," identifying the whale's injury with incarcerating restriction or constraint. Bent on such achievement and on overcoming such restriction, the way this self too proposes to establish itself is through an act of resistance: an immense discharge of aggression aimed to obliterate whatever would set limits to its power. "He piled upon the whale's white hump the sum of all the general rage and hate felt by his whole race from Adam down; and then, as if his chest had been a mortar, he burst his hot heart's shell upon it" (NN *MD* 184). Melville writes in truly astonishing figures of this manly resister, who is himself the bomb that he would throw.

If my reasoning here is correct, it would suggest that Melville's heightened interest in aggression has as one of its occasions the pressure on gender roles that attended the institution of a new social formation in the antebellum decades, the social order based on entrepreneurialism and professional achieverism on the one hand and enclosed domestic leisure on the other. That order, however obliquely engaged, is one referent of Melville's imagining of aggressive masculinity: I share David Leverenz's sense that Melville like many of his contemporaries addresses this larger social reality not directly but at the level of the men's and women's "personal" lives it mandated. If this is so, we could now ask, how does Melville stand toward this contemporaneous figure of masculinity so centrally founded on aggressive drives?

Melville is, it must first be said, no outsider to this conception. The most egregiously ambitious of antebellum American writers, Melville knows the psychodrama of unlimited self-assertion with the intimacy of one fully enlisted in it. In his work, further, Melville to a remarkable extent enters into such masculinity's self-conceptions. It is the nature of this model of selfhood to aggrandize itself; and in his heroic phase at least Melville aggrandizes his self-aggrandizers, confers upon them the dignity of mighty powers and woes. Nevertheless, part of the interest of this aspect of Melville's work is that, without ceasing to be deeply and even tormentedly involved in it, Melville also uses his fiction to plot the inner workings of the manly aggression syndrome and to chart its psychic strains.

To develop this case very briefly: as Melville understands it, aggression always intends a demonstration of power in a scene of power rivalry. "The man who, like Russia and the British Empire, declares himself a sovereign nature (in himself) . . . may perish," Melville writes Hawthorne in April 1851, "but so long as he exists he insists upon treating with all Powers on an equal basis." This self's assertion is an assertion of sovereignty over against an array of forces that would otherwise "make me tributary"; and the implication here—that aggression is the drive to secure personal autonomy or nonsubjugation—is consistent with Melville's other work. Ahab sees in Moby Dick "outrageous strength"—an unbearable superiority of power—that requires him, in his hunt and in his general defiance, to "dispute its unconditional, unintegral mastery in me." White-Jacket's aggression, similarly, is an aggression against an intolerable omnipotence: the monopoly of force that allows the Captain to visit his authority on a flogged man independent of his will.

What such scenarios imply, however, is that aggression's assertion of the self's manly sovereignty always operates in a situation of real or feared inferiority, and so that aggression is born out of a consciousness of a humiliating insufficiency of force. "If any of those other Powers choose to withhold certain secrets, let them," Melville's Imperial Self letter continues; "that does not impair my sovereignty in myself; that does not make me tributary." But the very denial expresses a felt threat of impairment, which his assertion of sovereignty can only be a denial of. Ahab's monomaniacal or projectile self is born together with the consciousness of himself as wholly vulnerable: when the hundred-foot-long whale attacks the bearer of the six-inch blade, an almost grotesque imparity of power gets enacted on his fragile, violable body, a scene he would undo by reversal in his intended revenge. To go to the bottommost motivation of Ahab's quest—to the Roman baths under the Hotel de Cluny metaphorically visited in chapter 41 of *Moby-Dick*—is to find as our forefather a deposed king or God in ruins: the deepest of human consciousnesses, Melville implies, is that man is not the sovereign he feels he should be, and this consciousness impels Ahab's drive to enact mastery through aggression. Billy Budd—admittedly the bearer of another model of manliness than the one under discussion here—has his aggression too born out of humiliating insufficiency. "Speak, man! Speak! Defend yourself!" Captain Vere exhorts him, already linking the speech he solicits with a crisis of exposure or undefendedness. But the consciousness of his need for defense blocks Billy's speech, hideously augmenting his felt insufficiency. Displaying his "vocal impediment," the gagging Billy exhibits himself to himself and others as a "startling impotence"; and here again the aggravated consciousness of undefendedness, physical impairment, embodiedness itself, and bodily impotence triggers aggression's counteractive blow.

Manly self-assertion, the frantic compulsion to demonstrate manly power, Melville implies, is not the expression of the conviction of such power but an attempt to erase the self's real conviction of its power's limits or lack. If this is so, Melville suggests by extension, the cultural system of entrepreneurial and high-achiever-oriented manhood—the system that invites a man to show he is a man through acts of individualistic self-assertion—works by inducing a sense of the given or natural self as a shameful insufficiency, an insufficiency culturally proposed forms of self-assertion then offer to repair. Having assented to have his manhood established within a scheme that mandates infinitude of power, Ahab is made to find his necessarily finite given, natural, bodily self an intolerable humiliation: it is his expectation of omnipotence, quite as much as the Whale, that makes his limited power feel like a shameful impotence. The aggressive drive toward great accomplishment offers, he thinks, to undo this shame; but in fact it renews it—through his attack on Moby Dick Ahab reexperiences his original helplessness (in "The Chase—First Day" Ahab's assault "placed him all alive and helpless in the very jaws he hated")— and this renewed feeling of powerlessness fuels his renewed aggressions. In such imagings, Melville figures the new social system of his time as driven by an interiorized inward drama in which a culturally induced sense of personal insufficiency produces a hunger for self-assertion, which in turn revives the sense of insufficiency, which in turn requires yet more self-assertion, thus guaranteeing the continuous or never-arriving drive of energy, to all appearances wholly inwardly impelled, that makes this system work.

The psychocultural logic of nineteenth-century American individualism is not the whole story of Melvillean aggression. But it is a striking part of that story, and it has much to teach us at our current stage of knowledge. For the now wholly successful excavation of women's sphere in mid-nineteenth-century America has created the odd impression that there is no comparably interesting men's history to tell. But the masculinity that the nineteenth-century middle-class world made normative was as much a cultural and historical product as the feminine self of that time; this "normal man" too had to be both ideologically projected and brought home to actual selves in their acculturation; and this ideal manliness too, we should now admit, must have brought the actual human subjects who engaged it a very mixed yield of psychic gains and tolls as part of the "selfhood" it offered. The inner history of this historical masculine self, with its interlinked glooms and glories, joyous assertions and mandatory anxieties, is a subject on which Melville sheds particularly strong light. One hundred years after his death, it is this story that his fables of aggression most excitingly bring to life.

10

"Counter Natures in Mankind":
Hebraism and Hellenism in *Clarel*

SHIRLEY M. DETTLAFF

A little more than halfway through Herman Melville's *Clarel* (1876), when the pilgrims visit the monastery of Mar Saba in the Judean desert, the bewildered title character attends a masque in which the Wandering Jew, portrayed by one of the monks, pours forth all the agony in his soul; no sooner has the doleful monk-actor left the stage than a cheerful Greek traveler is heard extolling the joys of life in a pagan song. The sudden juxtaposition of these opposites causes Clarel to question

> if in frames of thought
> And feeling, there be right and wrong;
> Whether the lesson Joel taught
> Confute what from the marble's caught
> In sylvan sculpture—Bacchant, Faun,
> Or shapes more lax by Titian drawn.
> Such counter natures in mankind—
> Mole, bird, not more unlike we find:
> Instincts adverse, nor less how true
> Each to itself. What clew, what clew? (NN *Clarel* 3.20.32–42)

What clue, indeed? Answering this question becomes a crucial problem for the main character in *Clarel*.[1] Although the surface story of *Clarel* features conflicting religious views that bewilder the title character during his pilgrimage to the Holy Land, what Melville has Clarel and the reader gradually realize is that these debates stem from the two opposing views of human personality generally expressed in the Greco-Roman and Judeo-Christian traditions. The issue involves, in Melville's words, the "old debate" whether man is "ape or angel" (4.35.12). But there is more to it than this rather general contrast: Melville's perception and expression of this dichotomy was influenced by a theory of human personality that eighteenth-century German literary critics had developed and that eventually made its way into English literary culture. It is the human typology that Friedrich Schiller and Friedrich Schlegel had worked out independently during the late eighteenth century and that A. W. Schlegel had popularized in the early nineteenth century. It is the theory of human character that, with a slight twist, Matthew Arnold, during the time that Melville was writing *Clarel,* proposed as Hellenism and Hebraism.

CLASSICISM AND ROMANTICISM IN GERMAN LITERARY THEORY

This basic dichotomy developed in Germany out of independent and slightly different attempts to distinguish between the ancients and the moderns, distinctions that were to some extent inspired by medieval romances, Shakespearean plays, English graveyard poetry, and *Sturm und Drang* literature, much of which Melville knew and admired. These attempts began as interpretations of cultural history but broadened to include a theory of human types. In *Naive and Sentimental Poetry* (1795–96) Schiller presented the more fully developed theory, influenced by Kantian philosophy, when he described ancient poets as "naive" and modern ones as "sentimental" but changed the terms to "realist" and "idealist" when broadening the concepts to distinguish between basic human types. Developing his own similar distinction independently in a series of articles (1797–1800), Friedrich Schlegel used the terms that finally prevailed, "classic" and "romantic," although it was his brother, August Wilhelm, who codified and popularized Friedrich's ideas, along with many of his own, in the well-known and influential *Lectures on Dramatic Art and Literature* (1809–11).

Despite the differences in meaning, the antitheses of these early theorists had a certain basic similarity. Following Winckelmann's familiar but now debunked theories about Greek art, they suggested that the ancient Greeks epitomized one type of human or artist, who was then labeled as naive, realistic, or classical. A. W. Schlegel, whose version of the antithesis in *Lectures on Dramatic Art and Literature* became better known outside of Germany than Schiller's, popularized the familiar stereotype of the Greeks as representatives of classical culture who were fully realized products of nature, healthy human beings raised to feel external harmony with a beautiful, hospitable environment. With objective minds relying primarily upon the operation of the senses and the intellect, they enjoyed internal "harmony of all their faculties" and felt little self-consciousness or internal conflict. They accepted their lot in life as a part of nature and spontaneously expressed this vision in art that was sensuous, beautiful, and full of joy. A major deficiency of their outlook, Schlegel charged, however, was that it never became much more than "a refined and ennobled sensuality," the highest development of "finite nature" (24).

The other kind of human personality, the one that moved beyond man's finite nature to aspire to the infinite and appeared in the most famous literary characters of the period, was the modern, which Schiller called "sentimental" or "idealist" and the Schlegels "romantic." The product of a hostile northern climate, a highly spiritualized Christianity, and a modern civilization alienated from nature, this also-familiar stereotype was seen as a very subjective, divided being. He was torn between his senses, which seek gratification in this world, and his spiritual faculties, which long for something so far transcending the senses that it can never be attained. This *Streben nach dem Unendlichen,* a key concept of *Sturm und Drang* romanticism, propels the typical romantic quest for some unreachable goal. This heightened sense of the ideal also creates an inner discord in the modern's faculties unknown among realists or the ancients, one that is exacerbated by modern introversion and can lead to moral paralysis. Both the northern climate and Christianity have turned the attention of the modern or romantic inward, causing him to be highly reflective and, according to Schlegel, to develop an "earnestness of mind" (25), all of which qualities, for example, made Hamlet the darling of the romantics. The unbridgeable gap that the idealist perceives between what his imagination intuits and what he experiences in actuality creates a pervasive melancholy, the *Weltschmerz* of Werther, in which, as Schlegel put it, "life has become shadow and darkness" (26). This idealism is not totally negative, however, Schiller noted, since it assumes a superior concept of humanity and a more lofty ethical system. Unlike the realist who, following the rule of practical use, seeks pleasure, happiness, and well-being, the idealist, following the rule of abstract value, longs mainly for a noble heroism and freedom from physical necessity (182–83). Schiller also warned that both types can lead to exaggerated behavior: the realist can sink into coarse, mindless activity, while the idealist can become a rigid, joyless fanatic locked into and enervated by his own mental system (183–84).

Central to the thinking of these theorists is the belief that these types of personality conflict with each other and, yet, both must be combined to provide a complete definition of man. In *Naive and Sentimental Poetry* Schiller asserted that the antithesis between the naive and the sentimental is a psychological antagonism that is as old as mankind, that is "based on inner mental dispositions," and that, being nearly insurmountable, makes true communication between the two types almost impossible (176). Despite the tendency for most humans to belong to one type or another, he felt that both opposites had to be synthesized to produce the fully human person. He held out the hope that the antagonism could be overcome "in a few rare individuals who . . . always existed and always will" (176). And he suggested that in society there should be a class of humans in which both tendencies were developed "so that each would preserve the other from its own extreme" (175). It must be remembered that the aesthetics of these writers were closely related to these theories about personality types, which originated in attempts to distinguish between types of poets. Since these writers believed that the truly great poet is one who can synthesize the senses and the spirit, he must be such a person himself.

It is this theory of characterization that is often dramatized in the *Bildungs-* or *Kunstlerroman* of romantic literature. As M. H. Abrams has observed, in many of the great works of this period that dramatize this dichotomy, like *Wilhelmmeisters Lehrjahr* or *Faust,* the poet's search for identity and fulfillment involves a dialectic between the actual and ideal worlds and eventually culminates in a synthesis of the two. In the typical *Bildungsweg,* the protagonist falls from his innocent, instinctive life of the senses. Some trauma, often an unhappy love affair or death of a loved one, shocks him out of this naive unity with nature, and he enters the romantic state, one characterized by alienation, obsessive thought, interior conflict, melancholy, and unfulfilled yearning. He sets off to search for truth and for a return to this earlier paradise, but he discovers that he cannot go back and instead must struggle forward dialectically through reflection and freedom to achieve a new wholeness or reintegration. In his new, mature state he appreciates both the life of the senses and that of the spirit. It is thus that he is able to create the true art that also unites the diametrically opposed worlds of the senses and of the spirit (Abrams 217–37).

Able to operate in both worlds, the man who achieves this synthesis is not the captive of either. He is free and independent, the most noble human whose development of self transcends the antithesis of the senses and the spirit. Yet even he can never achieve perfection. A crucial point the theorists make is that in the search for the infinite there can be no attainable goal, only progress toward it. As Schiller observed in his poem "The Pilgrim," a work that Melville probably read,

> While I live is never given
>   Bridge or wave the goal to near—
> Earth will never meet the Heaven,
>   Never can the THERE be HERE! (*Poems and Ballads* 35)

But the quest is not fruitless. Also important for the romanticist, as Abrams notes, citing Faust as an example, is that the fully developed human's "triumph consists simply in the experience of sustaining a desire which never relaxes into the stasis of a finite satisfaction" (245). The great artist, then, constantly striving for the infinite, creates works that are deliberately open-ended, that suggest more to the imagination than can the tidy resolutions that appeal merely to the intellect. The ambitious but inconclusive quest is not evidence of a pessimistic naturalism; it is, instead, evidence of a tragic view of life in which the human has a lofty mental potential in his imagination and a dignity in his ability to choose that surpass the limitations of his physical being or finite mind.

Schiller and the Schlegels, who were at the center of two very powerful German literary circles, influenced other romantic authors and theorists, as well as Coleridge, Byron, Shelley, Madame de Stael, and Carlyle. These were other sources from which Melville could have encountered this dichotomy directly or indirectly before the 1860s. Although there is no external evidence that Melville studied Schiller's theory in *Naive and Sentimental Poetry,* he did, early in his career, read a great deal of Schiller. Nor do we know if Melville actually read A. W. Schlegel's *Lectures on Dramatic Art and Literature,* which was probably Schlegel's most influential work, but apparently he knew enough in 1849 to report in his journal that he had discussed "Schlegel" with George Adler. There is no doubt, however, that Melville was fascinated by those literary characters who embodied to one degree or another the spirit of what Schiller called the sentimental and Schlegel the romantic: Hamlet, Werther, Faust, Childe Harold, Teufelsdrock. And Melville's early, rather general use of this antithesis can be seen already in *Moby-Dick* and *Pierre,* for instance, in the well-known passage from "The Lee Shore" in *Moby-Dick:* "But as in landless-ness alone resides the highest truth, shoreless, indefinite as God—so, better is it to perish in that howling infinite, than be ingloriously dashed upon the lee, even if that were safety! For worm-like, then oh! who would craven crawl to land!" (107).

Melville apparently became more deeply interested in the distinction when in 1862 he read and heavily annotated Madame de Stael's *Germany,* which provides a summary of the Schlegels' dichotomy in chapter 11, "Of Classic and Romantic Poetry." In fact, Melville checked in de Stael a key point that the Germans made, that modern writers stress the personality of the individual more than the ancients did: "In ancient times, men attended to events alone, but among the moderns character is of greater importance; and that uneasy reflection, which, like the vulture of Prometheus, often totally devours us, would have been folly amid circumstances and relations so clear and decided, as they existed in the civil and social state of the ancients" (Cowen 52). His reading of Schiller's poetry at the same time also had an impact on his imagi-nation.

But the culminating influence was probably Matthew Arnold's. Melville's in-tensive reading of Arnold in the 1860s and early 1870s, the gestation period for *Clarel,* exposed him to Arnold's version of that earlier German dichotomy. Arnold's antithesis was heavily indebted to Schiller and to the Schlegels, as well as to Heinrich Heine, from whom he took the terms "Hebraism" and "Hel-lenism."[2] Arnold used the dichotomy but not the terms in *Essays and Criticism,* which Melville read and carefully annotated. Melville surely recognized the distinction and its relationship to the earlier theory. Also, Arnold was popu-larizing the distinction and the terms in a series of essays that were eventually collected in the famous *Culture and Anarchy.* Melville's use of the dichotomy may have been influenced by one of the essays that was originally entitled "Anarchy and Authority":

Both Hellenism and Hebraism arise out of the wants of human nature, and address themselves to satisfying those wants. But their methods are so dif-ferent, they lay stress on such different points, and call into being by their respective disciplines such different activities, that the face which human nature presents when it passes from the hands of one of them to those of the other is no longer the same. To get rid of one's ignorance, to see things as they are, and by seeing them as they are to see them in their beauty, is the simple and attractive ideal which Hellenism holds out before human nature; and from the simplicity and charm of this ideal, Hellenism, and human life in the hands of Hellenism, is invested with a kind of aerial ease, clearness, and radiancy; they are full of what we call sweetness and light. Difficulties are kept out of view, and the beauty and rationality of the ideal have all our thoughts . . . . But there is a saying which I have heard attributed to Mr. Carlyle about Socrates,—a very happy saying, whether it is really Mr. Carlyle's or not,—which excellently marks the essential point in which Hebraism differs from Hellenism. "Socrates," this saying runs, "is terribly at ease in Zion." Hebraism—and here is the source of its wonderful strength— has always been severely preoccupied with a severe sense of the impossibility of being at ease in Zion; of the difficulties which oppose themselves to man's pursuit or attainment of that perfection of which Socrates talks so hopefully, and, as from this point of view one might almost say, so glibly. (802–03)[3]

However, it would be more accurate to suggest that, rather than being influenced by Arnold, Melville was inspired by Arnold's updating of the then old German dichotomy to present his own modification of it in *Clarel*. What Arnold was trying to achieve in his prose criticism of modern English culture, Melville decided to do for American and European culture, only better—that is, in poetry and according to his own version of the old antithesis.

"HEBREW" AND "HELLENE" IN *CLAREL*

The setting of *Clarel*, the Holy Land, where ancient Jewish history has been overlaid by centuries of Greek influence, offered Melville the perfect opportunity to use this dichotomy. Palestine abounds in historical evidence of "Isaiah's dark burden, malison" (4.26.116) as well as "gay Hellene lightheartedness" (3.4.110). Melville uses Arnold's very terms early in *Clarel* when he contrasts a barren tomb with a frieze sculptured on it, suggesting that both the decoration and the sepulcher represent "contraries in old belief— / Hellenic cheer, Hebraic grief" (1.28.33–34). Influenced by a theory of art that stresses the conflict and union of opposites, Melville uses the dichotomy not only to align the characters in opposing groups but to provide a pattern for their interplay. It suggests literary models and rationales for his characters. It supplies thematic as well as scenic contrasts. But, most important, it provides a kind of dialectical pattern for the story of the title character.

First, the Hebraic/Hellenic dichotomy determines character alignment in the story. Melville deliberately highlights the distinction between these "counter natures" and also gives both a mythical dimension when at Mar Saba he juxtaposes the Wandering Jew's complaint and the Greek Merchant's lyric. This pointed contrast suggests that one of Melville's narrative strategies is to confront the pilgrims touring Judea with the desert and all that it represents in order to give them a kind of reality test, during which they reveal their personality type. Regardless of their ethnic origin, characters can be considered "Hellenic" if, to follow Arnold's criterion, they manage to make themselves at ease in Judea, or "Hebraic" if they do not.[4] In responding to the desert, the characters also reveal their moral status, for the issue is not just the identification of personality types but the question of whether one type of life is superior to the other.

According to the paean to a Saturnian Golden Age sung by the Merchant from Lesbos, Melville's Hellenism is roughly the same as the German notion of classicism, a joyful naturalism which extols the worldly, focusing on the bright side of life rather than on the dark. It is represented in the mythic Golden Age, the prelapsarian childhood of the race, an Eden of agrarian peace and harmony, of glorious sensuousness, of culture and "gracious talk" with the gods. Those characters in *Clarel* who can be considered Hellenic, to one degree or another, try to create this world about them. They fail Melville's reality test of the Judean desert by attempting to ignore, trivialize, or escape what it represents: evil or nonbeing, the physical, moral, and intellectual negatives that constitute the dark underside of human existence. Like Schiller, Melville reveals attitudes toward them that vary from bemused tolerance to outright contempt. If they are very young, like Glaucon or the Cypriote, their innocent, mindless enjoyment of life stems from the charming, natural ebullience of youth that as yet has had little or no experience of physical or moral evil. But the older Hellenes, who Melville thinks should know better, have deliberately and thus reprehensibly prolonged their moral childhood. Whenever some evil looms into view, they blindly flee it and create only an environment of creature comforts or intellectual certainty. Sensualists such as the Greek Banker, the Merchant of Lesbos, and the Lyonese Jew have created for themselves false Edens in which financial success, convivial gatherings, or hedonistic delights provide a sense of security and block out painful realities. More intellectual Hellenes like Margoth or Derwent create an Arcadia of the mind, Margoth putting his faith in the scientific method, and the Anglican clergyman glossing over the troublesome nineteenth-century doubts about Christianity with an optimistic casuistry.

Even those characters who are ethnically Jewish may reveal a Hellenic temperament, as is the case with the Lyonese, Margoth, Agar, and Ruth. The two women, for instance, neither understand nor sympathize with Nathan's Zionist vision and shrink from the Judaic wasteland. They try, futilely, with potted plants and flowers, with the semblance of family life, to recreate the American homeland, a snug domestic retreat from unwelcome reality. Whether they obscure disturbing realities with food, drink, sex, fellowship, domesticity, success, or religious sophistry, these Hellenes do not have the type of human nature or strength of character to open their eyes to what the desert represents. Melville even extends his character test to the reader of the poem, warning that he may wish to turn back from the desert along with the Syrian Banker (2.13.112–19) or skip a disturbing description (2.35.38–41). Melville understands and appreciates this life but considers it to be limited, agreeing with Schiller in the poem "Guides of Life: The Beautiful and the Sublime," that one may enjoy the beauty of the physical world and yet not grant it the respect that one reserves for a higher experience, the sublime.

It is in his depiction of the Hebraic character that Melville is most indebted to the Hebraic/Hellenic dichotomy. This is the temperament that Melville does respect highly, the embodiment of the sentimental or romantic character whose *Streben nach dem Unendlichen* Melville was describing when he grouped Leopardi, Obermann, and St. Teresa as "all of earnest mind, / Unworldly yearners" (3.1.13–16). He is represented to a great extent by the Wandering Jew, a figure of mythic resonance whose vision is dark, otherworldly, and sublime. Early in *Clarel* (1.13.112–16) Melville recounts his version of the legend of Cartaphilus. In the masque at Mar Saba he dramatizes and renders more generally symbolic the Wandering Jew's anguish: his fall from grace, his guilt and alienation, his search for rest and peace.[5] The key point in Melville's depiction of Cartaphilus and the Hebrew in general is that both have been cast out of Eden and yet strive for the infinite with a "longing which cannot be uttered."[6] Since Melville's Hebrew character has high expectations of life, he is especially sensitive to evils that he encounters. When this type of character is thwarted by some catastrophe of fate and is traumatically shocked, he does not seek relief in the Hellenic joys of life. Goaded, like the German romantic, to search for a better world that his imagination suggests should exist somewhere, he embarks upon the quest to discover some explanation or justification for this evil as well as some respite from the alienation and pain he suffers. One type of Hebrew striver in *Clarel,* the religious zealot—like Nathan, Nehemiah, the Syrian monk, and Brother Salvaterra—having abandoned worldly joys and undertaken the journey, achieves some degree of peace through espousing one of the great religions. However, the more truly Hebraic personality finds institutionalized religion another Hellenic delusion and avoids that, too; he cannot be "at ease in Zion." He is like Moses Mendelssohn, who, according to Rolfe, "though his honest heart was scourged / By doubt Judaic, never laid / His burden at Christ's door" (2.22.86–88). This Hebraic doubter, a Byronic exaggeration of the type—represented also in Celio, Mortmain, Agath, and Ungar—is torn by disbelief and wracked by despair or anger. Like the Byronic hero, he wanders about the world, unable to find meaning or rest, gradually wearing himself out physically but never relaxing his *Streben nach dem Unendlichen* or lightening his *Weltschmerz.*

One specific way in which Melville develops this difference between Hebraism and Hellenism is through the Pilgrim / Tourist dichotomy presented in the first two cantos of the poem. Melville twice warns Clarel, as well as the reader, that a tour of the Holy Land requires a proper attitude, that of the Hebraic pilgrim, who realizes that the journey is a spiritual one like those taken by the great saints rather than the sightseeing trip taken by a Hellenic tourist. A fellow American traveler returning from Jerusalem points out that his countrymen especially need to put aside their provincial attitudes and adopt "the Semitic reverent mood, / Unworldly" (1.1.93–94), to interpret Palestine correctly, opening their minds to a more profound reality, which they are unaccustomed to and indeed repelled by. For, as the American traveler warns Clarel in what is a key line for understanding Clarel's actions in the poem, "To avoid the deep saves not from the storm" (1.1.99).

A poem entitled "Judaea," which Clarel discovers in his room in Jerusalem, expands on this point, contrasting what the worldly traveler, the tourist, expects from the Holy Land with what the "palmer," the true pilgrim, seeks. The shallow sightseer concentrates on "Sychem grapes," Tabor's garlands, "Sharon's rose," and "Solomon's Song," fabled tourist attractions that appeal to the superficial fancy, whatever diverts and cheers the soul. The true pilgrim, with his more profound imagination, "clings / About the precincts of Christ's tomb" (1.2.119–20) and brings with him out of Judea only a dusty palm. The pilgrim focuses on what for Melville was the most important symbol of the Christian story for modern man: the Crucifixion.

Imagination, earnest ever,
Recalls the Friday far away,
Re-lives the crucifixion day—
The passion and its sequel proves,
Sharing the three pale Marys' frame;
Through the eclipse with these she moves
Back to the house from which they came
To Golgotha. O empty room,
O leaden heaviness of doom—
O cowering hearts, which sore beset
Deem vain the promise now, and yet
Invoke him who returns no call;
And fears for more that may befall.
O terror linked with love which cried:
"Art gone? is't o'er? and crucified?" (1.3.181–96)

Of the great Christian mysteries, the Crucifixion and its immediate aftermath of doubt for Christ's followers are central for the sincere modern Christian who realizes that Christ has died again in the contemporary world, this time because of rationalism and science. When the imagination grasps this point, worldly existence loses its meaning, human death becomes terrifying, and the human has no recourse in dealing with evil. The modern Hebraic character is frustrated because his intense spiritual longings have lost their object and he cannot find another. This search is the real quest, the true pilgrimage that Melville is suggesting in *Clarel* as opposed to the conventional tour of the Holy Land.

The Hebrew doubters are on such a pilgrimage: not only have they, like Christ's followers immediately after his crucifixion, begun to doubt Christ, but like Christ they have taken up their cross and are struggling on the *Via Crucis* toward their own inevitable crucifixion. The Wandering Jew is a dark version of or mythic alternative to Christ, whose suffering and alienation may never reach the ultimate reward of reunion with God. As much as Melville admires these Hebraic doubters, he agrees with the German literary theorists and Arnold that they represent only one side of human nature and that characters who synthesize both the Hebraic and the Hellenic are the preferred, if rare, ideal. Obsessed with the dark side of life, the Hebraic doubters lose sight of its bright side and do not transcend and judge it from a tragic perspective, affirming its validity while still aware of its transience and triviality. Just as he had in his earlier works, Melville believed, like Schiller, that such a synthesis must be achieved, that psychological growth is dialectical. But his idea of the synthesis is not like that of some German romantics, a reintegration with nature or any other exterior forces. Unlike Matthew Arnold's synthesis, where balance is maintained by a movement away from the extremes toward the middle, Melville's more heroic idea requires an experience and balancing of the opposite extremes. Most humans cannot achieve this synthesis, perhaps because they lack a sufficiently strong, imaginative personality that can recognize the simultaneous validity of opposites and, what is even more difficult to do without losing their balance, develop an ethical system based upon such a dualistic vision.

In the divine Rama appears such a balance of the Hebraic and the Hellenic, of the classic with the romantic. According to the narrator, mortals with the divine heritage of Rama can experience crippling encounters with evil and still transcend it:

> Though the black frost nip, though the white frost chill,
> Nor white frost nor the black may kill
> The patient root, the vernal sense
> Surviving hard experience
> As grass the winter. (1.32.20–24)

Being both divine and human, spiritual and sensuous,

> Theirs be the thoughts that dive and skim,
> Theirs the spiced tears that overbrim,
> And theirs the dimple and lightsome whim. (1.32.35–37)

Potential guides or models for Clarel who have achieved some kind of Rama-like synthesis include Derwent, Vine, and Rolfe. However, Derwent's rather mindless, superficial attempt to achieve a middle way, which parallels Arnold's Hellenic latitudinarianism, while tempting to Clarel, proves ultimately unsatisfactory. And Vine's synthesis, which errs in the opposite direction, also fails Clarel. Vine represents the second-rate artist of the mere fancy, whose literary taste escapes to the romance of the past and the beauty of nature. An introvert of great personal beauty and sensuousness, he has learned that hedonism and aesthetic experiences do not quench his longing for the infinite. His similarities to Hawthorne have been much commented upon, but he also fits the more general romantic convention of the graveyard solitary and man of sensibility. Some tragic experience has made him a "funeral man," who is first introduced, significantly, reclining before and meditating upon a tomb, brooding about fate and death. Suffering and haunted by the tragic vision, he balances it, somewhat, with an appreciation of beauty, countering the void, not too effectively it turns out, with the sensuous and the symbolic. He has taken the dialectical journey, having been a "Sybarite" and now having become, for some reason that we are not told, a "Carthusian," yet

> Not beauty might he all forget,
> The beauty of the world, and charm:
> He prized it though it scarce might warm. (1.29.40–42)

The revelation of the moral weakness behind his reserve suggests the deficiencies of his synthesis as well.

Most closely resembling the Rama figure, however, is Rolfe, to a certain extent Melville's idealized self-portrait, but more significantly his depiction of the great artist. He possesses not the mere fancy, but a powerful imagination that can actively unite the past and the present as well as intuit the sublime in nature. And he possesses the great intellect that Melville considered crucial for the pursuit of truth. Rolfe has achieved a truer synthesis of the Hebraic and the Hellenic than has Derwent or Vine. Like the Hellenes, he has a very genial personality and is an active participant in the world, an erudite raconteur and persuasive debater whose search for the truth has made him knowledgeable about man's outer life, about the social, political, intellectual, and religious aspects of man's history. But all his knowledge of the world has not satisfied an Hebraic *Streben nach dem Unendlichen,* perhaps some explanation for all the evil that his study and personal experience of mankind have revealed to him. Despite his intellectual doubt, he continues his quest for truth, a *Kunstlerweg,* with that "earnestness of mind" that Schlegel stressed, apparently aware that although the goal may be unattainable, one must never relax "into the stasis of finite satisfaction." Not only does his personality represent a synthesis, but as an artist he tries to unite disparate experiences. Like the poet in Melville's poem "In a Garret," who desires to "grapple from Art's deep / One dripping trophy!" Rolfe has returned to the Holy Land

> where evermore
> Some lurking thing he hoped to gain—

> Slip quite behind the parrot-lore
> Conventional, and—what attain? (1.31.35–38)

Probing beyond official, sanitized versions of reality, he is the one who often tells stories about other characters' disastrous encounters with fate. Despite his awareness of evil, he is broadly tolerant of people and rejoices in convivial social situations, wholeheartedly joining in the drinking, the song, and even the whimsical talk. When another pilgrim overemphasizes the dark side of reality, Rolfe will contribute a story or comment that rights the balance (2.19.1–16). Rolfe's extremes in behavior reveal that "earnestness and levity" can be united in a "mind / Poised at self-center and mature" (4.3.124–25). Rolfe represents Melville's version of the German ideal, the free and independent, fully developed human and artist who synthesizes the Hebraic and Hellenic, the romantic and the classic, with a definite leaning toward the former. These are the reasons he is the mature model for Clarel, the tyro romantic or modern man of sensibility.

Beyond aligning most of the characters, the Hebraic / Hellenic dichotomy provides an adversarial pattern for the philosophical controversies about modern problems the pilgrims engage in as they travel in the desert. Representative Hebrews and Hellenes debate the issues from their respective viewpoints, the cast of minor characters changing but not the basically antithetical philosophical orientations. The latitudinarian Anglican Derwent can be trusted to argue for the Hellenic side, with the assistance of Margoth, the Merchant from Lesbos, and the Lyonese, all of whom represent well-defined and more extreme positions on the Hellenic spectrum. Speaking for various aspects of the Hebraic vision are Mortmain, Ungar, Rolfe, of course, and others.

The confrontation and alternation of the Hebraic and the Hellenic also function to control the mood of the poem. When a desolate scene or obsessed character threatens to take over, Melville introduces its opposite to remind Clarel and the reader that another choice is possible. Just before Clarel, Vine, and Nehemiah visit the Garden of Olives, the narrator answers his own question, "And wherefore by the convents be / Gardens? Ascetics roses entwine?" (1.3.1–2) by explaining that, like Christ suffering in the Garden, they "defend us from despair." Throughout the poem gardens, oases, and pastoral land punctuate the arid desert, as the pilgrims stop at the Jordan, Mar Saba, and Bethlehem while journeying in the Judean waste. Joyous or convivial episodes at these rest stops are juxtaposed with somber discussions and the deaths of Nehemiah and Mortmain.

CLAREL'S JOURNEY

The Hebraic / Hellenic dichotomy is perhaps most helpful in suggesting the form and significance of the central, if slight and somewhat confusing, story of Clarel's journey toward maturity. Melville casts Clarel as a tyro romantic and sets him on a *Bildungsweg,* during which the divinity student is tested to see which one of the "counter natures in mankind" is his own.[7] The question for Clarel at the beginning of the poem is whether or not he will become a true Hebraic pilgrim, opening his imagination to all the uncertainties that a sincere search for religious truth in the nineteenth century entails, or a Hellenic tourist, preferring merely a superficial, conventional tour of the Holy Land in which he merely exercises his fancy. The tests involve a dialectical process in which Clarel encounters Hellenic or Hebraic alternatives, not just in the intellectual discussions he hears but in his own personal life. Clarel's ultimate test, in the metaphor of the American traveler, is whether he will choose to brave the deep or try to avoid it.

During much of the poem Clarel tries to avoid it, although as a future clergyman on a trip to the Holy Land he would seem a person of Hebraic temperament. When he is first presented to the reader, Clarel is clearly portrayed as a young romantic, the contemplative solitary, in the traditions of Hamlet, Werther, the graveyard poet, and the Byronic hero. He reveals the characteristics that Schiller succinctly set forth in *Naive and Sentimental Poetry* and that Carlyle mocked in *Sartor Resartus.* In fact, the presentation of Clarel reveals all but one of the qualities of the sentimental character that Schiller saw concentrated in *Werther:* "sensitivity to nature, feeling for religion, a spirit of philosophical contemplation," "the gloomy, formless, melancholic Ossianic world," and a "tender effeminacy" (138). The one Wertherian characteristic not present in Clarel at the beginning—a "fanatically unhappy love"—does appear with full melodrama at the end of the poem. Like a graveyard poet, Clarel is first pictured in a tomblike cubicle of a Jerusalem hostel, reflecting very earnestly and rather self-consciously in the posture of the thinker brooding alone, as the last rays of the sun fade away. With features that are "pale, and all but feminine," he discontentedly questions the source of the melancholy that unexpectedly weighs down his spirit his first evening in the Holy City. Disturbed and depressed by the forbidding desert and barren city, he reflects upon their effect on the religious doubts that already plague him. "Earnest by nature" (1.1.107), Clarel is presented as an "Unworldly yearner" who opens his mind beyond book learning and society's official versions of reality to vague hints of another version of reality suggested by "nature's influx of control," even though he is made uneasy by the "clandestine" inklings, "underformings in the mind / Banked corals which ascend from far" (1.1.75–76).

Throughout his stay in Jerusalem, Clarel continues to exhibit characteristics of the tyro romantic. Like Hamlet, he is alienated, lonely, and melancholy; he is uncertain, irresolute, and passive; he is also sensitive and squeamish. Since the ruined city, with its deserted biblical landmarks, religious and cultural diversity, and commercial chicanery, has been stripped of any supernatural aura that he had associated with it, he wanders from one holy place to another, desperately hoping that one shrine or holy person will miraculously stem his increasing doubt. But he is disappointed by one false hope after another, including Nehemiah, the deluded Christian zealot who, ironically, becomes for a time his "guide." Also like the romantic hero, he is inexperienced, introverted, and full of fantasies, constantly reflecting and castigating himself. At the Church of the Holy Sepulcher Clarel's long-sustained reflection about the pilgrimages of various religions culminates in typical romantic inner conflict and self-loathing. Projecting his feeling of guilt upon the situation, he fancies that the sounds of the various religious services are curses aimed at him for his sacrilegious questioning of Christianity, and he actually flees the scene in self-condemnation.

However, Clarel's Hebraicism is superficial, more fanciful than truly imaginative. His increasing doubt opens up the "deep," and he begins to develop the imagination to see it; but he lacks the courage and resolution, the maturity and independence, the strong sense of self, to embark upon it. Because of his youth and inexperience, Clarel is naturally drawn to the more attractive and commonly accepted Hellenic attitude. Clarel unwittingly reveals his weakness when he answers Nehemiah's insistent question about the traditional Christian pilgrimage, "A pilgrim art thou? pilgrim thou?" (1.9.20), by acknowledging, "I am a traveler—no more" (1.9.28).

In key parts of the poem Melville puts Clarel in situations where he is drawn to these opposite poles, represented in Part I by Celio and Ruth. An understanding of Melville's dialectic reveals his attitude toward Clarel's behavior, showing that while Melville tempts the youth with a Hellenic alternative, here Ruth, he really expects Clarel to respond to the Hebraic or heroic alternative, as represented by Celio. Just how far Clarel has to go to become the true Hebraic doubter is suggested by Celio, whom Clarel meets while touring aimlessly with Nehemiah. He is a mature Hebraic doubter cast in the mold of a Byronic or Shelleyan rebel. When Celio wordlessly recognizes in Clarel "A brother that he well might own / In tie of spirit" (1.11.43–44) and hovers about, Clarel becomes "embarrassed" and does not acknowledge the tie that he too feels. They differ in that Celio has already worked out a way of dealing with his doubts, while Clarel scarcely knows what to do about them. Clarel realizes this fact when he reads the journal of the dead youth, whom he has searched out at last—when it is too late:

> A second self therein he found,
> But stronger—with the heart to brave
> All questions on that primal ground
> Laid bare by faith's receding wave. (1.19.26–28)

Unlike Clarel, Celio has had the intellectual and moral strength to move beyond the Christian framework and judge it. His Ecce Homo speech on the Via Crucis accuses Christ of misleading and betraying mankind with promises of immortality unknown to previous generations; it is a speech that, although much less vitriolic, recalls Ahasuerus's polemic against God in Shelley's *Queen Mab.* Celio's subsequent leaving the city walls and being accidentally locked out overnight in Jehoshaphat represents his confrontation with the heart of darkness and links him with the Wandering Jew, with whom he compares himself. Melville suggests that the Hebraic doubter can heroically descend into the dark night of the soul and courageously accept the alienation and anguish that such a journey creates. However, Clarel wanders about Jerusalem in Part I, still significantly more attached to Nehemiah than to Celio, and thus unable to take the first steps on this journey.

Instead, Clarel falls in love. Melville clearly suggests that this course of action, while natural, is an escape to Hellenism.[8] When the supernatural fails Clarel, he puts his faith into the natural—in human love, which gives emotional support but not complete spiritual satisfaction. With their pots of greenery and their family life, Ruth and her mother create for Clarel the only oasis that he knows in the city. Despite their ethnic background, both women close their eyes to the tragic vision. And they help Clarel close his eyes to it also, appealing to the Hellenic strain in his nature. There Clarel immerses himself in a youthful vision of Paradise, one whose power and beauty have fueled myth since the beginning of man, but which Melville sees as basically opposed to the tragic vision symbolized by the crucifix:

> Clarel and Ruth—might it but be
> That range they could green uplands free

By gala orchards, when they fling
Their bridal favors, buds of Spring;
And, dreaming in her morning swoon,
The lady of the night, the moon,
Looks pearly as the blossoming;
And youth and nature's fond accord
Wins Eden back, that tales abstruse
Of Christ, the crucified, Pain's Lord,
Seem foreign—forged—incongruous. (1.28.1–11)

It is to be expected that for someone of Clarel's age nature's lure is very strong and visions of the future should be idyllic. In this contrast between love's Eden and pain's Crucifixion, Melville makes one of the fullest statements of the Love or Bride / Death motif in the poem, a more specific version of the basic Hellenic / Hebraic dichotomy.

In the latter half of Part I, Clarel vacillates between the Hebraic / Hellenic dichotomy, as he moves back and forth between Ruth's home, on the one hand, and scenes of suffering or thoughts of Celio on the other. Clarel is ambivalent about following Celio's path, and his attraction to Ruth provides an excellent excuse for blocking out of his mind the serious problem of his faith. However, Clarel's need to decide between the two alternatives is succinctly pictured when the narrator describes Clarel's reaction to the arrival of a new group of pilgrims:

Dubieties of recent date—
Scenes, words, events—he thinks of all.
As, when the autumn sweeps the down,
And gray skies tell of summer gone,
The swallow hovers by the strait—
Impending on the passage long;
Upon a brink and poise he hung.
The bird in end must needs migrate
Over the sea: shall Clarel too
Launch o'er *his* gulf, e'en Doubt, and woo
Remote conclusions? (1.41.67–77)

In this call to the Hebraic quest, Clarel is compared to a bird reluctant to leave the shore and migrate over the sea because of the uncertainty, the hardship, and the possible disaster of the tragic journey. Drawn in opposite directions, Clarel remains indecisive.

Significantly, it is "Fate's herald" (1.42.40) that precipitates a decision, but a waffling one. When Clarel becomes indecisive because he is usually drawn to Hellenic temptations, disastrous events force him in the opposite direction—in this case, the murder of Nathan. Then, using the fact that Ruth and Agar are secluded in mourning as his rationale, Clarel finally does decide to join Rolfe, Vine, and some other travelers on a three-day journey to the Dead Sea and back. But here is no conscious, deliberate choice between the two ways of life represented by Celio and Ruth. Clarel still hopes to have it both ways. His journey into the desert begins as the pseudo-quest of a mere traveler, since he still does not understand the nature of the true pilgrimage.

THE HEART OF DARKNESS

Despite the fact that Clarel's story shifts into the background in Parts II and III, "The Wilderness" and "Mar Saba," his experience in the desert marks a significant advance in his education as he symbolically descends into Jehoshaphat just as Celio did. The trip into the Judean desert is, of course, the archetypal night journey that provides the main story line of the poem. It is a journey into the "heart of darkness," for the remote, uninhabitable wasteland, with its river of death, the Kedron, flowing through it into the Dead Sea, represents totally unmitigated evil, the core of which is nonbeing. "Wishful from everyone to learn" (2.5.10), Clarel observes carefully the responses of the travelers as they progress deeper into the desert. Their reactions, whether they are intellectual or moral, teach Clarel about human nature and prepare him vicariously for his own personal confrontation with death. Clarel begins to realize that there are "counter natures in mankind." Some of the "pilgrims" show themselves to be merely Hellenic tourists and flee. The Greek Banker, who refuses to say the word "death," turns back from the desert, along with his future son-in-law. And others become troubled or quiet. The effect on a Hebraic doubter like Mortmain is to increase his fascination with evil to a frenzy.

The characters that Clarel admires the most, the ones who have achieved some kind of synthesis between the Hebraic and Hellenic—Rolfe and Vine—neither shrink from the experience nor are overcome by it. Clarel is greatly impressed by both Vine and Rolfe in Jerusalem, seeing them both as extraordinary older men who can help him deal with his doubts. In the desert he studies them closely and observes that they take the bleak wasteland in stride, evidence, he thinks, of their already having confronted the specters of pain,

death, and doubt in their personal lives and having worked out ways of dealing with them. The youth watches them carefully to understand and emulate
their response, but he is still too inexperienced in life to be able to react as
they do. While Clarel does have the courage to continue on with the journey,
his experience of evil is still abstract and impersonal. Just as the other characters are tested, so is Clarel. Intellectually, he tries to figure out the "clew" to
which of the counter natures is right, but as he interacts with the other characters, fate in the form of the desert situation steps in and continues to force
him into a dialectic between the Hebraic and the Hellenic. His doubts about
religion have been a blow, but one that has not struck at the center of his
being; he assumes that there will be other Hellenic comforts in his life. However, Melville withdraws them, one by one, as he assesses Clarel's character.

One of the first Hellenic comforts that is undermined in the desert is
friendship. Early in the journey, the lonely, confused Clarel imagines that
the introverted, uncommunicative Vine will eventually share his solution to
the problem of doubt, that their similar concern with the dark side of life
will bind them together in a close friendship. But when, at the Jordan, Clarel's
desire for companionship and security becomes a homoerotic overture that
Vine repulses, Clarel begins to see that his ordeal must be a solitary one (2.27.
121–23) Later in the high desert, Clarel's accidental observation of the fear at
the center of Vine's being, a weakness camouflaged by his reserve, suggests
that the older man has not been completely successful in dealing with the
problems of death or doubt. Clarel reluctantly begins to face the essential isolation of the human condition.

Another of these Hellenic comforts that the desert experience undermines
is intellectual certainty. Ready to "woo / Remote conclusions," Clarel at first
trusts that there are intellectual avenues to faith, that others more learned
than he may have answered the religious questions that are disturbing him.
His need seems about to be fulfilled when in the desert the pilgrims bring
up and debate major modern questions such as the role of rationalism and
science in religion, the evolution and validity of Judaism, Catholicism, and
Protestantism, as well as many other topics. These debates constitute much
of Parts II and III of the poem and prove informative to Clarel, but they do
not provide a certain path to truth. When, at the end of one such discussion in the canto "Concerning Hebrews," Clarel naively asks, "whose the
eye that sees aright, / if any?" (2.22.129–30), even Rolfe turns aside "as over-
tasked." Clarel realizes that all this intellectualizing about faith has come
to nothing. He notes that in contrast to the European pilgrims, Djalea, the

desert dweller, has achieved a calm there and will not "fall / In waste of words, that waste of all" (3.5.181–82).

Because of his experience in the desert, Clarel's original romantic inner conflict and distrust of self deepens, especially as he contrasts his reactions to those of Rolfe. In his role of the sensitive young gentleman, he tends to shrink repeatedly from Rolfe's wide-ranging and nonpartisan intellectual inquiry, becoming increasingly aware of his own weakness and cowardice. Rolfe's ability to look objectively at everything, his ability to "Forego the state / Of local minds inveterate, / Tied to one poor and casual form" (1.1.96–98), frightens Clarel. Early in the journey Clarel chastises himself for being weak and resolves: "This pressure it need be endured: / Weakness to strength must get inured . . . " (2.21.127–28). He realizes that Rolfe's frankness is

> At variance with that parlor-strain
> Which counts each thought that borders pain
> A social treason. (2.21.130–32)

Yet much later in the poem Clarel still has enough of that genteel, Hellenic "parlor-strain" in him to shrink from Rolfe's "earnest comment's random force" (2.21.123) and to flinch when Rolfe broaches topics that pain or embarrass; for at Mar Saba Clarel feels "quick distaste" because Rolfe uses the sexual allusion "hermaphrodite" when discussing Derwent (3.16.174–76), and he actually turns his head when Rolfe refers to an old battle tactic of setting forth a "King a corpse in armor led / On a live horse" (3.16.208–09). This squeamishness, which reveals Clarel to be still conventional, narrow, and superficial, suggests that even at Mar Saba Clarel has not yet traveled very far in his own pilgrimage. Despite the waning of his faith, his growing distrust in rational discourse, and his disappointment in friendship, he has not yet received the kind of grave psychic wound that will make him so tragically aware of the dark side of reality that he realizes the triviality of mere social improprieties.

At the end of the Mar Saba section, however, Clarel does move closer to such a wound, when he sinks to a new emotional low, in his experience with the mad monk Cyril. It is still a second-hand encounter with death that only prefigures what is to come. But his reaction to it does begin to precipitate his choice of the two "counter natures in mankind." When Clarel is further disappointed in his last faint hope—the possibility that Derwent might offer some acceptable way to faith—and happens upon a grisly vault full of skulls, he is forced by the shrouded monk Cyril, to participate in a demented initiation ritual by uttering the password "death." The shock of fear that this experience arouses in Clarel galvanizes his imagination and marks a significant step forward in his becoming a true pilgrim. For the first time in the poem, he broods about the enigma of death without the Christian promise of an afterlife:

> Die—to die!
> To be, then not to be! to end,
> And yet time never, never suspend
> His going. (3.24.92–95)

In these lines, which echo Hamlet's famous soliloquy, Clarel applies his loss of faith to the central human mystery[9] as it relates to him personally, and the effect is profoundly disturbing.

CLAREL'S CHOICE: AN ANATOMY OF PSYCHOLOGICAL CONFLICT

This encounter brings about the major internal conflict that puts Clarel back in the center of the story during the last part of the poem, a crucial conflict that Melville develops in complex detail. The conflict has several stages in which Clarel continues to vacillate between the opposite poles, drawn by both but satisfied with neither, developing new arguments for both sides. At first, with Ruth and the Celibate representing the opposite responses to death, the power of the Hellenic attraction seems to wane. The thought of Ruth, previously such a comfort to him, no longer provides much guidance or solace. When Clarel broods about death after seeing the vault of skulls, the image of Ruth he envisions as solace is like a star seen only fitfully during a storm (3.30.6–10). A much more powerful antidote to his encounter with death is the celestial vision he experiences soon afterwards as he observes the celibate monk feeding doves under the Mar Saba palm. As superior to Plato's world of the mind as Plato is to "the Mammon kind" (3.30.51), the spiritual purity of the ascetic monk charms "away half Clarel's care" (3.30.59) and suggests to him that this kind of life is, after all, the best. Significantly, it is the Celibate who offers Clarel the old "hermit-rhyme" recording instances of women causing trouble for men throughout the Old Testament and thus causes Clarel to explore new arguments against this Hellenic alternative. He wonders if his idealized view of marital love can transcend the limitations of the flesh, as he imagined it would, and he questions, with new awareness, if such a love is really "locked, with Self impure" (3.31.48).

But Clarel can no more figure out whether the Celibate's path or marriage to Ruth is right than he could figure out previous riddles. At one point, trying to break out of his futile oscillation, he raises the larger question of whether there are any general or eternal truths at all (3.31.60–63), and later he expresses a thorough skepticism that shocks him.

> What may man know?
> (Here pondered Clarel;) let him rule—
> Pull down, build up, creed, system, school,
> And reason's endless battle wage,
> Make and remake his verbiage—
> But solve the world! Scarce that he'll do:
> Too wild it is, too wonderful.
> Since *this* world, then, can baffle so—
> Our natural harbor—it were strange
> If *that* alleged, which is afar,
> Should not confound us when we range
> In revery where its problems are.—
> Such thoughts! and can they e'en be mine
> In fount? (4.3.107–20)

This is the result of Clarel's launching "o'er *his* gulf, e'en Doubt," the logical conclusion that Clarel's experience in the desert has led him to. And his doubt about eternal truth, about worldly truth, and even about his own motives renders him, again like Hamlet, unable to act. When he considers leaving the pilgrimage to rejoin Ruth in Jerusalem, he does nothing:

> Nay,
> Doubt had unhinged so, that her sway,
> In minor things even, could retard
> The will and purpose. (4.16.108–12)

The Hamlet-like moral paralysis that sets in exacerbates his obsessive tendency toward internal debates and self-criticism.

At Bethlehem the conflict intensifies and reaches its climax, this time featuring the Lyonese and Brother Salvaterra. Clarel is attracted to the Franciscan monk from Tuscany for much the same reason that he admired the Celibate at Mar Saba—for his heroic asceticism. But when Ungar suggests that man is totally depraved, Clarel develops a new argument. If Ungar is right, Clarel infers, should not one then "sin out life's petty lease" if nothing is "left us but the senses' sway?" (4.22.64–65). Although he is immediately repelled by this proposition, he begins to toy with a pagan hedonism that along with an abdication of reason seems the legacy of doubt. The question at issue is whether a person with a Hebraic nature can yield himself to "the senses' sway." This question is immediately answered in Clarel's encounter with the Lyonese Jew, who has embraced such a hedonism and, in effect, denied his racial heritage. The Prodigal's arguments against the mysticism of Judaism and his profligate way of life dramatize for Clarel an affirmative answer to the question. Therefore, when Clarel dreams of a desert presided over by the "pale pure monk" and of a pagan city ruled by the prodigal, the power of the Hellenic attraction is revealed as "he felt the strain / Of clasping arms which would detain / His heart from such ascetic range" (4.26.308–10).

However, Clarel's movement toward the Hellenic creates a strong reaction in the opposite direction. At David's well, before he discovers that the Lyonese is an apostate Jew, he expresses that Hebraic yearning for the infinite that he has felt throughout the poem, comparing himself to the biblical David: "But who will bring to me / That living water which who drinks / He thirsteth not again!" (4.28.69–71). And when he naturalistically concludes that this longing of his may just disappear because it has never been fulfilled, he takes himself sternly to task in a crucial passage that suggests a deepened awareness of the "counter natures in mankind" and the demands of his higher nature:

> "But whither now, my heart? wouldst fly
> Each thing that keepeth not the pace
> Of common uninquiring life?
> What! fall back on clay commonplace?
> Yearnest for peace so? sick of strife?
> Yet how content thee with routine
> Worldly? how mix with tempers keen
> And narrow like the knife? how live
> At all, if once a fugitive
> From thy own nobler part, though pain
> Be portion inwrought with the grain?" (4.28.74–84)

Here Clarel definitely places himself with the Hebraic characters in the poem, chiding himself for the moral weakness that tempts him to shun the heroic way of life and betray his true self.

After this insight, Clarel's final choice seems puzzling, since he understands clearly at this point what the choices are and what kind of person he is. It is the Hellenic temptation that Clarel chooses after he learns that the Lyonese is by birth a Jew. He denies his Hebraic nature and, giving rein to an emotion that ends all debate, he decides to marry Ruth and take her away from the desert town. He concludes that "One thing was clear, one thing in sooth: / Stays not the prime of June or youth" (4.29.61–62). Although he has some misgivings about rejecting the heroic alternative, Clarel affirms a traditionally romantic naturalism as the only certainty in life, one that is validated by a corresponding impulse from the heart:

> At large here life proclaims the law:
> Unto embraces myriads draw
> Through sacred impulse. Take thy wife;
> Venture, and prove the soul of life,
> And let fate drive. (4.29.102–06)

The important question here is, "Has Clarel passed the test of choosing the right alternative, has he followed the "clew" to determine his true nature?

Melville suggests that Clarel has not, that he has fallen to temptation in reaching out to "pluck the nodding fruit to him, / Fruit of the tree of life" (4.29.56–57). Melville reveals his disapproval by forcing Clarel to experience the unmitigated terror of the void by removing the tempting alternative, by causing the sudden deaths of Ruth and Agar. Upon seeing the dead bodies of the two women in the Valley of Jehoshaphat, Clarel does finally encounter the heart of darkness and receives the serious psychic wound for which his experience in the desert has been preparing him. No longer abstractly and intellectually weighing arguments, he suffers for the first time what seems to him intolerable agony, melodramatically crying out, "art thou God?" Like a Byronic madman he storms:

> "O blind, blind, barren universe!
> Now am I like a bough torn down,
> And I must wither, cloud or sun!" (4.30.93–95)

When he feels the anguish that Celio, Mortmain, Ungar, and Agath as well as Rolfe and Vine have experienced, Clarel can truly understand and feel the significance of the crucifixion. Longing for some meaning, some sense of immortality or of a deity, Clarel does not leave Jerusalem when the rest of the travelers do and instead haunts the town during the rest of Lent, experiencing the liturgy, especially that of Good Friday, with new emotional impact. Finally, he has become the true pilgrim, having realized that his original quest for religious faith was a rather superficial one. After describing both animals and humans burdened by fate wending their way along the way of the Cross, the narrator asks,

> But, lagging after, who is he
> Called early every hope to test,
> And now, at close of rarer quest,
> Finds so much more the heavier tree? (4.34.45–48)

Clarel's *Bildungsweg* suggests Melville's belief that basically Hebraic personalities cannot escape their destiny of doubt and pain, nor can "Unworldly yearners" ever be satisfied with what is basically a Hellenic mode of life, whether it is the simple appeal to the heart and the senses that Ruth embodies or the more sophisticated religious *via media* that Derwent represents. Clarel's attempt to evade his destiny shows that he did not learn the lesson that Agath's story and Rolfe's story about the mariner were trying to teach. Although some people may try to avoid the evils that fate has in store for them, fate will triumph eventually and force them to assume the cross. This is the lesson that the biblical Jonah as well as Shakespeare's Hamlet had to learn. In choosing to return to Ruth and all that she represents, Clarel willfully challenged fate to "drive" (4.29.106). But now he takes his place with all the others on the *Via Crucis* as "in varied forms of fate they wend" (4.34.41).

While Clarel's story is thus the making of another heroic striver, a Hebraic doubter, Melville, following the path of the early Goethe and Schiller as well as Byron, leaves Clarel at the end of the poem still on his journey. He has not found truth, freedom, or wholeness. He does not achieve a synthesis of the Hebraic and the Hellenic, as did Rolfe. He does not accept his fate. He simply suffers. But the fact that he is last seen walking the *Via Crucis* suggests that he has learned some lessons. Apparently he realizes that the Hellenic path is not his; he has become a tragic figure whom fate, in the form of Ruth's death, forces to continue his quest. There is some question whether the painful loss of faith, friendship, intellectual certainty, and romantic love will actually foster the call to heroism, the *Streben nach dem Unendlichen* of which Clarel has shown only fitful evidence.

In the controversial epilogue of the poem, Melville walks the same tightrope between belief and disbelief in his comments about Clarel's final mental state. He allows the reader to speculate about whether Clarel will find faith or not. Such an open ending is another of Melville's character tests for the reader, who, in giving a Hellenic or Hebraic interpretation, reveals his own personality type and thus his philosophical orientation. Perhaps Melville suspected that future readers might argue learnedly about the "correct" interpretation of the enigmatic ending of the poem. But he understood quite well that Hellenic readers would project their own optimism upon his remarks about immortality and that Hebraic ones would stress the darker side. One's temperament determines his solution to "The running battle of the star and the clod." Melville points out in the Epilogue:

> Science the feud can only aggravate—
> No umpire she betwixt the chimes and knell:
> The running battle of the star and clod
> Shall run forever—if there be no God. (4.35.14–17)

But Melville surely admired the rare few who could resist falling into either category and who could sustain a desire for faith even while seriously considering reasons for disbelief. About the only way of determining whether man is "ape or angel," star or clod, is the purely subjective evidence of man's yearning for the infinite.

It is a measure of Melville's intelligence as well as of his erudition that he perceived so clearly the importance and implications of the early-nineteenth-century German dichotomy between the romantic and the classic, as well as Arnold's distinction between the Hebraic and the Hellenic. Among theorists and artists, this human typology continued to inspire new interpretive twists through the late nineteenth and early twentieth centuries, with Nietzsche taking it in one direction and renaming it Apollonian and Dionysian. Carl Jung, in his psychology of human types, took it in yet another direction, calling it introversion and extroversion. And Thomas Mann used it to dramatize the development of the artist in *Tonio Kroger*. Clearly, Melville's thoughtful application of this theory of personality to *Clarel* places him in the mainstream of late-nineteenth-century and early-twentieth-century European thought.

NOTES

1. A few critics have briefly mentioned that in *Clarel* Melville is more interested in human character and psychology than in ideas. Howard describes the poem as one in which Melville's "mind dwelt more upon people than upon philosophy" (307), and Bezanson notes that Clarel "goes increasingly from asking whose beliefs are right to asking who is the right kind of man" (lxix).

2. See Super, who notes that Arnold took the contrast from Heine's *Der Doktor Faust* "Erlauterungen" (439n).

3. See Dettlaff 214–16, where I argue that Melville had read enough of Arnold to understand and use these terms and that Melville may have read "Anarchy and Authority" when it appeared in 1868 (216n).

4. Early critics divided the characters into the ascetic and the worldly, a division that is very similar to the Hebraic and the Hellenic. Sedgwick distinguished "the lighthearted few" from the majority of serious "seekers after spiritual refreshment" (205), and Arvin categorized the youths as those who represent "pleasure-loving worldliness" or "ascetic spirituality" (277). Beginning an interpretation that has since predominated, Howard emphasized another, narrower dichotomy—that of faith *vs.* doubt—asserting that all the characters represent varying degrees in the range between these opposites. Apparently refining Howard, Bezanson suggested three clusters of characters: the centrists, the dark monomaniacs, and the optimistic believers. Brodwin, Knapp, and Kenny have followed basically that same dichotomy.

5. Rosenthal points out the importance of this motif for the poem. However, in not placing the Wandering Jew in the Hebraic part of the basic dichotomy in the poem, Rosenthal applies the motif indiscriminately, I believe, to almost all of the characters and thus weakens the significance of the symbol as an aid to understanding the poem.

6. Arnold uses this quotation from Romans 8:26 to describe Heinrich Heine's Hebraism in *Essays in Criticism* 166.

7. Although most critics have dealt with Clarel's search for faith, few have analyzed the inner drama of Clarel's education. Chase was the first to emphasize the poem as an educational one and to discuss the other main characters as symbolizing "modes of life or thought bearing upon the education of Clarel" (244), but he did not focus on the continuity of Clarel's interior reactions to these characters and the events of the poem. Bezanson saw Clarel as a "lost hero in search of a guide" (liv). Bowen, Miller, and Browne have continued the pattern of briefly discussing Clarel's state at the beginning and the end of the poem and have not analyzed the developing psychological drama. In the 1970s, however, critics began to look more carefully at Clarel's education. Brodwin argued that Clarel's real education involves not just the search for religious faith but a deeper, existential realization of an authentic self after experiencing pain, death, and freedom. Knapp and Ra'ad both looked beneath the surface; but Knapp's interpretation is too optimistic and Ra'ad's argument that Clarel's education develops dialectically only as a reaction to the deaths of characters in the story seems narrow, even though valid.

8. Baym concludes that the erotic "motif" is not just one thread in the complexly woven tapestry of Clarel but the framework for the entire design. Seeing the action of the story as Melville's sophisticated rendering of the conventional nineteenth-century conflict between intellect and nature, Baym asserts that Clarel's flight from feminine love into skeptical intellectualizing is ultimately sterile and that salvation lies only in a return to Ruth, a return that Clarel's neurotic fear of sex makes difficult. But the way that women in general are seen in the poem is the traditional biblical or Hebraic one, which while sometimes appearing to admire, still really sees woman as a trap, a snare that will lure man to his doom by personifying those very qualities in himself that he would like to yield to but must transcend if he is to achieve salvation. Thus woman is associated with youth, beauty, charm, pleasure—those very joys that the Hellenes celebrated. Baym, in following and overemphasizing a suggestion of Bezanson's, has pushed her naturalistic and psychological interpretation too far, with the result that it contradicts the major thrust of the poem's theme: the need for the person with the deep-diving imagination to deny the commonplace and become a heroic quester.

9. See Brodwin, who points out that death is the central problem underlying the question of faith and doubt in the poem and asserts that "Faith for Melville is in fact an end condition, a stance one finds oneself in only after confronting and resolving the question of death" (30).

WORKS CITED

Abrams, M. H. *Natural Supernaturalism: Tradition and Revolution in Romantic Literature.* New York: Norton, 1971.

Arnold, Matthew. "Anarchy and Authority." *Every Saturday* 5 (June 27, 1868): 802–03.

———. "Heinrich Heine." *Essays in Criticism.* Boston: Ticknor and Fields, 1866. 140–73.

Arvin, Newton. *Herman Melville: A Critical Biography.* New York: William Sloane Associates, 1950.

Baym, Nina. "Erotic Motif in Melville's Clarel." *Texas Studies in Literature and Language* 16 (Summer 1974): 315–28.

Bezanson, Walter, ed. Introduction. *Clarel: A Poem and Pilgrimage in the Holy Land.* By Herman Melville. New York: Hendricks House, 1960. ix–cxvii.

Bowen, Merlin. *The Long Encounter: Self and Experience in the Writings of Herman Melville.* Chicago: U of Chicago P, 1960.

Brodwin, Stanley. "Herman Melville's *Clarel:* An Existential Gospel." *PMLA* 86 (May 1971): 375–87.

Browne, Ray. *Melville's Drive to Humanism.* Lafayette, IN: Purdue UP, 1972.

Chase, Richard. *Herman Melville: A Critical Study.* New York: Macmillan, 1949.

Cowen, Wilson Walker. "Melville's Marginalia." Vol. 11. Ph.D. diss. Harvard University, 1965.

Dettlaff, Shirley. "Ionian Form and Esau's Waste: Melville's View of Art in *Clarel.*" *American Literature* 54 (May 1982): 212–28.

Howard, Leon. *Herman Melville: A Biography.* Los Angeles: U of California P, 1950.

Kenny, Vincent. *Herman Melville's "Clarel": A Spiritual Biography.* Hamden, CT: Archon, 1973.

Knapp, Joseph G. *Tortured Synthesis: The Meaning of Melville's* Clarel. New York: Philosophical Library, 1971.

Miller, James E. *A Reader's Guide to Herman Melville.* New York: Noonday Press, 1962.

Ra'ad, Basem L. "The Death Plot in Melville's Clarel." *Emerson Society Quarterly* 27 (1981): 14–27.

Rosenthal, Bernard. "Herman Melville's Wandering Jews." In *Puritan Influences in American Literature.* Ed. Emory Elliot. Urbana: U of Illinois P, 1979. 167–91.

Schiller, Friedrich. *Naive and Sentimental Poetry* and *On the Sublime.* Trans. Julius A. Elias. New York: Frederick Ungar, 1966.

———. *Poems and Ballads.* Trans. Edward Bulwer Lytton. London: George Routledge, 1887.

Schlegel, Augustus William. *Lectures on Dramatic Art and Literature.* Trans. John Black. London: Henry G. Bohn, 1861.

Sedgwick, William. *Herman Melville: The Tragedy of Mind.* New York: Russell and Russell, 1944.

Super, R. H., ed. *Lectures and Essays in Criticism.* Vol. 3: *By Matthew Arnold.* Ann Arbor: U of Michigan P, 1962.

The Art of Melville Biography

11

Biographers on Biography:
A Panel Discussion

PARTICIPANTS: STANTON GARNER, LYNN HORTH,
HERSHEL PARKER, ROBERT RYAN, AND DONALD YANNELLA

The Queries

1. What are the central, perplexing questions basic to Melville biography? Have they changed over the years? What episodes in Melville's life would you tell differently from Howard or Mumford or Miller?
2. What do we not know that we would like or need to know? How is our picture of Melville skewed by the many gaps in our knowledge?
3. Although the necessity of defending Melville against charges of insensitivity may be of more concern to critics, it may have implications for biographers. Have we done enough to explain Melville's impulses to address himself, for example, to the plight of the poor, the slave, the woman in the sweatshop, and the socially dispossessed?

DONALD YANNELLA: The questions that you have before you were drafted by the members of the panel; each person sent in several suggestions. We had a conference call about which questions seemed to be of most interest and which we could merge. We went through all that, and these are the results. We are going to proceed, having no illusion about completing the three questions. We'll go as far as we can. We would like this to be a dialogue—not only among the people sitting here at the table in front, but we'd like to invite members of the audience to participate as the discussion unfolds at appropriate times. But, you'll note, I'm sure, that each of the speakers up here is going to be quite precise, and certainly not prolix. We could all speak for an hour or two on any one of these items. But we agree that succinct answers are in order. I would hope that anyone in the audience who wants to participate will also be succinct.

STANTON GARNER: To me, one of the very central and very perplexing questions about Herman Melville has to do with the dichotomies or the contrariness of his character, or what we popularly call his ambiguities, such as: he appears very often to be a hypochondriac, yet he was also well known for his rugged physicality. He was certainly a patrician in orientation, the Vere de Vere of Pittsfield, and yet he very often appears to be dedicated to the common man. He needed companionship; [his father-in-law] Lemuel Shaw[1] complained that he was too lonely in Pittsfield, and yet he disliked crowds. Apparently he had a tremendous histrionic ability. There's the famous story about his recitation to the Hawthornes about the events of the South Sea Isles. Mrs. Hawthorne thought afterward that Melville had been wielding a war club, but he hadn't been; he had just convinced her that he had been.[2] And yet he was very often a failure as a lecturer, where he could have used his histrionic ability. He had an imposing presence. Apparently he was only 5'9" or 10" tall and impressed people as being . . .

ROBERT RYAN: Only?! *[laughter]*

SG: Well, I didn't mean to insult anybody.

RR: Awfully hard in this crowd.

SG: "Only" in comparison with those over six feet. He impressed people as standing [taller], and yet despite his imposing presence, apparently, he failed to inspire memoirs and anecdotes among an enormous number of people who encountered him.

HERSHEL PARKER: That's interesting.

SG: Those are some of the ambiguities that the biographer has to explain. At the same time, to go on to another part of Question 1, I think that that quality has attracted biographers. It certainly gives a lot of fodder for the biographer to chew on and critics, too, who pay attention to his ambiguities.

HP: A very brief comment on Query 1. There are moments when I get the feeling that in a time of crisis the Melville men would lie on the floor and kick their heels. On the other hand, you think about Mama being so worried about Herman's health and then you realize how fast her husband died and how suddenly Gansevoort died.[3] When she begins worrying about the strain on Herman's health in 1853, '54, and '55 she is, in realistic terms, fearing that she might lose another man of the family.

LYNN HORTH: And did lose one again.

HP: And did lose one again—Allan.[4]

RR: So she's not quite so hypochondriacal as [Melville biographer] Leon Howard—perhaps working out of his own interests—imagines her.

SG: Apparently Herman Melville himself was a hypochondriac in his own terms. One indication is that [in 1859] he dropped off the militia rolls in Pittsfield to which every able-bodied man of a certain age had to subscribe,[5] apparently because he felt he wasn't able-bodied; and yet as soon as the Civil War began, he went down and put himself down in the rolls.

RR: Except, out of my own peculiar history of having had a heart attack just last year, and as I read through the record again, and I see him in Italy, in the 1857 journal, saying, "I had a horrible pain through my chest and back,"[6] and as I think about the official postmortem analysis of how he died—the man, I would bet you, was having heart attacks all along.[7] Literal ones, not figurative ones, not hypochondriacal ones. I'll bet his heart was expanding, as they put it, all the way from at least the 1850s onward. So there may have been a real physical reason, not just a kind of psychic reason, for dropping off the militia rolls and so on. He may have despaired of not any longer being so physically competent to do the sorts of things he had done before. And it certainly "threw him off the wagon" when he was thrown off the wagon in 1862.[8] There was no doubt that he was physically injured.

SG: How do you mean "off the wagon?" *[laughter]*

RR: Well, I didn't mean the alcoholic wagon, though that might be a topic we'll address here in a moment. He was "thrown off the horse," in that figurative tale, where if you're thrown you're supposed to get back on immediately and then you won't have any problems. I think that it is easily inferable, demonstrable, plausible that he didn't get back on the horse for a while, maybe, in some people's terms, ever.

HP: Well, he clearly didn't. There's the recklessness, on the one hand, where he would terrify people by driving wildly on mountain roads, but then was excessively timid after that accident. You think of the descriptions of him in bookstores late in life—a wraith, a timid wraith—and that does fit with what J. E. A. Smith says about his behavior after the accident.[9] Melville also felt, when he left for the Levant in 1856, that he was an old man, a broken old man of thirty-seven. He was expecting as much pleasure as one could at his age.

SG: But, if we think about that accident, bringing the furniture back from Arrowhead into town: ten months later he left for a three-day driving trip with Lizzie . . .

HP: That's right.

SG: . . . and six months after that he rode in a cavalry scout for three days and made a charge with the cavalry, too.[10] So, he may not have driven as fast as he previously did, but he certainly was willing to drive.

LH: The big question with biography is not just what happened to Melville, but how this relates to all his books and to Melville as an author. It strikes me that all these ambiguities in just his health fit in with what Shirley Dett-laff was talking about this morning about the whole nineteenth century's sense of ambiguities and the straining between two extremes.[11] Maybe he's very typical of his age in that sense.

DY: Picking up the last question in Number 1—What episodes in Melville's life would you retell in a different way from Leon Howard, or from other biographers such as Lewis Mumford or Edwin Haviland Miller?[12]

HP: I would say I would go with Miller at one point. Miller is the first to have had access to Mrs. Eleanor Metcalf's volume, *Cycle and Epicycle,* and I think he is on the right track when he talks about Herman as a tyrant in the household.[13] This makes a lot of sense given the evidence in the Augusta Papers. As for [Leon] Howard, I more and more see that Leon did not have a basic sympathy with Melville: he disapproved of a lot of Melville's characteristics. Leon disapproved of reckless behavior. *[Addressing audience participant Harrison Hayford]* Is that not true, Harry, just in general? Again and again, he will try to tone Melville down. He will ignore some excessive emotionality and regularize everything. And it comes out in choices he makes as to what evidence he will run with for four pages.

LH: Such as?

HP: Well, one example of how dry and bland Leon can be is on the ninth of August of 1850, the day Melville wrote most of "Hawthorne and His *Mosses."* Leon is absolutely right that Melville wrote the bulk of the essay in the morning.[14] But he treats it very coolly. Melville wrote for several hours. But Howard doesn't at all get into any sense of Melville having a pent-up urge to express his aspiration to make this book as great as Shakespeare. He doesn't imply that Melville had been brooding for months about how there could be a great American book of Shakespearean qualities. Doesn't talk about the anxieties, tensions of the creative process. Doesn't even talk about the mechanical processes of how Melville went through *Mosses* marking passages to quote, and so on. But the basic comment about the morning, and the morning's work on that date, is that Leon doesn't recognize anxiety as being any part of the creative process, or exaltation in expressing things. He also misses what happened in the early afternoon: deflected sexuality. What happened is that Melville and [Evert] Duyckinck in two carriages drove to town, and you have an abduction of a bride.[15] What happened is that Herman got Mrs. Butler, who didn't know him from Adam, into the carriage and drove away fast to the Melvill place, leaving young William Allen Butler in the dust and not happy about it at all, coming along with Duyckinck in the wagon.[16] Duyckinck and Herman were determined that everyone was going to stay over for the masquerade. Young Butler said, "The hell with that" and got her back in there and ate waffles in town and got on to the other train station and got off to Springfield as he had intended to do. So this was a sexual excitement, arousal from the morning— well, you write a love letter to yourself and Hawthorne about creativity in America in the morning and then you go off and kidnap a bride . . . and then in the evening . . .

JOHN BRYANT *[in audience]:* What are you talking about?[17]

HP: I'm talking about *[laughter]* Butler's bride, Bill Butler's bride.

BRYANT: Whose bride?

DY: William Allen Butler.

HP: Herman just went on the railroad car, got hold of her, put her on the carriage and drove off with her, with Bill Butler left in the dust with Duyckinck. In the evening Leon has Herman and brother Allan dressing up in waiter's costume—I assume white—carrying around cherry cobblers. Hell no. The Augusta Papers show that he dressed up as a Turk.[18] You know, turban, scimitar, circumcized, you know, exotic—with a harem. Women, women! This was the result of that morning's writing. This was a wild night. *[laughter]* But to read it in Leon, the two waiters dressed as twins and served cherry cobblers. Hunh uh. No. And Leon has a way of doing that, of saying that it must have been Captain Taylor[19] who took the bride. He tended not to go beyond what Jay [Leyda] had in the Log, to the fuller documents, to see what Butler really wrote to George Duyckinck.

DY: Howard's account is much toned down even from the account in the *Literary World,* which appeared in two parts in August [1850], just shortly after the *"Mosses"* essay appeared also in the *Literary World.* Cornelius Mathews wrote back and told a lot more stories in his allegorical way about what really went on during that first encounter in this area than Howard did.[20] Leon truly did tone down what went on.

LH: So what did go on?

DY: Maybe we're opening up a new question that we might want to consider. Hershel on numerous occasions has suggested that the account of Lizzie and Herman's marriage that Leon wrote. . . . I'll let you articulate that.

HP: Well, as far as my biography is concerned, I will have to have a section in there on Herman as sex symbol. And this is something that never occurred to me until a couple of years ago because I didn't come at Melville through *Typee;* I came at Melville through *Moby-Dick* and *Pierre* and *Clarel* and then finally through *Typee* and *Omoo.* But a lot of the reviews show a range of attitudes toward sexuality in *Typee* and *Omoo.* Some really contorted ones a year after *Typee* was published expressed the way people felt after having had a whole year to find those descriptions working insidiously in their psyches. Also, Sophia Hawthorne—Remember that passage "I see Fayaway in his eyes."[21] You know, she looked in his eyes and saw this naked South Sea woman. She didn't say what else she thought about, but this is clearly like looking at Byron or looking at Mick Jagger. *[laughter]* Joyce and Fred Kennedy found that Lizzie was afraid to get married in church because of the groupies.[22] She got married at home, so the fans wouldn't storm. It's Herman as sex symbol for that time, for years.

DY: There's a lot of buzzing out there, anyone want to respond? *[laughter]* Hershel's been going to rock concerts for the past four years. He buys tickets in that place where people get crushed.

Unidentified audience member: Those were "groupies"?

HP: I won't call them that in the biography.

DY: Well, what I was actually alluding to was your suggestion that the account of the marriage that Leon Howard offers, which has become the essential version of it, is not very accurate. You've suggested to me and to others that it's more a description of Leon's marriage than it is of Herman's.

HP: Well, no, now, I'm not the authority on Leon and his wife Henrietta, but we have an authority in the house, and I'm not sure whether Harry [Hayford] wants to talk about it or not, but anybody who knew Leon and Henrietta would tell you that the portrait of Lizzie is not a portrait of Lizzie; it is a portrait of Henrietta. Do you want to say anything about that Harry?

Harrison Hayford *[in audience]:* No. I will say it's true, but I'd rather not elaborate.

DY: What are some of the characteristics so people can understand?

HP: Well, whining, nagging, kvetching . . .

DY: Kvetching?

HP: Let my wife say it. Say it, Heddy.

HEDDY RICHTER PARKER *[in audience]:* Don's saying it very well.

HP: Jay [Leyda] had almost no blinders, and yet even he wrote that he shared Leon's view of Henrietta, and it came out in really strange ways in [Jay's] transcription of some of the documents in the Augusta Papers. There are a couple of times when he misreads a word in a way that is extremely unfavorable to Lizzie. For example, he had—this is corrected now—but he had Augusta saying that a letter came addressed to Lizzie, of course, with "the eagle-eyed Lizzie *censoring* the contents." What it really said was, "the eagle-eyed Lizzie *scanning* the contents," and that's an example of how, when you have a prejudice against a person already formed . . .

LH: "Argus-eyed."

HP: Is it "argus-eyed"? But the word is "scanning," not "censoring." The point is, what you expect to find is what you find. If a word is hard to read, you can just misread it in a way that reflects your prejudice. Lizzie comes off much stronger in the Augusta Papers and other papers that have come to light recently.

DY: More favorably.

HP: Oh yes, much more favorably. Yes.

ROBERT MILDER *[in audience]:* Could you say something about the character of Lizzie and what you think makes her the attraction?

RR: Bob, I've been thinking about that one, and it is all speculation. Part of what this is all about is that biography, as you well know, is a compound of fact and a whole lot of surmise, more or less plausible. We do have the fact of Herman's being in the right place at the right time, or she was in the right place. What was he doing? What was he up to in marrying Lizzie if Fayaway was in his eyes or if somebody else was in his heart? One ordinary surmise for an American boy of his origins in recent failed prospects is that in Lizzie he saw, most obviously, what we would all see: the daughter of the chief justice of the Commonwealth of Massachusetts. And furthermore, one that was a friend of his sisters. In many ways that we could specify, Lizzie was indistinguishable from the Melville sisters, except that the incest taboo did not apply to her. If you don't want to psychologize or socioeconomicalize, or whatever, you can, at the very least, imagine her in some terms as the safe one to marry who also had other advantages, at least as I would understand them. Do you want to make something of this?

HP: No. No. She loved him for the dangers he had passed, and he loved her that she did pity them—as in Othello.[23]

RR: Well, all right. She gets demonized all over the place and it's a bum rap. She was "eminently safe," but she was not as dumb as she has been passed off as being. She was not malicious. She was not, as Walker Cowen and many others have said quite without substantiation, one who went through his books erasing things he had written.[24] As far as we can tell, that's not demonstrable; it's possible that she or someone after Herman died did do such things. She was level headed. As we know, I'm just recounting some of those things that we do know—she took charge of the family finances, and Herman heaved a sigh of relief when she did, and, even though he was a good businessman, turned it all over to her so that he could contemplate The Beyond on a full-time basis. *[laughter]*

HP: No!

LH: She could have made a very advantageous marriage, but she wanted to marry this more adventurous, unusual man and was willing to go off into the wilds of Massachusetts or Manhattan rather than stay home.

HP: There's something else about her. I totally agree with what they're saying, and she was very reasonable and patient.

RR: Oh God, [yes]!

HP: Even when she was young, she wanted to go see [John] Oakes Shaw, her brother, out there in Chicago, which was the wilds of the world; ten years before, it had been just four log cabins on a big lake. She wouldn't say "I have to go, I have to go." Oakes would arrange an escort for her, and she would think about it and say "I'd better defer to my father on that." She would say to her father, "You should think about it, whether this would be the most fitting thing for me to do." But she could be a tough cookie as well as patient. [Melville's mother] Maria was determined that Lizzie and Herman were going to come and live in Lansingburgh.[25] Lizzie just sweetly and calmly wouldn't do it, and Maria was determined still, and Maria was a powerful opponent. But Lizzie won on that; Lizzie waited for the marriage until someone came up with the bright idea that Judge Shaw would set up the two couples in Manhattan, and that happened. And Lizzie prevailed on that.[26]

DY: I'd just like to add something here. I've read a number of these letters in the Shaw Papers at the Massachusetts Historical Society, and I have not found any evidence that there was an overbearing strain in her character. No evidence at all before or after the marriage. No indication at all that she was as matriarchal as has been understood by most of us from the work of

Leon Howard and others over the past fifty years. The word that always pops into my mind—and I don't mean to be at all patronizing about this—is that she was sweet. Hennig Cohen and I have talked about the roles of Herman and Lizzie as parents in the household of the four children.[27] In analyzing the sort of child rearing and family perception practices in what we call the Gansevoort-Melville side of the family, we found a remarkably distinct difference from those in the Shaw side of the family. The general impression most of us have of Judge Shaw is that he's the "hanging Judge," and a good number of Melville scholars, I have found through the years, have that image of Shaw from those pictures that have survived, the daguerreotype of a very strong-willed patriarchal man. But what Hennig and I have discovered in reading a lot of the Shaw papers, especially letters to his son Lemuel Jr., who is a near-contemporary of Lizzie's, is that the Judge treated that boy, when he was having difficulties at boarding school, with so much gentleness and understanding and empathy that he couldn't be conceived of as coming from the household of a Peter Gansevoort.[28] Peter Gansevoort is one we've come to know quite well. And so, Lizzie's and Herman's views of how a household was structured, how it ran, who did what, how the children behaved, were in large measure, if not entirely, the product of their own upbringings and understandings and the culture that they lived in. They lived in different worlds; they were brought up much differently. Lizzie was a very sweet person.

MOLLY GELLER [*in audience*]: I want to talk about the Judge. Dr. Oliver Wendell Holmes lived for years across the street from where Melville lived, on what is now Holmes Road. He treated Melville at a time when Melville had a psychological illness, or maybe a physical one. Melville was working in the dark room, under the north side, and the writings that he was producing looked to him like pieces of the wire, broken on a white page. And Holmes, in writing about Melville says "I don't know why Herman complains about his wife, she is running this household . . ."

RR: Where's this?

HP: Where's this? You know more than we know.

GELLER: Well, I read his story on local authors.

HP: Well, very good. Will you come see us after we finish?

GELLER: [*continuing in paraphrase of Holmes*] "I feel sorry for Liz. I don't know why Herman's doing all of this complaining because he lives in this house with his wife and his mother-in-law and his brother and his wife. She's jumping around with the bills, and he's complaining."[29]

DY: Is there anyone else with any unknown documentary evidence? *[laughter]*

HP: That's terrific.

DY: What is the document, ma'am? What is your name?

GELLER: My name is Dr. Molly Geller. I'm an ecologist who has studied the history of this area because I have lived here.

HENNIG COHEN *[in audience]:* What have you done with this?

GELLER: Well, I don't have it now; I have it in my notes.

DY: Is it from manuscript sources, do you recall, or is it printed?

GELLER: No, printed sources. It's by Judge Holmes, with whom I got very involved after that hike up Monument Mountain.[30]

DY: Shall we continue talking about Lizzie? Herman? The marriage?

RR: I want to say one thing. Probably other people want to say something about that, too. If you look at the later record, and especially in the wake of the wonderfully reticent and persuasive work that [Merton M.] Sealts has done on the later years, you get—or at least I get—the conviction that Lizzie was quite right in 1877 when she said that Herman suffers so needlessly.[31] What she meant, probably, is that he suffers so needlessly over matters that can be resolved, in Lizzie's terms, more practically. Matters we would think of as metaphysical or extraphysical, matters of The Beyond. Matters that we, at least in a literary mode, tend to value very highly, though we would ourselves be probably terribly impatient to have Herman around the house.

HP: *[to Robert Ryan]* Talk about pride. Talk about Herman's pride.

RR: I'm not sure about the pride. I'm sure he had it. I want to say one thing first before I forget it, and that is that even though Lizzie has gotten a bum rap, largely I think because most of us here come to Melville as sympathizers with Herman, nonetheless something should be said from Herman's point of view. He is said, as you probably know, in the family, to have always challenged her and that she did not understand. It sounds utterly plausible that he could have done that, that that could have been a repeated charge. It might also have been an irrelevant charge, that she did not understand his more complex divagations; but we should say about Herman's impatience or inability to take her plainness or her practicality or whatever—we have to say about his attitude toward her, that it was, from his point of view, justified. He wanted, at that point, to have that impossible compound of all things including the one who could and would sympathize with and participate in his more imaginative venturing.

HP: Sophia Hawthorne.

RR: Sophia Hawthorne, who did *not* have Fayaway in her eyes . . .

DY: But now, we're back to the marriage, and a couple of people have suggested that it was a *safe* marriage. Lizzie was in the same crowd as Herman's sisters; that's very true. As a matter of fact, Lemuel Shaw's connection with the Melville family, the Gansevoort-Melville side, was not only by [Lemuel Shaw's] engagement to Nancy Melvill.[32] Beginning in 1818 and running through 1822 there's an extensive correspondence between Lemuel Shaw and Peter Gansevoort about the purchase of a large tract of land in New York State known as the Goldthwaite Patent, and these two men really made a connection that I suspect had more of an impact on the Judge and on Peter than any romantic connection Lemuel had with the Melvill girl earlier on. This was really substantial, so that when Herman was ready to marry into that safe world, there were historical [business] connections between the two families that go back into the late 1810s, early '20s, and no doubt continued further on. But I haven't read in the correspondence thoroughly, you know, just turned the papers in the Shaw correspondence past 1825. So there may well have been other correspondence on other issues between 1825 and 1840 where I picked up again.

HP: My sense of it is that after Allan Sr. and Thomas [Melville's father and grandfather] died in 1832, and the Melvill siblings had to sue Maria and her children in order to protect their own inheritance since Judge Shaw and John D' Wolf were the trustees, Judge Shaw, probably deliberately, dropped all direct contact with Maria Gansevoort Melville.[33] And it didn't start up again until 1841 when Gansevoort went to Boston in January and that fall, when Judge Shaw came for his annual court appearance at Lenox, and [brother] Gansevoort and [sister] Helen were there, she visiting her old teacher.

DY: Eliza Sedgwick. Helen had gone to her school in 1836.

HP: Gansevoort appeared and charmed Hope [Mrs. Shaw] and the Judge, and the connection was made. From that came the invitation to [Herman's sister] Helen to spend the winter in Boston and then Lizzie's trips to Lansingburgh. So that exchanges had been made. The Shaws regularly had young girls there for winters: cousins, fairly distant cousins, friends of the family. Hope Shaw liked to be surrounded by adoring young girls—I don't know quite what's going on there—daughter substitutes maybe, or additional daughters, something like that, but she liked that.

DY: And Lizzie would like it, too

HP: And Judge Shaw liked having the girls around.

DY: For example, there's one lovely letter—I have no idea of the date; I would say it's late 1840s—an omnibus letter, written from Boston to the Judge who was riding circuit, by five young ladies who were staying over. Lizzie wrote the first part of the letter to Judge Shaw and the other four added a couple of paragraphs each to it, all of them addressing him very respectfully, as dear Judge Shaw or dear Mr. Shaw. They report in sort of a giggly way that they were not uncomfortable and they were not unknown in that house and to him.

SG: However, in that hiatus, between the deaths of Allan Melvill [January 1832] and Major Melvill [September 1832], there was a continuing relationship between Judge Shaw and the Uncle Thomas Melvill and, also a relationship between Judge Shaw and Amos Nourse [Aunt Lucy Melvill's second husband, ca. 1833].[34]

HP: And Aunt Priscilla.[35]

SG: And Cousin Robert to Melville.[36]

HP: To correct my own earlier impression, Shaw wasn't doling out money to them out of his own pocket; he was trustee for the estate and giving them the money that was coming to them. Sometimes they had to ask him twice after the time had come if he was very busy on a given date. So, the impression of [Uncle] Thomas Melvill *begging* for money is not quite right.

I want to say one thing else. I would not minimize the romance of it. Think about Lizzie making herself "look as bewitchingly as possible" for Herman.[37] I was not being flippant about the Othello reference, which all reviewers of *Typee* have made about the hair-breadth escapes. Herman came home and pretty clearly had those days in Boston. We now know from the letter that Allan wrote (it just turned up last year), that he had some days there, and since Helen had been a regular, I think the chances are extremely great, given when they got engaged, that he went to the Shaws then and told his story and that Lizzie fell in love. And that Herman probably fell in love.

DY: I think that 1844 letter has been given by Nina Murray to the Athenaeum.[38]

MILDER: What I have trouble seeing, from the limited bit that I know, is the love. I can see Lizzie staying home and being enthralled. I can't see the attraction [on Herman's side].

LH: Well, there's a wonderful letter in the new Savage Family Papers at the Massachusetts Historical Society. The Savages were in-laws of the Shaws,[39] and one of the boys is writing to [brother] Allan Melville and saying that Herman is in Boston and that he's hanging around the Shaw house because

Lizzie is there. There's a clear sense that there's this attraction and fasci-nation between the two of them. And then Lizzie at the end of her life defending this husband and writing up all that he had done even though he was no longer considered the great author.

RR: What seems obvious to me, Bob, if I can explain further, is that Lizzie was precisely the safe sort of good girl that—in his otherwise tending toward flightiness, perhaps more adventurousness than he could quite stand—Herman would be attracted to. She is not only prosperous and privileged: she is on an even keel, and this is rather obvious. Lots of wild boys marry very safe girls, and later regret it. Or perhaps come to the point where—and I think maybe Herman arguably did come to it—where they learn not any longer to regret it, as perhaps they grow into their earlier decision, or some-thing like that.

MILDER: Is there any evidence that Melville, later in life, became interested in or involved with [other women].

RR: Good question.

HP: No, absolutely not.

LH: What about abducting the bride, Hersh?

HP: Oh, well, that was deflected sexuality because he was excited by writing the *"Mosses"* essay . . .

RR: How about: since he and Hawthorne were great writers . . .

HP: No.

DY: Oh no, not with Herman. Now, Sarah Morewood with George Duyck-inck.[40] [Former Berkshire Athenaeum director] Bob Newman will remem-ber a while back my shock and dismay when I visited the Athenaeum in 1980, and I don't think the Melville Room was open. Bob knew what I was here for: "The Other Ends," that is George Duyckinck's letters to Sarah Morewood. There are loads of very suggestive letters from Sarah to George in the early 1850s. Bob opened this big folio scrapbook and there was the one letter from George to Sarah Morewood which was thoroughly innocuous, whereas hers bordered on, and occasionally slipped into, the passionate.

HP: Well, I don't believe that. She was a religious woman.

DY: Here he goes. . . . I've got xeroxes of those. You don't even have to go to the library to read those. I'll give you the xeroxes.

SG: I think this whole picture of the Melville marriage is looking more and more like a Harlequin Romance in which the blameless young lady is mar-ried to a somewhat dastardly man and in the end, why, she converts him.

I have the idea that, although Lizzie was almost invariably referred to as "sweet Lizzie," that she was really fairly human and that Herman Melville's continued pressures on her from an intellectual point of view, the claims that she was inadequate, were followed by a kind of revenge on her part. It's very difficult to document this, except when one realizes that Lizzie was the primary correspondent in the family with the rest. Herman rarely wrote his own family, except for letters we don't have with Allan and so on. But the women corresponded. So Lizzie wrote to Gansevoort, New York; she wrote to Albany; she wrote to Brookline, Massachusetts; she wrote to Lawrence, Massachusetts, and they got their impression of Herman from her.[41] In addition to that, she spent a lot of time at home, when she could, in Boston, and I have an idea that she unloaded a lot of things in sly ways.

For one thing, Herman was not as incompetent as he would appear from the family traditions. Her revenge was to picture him as an incompetent, and there's some evidence that a fairly clear antagonism existed in the Shaw household against Herman. [Mother-in-law] Hope Shaw, for instance, when Melville was applying for a consulship, said in effect, "Why send a man off to handle the government's affairs when he can't handle his own affairs."[42] The Shaw brothers invariably said bad things about Herman's literary work. Whether Lizzie had anything to do with that, I don't know, but there's one very telling instance of that. She wanted to go to Boston, and she wanted Augusta to come stay at Arrowhead with Herman and the children because she couldn't leave them alone. Well, the picture that we've gotten from that is that Herman was beating the children, or starving them to death, or keeping them up all night, or something like that. But the subsidiary correspondence—for instance, letters that [sister] Helen Griggs wrote about leaving Herman alone with children which say that if the two boys couldn't obey for two weeks they ought to go to a training school for boys or reform school—implies that Herman was not really cruel to the children. What he did was *neglect* them and let them run around and get out all the pots and pans and play.

HP: I think Lynn and I both want to challenge some of that. One of the main reasons for [Lizzie's] being afraid to leave was that he would give the cook such a hard time that the cook would leave. What we didn't realize is that the Melvilles always had a cook. They were generic: you could always go down to the boat and get one, and Mama was good about going down to the boat and picking one off; she would pick an Irishman or another cook. But the point is that Lizzie was servant-ridden till the end of her days. Herman would drive away these women, [leaving Lizzie to say,] "we've had her for over two months now, and I'd like to keep her through the summer." One of the reasons she sold the house as fast as she could and went to the Florence apartments in Manhattan is that she would be rid of servants whom she had to hire.[43] She could ring down and have a servant bring up dinner for her and [her daughter] Bessie when they wanted it. But [the idea of] Herman as domestic tyrant interfering and demanding that the coffee water be just so probably started very early. The need to replace the last cook and the foibles of the cooks run through the Augusta Papers. Also, Melville had been irresponsible financially, and some of that is just emerging with Patricia Barber's publication of the two letters back in the mid-1970s.[44]

But it's not all out, even yet. My wife Heddy was digging around in the Berkshire Athenaeum last summer, getting some things that I haven't quite assimilated yet, but it's very clear, that in the 1847 purchase of the New York York house, for example, the downpayment was Shaw's. And Herman, if he were a very practical man, would naturally sell that house in New York before insisting on buying Arrowhead. But did Herman do that? Of course not. He got Shaw to buy him Arrowhead before selling the house in New York, and then it didn't sell, and it didn't sell.

Let me just say one thing more. When the time bomb exploded in 1856, Melville not only had been remiss in the interest payments to T. D. Stewart ever since May of 1852, he was also a year late with the payment to [Dr. John] Brewster,[45] so Melville had, basically, mortgaged the same property to two different lenders, at the same time, and Shaw didn't know about this.

I would not want to malign Lizzie on this. Herman had been financially irresponsible, and Shaw bailed him out and sent him off on that trip to the Levant.

SG: That may be true, but I want to go back to the specific instance I was talking about when Lizzie wanted Augusta to come to stay with Herman while she went to Boston. Helen Griggs was very explicit about what the problem of leaving Herman alone was. It was because he would allow the boys to misbehave.

DY: And I just have one footnote to put in here, for those of you who haven't read Helen Griggs's correspondence. She strikes me as the least capable, intellectually. *[Pandemonium ensues in panel and audience.]*

HP: Oh no . . . Oh no!!

LH: No, she's hilarious.

DY: She's an airhead.

SG: She's a Republican.[46] *[laughter]*

LH: She's incredibly funny. She wrote a long, long letter all about . . .

DY: Helen is the woman who writes a long letter to one of the sisters about the horrors, the wasting of one's life, on novel writing. If one were going to be serious, and be in what we today refer to as the humanities, one could at least be a respected historian, a writer of nonfictional prose. But a fiction writer? You could imagine. She was responding to one of Herman's books, which she found intolerable.[47]

LH: But she herself . . .

DY: Which caused me to say, this woman's an airhead.

LH: She herself is incredibly funny.

JOYCE DEVEAU KENNEDY *[in audience]:* I wanted to mention that in the correspondence that we [Frederick Kennedy and I] found in Boston, there is a very interesting letter that Elizabeth wrote to her cousin Sam when he was in Illinois. And we tried to track down the persons mentioned in that letter but were unsuccessful. But the gist of it was that she probably went to Chicago not just for family reasons but because there was a man there she was interested in. He was a man named McIlroy, a Roman Catholic, who had lectured in Boston.[48] But all the papers perished in the Chicago fire so we weren't able to find out any more about it. Lizzie wrote this letter after her marriage saying if you happen to see Mr. McIlroy tell him that this marriage was definitely unexpected. Well, if you read something like that and you start tracking who this person was and see that he was a little firebrand who was speaking in Boston—I mean, Lizzie's marriage to Herman was maybe the other way around; that is, she had apparently other admirers at least as exciting as Herman.

DY: Good, Joyce. *[applause]* This might be a good point to ask. What do we know, what do we not know that we would like or need to know? Maybe we could address ourselves to some facets of Melville's biography by commenting on some portion of Question Number 2.

LH: "What are the gaps?"

DY: Well, the Hawthorne [relationship], that's the big example, and one of the letters Joyce [Deveau Kennedy] found was that very funny letter that Herman wrote to Sam [Savage].[49]

LH: It's all the people we *don't* know about. One new letter turned up from Melville to Richard Lathers,[50] and there's obviously a friendship there. And yet, we have no sense of what this friendship was. We just know that he was another man in Melville's acquaintance. We focus on Hawthorne because we have the letters to Hawthorne, although we don't know everything there either. But, there must have been a whole range of people that Melville knew that we have no sense of.

HP: Willis.

LH: N. P. Willis.[51]

DY: Because the [Willis] papers, to use one phrase that is rather euphemistic, have not yet been recovered.

LH: Or it would be like imagining what we know about Melville and then subtracting the Duyckinck papers, say. If you had none of that, you would have just a whole section of Melville cut off.

HP: Willis's papers survived his death and were used by that first biographer Beers,[52] but Mrs. Willis and the children had every reason to destroy those papers because fresh in their minds was the horror of the Forrest divorce trial with all those lurid, detailed accusations of adultery, what hours of the day and night the Willis brothers came to the Forrest house, and whether they slept over, how many times they slept over. Was it seven or ten times? It was way the hell out of town on Twenty-second Street, and they couldn't get an omnibus back into town, so naturally they had to sleep over with Mrs. Forrest. But this was a horrible thing. Mrs. Willis had to go to the trial and sit there every day and had to be the good wife and show that she believed him. So, all of these papers that must have mentioned Melville, all have disappeared.

DY: There's another part to Question 2 that becomes rather interesting: "Do these gaps about his friendships tend to overemphasize what we do know?" Such as his friendship with Hawthorne. Is there any way, wanting documentation or imagination, of correcting the imbalances? Or are we locked into a version of Melville forever based upon the surviving evidence?

SG: It is a commonplace that biography in general is skewed by the particular facts that survive, so that a minor friendship might be overcelebrated because there are a lot of letters about it that survive and a major friendship may tend to diminish in the biographer's eyes. But there are certainly areas that need to be explored more. For instance, a man by the name of George Henry Brewster was a good friend of Melville's from 1861 until his death; the fellow showed up for his funeral. We really know almost nothing about him.

HP: He worked *with* Allan? *For* Allan?

SG & LH: He was Allan's law partner.

LH: But he went out West.

SG: No, he didn't. A brother [Charles Brewster] of his went out West. He stayed in New York. He was a friend of Melville's.

HP: He came to visit at Arrowhead in the summer.

SG: Yes.

LEA NEWMAN *[in audience]:* What do you mean we're exaggerating the facts [about Hawthorne]? What are you saying? *[laughter]*

DY: I think what's being said is that there certainly was a very close relationship that lasted for at least several years in the early 1850s. But it may not have been the closest intellectual relationship that Herman Melville had. There may have been others before, or more likely after, or concurrently that we don't know a damn thing about, because there's been no evidence that survives, in one or another archive, or it's not been forthcoming or no one has gone and gotten it in some attic.

NEWMAN: Would any of us be here if he had not written *Moby-Dick*? Isn't the friendship in that book the heart of the matter for many people?

SG: But we're not saying that the friendship with Hawthorne was any less important than it's been depicted but that Melville's biography might be a much wider book if we had more information about other friends.

HP: I think that the friendship has been overemphasized. I think that Hawthorne has been given extensive credit for changing the direction of *Moby-Dick*. I've said for years—and people don't believe me until they look around the Berkshires and see—that coming back to the Berkshires was a wonderful, climactic, emotional, liberating experience for Melville. The memories so flooded over him that he felt that he couldn't finish *Moby-Dick* confined in the city; he had to be out here with Mount Greylock—with Hawthorne over there but also with Greylock. Getting here wasn't just to follow Hawthorne; it was to be in the Berkshires again where he could write as big a book as he was capable of writing.

SG: Even so, Hershel, according to something Lynn said, I think that we would still regard the friendship as being very important simply because of the letters involved. The letters from Melville to Hawthorne reveal something about Melville that we've spent a lot of time on.

HOWARD HORSFORD *[in audience]:* Something that I wouldn't want to make too much out of, but it bears on the relationship with Hawthorne. Whatever Melville's affection for Hawthorne, it was not entirely reciprocated. When Hawthorne's best friend in England, Henry Arthur Bright, came to this country, Hawthorne sent him on to many people, but he did not send him on to Melville.

LH: Although, Melville met Bright when he was in England and *was* introduced to him, so there was that connection. But probably the Hawthorne letters are the best letters that Melville wrote. They're the most . . .

MILDER: But they're one-sided.

HP: It's not Melville's fault. Or it *is* Melville's fault.

SG: In throwing away Hawthorne's letters.

JOYCE KENNEDY: I just wanted to ask you about this. This concerns what Richard Brodhead said this morning about aggression.[53] When you are dealing with biographical fact, you have to take into account the effect of those depressive mind states so that when you are looking to Lizzie's behavior for answers about Herman's state of mind—and this fits in with the types of things we never can really know—isn't it true that to a large extent the state of mind, even maybe the sort of somatic states that Melville was in, were caused by what he calls in *Pierre* "the black vein of the Glendinnings." And by that temperamental predisposition which made him swing back and forth between feelings of inadequacy on one hand and anger on the other. How do you factor that in when you are trying to decide why Herman was in that particular mood?

HP: One thing you can do is look at the barometer reading for that day— if you can establish it—maybe it was seasonal. Maybe it was climatic. *[laughter]*

RR: But not to dodge [the question]. Well, why don't we get over to Joyce Adler.

JOYCE ADLER *[in audience]:* It seems to me that a great genius like Melville would have had great yearning for some kind of community of imagination. And he found it in Hawthorne. But whether it was reciprocated I think is very questionable. I'll never forget the day in the New York Public Library when there had been a find of material and there was this very cool letter from Hawthorne: "Dear Mr. Melville, I am sending you a trunk . . ."

DY: ". . . Pick up my shoes."

ADLER: And so forth. "Would you kindly pick it up." It read like a real business letter.

LH: Well, it's a note of a neighbor. It's a business letter in a sense—that's its purpose; it's not an outpouring of his heart. It's "get my trunk."[54]

HP: Hawthorne invited Melville to stay overnight. That's extraordinary.

LAURIE ROBERTSON-LORANT *[in audience]:* Two questions I'm going to throw out right now. One is about the so-called other woman, and my question is do we know at this point who that uptown woman was?[55] And the more important question which someone alluded to and brushed off earlier: the question of Melville's drinking.

HP: I thought at first that the woman could have been Ellen Oxenham who was up at Hellgate, which is really way the hell uptown. But apparently not.

Ellen Oxenham was a very forward English woman who was making overt passes at Melville. That's a little shocking to read. But, chances are Melville's reference to "uptown" is innocuous. Chances are it's someone who lived on Fifteenth Street, which was uptown, but not so far north as Spuyten Duyvel. I defer on alcoholism to Bob Ryan. *[laughter]*

RR: That's great. What a line.

DY: The sins of graduate school—the old school rivals.

HP: I was on his dissertation committee.

RR: On this issue as on so many, I don't know that we can say anything for sure about the drinking. I think the one who makes out the most persuasive case on the matter is Haviland Miller. That is, rhetorically. I think it's a question for discourse finally, and unfortunately, in the absence of information, but there is indirect information in the Burgundy Club Sketches and elsewhere. All of the celebration which may strike some, especially in the case of the Burgundy Club Sketches, as mere pottering amounting to a kind of nostalgic or sentimental idealizing of tippling. There is that, although you don't have to interpret it that way.

DY: The two kids in the Berkshires who visited him at Arrowhead, they found him in the afternoon, flushed.[56]

RR: Yes. That's right.

HP: No, they didn't find him flushed; he may not have been used to drinking and he may have gotten flushed real fast.

RR: But the rest of it, I don't know where the evidence would be offhand for the effect of drinking on him, though this interpretation is an interesting one that perhaps he did not take readily or kindly to drink and therefore, like Poe, didn't have any business drinking.

HP: Howard [Horsford], do you want to comment on the joy of drinking in the London journal, and the absence, or relative absence of comment on drink in the journal of 1856 and '57?

HORSFORD *[in audience]:* I'm not certain if there is anything particular to say except that obviously he did enjoy big dinners. There were about three or four of them. And at the Paradise of Bachelors this was certainly tolerated.[57] But there is no evidence whatsoever, that I can remember now, that he did much of any drinking in 1856–57. But on those ships you wouldn't get much.

LH: Right. It's two different trips. London is a social, convivial place, and in the Mideast they're traveling to the Holy Land.

DY: Well, in 1849 he met David Davidson, who was a very personable young man. He was the one with whom he "blue-posted a dinner" in London.[58] He didn't meet such a convivial person in the second trip.

HP: But he drank in France, Germany, and Brussels, and he's always listing what he drank and enjoyed it immensely.

RR: That's why I would say to Laurie, or to all, that there is a danger, as always, in linking drinking with depression. *If* that's chargeable as well. There are happy drunks and sad drunks; there always were, there still are.

HP: And the only real authority is Paul Metcalf, or Melville Chapin.[59] Maybe Melville Chapin knows more. Paul Metcalf recounted a story that he got through Charles Olson, who presumably got it from Mrs. Metcalf, who wouldn't trust Paul with that kind of nasty news, about Herman getting drunk and pushing Lizzie down the back stairs, and it leaves unanswered—accidentally—whether this was every Saturday night? One Saturday night? Once? This is not direct information. Mr. Chapin do you have any . . .

MELVILLE CHAPIN *[in audience]:* I have no such information. I like a drink myself. *[laughter]*

DY: Shall we now shift the discussion to genetic considerations? *[laughter]* You know, there's much less drinking of hard alcohol in our period than there was thirty years ago, and there was two and a half times the amount of consumption in the middle nineteenth century as compared to the third quarter of the twentieth century in the United States. So from our more chaste period we might be learning more about standards in the 1990s rather than Melville's behavior within his cultural context in 1850 or '60. After a while, you do build up a tolerance for alcohol. And, yes, he may not have been used to having drinks. One or two may have knocked him on his ear. One suggestion about Poe's problems with alcohol came to me from Dwight MacDonald, who heard from a doctor that it sounded to her an awful lot like Poe was suffering from diabetes, probably undiagnosed, so that two or three stiff drinks would knock him reeling.

SG: Nevertheless, I remember in Eleanor Metcalf's book that she said in Melville's late years he drowned himself in a brandy bottle.[60]

GAIL COFFLER *[in audience]:* To return to the question of Melville's affection for Hawthorne not being reciprocated, it seems that this kind of thing repeated itself. And I ask this to you, Don. What about his relationship to [Evert] Duyckinck? Duyckinck seemed to favor Cornelius Mathews. And then we have Hawthorne who seems to favor Franklin Pierce.[61] Couple that to the family actually preferring [Melville's brother] Gansevoort, in the beginning, over Herman, with the family's honor resting on the shoulders of Gansevoort.[62] It seems that this is a kind of repetition that occurred frequently with Melville's being disappointed or frustrated in this way. Have you ever seen any irony there?

DY: You mean his disappointment with his relationships with, for example, Duyckinck?

COFFLER: Right. Duyckinck never appreciated Melville's genius. But he thought he saw genius in Mathews. He preferred his friendship with Mathews.

DY: That's difficult to talk about. Something I just recently discovered was why Mathews simply disappeared from the scene after 1852. He was drifting in a direction that the nationalistic literary movement would almost inevitably lead some people. In June of 1855, there's a one-column report in the *New York Evening Post* of a Know-Nothing meeting that was called in New York,[63] and Mathews was one of the foremen of the meeting and at this particular Know-Nothing group; he was the secretary, which was the major position.

HP: Jesus Christ.

DY: I think it was June 11, 1855. You know where that information showed up? In Spann's book that came out in 1981[64]; it's a history book. And as with most people in here, I find myself, most of the time when I'm reading an academic book, reading the footnotes first. I get a sense of where the person has been. I can get an idea of what the probable quality is going to be, and this just jumped up off the page in Spann's footnotes. I found exactly where he told me to go and read the report of the Know-Nothing meetings, and Mathews was probably engaged in that among other political activities from there on. So he was out [of favor with Duyckinck]; he was out. But as far as the breach between Duyckinck and Melville . . .

COFFLER: It's not a breach, but don't you think that Duyckinck preferred his friendship with Mathews?

DY: No. No. Their relationship dissolved after '53. The only document that survives between '53 and '63, is the document of '63 and that ends it. Mathews writes two or three lines saying that he's sorry that Duyckinck's brother George died.

COFFLER: This is after *Moby-Dick,* but what about before *Moby-Dick*? Again, Melville could not get the same kind of friendship in return that he sought.

LH: But we don't really know. We don't have the letters to Melville.

HP: Remember how many people found the young Melville enthralling, fascinating. How many people have named sons for Don or Bob or me or Stan (before we got to be full professors) the way people were naming their sons after Melville?

DY: Are we talking about bastards? *[laughter]*

HP: No, we're talking about his shipmates who named sons for him and wrote to him saying, "little did I know you'd be famous one day." So he had this extraordinarily winning personality. From Willis's description he must have been, and from Dana's description of him as incomparable at dramatic story-telling.

LH: Well, he won over that publisher that he went to visit in England, that seemed so cold at first.

HP: [Edward] Moxon.[65]

LH: And he wins him over and walks out quite warm and friendly.

NEWMAN *[in audience]:* I just wanted to say that if anybody is lacking in the [Melville-Hawthorne] friendship, it's Hawthorne. I don't think there's a Hawthornian that will not say that.

LAWRENCE BUELL *[in audience]:* I want to speak to the mentoring dynamics of the difference in age. You have [in Hawthorne] a relatively old and early-fiftyish person, always laid back. It is predictable and humanly understandable that Melville would have meant somewhat less to Hawthorne than Hawthorne would have to Melville. We can read Sophia writing about this boy who is gushing his rhetoric up against Mr. Hawthorne's silences in a pretty damning way. But I think we have to watch that.

HP: I think that Larry is right on that. Let me say something about the context of Melville's meeting with Hawthorne. He had written roughly half, some large proportion of *Moby-Dick.* I think he must have known—Leon Howard says otherwise—how good a book he was writing when he was writing it, and he had not talked to anybody about it as far as we know. The letter to Dana on the first of May expresses some of the tensions already: you can tell the truth and you're going to get poetry out of the blubber.[66] So some of the problems were already defined in his mind that early. I also now know that he was thinking about Shakespeare on the basis of Collier's "Life of Shakespeare."[67] He was thinking about contemporaries of Shakespeare in the way that he refers to [them] in the *"Mosses"* essay. I am convinced—well, I know because of the Thomas Powell affair[68]—he was thinking about the problem of Shakespeare and originality and how real originality tends to come in a form that is charged with imitation. Before he got to Pittsfield these things were on his mind. Maybe he invited Duyckinck and Mathews because Mathews had just started the *Prompter,* which was a dramatic magazine, although it was a contemporary dramatic magazine, as you know. Anyhow, Melville was thinking about Shakespeare when he got to the Berkshires; he wasn't thinking about Hawthorne. Aunt Mary gave him the *Mosses* volume.[69]

So when he met Hawthorne and was enthralled, charmed. You know, this man was drop-dead gorgeous (like Robert Taylor in *Camille*); this was an enthralling man. Melville needed to see an American whom he could think of as a very great writer approaching Shakespeare. He had not been talking to Duyckinck. We know this because of the letter Duyckinck writes to his brother George saying that Melville has a new work mostly done.[70] All those months he had holed up in the house and written, and written, and written. Maybe he went to West Point in the spring, judging by a letter in which Augusta refers to an excursion. But as far as we know he worked until he broke, at the time of ordering and getting the whaling books all lined up, and trying to plan for the future. So he was all primed to admire Hawthorne, because it took the burden off. Think of the crazy things, the thoughts he was thinking all those months, "I am writing a book as great as Shakespeare. Am I nuts? To whom do I tell this? Do I share this with Lizzie?" Well, praising Hawthorne, not himself but another American, was a way of verbalizing it, expressing it. It could be done. He didn't read *Mosses* carefully before praising Hawthorne. Look at the way he composed the *"Mosses"* essay where he wouldn't even copy out the quotations, but marked them for Lizzie to copy. He wasn't reading carefully. We now know because of the Augusta Papers when he was able to glance at the *Mosses* stories on Wednesday, two days before meeting Hawthorne.

In any case, Hawthorne was wonderful for Melville to meet at that time, because he'd get these thoughts off his mind. Just look at the way the essay was written. He pours out the Shakespeare stuff, which he had been brooding about before Hawthorne got there, and it is all very routine: look at this Hawthorne story, quote a few lines here; look at that story of Hawthorne's and quote a few lines there; say a few more obvious things about Hawthorne. *[singing]* "This is the way we write a review, write a review." This is the way Duyckinck reviewed Wordsworth's *Prelude*, by quoting vast passages of it, from Pittsfield here.

DY: Let me just throw in a question here. It might have crossed a number of minds. How do you respond to the information that Gary Scharnhorst turned up a while back: Lizzie's reporting to the fellow who is writing the introduction to one of Hawthorne's books that Melville had been, for quite some time, at work on the *"Mosses"* essay?[71]

HP: Well, Harry Hayford worked this out some years ago in '44, '43 . . .

HAYFORD: *Nineteen* hundred. *[laughter]*

HP: Leon Howard was wrong about J. T. Headley.[72] He didn't know that Headley came unexpectedly and stayed the whole day and that Mama was put out because he stayed six hours the first day he called, which meant that on that day, Tuesday, Herman couldn't have worked at the *"Mosses"* essay as Leon had thought he had done. But Leon is basically right on the button as far as the schedule goes.

DY: So the information that Lizzie gave the writer of the introduction after the death is a failure of memory.

HP: That's right. That's right. And another thing is that on this August vacation she was Melville's copyist, but she had *not* been copyist in 1849. She was relieved of copyist duties the moment Malcolm was born [February 16, 1847]. [Sister] Helen Griggs copied. We didn't know who the copyist was at the time we prepared the Northwestern-Newberry *White-Jacket* because we didn't have enough of Helen's letters, but Helen was the one who was copying that draft of the *White-Jacket* preface that we printed.[73] Helen and Augusta took over after Malcolm was born.

BRYANT: Hershel, you said something earlier that intrigued me, that Melville had to get out of the city and to the Berkshires to get into *Moby-Dick,* and yet the ironic thing is that apparently he had to get back to the city in order to finish it. Whatever the reasons, he found himself back in New York, and although we don't really know what parts of the book he was working on there, he was probably writing the last chapters at that time, which are the three chase chapters, in particular. The rhetoric in those three chapters, the style, is remarkably different from the preceding dramatic chapters ("The Candles," "The Needle") or even the Ishmaelean first-person chapters. Do you think that being in the city, being under the pressure of all that, compressed his creative process? This is a large speculative kind of question, and I'm not looking for some sort of easy answer that says the city was a dynamic creative force for Melville. But the quality of the language is so different, I was wondering if you had thought about that?

HP: He did what he had to do, and he just had to be there in that. It must have been terribly hot in that third-floor room, I would think. It must have been just miserable.

BRYANT: But the writing is so brilliant.

HP: Well, what he wanted though was that "silent grass-growing mood"[74] and couldn't get it, and so that was part of its being a botch. He finished the best he could under the circumstances.

BRYANT: I'm not sure it was such a botch.

SHEILA POST-LAURIA [*in audience*]: I'd just like to relate to what you've just been talking about previously regarding Question 3. In your discussions of Melville's relationship with Hawthorne, and Melville's publishing of his novels, you mentioned Anne Lynch,[75] N. P. Willis, Mathews. And given the way we have formulated Question 3, I wonder if you could address the issues about the responsibility of the biographer to account for the writer's relationship to the larger culture.

HP: A specific part of the culture is the literary world of New York. I've been spending far too much time for my own good on a collection of documents called the Powell Papers, because it turns out that Thomas Powell had a startling impact on the Duyckinck clique in 1849 after he fled from England where he had been embezzling and leaving Dickens outraged, Browning outraged, the whole literary society in London outraged and moving into the Duyckinck circle here as a con man from England. What he did was precipitate a scandal by charging Irving with plagiarism. You could not say anything bad about Irving. And the other thing he did was create an international scandal involving Charles Dickens, in which Dickens, by the end of 1849, was terrified that he was going to be charged in a libel suit lodged by Powell merely because he had told the truth writing to Lewis Gaylord Clark about Powell's embezzlement in England. In the Historical Note to *Moby-Dick,* I put three or four pages in about the tensions in the New York literary cliques that met Melville when he returned home from England and the Continent. I think there's probably good reason to think that one reason he wanted to get out of town this summer was to get away from these people. One reason why he didn't talk to Duyckinck a lot was because Duyckinck and Willis were feuding and everyone was being incredibly nasty to each other, and Melville had already, two years before, gone through the period of disgust with the cliques, as you know from *Mardi.* He was ready to get away from these little people and go out to the hills, and ready to meet Hawthorne, someone his equal. A man up there in the mountains, a profound thinker. So, drawing the literary milieu is very difficult because we lack a lot of evidence. Again, if we had Nathaniel Parker Willis's papers, for instance, we probably would have a lot. This is a man who was a friend of Melville, who had been a friend of Gansevoort's in London. Gansevoort knew Willis's brother-in-law. There was an intimacy there. There are so many other writers who knew Melville, and we know almost nothing. Things keep coming up just by accident.

I was in New Orleans a couple of years ago, wanting to look at the *Picayune.* They wouldn't let me see the *Picayune* in hard copy so I looked at the *Commercial Bulletin* and found there hundreds, several hundred, letters from someone in the Duyckinck clique, Oakey Hall, who later became mayor of New Orleans, the elegant Oakey. And there's a lot of biographical information about Melville in there. How many days it took him to write *White-Jacket,* for instance. The evidence is still out there. Joyce and Fred Kennedy haven't been going looking for it in the last decade, more is the pity. We can't recreate what's lost. You have to hint, suggest, what connections there were. There are a lot of descriptions of literary salons and who went there in *The Trippings of Tom Pepper* and *New York by Gaslight.* There are lots and lots of descriptions of Anne Lynch's parties. [Thomas] Powell has one where he describes Duyckinck and Mathews and Irving and Anne Lynch's salon, so we know something about that milieu. We know about the Valentine that Bayard Taylor wrote for Melville. But knowledge has got to be impressionistic as far as I'm concerned at this stage because we just don't have the details, and I've got to piece together a typical Anne Lynch soirée from Bayard Taylor's. There are just pieces, pieces, hints.

LH: We also know that Melville was not at the center of this social activity because he just doesn't show up again and again.

HP: Right.

SG: Nevertheless, there are some things we can find out, not perhaps about what happened in Duyckinck's house but other things that Melville did that we simply have not looked at hard enough. For instance, Duyckinck left the information that he and Herman Melville had gone out to the Brooklyn Navy Yard at the end of June or the beginning of July in 1861 [*Log* 641]. Leon Howard, who could investigate little things like that very well but did no investigation there, said that they visited the Navy Yard perhaps because Herman Melville wanted to enlist in the navy. Nevertheless, if one takes the pains to look at an incident like that, one finds out that the third in command at the Brooklyn Navy Yard on that day was Guert Gansevoort, Herman's cousin, and that the Brooklyn Navy Yard was the scene of the arming of the navy at the moment and that Gansevoort was bringing in merchant ships and putting guns on them. One can see the excitement that brought Melville and Duyckinck out there. Then by going to the newspapers to see what was going on in those days, it becomes apparent that the Navy Yard was a focus of national attention for just a few days at that moment because Commander James Ward of the navy had become the first naval officer to be killed in action, and his body was very ceremoniously brought to the Brooklyn Navy Yard; it was placed upon his former ship, the station ship in the yard. The public went over in hordes to look at the body, which was very beautifully decorated. As a matter of fact, Herman Melville and Duyckinck went up to see this sight that had the whole country interested. And apparently Gansevoort arranged for them to get a tour of some ships that had just come back from the African station. They got lectures on the new guns. By the time one finishes setting this sort of thing into its context then the idea that Herman Melville must have gotten a sudden urge to be a seaman on a Union warship begins to disappear.[76]

HP: That's terrific. May I say something about what Stan just said. This is the time, if you want new information to go into *The Melville Log*, for God's sake; do what Fred and Joyce Kennedy did ten years ago when they turned up wonderful things just by going out and looking. There are so many things that Stan hasn't looked at, that I haven't looked at, that Lynn hasn't looked at, that Don hasn't looked at, that Bob hasn't looked at. We've stopped, as a profession, going out and getting our hands dirty in the manuscripts and . . . . Where has she [Molly Geller] gone. Grab that woman; she's disappeared with . . .

Now's the time to go looking for things if you want them to be in the big, expanded *Log*.

NOTES (PREPARED BY JOHN BRYANT)

1. Lemuel Shaw (1781–1861) was the highly influential chief justice of the Massachusetts Supreme Court who ruled on several nationally important civil and criminal cases in the decades before the Civil War. Shaw's first wife died giving birth to Elizabeth, Melville's wife. His second marriage to Hope Savage produced two sons, Lizzie's half-brothers Lemuel Jr. and Samuel. The Judge had been good friends with Melville's father, Allan Melvill, and had even been engaged to marry one of Allan's sisters, who died before the nuptials. Shaw helped Herman and Lizzie through various financial embarrassments and emotional hard times, and Melville dedicated his first book, *Typee*, to him.

2. The anecdote of Melville seemingly to have wielded a club while telling his tale is related in several publications by Hawthorne's son Julian, most notably in his *Nathaniel Hawthorne and His Wife* 1:407.

3. Melville's mother, Maria Gansevoort Melville (1791–1872), was the last child of General Peter Gansevoort (distinguished in service during the Revolutionary War) and Catherine Van Schaick. She married Allan Melvill in 1814. After Allan died in 1832, the family added an "e" to their name. Gansevoort Melville, Herman's older brother, died suddenly, like his father, in 1847 while serving in the United States legation to England.

4. One of Herman's younger brothers, Allan Melville (1823–72), was a successful lawyer who in 1872 predeceased their mother by two months.

5. Garner 37.

6. In his 1857 journal Melville wrote on Sunday, March 15, that he was "Attacked by singular pain across chest & in back" (NN *Journals* 112).

7. Herman died just after midnight on September 28, 1891, of "Cardiac dilatation, Mitral regurgitation . . . Contributory Asthenia"—or, as Lizzie put it in her memoirs, an "enlargement of the heart" (*Log* 836).

8. While transporting furniture in Pittsfield on November 7, 1862, Melville was thrown from his horse-drawn wagon and suffered a broken shoulder blade. See *Log* 655; Sealts 136.

9. Pittsfield poet and journalist, J. E. A. Smith (1822–1896) supported Melville's work throughout the century and was Melville's first biographer in the pages of the *Berkshire Evening Journal*.

10. Melville's Civil War adventure behind the lines in Virginia and its relation to his *Battle-Pieces* poem "The Scout toward Aldie" is examined in Garner 294–344.

11. See chapter 10 above for Dettlaff's essay "'Counter Natures in Mankind.'"

12. See Mumford; also Edwin Havilland Miller.

13. See Eleanor Melville Metcalf. According to James Barbour, Metcalf's biographical volume "evoke[s] a sense of Melville's life within the setting of family and friends" (25). This important resource for Melville family history was published after Leyda's *Log* and Howard's biography (both in 1951) and preceded Miller's (1975) by two decades.

14. Howard 158. Melville's aunt, Mary D'Wolf, had given him a copy of Hawthorne's *Mosses from an Old Manse* in July 1850, but he only began reading it at his first meeting with the author as a scheduled August gathering at Arrowhead (later to become one of the most famous events in American literary history) drew near. Evert Duyckinck had assigned him to review the book for *Literary World*, and the result of the assignment was the epic / love letter / literary manifesto "Hawthorne and His *Mosses*," which Melville began writing on the morning of August 9, 1850. Hawthorne did not know until a month later that this review essay "By a Virginian" was actually written by his new friend, Herman Melville. For a full treatment of the August gathering, see Howard 154–60.

15. Evert Duyckinck (1816–1878) was perhaps Melville's longest-standing literary friend. He helped launch Melville's career during the 1840s by editing *Typee*, by introducing the writer to his circle of New York literati known as Young America, by opening up his extensive library to him, by facilitating the meeting with Hawthorne, and by assigning him reviews in the Young America journal *Literary World*. Duyckinck describes the August gathering in a series of letters to his wife, and a month later he published Cornelius Mathews's account in *Literary World*. There seems to have been a falling-out between Melville and Duyckinck after the publication of *Moby-Dick*, but the friendship survived until Evert's death.

16. William Allen Butler (1825–1902) was a New York lawyer, columnist, and socialite who later achieved some literary fame as author of the satire *Nothing to Wear* (1857). He relates his brief adventure in Pittsfield in an August 20, 1850 letter to Evert Duyckinck's brother George (*Log* 386).

17. At issue is one bumptious episode in the famous August gathering in Pittsfield, hosted by the Melville and Morewood families. According to Howard, Melville planned the ten-day party for literary friends and family as a final fling before the Melvill homestead (Broadhall) was to be sold to John and Sarah Morewood. In attendance were (among others) Evert Duyckinck, Cornelius Mathews, Hawthorne, his editor and friend James T. Fields, David Dudley Field, and Oliver Wendell Holmes. The festivities included picnics, a climb atop Monument Mountain, and a masquerade party. As Parker explains, Melville and Duyckinck conspired to include the Butlers, who by chance had just arrived by train at one of the two Pittsfield depots, by pretending to abduct Mrs. Butler. However, the Butlers would have nothing to do with this and continued with their journey.

18. Publishing his biography in 1951, Howard did not have access to the Augusta Papers, a trove of over five hundred letters discovered along with the *Typee* manuscript fragment in 1983.

The correspondence, now located in the New York Public Library, is mostly from and to several of Herman's closest female relatives—his mother, Maria, and sisters Augusta and Helen. It is a remarkable new source for understanding the Melville family relationships.

19. "Captain Taylor of the 'Pittsfield Artillery'" is given no further identification in Howard 159.

20. Cornelius Mathews (1817–1889), author of *The Career of Puffer Hopkins* (1841), was a literary champion of Duyckinck's Young America set. His rise and fall are depicted in Perry Miller.

21. Since this creative misquotation is picked up by other members of the panel, it is worth calling attention to the correction here. Sophia Hawthorne wrote her sister Elizabeth Peabody on August 8, 1850, that "I see Fayaway in his face" (*Log* Supplement 923), not "eyes." But a month later in a September 4 letter, Sophia does discuss Herman's eyes: "He has very keen perceptive power, but what astonishes me is, that his eyes are not large & deep (Log 393). Still, she seemed impressed by Melville's penetrating glance: "It is a strange, lazy glance, but with a power in it quite unique—It does not seem to penetrate through you, but to take you into himself" (*Log* 394).

22. In September 1847, shortly after her wedding to Herman, Elizabeth wrote to her cousin Samuel Savage: "At first I had some idea of being married in church and ordinarily I think it the most appropriate place for such a solemn ceremony—but we all thought if it were to get about previously that '*Typee*' was to be seen on such a day, a great crowd might rush out of mere curiosity to see 'the author'. . ." See Kennedy and Kennedy, "Herman and Elizabeth" 7.

23. "She loved me for the dangers I had pass'd / And I loved her that she did pity them" (*Othello* 1.3.167–68).

24. See Cowen. This five-thousand-page, multivolume Harvard dissertation has been reproduced by Garland Press.

25. One of several Melville residences in the 1830s. After the failure of his New York business in 1830, Allan Melvill moved his family to Albany, where they stayed after his death in 1832 until May 1838. Economy once again forced them to move across the Hudson to the community of Lansingburgh, now part of Troy, New York. It was in this house that Herman, upon his return from the Pacific, began writing *Typee*.

26. In September 1847, shortly after the weddings of Herman and Lizzie (August 4) and brother Allan Melville and Sophia Thurston (September 22), the two couples moved into a townhouse just off Astor Place. They were joined by mother Maria and the Melville sisters Helen, Augusta, Catherine, and Frances. Even so, the house had two empty rooms, enough for Lizzie to invite her cousin Samuel Savage to visit for a while. Later the population was augmented by the arrivals of Malcolm (to Herman and Lizzie on February 16, 1848) and Maria (to Allan and Sophia on February 18, 1848).

27. See Cohen and Yannella.

28. Peter Gansevoort (1788–1876), the son of General Peter Gansevoort, was Maria Melville's older brother. Uncle Peter was stern but invariably helpful in supporting his widowed sister and her family. Herman dedicated *Clarel* to his memory.

29. As of this printing, Geller's claim remains unsubstantiated.

30. The reference here is to one of the annual hikes up Monument Mountain in celebration of the original adventure on August 2, 1850, sponsored by the Berkshire Historical Society.

31. In a letter to her sister-in-law Catherine Lansing (June 5, 1877), Elizabeth writes, ". . . poor fellow he has so much mental suffering to undergo (and oh how all unnecessary) I am rejoiced when anything comes into his life to give him even a moment's relief" (*Log* 762).

32. Nancy Wroe Melvill (1780–1813) was one of father Allan's older sisters whose engagement to Allan's good friend Lemuel Shaw was cut short by her untimely death.

33. When Major Thomas Melvill followed his son Allan (Herman's father) in death in 1832, and his will was probated, Maria discovered that Allan had borrowed against his inheritance. To protect themselves from Allan's creditors attempting to claim a right to their inheritance, Allan's brother Thomas Jr. and his side of the family entered a friendly suit claiming no responsibility for Allan's debts. Although this could not be construed as harmful to Maria, she felt hurt by the litigation and isolated herself from the Melvill branch of the family. See Howard 8; *Log* 59. Massachusetts Supreme Court Justice Lemuel Shaw was Allan's best friend and a logical choice to be co-executor of the estate. John D'Wolf was Melville's uncle, the husband of his Aunt Mary Melvill (Allan's sister) and a former sea captain whose tales of the South Seas fueled young Herman's desire to go whaling.

34. Major Thomas Melvill (1751–1832), the patriarch of the Melville family, was noted for his participation in the Boston Tea Party and his continuing to wear his cock hat and breeches until his death. Uncle Thomas Melvill (1776–1845) was Allan's older brother and one of Herman's most cherished older relatives; he resided at Broadhall until debts forced him to leave the vicinity and start fresh in Galena, Illinois. Herman's father, Allan (1782–1832), failed in his business as a New York City merchant of fine imported clothing and died after suffering brain fever, leaving Herman fatherless at age twelve. Lucy Melvill was one of Allan and Thomas's younger sisters.

35. Priscilla Melvill (1784–1862) was father Allan's unmarried sister.

36. Robert Melvill (1817–1881) was Uncle Thomas's oldest son by his second wife, Mary Hobart.

37. In her December 23, 1847, letter to her step-mother, Hope Shaw, newlywed Elizabeth Melville describes her day: "By the time I come home [from a daily walk] it is two o'clock and after, and then I must make myself look as bewitchingly as possible to meet Herman at dinner" (*Log* 266).

38. As of this writing, the letter belongs to William Reese, bookseller, New Haven.

39. Hope Savage Shaw (1793–1879) was Judge Lemuel Shaw's second wife and Elizabeth Shaw's step-mother.

40. John and Sarah Morewood purchased the Melvill family residence, Broadhall, in Pittsfield in 1850 just as Herman and his family moved into Arrowhead, the adjoining property. The two families enjoyed a long friendship.

41. Gansevoort, New York: By the 1860s Melville's mother, his uncles Herman and Leonard, and his cousin Guert, among others, had settled in this upstate town near picturesque Glens Falls. Albany, New York: The more successful side of the Gansevoort family lived in the state's capital, including the family patriarch and benefactor Uncle Peter Gansevoort and cousin Catherine Gansevoort Lansing. Brookline, Massachusetts: One of Melville's sisters Helen lived here with her husband George Griggs. Lawrence, Massachusetts: Melville's sister Catherine (Kate) and John Hoadley were two of the author's more liberal-minded relatives. Hoadley, an inventive and enterprising engineer, became one of Herman's best friends. The Hoadley's daughter, Herman's niece Maria, married Herman's neighbors John and Sarah Morewood's son.

42. In February 1861 Melville, with the support of family and friends, attempted unsuccessfully to secure a consulship to Italy. Of the enterprise, Hope Shaw wrote in her diary (February 21, 1861): "I have no faith in sending away a *person* that is not able to see to his own business at Home" (Garner 80).

43. The Florence apartment building was a pioneer project in affordable urban dwelling that provided a staff of servants for the residents.

44. Barber, "Two New Melville Letters" 18–21. The letters of May 12 and 22, 1856, to Judge Shaw discuss Herman's failure to repay a loan that might result in his having to sell Arrowhead

(NN *Correspondence* 290–95). At this time, Melville considered moving to a smaller house in Pittsfield. A year later he contracted but then reneged on a house in Brooklyn. See Barber, "Melville's House" 433–34.

45. Tertullus D. Stewart, a Lansingburgh friend, loaned Melville two thousand dollars in 1851 to help in the renovations of Arrowhead. On purchasing Arrowhead, Melville also took on a mortgage from the former owner, Dr. John M. Brewster. Melville also accepted a loan of three thousand dollars from his father-in-law, Lemuel Shaw (NN *Correspondence* 291).

46. Most of Melville's family were Union-supporting Democrats, which is to say they were not abolitionists but reviled slavery and secession. Helen and George Griggs, however, were outspoken Republicans (Garner 6–7). No actual record exists of Herman's party affiliation.

47. Yannella elaborates his view in Cohen and Yannella, Appendix J. In a letter to her sister Kate on October 6, 1867, Helen Griggs writes: "One reads a novel to be amused, a sort of agreeable pastime, tho' not a useful one perhaps" (213).

48. In September 1847 Elizabeth wrote to her cousin Sam Savage asking him to convey a message to her friend, Daniel McIlroy: "If you have a good opportunity, *not without*[,] tell Mr. McIlroy for yourself, *not from* me, that my marriage was very unexpected, and scarcely thought of until about two months before it actually took place. I have some reason for wishing him to know this fact but I want you to mention it casually on your own account—." See Kennedy and Kennedy, "Herman and Elizabeth" 8.

49. Samuel H. Savage was Elizabeth Melville's step-mother's nephew (i.e., Herman's step-cousin-in-law). See NN *Correspondence* 201–03; Kennedy and Kennedy, "Melville and Samuel Savage" 1–10.

50. Although only distantly related by marriage—he was the husband of Abby Thurston, the sister of Herman's brother Allan's first wife, Sophia Thurston—Richard Lathers (1820–1903) was a wealthy companion, sharing books and his art collection with Melville throughout his later decades.

51. Magazine editor, correspondent, and man of letters, Nathaniel Parker Willis (1806–1867) was an early supporter of Melville's who was involved in an adulterous affair with the wife of American stage actor Edwin Forrest. The subsequent divorce trial was a national scandal.

52. See Beers.

53. See chapter 9 above for Brodhead's essay "Melville; or, Aggression."

54. Two letters are under discussion here. The March 27, 1851, letter from both Nathaniel and Sophia Hawthorne asks Melville to pick up "a large box" at the Pittsfield depot. The Melvilles lived considerably closer to town than the Hawthornes, and Herman was apparently happy to perform such errands. There is, however, no mention here of shoes in this letter (NN *Correspondence* 607–09). Upon delivery of the box, Melville received an inscribed copy of *The House of the Seven Gables,* only just published, and dated April 11, 1851. Apparently at this time the Hawthornes asked Melville to purchase for them a pair of shoes for their child, Julian, whenever he was to be in town again. About five days later Melville wrote Hawthorne in praise of *Seven Gables,* beginning the letter with a reference to his search for "the young gentleman's shoes" or "booties" (NN *Correspondence* 184–85).

55. *Log* 229.

56. The two Williams College students, John Thomas Gulick and Titus Munson Coan, visited Melville at Arrowhead on April 20, 1859. Only Gulick alludes to alcohol: "His countenance is slightly flushed with whiskey drinking, but not without expression" (*Log* 604–06).

57. "The Paradise of Bachelors," the first part of one of Melville's three double tales, or diptychs, is based on dining experiences at London's Inns of Court and is replete with drinking and eating imagery.

58. David Davidson was a London agent for the American publishers Wiley and Putnam's when Melville visited London in 1849 (NN *Journals* 302). Yannella is quoting Davidson's usage of "blue-posted," found in a letter to George Duyckinck (December 24, 1849), which refers to dining at the Blue Post Tavern in London (NN *Journals* 329; *Log* 340).

59. Novelist Paul Metcalf (*Genoa* [1965]) is Melville's great-grandson, the son of Eleanor Melville Metcalf. Melville Chapin, a Boston lawyer, is also a great-grandson of Melville's.

60. Eleanor Melville Metcalf 215.

61. Hawthorne and the fourteenth president of the United States, Franklin Pierce (1804–1869), were schoolmates at Bowdoin College. Their friendship continued until Hawthorne's death in 1864. In 1852 Hawthorne wrote Pierce's presidential campaign biography and was later rewarded for this job with a consulship to Liverpool.

62. Gansevoort Melville (1815–1846) was Melville's active older brother. He took over the family business when father Allan suddenly died; he became a politically active Jacksonian and served in the American legation to England during the Polk Administration. He died in London while helping to see *Typee* through its British publication.

63. The American, or Know-Nothing, party was a reactionary, racist, and anti-Catholic movement of the 1850s that had its roots in nativist organizations begun as early as 1845 in Philadelphia, the city of brotherly love. The party was structured on local secret lodges, and their password was "I know nothing"; hence, the party's sobriquet.

64. See Spann 498n53.

65. Edward Moxon (1801–1858), British publisher, was a close friend and literary associate of Charles Lamb's. Richard Henry Dana, Jr., provided Melville with a letter of introduction to Moxon, and Melville later recounted to Dana how the two met in Moxon's icy offices on November 20, 1849. *Log* 335; NN *Journals* 23.

66. Melville's May 1, 1850, letter to Dana, written soon after his return from England, helps date the composition of *Moby-Dick,* for he indicates that he is already "half way" done. Even so, it would be another year or so before the work was complete. Parker is paraphrasing from the letter's last paragraph: "It will be a strange sort of a book, tho', I fear; blubber is blubber you know; tho' you may get oil out of it, the poetry runs as hard as sap from a frozen maple tree;—& to cook the thing up, one must needs throw in a little fancy, which from the nature of the thing, must be ungainly as the gambols of the whales themselves. Yet I mean to give the truth of the thing, spite of this" (NN *Correspondence* 162; *Log* 374).

67. See Collier.

68. Thomas Powell, a British litterateur of dubious character, had come to New York in 1849 to flee forgery charges in England. There he had made numerous enemies, including Dickens, whom he continued to vilify in various New York publications. He was briefly lionized by the Young America crowd, but when Dickens wrote to the *Knickerbocker* about Powell and when Powell began to attack Irving and later Melville, he fell quickly out of favor. Parker suggests in the Historical Note to the Northwestern-Newberry *Moby-Dick* that these events were enough to reinforce Melville's desire to leave the city for Arrowhead (606–10).

69. Mary D'Wolf (1778–1859) was father Allan's older sister and wife of sea captain John D'Wolf. She gave Melville a copy of Hawthorne's *Mosses from an Old Manse* in July 1850, but the author did not begin reading until his guests for the August party arrived, and he was scheduled to meet Hawthorne in person, who was himself newly ensconced in neighboring Lenox, Massachusetts.

70. In his August 7, 1850, letter to George, Evert writes, "Melville has a new book mostly done—a romantic, fanciful & literal & most enjoyable presentment of the Whale fishery—something quite new" (*Log* 385).

71. Based on information from Elizabeth Shaw Melville, critic Moncure D. Conway (friend and later editor of Melville) wrote in the introduction to his edition of *Blithedale Romance* that "he had never yet seen Hawthorne" before writing the *Mosses* review (as quoted in Scharnhorst 2).

72. Berkshire author Joel T. Headley participated in some of the dining and excursions at the August 1850 party, in particular a tour of Stockbridge's Ice Glen (Howard 157–59). According to Howard, "The arrival of Headley may have interrupted [Melville's] reading of [Hawthorne's *Mosses*] before he finished the volume, but he could have started meditating that evening an essay which would express his genuine enthusiasm for the work" (158).

73. See NN *WJ* 489ff.

74. Anticipating a trip to New York City in order to put the finishing touches to *Moby-Dick*, Melville wrote Hawthorne [June 1, 1851?], "I am so pulled hither and thither by circumstances. The calm, the coolness, the silent grass-growing mood in which a man ought to compose—that, I fear, can seldom be mine" (NN *Correspondence* 191).

75. New York socialite Anne Lynch invited Melville to a Valentine's Day party in 1848. In attendance were various artists and literary figures, including travel writer Bayard Taylor, who composed and recited several valentine poems to party guests, among them Herman Melville. See Howard 118; *Log* 272.

76. See Garner 101–03.

WORKS CITED

Barber, Patricia. "Melville's House in Brooklyn." *American Literature* 45 (November 1973): 433–34.
———. "Two New Melville Letters." *American Literature* 49 (November 1977): 18–21.
Beers, Henry Augustin. *Nathaniel Parker Willis.* American Men of Letters Series. Boston: Houghton, Mifflin, 1885.
Bryant, John, ed. *A Companion to Melville Studies.* Westport, CT: Greenwood, 1986.
Cohen, Hennig, and Donald Yannella. *Herman Melville's Malcolm Letter: "Man's Final Lore."* New York: Fordham UP and the New York Public Library, 1992.
Collier, John Payne. "The Life of William Shakespeare." In *Shakespeare's Plays and Poems.* London: Whittaker, 1844.
Cowen, Wilson Walker. *Melville's Marginalia.* New York: Garland, 1987.
Garner, Stanton. *The Civil War World of Herman Melville.* Lawrence: UP of Kansas, 1993.
Hawthorne, Julian. *Nathaniel Hawthorne and His Wife: A Biography.* 2 vols. Boston: Ticknor, 1888.
Howard, Leon. *Herman Melville: A Biography.* Berkeley: U of California P, 1951.
Kennedy, Joyce Deveau, and Frederick J. Kennedy. "Herman and Elizabeth." *Melville Society Extracts* no. 33 (1978): 8.
———. "Herman Melville and Samuel Hay Savage, 1847–1851." *Melville Society Extracts* no. 35 (September 1978): 1–10.
Metcalf, Eleanor Melville. *Herman Melville: Cycle and Epicycle.* Cambridge, MA: Harvard UP, 1953.
Metcalf, Paul. *Genoa: A Telling of Wonders.* Millerton, NY: The Book Organization, 1965.

Miller, Edwin Havilland. *Herman Melville: A Biography.* New York: Braziller, 1975.

Miller, Perry. *The Raven and the Whale: The War of Words and Wits in the Era of Poe and Melville.* New York: Harcourt, 1956.

Mumford, Lewis. *Herman Melville.* New York, Harcourt, 1929.

Scharnhorst, Gary. "Melville's Authorship of 'Hawthorne and His *Mosses*': The First Public Attribution." *Melville Society Extracts* no. 73 (May 1988): 1–3.

Sealts, Merton M., Jr. *The Early Lives of Herman Melville: Nineteenth-Century Biographical Sketches and Their Authors.* Madison: U of Wisconsin P, 1974.

Spann, Edward K. *The New Metropolis: New York, 1840–1857.* New York: Columbia UP, 1982.

12

The Lost *Poems* (1860) and Melville's
First Urge to Write an Epic Poem

HERSHEL PARKER

If Melville had not been prevented from publishing two books he had completed, we would know him as the man who published these volumes between 1846 and 1876: *Typee, Omoo, Mardi, Redburn, White-Jacket, Moby-Dick, Pierre, The Isle of the Cross* (1853), *Israel Potter, The Piazza Tales, The Confidence-Man, Poems* (1860), *Battle-Pieces,* and *Clarel.* We might or might not have known him also as the man who published *John Marr* (1888) and *Timoleon* (1891), since in these little books, particularly in the latter, he may have salvaged some pieces from *Poems,* which he tried to publish in 1860. However much we learn about the circumstances of its creation, we find it hard to take account of a real, completed book-length manuscript if it was (as far as we know) never published and if it is not known to be extant. If I had the money, I would order dummies in the Northwestern-Newberry format, so that when I look up at my row of Melville volumes the spines of *The Isle of the Cross* (between *Pierre* and *Israel Potter*) and *Poems* (between *The Confidence-Man* and *Battle-Pieces*) would forcibly remind me that those books were real to Melville.

If the Harpers had published *The Isle of the Cross* soon after Melville offered it to them in June 1853, and if Melville had gone on to write "Bartleby" and other stories, as he did, then we would make appropriate use of the letters from late 1852 in which Melville tried to persuade Hawthorne to write the story of Agatha Hatch before he decided to write it himself. Then we would talk about the aesthetic advances Melville had made after *Pierre,* during the composition of *The Isle of the Cross,* and explore "Bartleby" in light of that book. As it is, having discovered belatedly that Melville completed a book called *The Isle of the Cross,* which must be the "Agatha" story, we have scarcely begun to think of the likelihood that whatever he learned in writing it affected the way he wrote "Bartleby" and the other stories in the summer of 1853.

Similarly, because it was never published, we treat the 1860 *Poems* by Herman Melville not as if it were lost but as if it never existed. It existed. Melville wrote it, his wife Elizabeth Shaw Melville copied it, the New York editors Evert and George Duyckinck read it, at least two publishers looked at it. When Melville sailed from Boston on May 30, 1860, in the clipper ship *Meteor,* commanded by his brother Thomas, he was sure a copy of his *Poems,* printed in the interval and shipped by way of Panama, would be waiting for him when he reached San Francisco after the long voyage around the Horn.

To comprehend Melville's transforming himself into a poet after his travels in the Mediterranean and in Europe in 1856 and 1857, we need to remember the relative status of prose fiction and poetry in Great Britain and the United States in the 1840s and the 1850s. The theory still prevailed that the greatest writers were poets and that for a lover of literature the highest and richest rewards were to be found in poetry. When the sailor Herman Melville took up his pen in Manhattan late in 1844, he learned, fast enough, that most critics who hoped for the emergence of great American literature were looking for it to come in the form of poetry, not prose. Late in 1847 and early in 1848, the months he was working his way deep into the manuscript of *Mardi,* Melville knew that some critics were hailing Longfellow's *Evangeline* as the great literary work they had been calling for.

Through the 1850s, American critics regularly gave more space in reviews even to routine books of poetry than they did to routine works of fiction. Through the 1850s, poems such as Longfellow's *The Golden Legend* and *Hiawatha* received far more extensive coverage in the press than Melville's own books. Melville knew this disparity well, for in the course of looking for reviews of his own books he inevitably took note of the books being reviewed alongside his own. One example can show the pattern. During the spring of 1855, Charles Kingsley's novel *Westward Ho!* received only slightly longer reviews in the United States than Melville's *Israel Potter* (as a British novelist deserved). The next year, however, while *The Piazza Tales* was receiving mainly short polite reviews, the *New York Tribune* (on May 10, 1856) lavished five columns on Kingsley's *Poems*. Kingsley the fiction writer did not deserve such space, but Kingsley the poet *did*.

Well before he returned from his Mediterranean and European trip in 1857 and announced that he was not going to write any more at present, Melville's prose in *Mardi, The Whale* and *Moby-Dick*, and *The Piazza Tales*, especially, had been described by reviewers as poetic. His only known verse from his early career is what he ascribed to (and presumably wrote for the voice of) the sentimental Yoomy in *Mardi*. Within a year or two of the utter failure of his career as a prose writer (when he earned not a penny from *The Confidence-Man* to pay for the paper and ink expended upon it), Melville had begun to think of himself as a poet—not as a closet scribbler of verses but as a writer who would reemerge into the literary scene as a poet, like Bryant, Halleck, Longfellow, Willis, Hoffman, most of whom were friends or acquaintances of his.

On July 26, 1858, George Duyckinck, the younger of the Duyckincks, gave news about his visit to Arrowhead, Melville's farm two miles south of Pittsfield, Massachusetts. Melville, he had learned, was "busy on a new book," but he had apparently been told nothing about its nature. It is possible that Melville was then writing a new work in prose, but more likely it was a book of poetry, since when *Poems* was ready for publication two years later, Melville's wife said that she and her husband had kept its existence "a profound secret" between them for a long time. In 1858 the secret was not that Melville was working on another book but that what he was writing was poetry.

Early in 1860 Melville's abrupt decision to sail around the world on the *Meteor* precipitated complex legal machinations to protect his wife in the event of his death on his voyage, and also precipitated the literary decision to try to publish the book of poems. On May 21 Melville wrote Evert Duyckinck: "If you have met Allan [Herman's younger brother, and his lawyer] lately he has perhaps informed you that in a few days I go with my brother Tom a voyage round Cape Horn. It was only determined upon a short time since; and I am at present busy, as you may imagine in getting ready for a somewhat long absence, and likewise in prepareing for type certain M.S.S."[1] This was preliminary to a request for Duyckinck's editorial services in his absence:

Now may I with propriety ask of you, conditionally, a favor? Will you, upon the arrival of the M.S.S. in New York—that is, in the course of two weeks, or less—look over them and if they seem of a sort that you care to be any way concerned with, advice with Allan as to a publisher, and form of volume, &c. . . . In short, may I, without seeming too confident, ask you, as a veteran & expert in these matters, and as an old acquaintance, to lend something of an overseeing eye to the launching of this craft—the committing of it to the elements?

Evert's response, "a very welcome one—quite a wind from the fields of old times" (as Melville wrote on May 28), included an agreement to help see the poems into print.

The next day after he wrote Duyckinck, May 22, Melville hastily jotted down what he labeled "Memoranda for Allan concerning the publication of my verses," the fullest instructions he had ever given for the publication of one of his works and powerful evidence of how seriously he took his new role as poet:

1—Don't stand on terms much with the publisher—half profits after expenses are paid will content me—not that I expect much "profits"—but that will be a fair nominal arrangement. . . .

2—Don't have the Harpers.—I should like the Appletons or Scribner—But Duyckinck's advice will be good here.

3—The sooner the thing is printed and published, the better. The "season" will make little or no difference, I fancy, in this case.

4—After printing, dont let the book hang back—but publish & have done.

5—For God's sake don't have *By the author of "Typee" "Piddledee" &c* on the title-page.

6—Let the title-page be simply,

Poems

by

Herman Melville.

7—Dont have any clap-trap announcements and "sensation" puffs—nor any extracts published previous to publication of book—Have a decent publisher, in short.

8—Don't take any measures, or make inquiries as to expediency of an English edition simultaneous with the American—as in case of "Confidence-Man."

9—In the M.S.S. each piece is on a page by itself, however small the piece. This was done merely for convenience in the final classification; and should be no guide for the printer—Of course in printing two or more pieces will sometimes appear on the same page—according to length of pieces &c . . .

10—The poems are divided into books as you will see; but the divisions are not *called* books—they are only numbered . . . .

11—Anything not perfectly plain in the M.S.S. can be referred to Lizzie . . .

12—Lizzie should by all means see the printed sheets *before* being bound, in order to detect any gross errors consequent upon misconstruing the M.S.S.

Melville added, self-deprecatingly yet soberly, "Of all human events, perhaps, the publication of a first volume of verses is the most insignificant; but though a matter of no moment to the world, it is still of some concern to the author,—as these *Mem.* show—Pray therefore, don't laugh at my *Mem.* but give heed to them."

Only a few of the points in the memorandum need comment. Melville may have put in the second item because the Harpers had turned down poems he submitted to their magazine in 1858, although what they rejected then is uncertain; in any case, he held old resentments against the firm. Items 11 and 12 constitute the earliest evidence that Mrs. Melville was so intimately familiar with the poems that she could explain anything that was confusing and would have to be the one to exercise final judgment over the proofs. No one preserved a table of contents, so we are left to guess about such matters as the numbered sections (not called books, the way the sections of *Paradise Lost* are called books, but nevertheless constituting books in the sense that they were separate sections unrelated to other sections). In the letter Melville wrote to Duyckinck on board the *Meteor* in Boston Harbor on May 28, he explained that his wife would send "the parcel" of poems "in the course of a week or so—there remaining something to be finished in copying the M.S.S." His wife, he explained, had "interested herself a good deal in this matter," to the point that she seemed "to know more about it" than he did, "at least about the *merits* of the performance." George, he hoped, would also look over his "scribblings"—this he added before breaking off his "egotistical" requests.

Melville loathed asking favors of anyone, as his mother had observed long before, so his "egotistical" placing of his poetry in the capable editorial hands of Evert Duyckinck reveals how momentous to him the publication of his *Poems* was. Evert's acquiescence took the burden off his mind: Lizzie could answer any questions of reading or design, Allan could handle all legal matters (expeditiously, since no English publication would have to be arranged), and the most professional literary man in New York would see *Poems* by Herman Melville into print. It was a done deal, and Melville would not have to suffer any of the annoyances of negotiating with publishers and correcting proofs.

When he had reached London in 1857 *The Confidence-Man* had been waiting for him, brought into print by the combined efforts of his brother Allan and Nathaniel Hawthorne; now when he reached San Francisco his *Poems* would be waiting for him, brought into print by the united agencies of Lizzie, Allan, and not one but two Duyckincks. Melville would open his package from Lizzie and take out a little decorously bound volume. On the shores where Sir Francis Drake was said to have anchored his *Golden Hind,* Melville could see his poems in print for the first time. The voyage by Panama would be a fit initiation for some of the poems, if, as seems likely, the volume included verses based on his experiences in the Mediterranean. Nothing would go wrong: the poet would leave early and take the long way, *Poems* would leave late but take one of two shorter ways, and the poet and his *Poems* would be reunited in San Francisco.

In the next weeks after Melville's departure, his wife did her best by his poems. On June 1 she informed Duyckinck of an instruction her husband had "omitted in his haste," that the book should be "plainly bound." Melville, she explained, had "a decided aversion" to the recent fashion of packaging poetry in "'blue and gold'" bindings, gaudily "over-gilt." On June 4 she accompanied the "parcel" with a letter in which she begged Duyckinck to tell her his honest opinion of the poems, an opinion she was especially anxious to hear since no one had seen the sheets, "excepting two of Herman's sisters, who are now with me—and I want to know how they would strike an unprejudiced person." Having read the poems, Evert reassured her of their merit. Promptly enough he sent the manuscript to Charles Scribner, who had published the Duyckinck brothers' *Cyclopaedia of American Literature.* Feeling no excess of loyalty to the Duyckincks, Scribner returned the poems on June 19 with a perfunctory comment ("I have no doubt they are excellent, they seem so to me, and I have confidence in your judgement") and the cool decision that he had issued enough poetry for the season, a volume by E. C. Stedman and another by G. P. Morris, neither of which he expected to pay. After receiving the news, Elizabeth on June 23 expressed her gratitude to the Duyckincks for their help as well as their praise of the poetry. She acknowledged that rejection by a publisher was not necessarily an indication of low literary merit: "I suppose that if John Milton were to offer 'Paradise Lost' to the Harpers tomorrow, it would be promptly rejected as 'unsuitable' not to say, denounced as dull" (*Log* 620). Whatever the fate of her husband's volume of poetry, Evert and George had confirmed her "own prejudice in its favor." Herman's being away might even work in the book's favor: "he might be disheartened at the outset, by its rejection, and perhaps withhold it altogether, which would be a great disappointment to me." Evert Duyckinck tried again, sending the manuscript to Rudd & Carleton, who were then intent on pushing forward their translations from the French classics (according to Blox, the correspondent of Washington's *National Intelligencer,* November 1, 1860). They soon rejected it in turn. Then Duyckinck probably gave up and returned the manuscript to Allan or sent it to Mrs. Melville.

Some or many of the poems may have survived, and some may have been published in the two volumes Melville issued at the end of his life. So far there is no way of identifying a single one of the poems in what, by the grace of Charles Scribner or another publisher, would have appeared in 1860 as *Poems,* by Herman Melville. It is possible that not one of the poems survives in any form, revised or unrevised, although the reasonable assumption is that some of them do survive, however revised, most likely among the group "Fruit of Travel Long Ago," which he published in *Timoleon* in the year of his death.

In the last days before sailing, Melville had packed "a good lot of books," he wrote to Evert Duyckinck, and "plenty of old periodicals—lazy reading for lazy latitudes." During the early weeks of the voyage, Melville's reading was desultory, his journal entries show. On June 18 he spent the day "dipping into the 'Quarterlies,'" but he found "methodical reading out of the question." The day they crossed the Line, June 29, he gave to his brother Tom *Sketches of Life and Character,* by Alexander Campbell (Edinburgh, 1842), a fair indication that he had just finished reading it (just as the almost total absence of marks indicates that he found little of value in it). In July he read some or all of *The Marble Faun,* which his neighbor Sarah Morewood had given him as a going-away present (the time being long past when Hawthorne would ask Ticknor and Fields to include Melville among those to be sent presentation copies). He ignored most of Hawthorne's inept art criticism but took issue with the assertion in chapter 12 that "Perugino was evidently a devout man": "On the contrary, if I remember right, he is said, in 'Lives of the Painters,' to have been a jeerer at all religion" (*Log* 621). (He had made good use of Duyckinck's loan-volumes of Vasari's *Lives.*) During the later stages of the voyage down the Atlantic and round the Cape, he made a few more journal entries, none of which mentions any current reading.

Instead of reading, even in desultory fashion, Melville may have been writing poetry. One moonlight night he overflowed to Tom with verse, some of which he may have written on the voyage:

I cant help thinking what a luckless chap you were that voyage you had a poetaster with you. You remember the romantic moonlight night, when the
conceited donkey repeated to you about three cables' length of his verses.
But you bore it like a hero. I cant in fact recall so much as a single *wince.* To
be sure, you went to bed immediately upon the conclusion of the entertainment; but this much I am sure of, whatever were your sufferings, you never
gave them utterance. Tom, my boy, I admire you. I say again, you are a hero.

This was in a letter of May 25, 1862, in which he facetiously assured his brother
that he had disposed of his doggerel to a trunkmaker for linings. But in the
late summer of 1860, Captain Melville may have been listening to a genuine
poet aboard the *Meteor,* not a mere poetaster.

Once Cape Horn had been rounded, Melville made no journal entries at all.
As the *Meteor* sailed up the coast toward the equator, from mid-August to mid-
September, he was at last reading methodically and purposefully. Besides many
old quarterlies, he had taken with him a good lot of books, as he had told Evert
Duyckinck, being free to carry all he wanted, since once they were installed
in his cabin they could stay there as the *Meteor* sailed around the world. Writing to Duyckinck in a confidential tone, and feeling in a confidential mood,
Melville nevertheless had given no indication that there was anything systematic in his choice of books for the voyage. In fact there were disparate items
among them, carried aboard for personal, incidental reasons, as the Hawthorne book was, but he had exercised a rigorous selection policy. A sufficient number of books have been identified so that we can be reasonably sure
about what he was doing, day by day. Chances are that he was not, for instance,
steeping himself in contemporary fiction. Rather than stuffing a shirt or two
into his old carpetbag and heading for Cape Horn and the Pacific (like himself
in 1840, or his Ishmael in *Moby-Dick*), he had taken a small library of great
poetry, classical epic poetry in English translation, modern European poetry in
translation, and English poetry with an emphasis on the epic or very long
poem. Some of these works he had already read with great care over a period of
a decade or more (even longer, in the case of Spenser); some he had owned for
at least two years and may or may not yet have worked through with great care.

Melville did not mention these volumes of poetry in his journal or in surviving letters, but he identified them as having been read at certain points
on the voyage. Conscious of the grandeur of this episode in his life, his voyag-
ing round the world, he noted expansively "Cape Horn" and "Pacific Ocean."

Thinking of this voyage as "Cape Horn 2," the second time he had doubled the Cape from the Atlantic to the Pacific, he inscribed "C.H.2" or some other variant (e.g., "C. Horn 1860") in several books. In his father's eight-volumes-in-four set of Spenser, he marked "C.H.2" in the upper left front flyleaf of at least two volumes. Mindful of the fact that he was headed for Indian waters, if not for specifically for the port of Calcutta, he had taken Thomas Duer Broughton's *Selections from the Popular Poetry of the Hindoos* (on which he wrote "C.H.2" in pencil on the recto of the front flyleaf). Sometimes he relocated himself even in books with a new date and location: even though he had already inscribed "H.Melville/N.Y. 1849" in his two-volume Milton, he marked the volumes with a new date in one and a nautical location in another.

In some volumes Melville noted date, location, or both. In his copy of Beranger's *Songs* he wrote "Pacific Ocean / Sep 4th 1860 / 19 S.L." After crossing the Equator, he wrote "Pacific Ocean, Sep. 14th 1860 / 5° 60" N.L." in his copy of Wordsworth's poems. In the set of Milton's poems he wrote on the flyleaf of the first volume "C. Horn 1860" and in the second volume "Pacific Ocean / N.L. 15° / Sep. 21th 1860." In a copy of Dante he wrote "Pacific Ocean / Sunday Afternoon / Sep 22 1860." In a copy of Schiller's *Poems and Ballads,* by the last stanza of "To Emma," he wrote: "Sept 25th 1860 / North Pacific." On the front flyleaf of the first volume of George Chapman's translation of excerpts from Homer, Hesiod, Musaeus, and Juvenal (the set of Chapman that George Duyckinck had given him in 1858), Melville wrote "C.H.2." On the front flyleaf of the first volume of the *Iliad* in the same set he inscribed "C.H.2"; in the front flyleaf of the second volume he wrote "'Meteor & Derby'" (a note about a ship sighting as they neared San Francisco) and "Cape Horn 2." On the front flyleaf of the first volume of Chapman's *Odyssey* he wrote "Pacific Ocean / Oct 3d 1860 / 700 miles from San Francisco / CH2." These unsystematic notations in these volumes which happen to survive do not establish anything like the precise sequence and intensity of Melville's reading, yet they are highly suggestive.

In the Spenser he carried, Melville not only noted a Wordsworth borrowing but shared vicariously in Wordsworth's own joy in Spenser: "How W. W. must have delighted in this stanza." In his Spenser he copied the tribute from "The Passionate Pilgrim," assuming it was by Shakespeare, and recalled Spenser's tribute to "Dan Chaucer," the *"well of English undefyled."* In other places in the Spenser he traced borrowings by Shakespeare (repeatedly, *Macbeth*), Milton, Pope, Keats, and Poe, besides Wordsworth. (This set of Spenser is the only known extant place where Melville wrote Poe's name; he gave his wife his now-lost Poe on New Year's Day 1861, perhaps because he was through with it.) In reading Wordsworth's "The Excursion," he noticed a debt and copied lines from Spenser for comparison: "Sleepe after toyle, port after stormie seas, / Ease after warre, death after life does greatly please"—exactly the reading in his father's copy, except for his omission of a comma after "life." Elsewhere he saw a similarity between something in Wordsworth's "Character of the Happy Warrior" and a line from Schiller's *Don Carlos,* "'Keep true to the dream of thy youth.'" In reading "Laodamia" Melville turned a criticism Wordsworth made of tautology in Dr. Johnson back on Wordsworth, remembering something he had read in Hazlitt's *The Spirit of the Age.* In the Milton volumes Melville marked comparisons to Virgil, Tasso, Ariosto, Dante, Johnson, Shakespeare, Campbell, Lucan, Sir Thomas Browne, Byron, Spenser, Plutarch. Into his Dante he inscribed a quotation from Walter Savage Landor. Reading Dante, he was reminded of Blake (and Botticelli). On a free leaf in the back he jotted down several lines and the initials "J. Q. A."—apparently unidentified lines of poetry, and not from Adams's epic of Irish history or his *Poems of Religion and Society* (1848). For Melville, all such markings and annotations went under the heading "methodical reading."

The generalizations we can make about Melville's reading on this voyage will change, very likely, as still more volumes from his library turn up (as the Wordsworth did in the 1970s, the Milton and Dante in the 1980s, and the Spenser in the 1990s). But the nature of the books he carried is clear: mainly he carried poetry, and most often volumes that contained epic poems or else very long poems (such as Wordsworth's "The Excursion"). Now, in the Pacific Ocean, he gave himself over to a prolonged study of the interconnections between earlier and later Western poetry, and especially English poetry. He was tracing what a recent fad in literary criticism called "intertextuality," the sort of technical term he eschewed. Melville took hints from the editors of the poetry he was reading, and he read about poetry in essays in his periodicals; but mainly he had amassed and was amassing in his brain lines of poetry that set off signals of recognition when he came across sources for them or echoes of them.

These particular surviving volumes that he marked during the voyage cannot be the only volumes Melville took with him: others must now be lost, and others may survive with no record that they went round the Horn. Some guesses may be hazarded. Melville may have carried with him the epic by John Quincy Adams, *Dermot MacMorrogh, or, The Conquest of Ireland: An Historical Tale of the 12th Century, in Four Cantos,* for he referred contemptuously to it in an annotation in the Milton. Adams's poetry was on his mind, for he seems to have copied out a passage of the former president's poetry into his Dante (now erased, leaving only a few words visible). He may have had his copy of Ossian, James Macpherson's *Fingal, An Ancient Epic Poem,* which he had bought in 1848 and remembered well in March 1862, as shown by an annotation in William Hazlitt's *Lectures on the English Comic Writers* and *Lectures on the English Poets.* In books he carried with him he refers to other writers, including Byron, Keats, and Poe, whose poetry he may have had at hand.

At this stage of his life, Melville was in the habit of reading a translation of an epic poem with a second translation at hand, but no translations are known to contain his label "C.H.2." The fact that he repeatedly made cross-references between writers he had with him (Milton and Spenser, Spenser and Wordsworth) suggests, but does not prove, that his frequent citations of lines from Pope's Homer in his annotations in books he had with him means that he had the Pope *Iliad* of the Harper's Classical Library with him too. (Such annotations could have been made before or after the voyage.) He may have had with him his Classical Library copy of Dryden's translation of Virgil's *Aeneid,* and it is hard to imagine that he traveled with no Shakespeare, although the good set he bought in 1849 does not bear any indication that he had it along. (Tom might have kept a set of Shakespeare on board.) It is possible that he had Tasso and Ariosto. He may have had with him Chaucer (perhaps in the 1835 expurgated, modernized edition he picked up at some time). Either on this voyage or about this time, he wrote onto the pages of Chapman's Homer many of Pope's renderings of particular lines. In the Dante he noted a variant rendering of a line by the translator John Carlyle, although in this case there is no other evidence that he had further knowledge of the Carlyle translation. I make these speculations because Melville refers to Pope and these other authors in his annotations in some of the volumes he demonstrably took.

Inevitably, the magazines Melville took with him contained essays on poetry, and by "old periodicals" he may have referred to selections *from* periodicals, such as the volumes in the set of *Modern British Essayists* he had bought in 1849. In that set the Francis Jeffrey volume contained classic *Edinburgh Review* reviews of recent poetry such as *Manfred, Reliques of Robert Burns, Gertrude of Wyoming, Endymion, Childe Harold's Pilgrimage, The Prisoner of Chillon, The Excursion,* and *The White Doe of Rylstone.* The Jeffrey volume in itself was a library of practical criticism on poetry. More importantly, Jeffrey insisted in his 1843 Preface, his reviews demonstrated "the

Principles" on which his literary judgments had been based. That is, Jeffrey thought of himself as having contributed significantly to what we would call "theory." Whether or not Melville took the Jeffrey volume, he had old periodicals with him. Lazy reading for lazy latitudes indeed!

On the *Meteor* Melville was going to the best authorities. Just as he had once gone to books on whaling, he now went to the poets themselves and to their editors and critics, not only to learn to understand poetry but to determine what he might achieve as a poet. Melville read carefully Milton's justification "Of that Sort of Dramatic Poem which is Called Tragedy," his preface to *Samson Agonistes*. There he absorbed the idea that "Heretofore men in highest dignity have laboured not a little to be thought able to compose a tragedy": "Of that honour Dionysius the elder was no less ambitious, than before of his attaining to the tyranny. Augustus Caesar also had begun his Ajax, but unable to please his own judgment with what he had begun, left it unfinished. Seneca, the philosopher, is by some thought the author of those tragedies, (at least the best of them,) that to under that name."[2] Melville put an *x* in the margin by the passage on Augustus's leaving his tragedy about Ajax unfinished and at the bottom of the page adduced a contrary example from the history of the young American republic: "J.Q.A. might have followed his example." This means, as I indicated earlier, that Melville knew *Dermot MacMorrogh, or, The Conquest of Ireland: An Historical Tale of the 12th Century* and had brooded both over the Massachusettsean's high intention and his failure. He read Michael Drayton's praise of Chapman's translation of the *Georgics* of Hesiod:

> CHAPMAN, we find, by the past-prized fraught,
> What wealth thou dost upon this land confer,
> Th' old Grecian prophets hither that hast brought,
> Of their full words the true interpreter;
> And by thy travall strongly hast exprest
> The large dimensions of the English tongue.

Melville's check mark by this last line identified an ambitious hope for his future influence as a poet. Similarly, Melville checked and underlined *"To build with level of my lofty stile"* in Spenser's "The Ruins of Rome" and wrote at the foot of the page, "Build the lofty rhyme / Milton."

Paying attention, as he had always done, to what the scholarly editors said in their biographical and critical material, Melville in Richard Hooper's introduction to the *Iliad* drew a box around the word "passion," underlined "the all in all in poetry" and put brackets around this entire sentence: "But passion (the all in all in poetry) is everywhere present [in Chapman's translation], raising the low, dignifying the mean, and putting sense into the absurd." There he also boxed a reference to Chapman's "primitive power" and was struck by this sentence:

> When we consider the subtile influence of poetry upon the rising spirits of the age, it tempts me to hazard the speculation that, if Chapman's noble paraphrase had been read instead of Pope's enervating monotony, and as extensively, the present class of general readers would not only have been a more poetical class—as the fountain-head from the rock is above the artificial cascade in a pleasure-ground—but a finer order of human beings in respect of energy, love of nature at first-hand, and faith in their own impulses and aspirations. (Cowen 2:5–6)

Melville drew three vertical lines along "subtile influence of poetry upon the rising spirits of the age" and underlined those words, and he underlined from "but a finer order" on through the rest of the sentence. Far from remaining in his state of alienation from the contemporary world, Melville was now thinking of how through poetry he might arouse "a finer order of human beings," at least among the English-reading world. In a copy of the New Testament he had with him, he underscored in Romans 14 "Hast thou faith? have it to thyself before God" and commented, "The only kind of Faith—one's own." He had that kind of faith now, as a published poet, his apprentice work behind him and a major work ahead.

Melville's ultimate purpose in reading epics of Western civilization and reading criticism on them was to learn how he could learn to write great poetry in his own time. The point needs to be made strongly, since it is often assumed that after the failure of *The Confidence-Man* Melville renounced his attempts to have a further career as a published author and began writing poetry, privately, as a trivial hobby, with no thought of trying to publish it. By the time the *Meteor* doubled the Horn, he assumed that his *Poems* had already been published and was being reviewed. When he read poets in the Pacific, he (in his own mind) was reading *other* poets, Spenser, Milton, Wordsworth. He was, he had every reason to think, already a *published* poet, and he was not merely deluded in thinking that his next step, the way of achieving the greatest prestige as a poet, lay in writing a long, ambitious poem. All the way to San Francisco he was expecting to find waiting for him a precious volume—*Poems,* by Herman Melville, perhaps accompanied by a few early New York reviews. After a brief stay he and Tom would be off, his library of poetry augmented by his own *Poems,* and on his dear Pacific he would write his own poetic epic.

Melville noted in the *Odysseys* (plural) on October 3 that he was in the Pacific Ocean "700 miles from San Francisco." As the *Meteor* approached the California coast, it came in sight of another clipper ship, the *Derby,* Captain Hutchinson, and Melville noted in the front flyleaf of the second volume of the *Iliad* "'Meteor & Derby.'" The *Meteor* anchored temporarily on the bar off San Francisco at 8:30 P.M. on October 11 and the next day made its way into the bay in hazy weather, with a light wind from the west, 134 days from Boston. Tom anchored the *Meteor* at the Vallejo Street wharf and prepared to deliver his cargo of merchandise to C. T. Meader & Co.

Tom was already well experienced in the fastest way to get his letters from home, for letters always awaited him there (and he always made it clear that he expected "many"). Now letters awaited Herman too. When he looked at his mail, Melville saw at a glance that there was no package big enough to contain the book he was expecting, so he knew what he would read even before he opened a letter from his wife. Lizzie's letter (or one of her letters) must have laid out what had happened—that first Charles Scribner then Carleton & Rudd had refused the manuscript and then or later Allan, Lizzie, and Evert Duyckinck had given up. No documentary evidence survives to prove that Melville was deeply disappointed at the news that his poems had not been published, but his behavior compellingly suggests he took the news as a violent psychological blow. Tom (opening his own mail) learned that he would not take on a cargo immediately for Manila, as he had planned, but instead would soon begin taking on a cargo of a hundred tons of wheat to transport not to the Far East but back around the Horn to Falmouth, England. (The loading had begun by October 31, according to the *New York Times* on November 12.) Herman decided at once to turn around and go home as soon as he could and by the fastest way, for he would be stuck for many days in San Francisco, if not weeks, if he decided to continue with Tom (on a comparatively mundane voyage). Besides, a genuine poet had a right to indulge himself in more months of reading epic poetry, but a mere unpublished "poetaster" (as he later called himself in his letter to Tom) had no such right—and certainly had no right to attempt an epic poem himself. Later, he could draw on the riches he had gained from his reading of great poetry in the Pacific, but the news in San Francisco had annihilated all his ambition to write, in 1860 and 1861, an American epic poem. His next serious course of reading, in 1862, would be for quite another purpose than to learn how to write epic poetry, and the full epic impulse would not gather strength again until almost a decade had passed.

Melville knew as well as anyone that there was never one reason for an action of a human being, the simplest of whom are fearfully and wonderfully made, but he settled at once on the reason to be given the public: the voyage had not benefited him. Perhaps it hadn't. Melville soon wrote Lizzie by the expensive new Pony Express, and the November 8 issue the *Berkshire County Eagle* printed the public version of events, from Lizzie or indirectly from another source: "Mr. Melville's health is better in some particulars than when he left home, but we regret to learn that he has not experienced the full benefit hoped from the trip, and as the voyage will be prolonged beyond what was first anticipated, Mr. Melville will return via the Isthmus, and reach home early in the winter." The voyage was not being prolonged but shortened; only the stay by the Golden Gate was being prolonged. There was no being precise in anything involving human psychology. Perhaps the voyage had benefited Melville immensely, until he got his news in San Francisco.

On the day of Melville's arrival, the *San Francisco Daily Evening Bulletin*—on the basis of private letters from Boston—announced his presence on the *Meteor,* "A Noted Author Coming to San Francisco." The item explained: "Mr. Melville is traveling in pursuit of health, and new experiences to turn to account in a literary way. He will remain in San Francisco some time; and our Mercantile Library Association, or some other society, might possibly secure his services for a series of lectures. We like to taste the quality of all the celebrities who fall upon our shores" (*Log* 627). This was a warm welcome, and if Melville had seen it before disembarking he might have looked forward to earning some money while reciting his verses during the days Tom was unloading and taking on cargo. More likely he saw it after he had received the bad news from home.

Word got out at once in San Francisco that Melville planned to turn around and go back home on the next steamer, so on October 18 the *Daily Alta* suggested urgently that "some of the literary Institutions might prevail on him to favor us with a lecture or two before his departure." If *Poems* had been waiting for him, elegantly printed by Scribner's, he might willingly have read some of his verses aloud. He might have talked about intertextuality in heroic poetry (using his own unpedantic imagery he could talk about the "joint-stock" or "monkey-rope" condition in which all great poets found themselves in relation to their predecessors). He might have held forth about monumental poems in the English language and their power to energize a sluggish populace. A poet is a writer of verses whose poems are printed. As a mere unpublished poetaster, Melville had nothing to say to the "present class of general readers" in San Francisco.

When he wrote his wife "saying he was not at all benefitted by the Voyage," Melville asked her to convey to his mother and the others at Gansevoort, New York, that he had written them a letter "to come by Steamer," more economically. On October 20, the first nasty day of the season, Melville boarded the *Cortes*. (It "rained in the morning enough to convert the dust into mud," wrote "Glaucon" in a letter from San Francisco published in the *New York Times* on November 15.) Tom had hands who could stow his brother's books onto the steamship for him, but without porters Herman would not easily get them off ship and onto the train across the Isthmus then onto another ship and off ship in New York. He kept at least the Wordsworth and the Schiller, for he had them with him in the Caribbean on the *North Star,* but it is possible that he left some of the bulkier and heavier volumes aboard the *Meteor,* for Tom to carry back around the Horn and up and across the Atlantic. The urgency of Melville's need to have Homer and Milton and other epic volumes at hand had evaporated when *Poems* was not awaiting him in San Francisco. His books taken care of, one way or the other, he left for Panama. Nothing is known of Melville's companions or his states of mind on his return voyage, other than that he did some reading in Wordsworth and Schiller after he crossed the Isthmus. When the *North Star* docked in New York at 10 P.M. on November 13, Melville probably went ashore, late as it was. He set foot in New York as a failed poetaster, not as Herman Melville, the author of a published volume of minor (shorter) poems and a great soon-to-be-published American epic poem.

NOTES

1. All quotations from Melville's letters are from NN *Correspondence*.
2. Melville's copy of Milton is at the Firestone Library, Princeton University.

WORKS CITED

Adams, John Quincy. *Dermot MacMorrogh, or, The Conquest of Ireland: An Historical Tale of the 12th Century, in Four Cantos.* Boston: Carter and Hendee, 1832.
Cowen, Walker. *Melville's Marginalia.* New York: Garland, 1987.

13

Herman Melville
and the Customs Service

STANTON GARNER

In the last two and a half decades of his life, Herman Melville surely devoted far more time and energy to his employment in the New York Custom House than he did to his literary pursuits. Therefore, it follows that to know something about his experience in the federal civil service is to understand his later life from a novel and significant perspective. The purpose of the present remarks is to facilitate that understanding by presenting some factual material about his employment and, to the limited extent possible, to assess its effect on his life and works.

According to most Melville biographers, for one of America's greatest authors the position of inspector of customs was unsuitable, degrading, and humiliating. It was as low as he could be carried (Mumford 307), "somewhat" patronizing (Arvin 259–60), "not a position of great responsibility or of social distinction" (Hillway 62), "not quite up to the dignity of a Melville and a son-in-law of the late chief justice of the Commonwealth of Massachusetts" (Howard 283). Lewis Mumford bewailed Melville's situation the most mournfully when he wrote that it was "one of the lowest political positions open to patronage" and that while holding it Melville was "an Ishmael among Ishmaels, and a pariah among outcasts" (329). There may be some truth to these speculations, but it is also true that in them one detects a twentieth-century American attitude toward mere sustenance. For many in this favored time and place, life with dignity and sufficiency has become a norm so confidently expected that its achievement is hardly a measure of success. Rather, success is more likely to be measured by display and consumption, éclat, status, and sufficient power to permit and excuse impudence, benefits that Melville's position largely lacked. However, the record suggests that during his adult life a position such as inspector of customs did not stigmatize the holder as an Ishmael and a pariah but was welcomed, often coveted, even in the higher strata of society and the literary community.

True, the civil service was a notorious haven for the loyal mediocrity of the dominant political party. But in Melville's own family, his grandfather, Thomas Melvill, had been for many years naval officer for the Port of Boston; his uncle, Amos Nourse, a physician and professor, was the long-time postmaster of Hallowell, Maine, and then collector of customs for the port of Bath, Maine; and Edward Curtis, a brother-in-law of a sort to Guert Gansevoort, was collector of customs for the port of New York before his untimely death.[1] Although these positions were elevated enough to meet any test of suitability for a member of the Melville-Gansevoort family, other relatives were happy to occupy lower posts equivalent to Melville's. Guert's blood brother, Leonard Gansevoort, was an inspector in the New York Custom House for a number of years; Guert's nephew, Edward Gansevoort Curtis, was for many years an inspector of customs in Washington, D.C.; and Melville's brother-in-law, Oakes Shaw, made a career far longer than Melville's of various clerkships in the Boston Custom House.

Among authors, any government office, however low (providing it bore the cachet of respectability) was diligently sought and gratefully accepted. The undisputed winner of the brass ring of the spoils system was Nathaniel Hawthorne, who graduated from weigher in the Boston Custom House to surveyor in the Salem Custom House and capped his career on the government dole as U.S. consul in Liverpool, England. The most notable loser was Edgar Allan Poe, who, failing in his attempt to burrow his way out of penury through patronage, would have been grateful to receive a position such as Melville's. Walt Whitman worked as a lowly government clerk in Washington, and, although he did not seek spoils for himself, when his party won the presidency for the first time John Greenleaf Whittier cashed in his political credits by demanding a clerkship in the customs service for his brother Matthew (Whittier 13–15). Matthew was given one paying at least $1,300, the salary Whittier had specified, and occupied it for twenty contented years. In the younger generation, William Dean Howells escaped the Civil War by accepting a minor diplomatic office in Italy.

Although the New York Custom House was far from being an eleemosynary institution, it harbored in inferior positions a number of literary figures of some contemporary note. Charles Fenno Hoffman, Melville's one-legged friend, worked for the government there (and in the nation's capital), as did William Cullen Bryant's son-in-law, Parke Godwin (later editor of the *New York Evening Post*); Thomas Dunn English; Charles Frederick Briggs, who wrote fiction under the pen name "Harry Franco"; Robert Barry Coffin, whose pen name was "Barry Gray"; Richard Henry Stoddard, editor and literary critic; Thomas Bangs Thorpe, remembered for his southwestern humor story "The Big Bear of Arkansas"; and Melville's close friend George Long Duyckinck. For good measure, a composer, Harrison Millard, also found refuge there. Most of them were content to remain buried in the anonymous mass of foot-soldiery of this large office, performing the duties that earned them modest salaries; but an occasional literary figure with career aspirations ascended to the rarefied air of the higher federal bureaucracy. Thorpe promised to do so until his dishonesty arrested his ascent (Garner, "Thomas Bangs Thorpe"), but others were more successful. Richard Grant White, editor, critic, and Shakespeare scholar, worked his way up to an important position in the collector's office, and Charles Powell Clinch, dramatist and erstwhile member of the Drake-Halleck literary coterie, became the permanent assistant collector and, for six months, acting collector. The latter two were true civil servants of the type who ensured that the work of the New York office would continue as the senior political appointees were blown in and out of office by the periodic gales of electoral change.

Melville had been seeking a federal sinecure for almost twenty years, without success, and 1866 seemed, in one respect, to be an unfavorable year in which to obtain one. Because many Civil War veterans were unable to find employment, government officials were instructed to give them preferential consideration (Dearing 54–55). But it was also a serendipitous year, perhaps the only one in which Melville could have succeeded. That was because he enjoyed an ideological advantage due to the battle over the treatment to be accorded the defeated Confederate states that was being waged during that year between the national administration and the Congress. Shortly after the marching and volleying of the great conflict had ended in 1865, while Congress had been in recess, President Johnson had begun to reconstitute the

Union, generally in accordance with Lincoln's principle of "malice toward none." He had allowed the Southern legislatures to meet, organize, and elect representatives to Congress. But when the Congress reconvened at the end of the year, it refused to seat the Southern delegations and embarked on a punitive Reconstruction program. Soon the two branches of government locked into a struggle of legislative against executive, conservative against radical, and Johnson began to use his appointive power to reward those conservatives who sympathized with his policies and to fill federal offices with political allies. One of these was the banker Henry Augustus Smythe, who, as the Collector for the Port of New York, was the chief executive officer of the custom house. As such, he was Johnson's principal agent and adviser in the City (Cox and Cox 273n) and a ruthlessly partisan wielder of the massive patronage power of his position (Eaton 22). Thus it was fortuitous that in August 1866 Melville published his book of Civil War poems, *Battle-Pieces and Aspects of the War*. In their combined thrust, the poems called for renewed brotherhood with the defeated Southerners, and the prose "Supplement" solidly endorsed President Johnson's political position. Although it is doubtful that Melville intended the book to be an instrument of self-advancement, since it said no more than what he believed, it was, politically speaking, timely.

Despite a gallant effort, Melville had not succeeded in obtaining government employment in 1861, when Lincoln had taken office, and the advent of the Johnson presidency in 1865 offered him the next logical opportunity. In 1866, with *Battle-Pieces* in print, he wanted a position in the custom house. Since all appointments were political, he set about to collect, probably with some assistance from his brother Allan, his politician-uncle Peter Gansevoort, and his brother-in-law Richard Lathers, whose pro-Southern politics were newly returned to favor, the three required endorsements from influential politicians. There is evidence that he solicited one from a New York senator (Croswell), but he then abandoned that approach and used, instead, his personal influence in the customs house and that of Allan and of Lathers (NN *Correspondence* 397). By coincidence, he had become acquainted with Smythe in the spring of 1857, when the two men had toured together in Europe (*Log* 573–74). That alone might have ensured his employment. However, it happened that another of the three top customs officers, Abram Wakeman, the surveyor, was a friend of Allan's who had previously offered to place his influence at Allan's disposal (Garner, *Civil War* 117, 217). Then in an incredible stroke of luck, Major General John Adams Dix was given a temporary appointment as naval officer, the third and last top position, while awaiting an ambassadorship (Dix 148–50). Dix knew and had been allied with members of Melville's family and had twice before recommended Melville for government positions (*Log* 236, 635). Earlier in the century, Dix had been a member of the Albany Regency with Uncle Peter Gansevoort, and for years (except during the war, when he could not) he had been a political cohort of Richard Lathers. Since Melville could count on the support of *all three* of the principal officers, it would have been wretched luck indeed had he failed to obtain the inspectorship for which he applied.

On or about December 5, 1866, Melville took the loyalty oath, a formality held over from the war, and became a government employee over the figuratively headless body of his "decapitated" predecessor, one George S. Swackhammer. That put Melville on the government payroll at a rate of four dollars per day, which was, and remained, with the exception of a reduction during a ten-month period in the mid-1870s (*Log* 745, 755), the uniform pay of all regular inspectors. Before beginning work, he reported to James L. Benedict, the deputy surveyor under Wakeman. Although I have been able to discover little about Benedict, other than the fact that he was a man of probity and ability, he was one of those permanent employees who actually ran the custom house until he erred by accepting an appointment as surveyor, which gave him the impermanence of a political appointee. He seems to have known Melville by reputation and to have valued him, since he gave him favorable assignments and seems from time to time to have shielded him from official unpleasantness. After some preliminaries, he turned Melville over to Richard Henry Stoddard, a debenture clerk, for processing. That probably involved a cursory explanation of his duties, but it was required that a new inspector be issued forms, locks, and a badge. Then Melville was ready to commence his duties.[2]

On his first day on the waterfront, Melville appeared at the District Four office, along the North River at 207 West Street, displaying his badge prominently on the lapel of his usual civilian clothing, as regulations required him to do—at that time, inspectors were not yet uniformed. It was probably there that he first met his postmate, Colonel Henry Langdon Potter, a native of Berkshire (Potter obit.). The two men seem to have gotten along very well—two weeks later Melville gave him a copy of *Battle-Pieces,* and during their time together Potter did favors for him, such as drawing his pay during vacation periods, and Melville probably responded in kind.

Because the two men were compatible, knowing something about Potter may help one to understand Melville a little better. Although Potter was not large—somewhat smaller than Melville—in the army he had shown himself to be a feisty man capable of ferocious brawling when intoxicated. A veteran who had served as second-in-command and then commander of a New York volunteer infantry regiment in Dan Sickles's Excelsior Brigade, prior to 1864 he had fought in most of the engagements of the Army of the Potomac, notably Gettysburg, where he had merged three shattered regiments into one and returned them to the battle. Then in 1864, when he was in New York City recruiting replacements for those of his regiment whose enlistments had expired, he had been cashiered from the army. Despite his valiant service and his many wounds (he wore one of the offending bullets on his watch chain), he had been accused of profiting financially from his dealings with recruits. Fortunately, a later pardon from General Dix had made it possible for him to obtain his government position.[3]

It was a fortunate thing that their personalities did not conflict, for the two men were attached to each other by a monkey-rope of a sort. The official schedule required that they work together from sunrise to sunset, six days a week, during rush periods, when shipping traffic was at its densest. During slow periods, the services of two men were not needed: Potter could mind the office while Melville tended to his personal business of inspecting bookstores, combing through libraries and art galleries, strolling through the streets to observe the human comedy and tragedy enacted there and to peer into the store windows, or perhaps even returning home for lunch. When Melville took his turn, manning the office or patrolling the waterfront, Potter could escape the tedium. When sunset came and the revenue work ended for the day, the two men, or the one still on duty, handed over the district to the night inspector force, watchmen, in effect, and went home.

Newton Arvin has written of Melville "boarding and inspecting incoming vessels, weighing and gauging their merchandise, [and] inspecting the baggage of arriving passengers" (260). Others have believed either that his family invented the title "district" inspector for him, perhaps to give his position added respectability (Howard 283), or that he became a "district" inspector through promotion (Mumford 230). But in fact, he was from the beginning a district inspector, not an elevated position but rather an ordinary classification of inspector that exempted him, in most cases, from boarding and inspecting vessels and combing through luggage, which was done by the male and female discharging inspectors, and from weighing and gauging cargo, which was done by the weighers and gaugers.

That is not to say that the work of a district inspector was wholly custodial. Whenever a ship from a foreign port tied up at a pier in his district, he (in this case either Melville or Potter) had to be present to ensure that she had been boarded downstream by discharging inspectors. If she had, he could go about his business; but in the rare instance in which she had not, he was required to board the ship, lock her holds, and send for inspectors to discharge her. In an emergency he might be ordered to do the job himself, but, since that was not a duty for which daily experience prepared him, he was probably seldom required to do it. When he did, he would not have discharged passenger ships, since only female officers could inspect the luggage of female passengers. Thus if Melville ever did discharging work, he probably handled cargo ships, reporting the material carried and ensuring that banned goods—such as contraceptives and obscene materials, most cattle and hides, and cigars and liquor packed in unauthorized quantities—were not landed. If a ship was involved in the coastal trade, she did not have to be discharged, since her cargo was not subject to import duties; but the district inspector was required from time to time to inspect the ship to ensure that she was properly marked and that her papers conformed to regulations.

Other than this, his duties concerned, literally, the district. The district inspector was in charge of all customs-related matters along the shore. That meant keeping an eye on the ships at the piers to ensure that they did not violate any revenue laws. He was also responsible for goods in the hands of the customs service, those being loaded aboard ship from customs storage or those unloaded with customs storage as their destination. In each case, he was required to escort the cart-man or lighter-man to ensure the integrity of the shipment and, in the case of goods delivered to a ship, to supervise the loading. In addition, he might be required to take charge of goods being transported up or down the coast under bond or goods being transferred from ship to ship without being landed. He also had to take charge of sea stores, or "slops," which, while not dutiable, had to be accounted for. In any case, he was required to report to the custom house daily all merchandise transferred and all ships arriving. He had also to keep a journal of his daily activities and a record of his examinations of ships, both of which were subject to inspection by his supervisors.

Inspectors worked under a complex of rules and prohibitions. The most genial of these was an allowance for a two-week vacation each year, with additional time, other than sick leave, allowed only upon application to the secretary of the treasury. Other rules were designed to prevent corruption and sloth by imposing standards of reliability, diligence, and honesty. Inspectors were not allowed to have financial dealings with anyone who did business with the customs service or to act as agents in customs transactions; they were not to divulge unnecessary information about customs business; and they were not to lend money at usurious rates to fellow employees or to commit any act that might bring discredit on the service. Punishments included fines of from fifty dollars to five hundred dollars and/or dismissal from the service. On the other hand, as officers of the United States, they were armed with impressive powers. They were permitted to use all necessary force to board and inspect a vessel and to seize it, if appropriate. They could also stop and search any vehicle or person who might be carrying suspect goods, and they could procure search warrants, invade buildings other than residences, arrest violators, and deputize any person within three miles to assist them in enforcing the law.

How did Melville respond to his employment? Only three months after he began, his family believed that he was flourishing in it. His mother wrote that "Herman's health is much better since he has been compelled to go out daily to attend to his business," and a cousin wrote that "he is less of a misanthrope" (*Log* 686). The poet W. H. Auden has written, speculatively, of his "extraordinary mildness" during the customs period and of his employment as "another island," as though it isolated him from the mainland of annoyances and sorrows (Auden 200). As for Melville himself, it is doubtful that he thought as poorly of his position and its emolument as have his biographers, with the signal exception of Leon Howard (284). He was not ambitious for a job in which high pay meant large responsibilities (and attendant distractions, such as representing the service to the public and participating in political warfare), since he was, after all, only a poet desirous of a regular income. His salary, while it did not equal that of Matthew Whittier or Richard Henry Stoddard, was generous in comparison with the pay of the consulships he had sought in 1861, though wartime inflation had muddied that comparison. Although the other rank-and-file position he might have obtained, clerk, paid less for beginners, it could eventually, through promotion unavailable to inspectors, pay about twice as much. But Melville could not have survived life as a clerk, crowded daily into the rotunda of the main custom house building, seated at a desk performing the chores of a Bartleby, and his handwriting was simply too villainous for such service. In contrast, the duties of an inspector offered him a partial exemption from clerical responsibilities, fresh air, bustle, exercise, and some companionship, which his family believed he needed, and some independence and, probably, a little more privacy than his family suspected. If the job was undistinguished, it was, at least, relatively suitable.

But despite Auden's romantic vision of Customs District Four as an insular Tahiti, Melville's work subjected him to a number of annoyances and cares, as he suggested in his own (occluded) statement, written at about the time of one of the most anxious periods of his service: "99 hundreths of all the *work* done in the world is either foolish and unnecessary, or harmful and wicked" (NN *Correspondence* 464). For one thing, his salary was *de facto* less than *de jure* it was supposed to be. Although the regulations specified that he and Potter maintain an office, no funds were allocated for one, meaning that the two of them had either to pay the rent for theirs out of their own pockets or to cajole a genial landlord into letting them occupy it rent free. In addition, they had literally to pay to keep their jobs. The New York Custom House was one of the largest federal offices in the land, and two-thirds of the income of the government was collected there. That made the collector the second most powerful officer in the federal bureaucracy, after the secretary of the treasury, and, because of certain perquisites, the highest paid official, including the president (Hartman 11–19). Because of the enormous amount of patronage at his disposal, the collector was also the political boss of the administration party in New York City. That the custom house operation was blatantly political was no secret: it sent a raucous delegation known as "the custom house gang" to both state and national conventions. That set of circumstances made the practice of assessing all of the employees a percentage of their salaries to replenish the campaign chests of the party particularly important and sadly inescapable. There were separate solicitations for the municipal, state, and national organizations, and one could expect to contribute—on penalty of dismissal—perhaps 2 percent of his salary to each, or, in Melville's case, a total of around seventy-two much-needed dollars per year. The practice was justified by the excuse that the employees were simply paying job insurance, since the loss of an election, to the other party or to a different wing of the same party, was likely to lead to wholesale dismissals. It is unlikely that Melville risked martyrdom in order to resist the levy.

Despite this insurance, every election was followed by decapitations. Melville seems to have worried about the "infirmity of temper" of the federal eagle, which, as Nathaniel Hawthorne wrote, was vixenly: despite the fact that many office seekers sought shelter under her wings, she was "apt to fling off her nestlings, with a scratch of her claw, a dab of her beak, or a rankling wound from her barbed arrows" (*Scarlet Letter* 5). No doubt Melville performed his duties well and avoided conduct that might endanger his position, but the spoils system rewarded political loyalty rather than efficiency. Nevertheless,

Melville managed to survive for nineteen years, at the end of which he left voluntarily. The remarkable character of that survival is evident in the fact that (by my count) of the 211 male inspectors employed at the time of his arrival, only ten remained at the time of his departure. One of his defenses seems to have been the protection of Benedict, but Melville had another protector, his near-anonymity. It is nearly impossible to find any mention of him in the records of the custom house, save for a book containing a list of employees and their political sponsors (U.S. Treasury, Register). Using this record, officials kept track of the loyalties and affiliations of each man so they could determine at a glance who could and should be fired. But because of the peculiar manner in which Melville had obtained his position, his sponsorship was specified as "nil." Thus the book did not reveal whether his affiliation was with the "wrong" faction or the "right" one, and it is probably true that no one dared risk offending important patrons to find out.

Considering Melville's peculiar form of idealism, or, perhaps better, his disgust with cynicism, one can easily imagine that he was also irritated by the widespread incompetency, sloth, avarice, and lawlessness that surrounded him. One need only read Hawthorne's description, in his essay "The Custom House," of his Salem employees to form an idea of the unsuitability for public service of typical officers. Yet the greatest irritation must have been the rampant fraud on all sides. With an enormous amount of money changing hands, with officers dedicated to self-interest rather than to the public good, and with the profits available to Gilded Age merchants by evading duties on their merchandise, bribery was rampant. Inspectors turned their backs on irregularities and weighers and gaugers recorded short weights and volumes while importers happily rewarded them. That Melville was offered such inducements is patent in a letter written on his behalf by his brother-in-law, John C. Hoadley. "Surrounded by low venality, he puts it quietly aside," Hoadley wrote, "quietly declining offers of money for special services,—quietly returning money which has been thrust into his pockets behind his back, avoiding offence alike to the corrupting merchants and their clerks and runners, who think that all men can be bought, and to the corrupt swarms who shamelessly seek their price;—quietly, steadfastly doing his duty, and happy in retaining his own self-respect—" (*Log* 730–31).

If Melville was disgusted, he was not alone. During many of the later years of his employment, the outrages were exposed by the New York Civil Service Reform Association, consisting prominently of radical abolitionists of past times, and over the years it became more and more powerful, publishing exposés and lobbying for corrective legislation (Fish 217). But it was a difficult battle, since those who had the power to reform were the same incumbent politicians whose patronage and power were under attack. The practice of assessing employees' salaries for campaign funds was discouraged and banned from time to time, but such constraints were, at first, almost impossible to enforce. Assessments continued brazenly, until, gradually, the reform pressures eroded the politicians' power of intimidation and employees resisted paying (Hoogenboom 225). Corruption was constantly exposed and deplored, but, pervasive and elusive, it seemed impossible to prevent. The same was true of incompetency. The solution to both problems was a civil service meritocracy, but that was easier to advocate than it was to achieve.

In 1877, a committee, headed by John Jay, was appointed to investigate the New York Custom House. It rediscovered and rereported the obvious abuses, but it also recommended that one-fifth of the employees be discharged, that the remainder be required to remain on the job for the full working day, that officers be banned from political party offices, and that the collector, Chester A. Arthur, and the naval officer, Alonzo B. Cornell, be fired (Fish 216). The custom house officials resisted the measures, but they were forced to acquiesce to those that fell under their authority. A three-man committee, including Richard Grant White, selected those to be terminated (*Log* 762). This peril, different from the periodic political purges, must have caused Melville acute anxiety; but when fifty-six inspectors were designated for removal, he was spared, perhaps through Benedict's intercession, though Colonel Potter was terminated. The committee also found flagrant improprieties in the weigher force and recommended wholesale firings, with the result that author Thomas Bangs Thorpe was removed. Later, however, the discharge was revoked and Thorpe was allowed to resign. Attempts to fire Arthur failed when his powerful allies intervened, and eventually, as was often the case, both Thorpe and Colonel Potter were reinstated.

By now, the entire civil service was headed toward fundamental and lasting reform that included, incidentally, uniforming the entire inspector force, not excepting Melville (*NY Times;* Arthur). Examinations for promotion were instituted, and there is evidence that Melville made an attempt, at least, to improve his handwriting to the level of legibility required in the examinations (Garner, "Melville in the Custom House"). Finally, the spoils system itself was abandoned. The instrument, surprisingly, was Collector Arthur, who, in 1879, was finally removed, not because he was personally corrupt but because he resisted reforms. In the following year, 1880, he was elected vice president of the

United States, and in 1881 he became president when James Garfield was assassinated. As president, he confounded history by supporting the Pendleton Act of 1883, which made the civil service a professional, rather than a political, organ of government. Thus when Melville resigned from the service in 1885, his tenure had covered the entire period from the worst days of divided government and postwar corruption to the opening of a new era of civil service professionalism. Although his reaction to this new era is not recorded, he may have had some feeling, even in his last days of nostalgia for an earlier republicanism, that there was yet hope for the future of his country.

There can be little doubt that this drudgery, repeated day after day, month after month, year after year, left its impression on every aspect of Melville's later life and work, though sometimes in subtle ways that may never be discovered. Perhaps it will be of some help that the above remarks have presented his experience in a different light from the one to which we have been accustomed. In obtaining his appointment, Melville was not surrendering to a dire necessity but was, rather, winning a prize that had long eluded him. Nor was he debasing himself by being a customs inspector. That was a normal, desirable goal for a man of letters: the salary was not really as inadequate as has been thought, the position was one of trust and responsibility, and it was hardly inferior in social status to the job of dirt farming at which he had been employed for years, though on his own farm. In short, Melville was not dragged into the service as to a prison or a gallows.

Yet the ideas of scholars in the past have not been completely wrong. Whatever its benefits in fresh air and diversion from melancholy, the office was not a happy occupation for this "proud, shy, sensitively honorable" man, as Hoadley described him (*Log* 730–31). Melville was suited by nature to freedom from routine and to freedom to roam, not to the confinement of a regular job; Hoadley said as much when he added that his brother-in-law "had much to overcome, and has much to endure." Although he was always a difficult husband, the frustrations of his job appear to have led to the "desperate irascibility and solace of brandy" of his later years, as family tradition maintained (Metcalf 215). It was only a half-year after his appointment that his wife, Lizzie, attempted a separation from him, and only a few months after that when, for reasons only to be guessed at, his oldest son, Malcolm, shot himself fatally. Surely there were other sources of Melville's black moods, including the adverse course of postwar Reconstruction (adverse to a man of his political persuasions), but his unhappiness in office must have been a contributing factor. The strain in the family appears to have continued throughout these years and to have abated only after his retirement, when his home became his insular Tahiti.

Because of the inherent indirection of imaginative literature, assessing the effect of Melville's federal service on his writing is a treacherous task. It is no surprise that *Clarel* (published in 1876) does not exhibit any obvious influence, despite the fact that there are references to the Civil War in it. That may be because of its concentration on religious themes, since a custom house is a poor place from which to embark on a search for eternal truths (unless one discover a scarlet letter there), but it may also be that the inception of the work, including decisions concerning its general plan and its materials, preceded the stresses of the inspectorship on the waterfront. More suggestive of the effect of his employment is the fact that he published nothing else during this period except for a few verses in newspapers, and those not long before his resignation. It was not that he was not writing: he made several unsuccessful attempts during those silent years to find a viable avenue for expression, failing but leaving behind hints of the nature of his imaginative wanderings.

The least successful of these was the fragment "Rammon." As I have suggested elsewhere (*Civil War World* 447–48), the rejection by the king, Rehoboam, of his brother Rammon's advice to deal generously with the rebel Jereboam, and Rehoboam's acceptance of the contrary advice of his council of utilitarians, appears to reflect Melville's bitterness about the rejection of his own counsel in *Battle-Pieces* regarding Congress's treatment of the late Confederate states after the Civil War; and Rammon's subsequent retirement from the affairs of men into Buddhism may reflect and justify Melville's retreat into the anonymity of his customs position and into his meditations. However, it appears that the "Rammon" project was doomed to fail because it barricaded the author into a creative corner—that is, because the act of withdrawal of a protagonist is better suited to the conclusion of a discourse than it is to the inception and development of one.

Only slightly more promising were the Burgundy Club sketches, a principal purpose of which was, it would seem, to present and develop a protagonist, Major Jack Gentian, who was both a representative of genial American virtue and a defender of that virtue against the frivolities, impudencies, and evils of post–Civil War society. But this veteran, who has been wounded in the struggles of human existence, who (despite somewhat lax habits) cherishes the family Order of the Cincinnati and the manners and traditions of America's past (such as fireworks on Independence Day), who shares Melville's feelings of brotherhood toward the late Confederates, and who deplores the entrepreneurial patriotica of the Grand Army of the Republic and the development of a smug and self-seeking class of merchants in the club world of New York City, dramatizes Melville's general antagonism to the age, not to the specific irritations of the customs service. However, the latter are inherent in a contretemps between Gentian and Colonel Josiah Bunkum, who challenges Gentian's patriotism and his qualification to hold government office. Bunkum's wartime experiences bring to mind those of Melville's fellow customs employee Colonel Thomas Bangs Thorpe, a loud-mouthed Republican with a dubious claim to military rank ("Colonel" was an honorary title dating from the Mexican War). Bunkum was supposed to have marched to the Gulf with a load of spelling books with which to redeem the ignorant Southerners there, while in 1862 Thorpe obtained a civilian position in the Union military government of New Orleans (as one of the first of the carpetbaggers), where he was involved in public-service projects (Garner, "Thomas Bangs Thorpe"). Interesting as these sketches are for biographical reasons, they did not develop a coherent direction and therefore led Melville nowhere. Virtuous characters may scratch an author's ideological itches, but they may also lack the vigor necessary to generate fictional energy.

Better yet, and more closely identifiable with the custom house experience, are two poems that Melville never published, but which he was revising as late as mid-1882, "Naples in the Time of Bomba" and "At the Hostelry," and a related poem, "Pausilippo," in *Timoleon* (1891). Narrated by Jack Gentian and by Gentian's mentor, the Marquis de Grandvin (a kind of muse of wine), the first two are of considerable interest and of slender promise of leading Melville out of the creative impasse in which he was stalled. The first is a portrait of a seemingly joyous Neapolitan population threatened and oppressed by a tyrannous Bourbon monarchy, while the second gathers artists of long ago in a retreat where

> Never comes the mart's intrusive roar,
> Nor heard the shriek that starts the train,
> Nor teasing telegraph clicks again,
> No news is cried, and hurry is no more—(*Collected Poems* 334)

The hostelry is a friendly sanctuary where creativity, or at least creative people, flourish; Bomba's Naples is, like Melville's bureaucratic place of employment, a government-controlled society in which one must struggle to attain a tenuous spontaneity and individuality. "Pausilippo" is, in effect, an excerpt from

"Naples in the Time of Bomba" in which extended imprisonment has rendered a bard wan and voiceless. Taken together, the three poems suggest the basic difficulty that confinement in the federal service caused him: a man who belonged at the hostelry, he was mislocated in the customs service, his Naples. Melville made the struggle between art and commerce even clearer in some of his later lyrics, such as "The Ravaged Village":

> The weed exiles the flower:
> And, flung to kiln, Apollo's bust
> Makes lime for Mammon's tower. (*Collected Poems* 222)

But in those later poems he also found a more useful trope, representing artists as "sailors," as in "John Marr": "Barbarians of man's simpler nature, / Unworldly servers of the world" (*Collected Poems* 166). In the prose introduction to that poem, the old seaman, marooned in an alien society, unable to communicate with his unimaginative neighbors, is a type of Melville himself, the old artist marooned in the customs service whose works had never communicated with his fellow citizens as he may have hoped that they would (*Collected Poems* 159–64).

The final step was *Billy Budd, Sailor,* in which the full implications of his customs service are laid out. (I hasten to add that the romance is far more complex than that, incorporating, as it does, the gist of many of his works going back as far as *Typee.*) In it, the world of the *Rights-of-Man* is free, a place where sailors govern themselves, resolve their own disputes, and proceed about their work or play without constraint. It is a world in which the artist could survive, but it is no more than a hypothetical world, like that of the hostelry, laid before us for our contemplation and judgment about how matters might be arranged had we the ability and wisdom to make such arrangements. In the real world of the *Bellipotent,* as in that of the custom house, the artist cannot flourish. This ship is commanded by powerful bureaucrats who, whatever their virtues, did not gain their positions through merit. Under them, the common sailor, like the common customs inspector, is in constant danger of victimization by his superiors and of the consequent summary, terminal punishment, regardless of his innocence and sincere dedication to his duties. Melville's saddest response to his experience is his conclusion, patent in *Billy Budd,* that the American system of government had faltered by bestowing power on the mediocre, even though the ballot had made it possible, ideally, to bring about the rule of the best of men.

Thus was Melville affected by his federal service. In some ways, it was an agreeable occupation: close to the ships and the seamen he loved; free of dealings with tourists and their baggage, which he would not have enjoyed; flexible enough in its work schedule to allow him some leisure free of close supervision; and fairly if not amply paid. In other ways, it must have been like a sentence to prison for a man who had for many years made his own schedules, arranging for himself the hours in which he could work and think in seclusion, in which he could devote himself to his family, and in which he could socialize and travel, all of which were compromised by the service. Working at the custom house, with its schedules and its rules, must have reminded him of his service many years earlier as an enlisted man aboard the frigate *United States:* he would serve and serve competently, but he could not flourish.

Perhaps the most deplorable effect of his custom service was the toll it took on his authorship. These were years in which, instead of perfecting and exploiting his poetic voice and following other creative paths, he sat perplexed at his desk, attempting to work his way out of imaginative labyrinths from which there were no exits. Had it been otherwise, his late works might have been different from the ones he actually wrote. As it was, after the end of his years of employment he had to reach, poetically, for what remained of his enthusiasms, for his past as a sailor and for the classical past that he had always admired— until the great reaction to his years of service came. Then he took his revenge by writing *Billy Budd*. In it he set his Handsome Sailor—full of youth, beauty, strength, skill, loyalty, and spirituality—on the decks of the world-ship Melville had found in the custom house, and he presented his readers with the distressing sight of human goodness destroyed by the misguided imperatives of the bureaucratic world. With that, he demonstrated the costs and the consequences of pedestrian governance, regulations valued more highly than the people regulated, and the absolute obedience demanded of citizens, not to leaders whom they choose to follow, but to the idea of office for its own sake. This is only one way to read this work, and others may disagree with it, but it is the one most harmonious with Melville's experience. If it is correct, then it says more about his years of service than could any amount of speculation and assessment by biographers.

NOTES

Because of the circumstances under which the original version of this paper was presented, I echo here some material that I published earlier in "Surviving in the Gilded Age."

1. Federal officers, here and below, are found in U.S. *Register.* This biennial publication lists all current occupants of all federal government offices.

2. The regulations under which Melville worked are found in two pocket-size books, apparently furnished to employees, U.S. Treasury Department, *Laws and Regulations* and *Regulations.*

3. See Potter obituary; U.S. War Department; U.S. Veterans Administration; Phisterer 1:725–26, 4:2722–23, 2732; Dyer 3:1432. An incident at the Battle of Gettysburg linked Potter to Melville's family. During the battle, at a time when Melville's cousin, Henry Gansevoort, was detached from the regular army to serve in the volunteer cavalry, his U.S. artillery battery was shattered and its cannon captured. After Potter returned his regiments to the attack, he recaptured the battery's guns.

WORKS CITED

Arthur, Chester A. Letter to John Sherman. February 4, 1878. Correspondence Relating Mainly to Personnel Matters, August 6, 1875–January 16, 1879. Records of the U.S. Customs Service, 1815–1942, Record Group 36, Department of the Treasury. Federal Archives and Records Center, New York City.

Arvin, Newton. *Herman Melville.* New York: Sloane, 1950.

Auden, Wystan Hugh. "Herman Melville *(for Lincoln Kirstein)."* *W. H. Auden: Collected Poems.* Ed. Edward Mendelson. New York: Random House, 1976.

Cox, Lawanda, and John H. Cox. *Politics, Principle, and Prejudice: Dilemma of Reconstruction.* London: Free Press, 1963.

Croswell, Edwin. Letter to Peter Gansevoort. N.d. Gansevoort-Lansing Collection. Astor, Lenox, Tilden Foundations. New York Public Library, New York City.

Dearing, Mary R. *Veterans in Politics: The Story of the G.A.R.* Baton Rouge: Louisiana State UP, 1952.

Dix, Morgan. *Memoirs of John Adams Dix.* Vol. 2. New York: Harper, 1883.

Dyer, Frederick Henry, comp. *A Compendium of the War of the Rebellion . . . .* Vol. 3. Des Moines: Dyer, 1908.

Eaton, Dorman B. *The "Spoils" System and Civil Service Reform in the Custom-House and Post-Office at New York.* New York: Putnam, 1881.

Fish, Carl Russell. *The Civil Service and the Patronage.* New York: Russell, 1963.

Garner, Stanton. *The Civil War World of Herman Melville.* Lawrence: UP of Kansas, 1993.

———. "Melville in the Custom House, 1881–1882: A Rustic Beauty among the Highborn Dames of Court." *Melville Society Extracts* no. 35 (September 1978): 12–14.

———. "Surviving the Gilded Age: Herman Melville in the Custom Service." *Essays in Arts and Sciences* 15 (June 1986): 1–13.

———. "Thomas Bangs Thorpe in the Gilded Age: Shifty in a New Country." *Mississippi Quarterly* 36 (Winter 1982–83): 35–52.

Hartman, William J. "Politics and Patronage: The New York Custom House, 1852–1902." Ph.D. diss. Columbia University, 1952.

Hawthorne, Nathaniel. *The Scarlet Letter.* Ed. William Charvat, Roy Harvey Pearce, Claude M. Simpson, Fredson Bowers, and Matthew J. Bruccoli. Columbus: Ohio State UP, 1962.

Hillway, Tyrus. *Herman Melville.* Boston: Twayne, 1979.

Hoogenboom, Ari. *Outlawing the Spoils: A History of the Civil Service Reform Movement, 1865–1883.* Urbana: U of Illinois P, 1968.

Howard, Leon. *Herman Melville: A Biography.* Berkeley: U of California P, 1951.

Melville, Herman. *The Collected Poems of Herman Melville.* Ed. Howard P. Vincent. Chicago: Hendricks, 1947.

Metcalf, Eleanor. *Herman Melville: Cycle and Epicycle.* Cambridge, MA: Harvard UP, 1953.

Mumford, Lewis. *Herman Melville.* New York: Literary Guild, 1929.

New York Times. May 2, 1871.

Phisterer, Frederick. *New York in the War of the Rebellion, 1861 to 1865.* 3d ed. 5 vols. Albany: Lyon, 1912.

Potter, Henry L. Obituary. *New York Times* March 31, 1907.

United States. *Register of Officers and Agents, Civil, Military, and Naval, in the Service of the United States, on* . . . [also *Register of All Officers* . . . and *Biennial Register of All Officers* . . .]. Washington, DC: GPO and others, biennial (on September 30 of each odd-numbered year).

———. Treasury Department. *Laws and Regulations for the Government of Officers of Customs, under the Superintendence and Direction of the Surveyor of the Port of New York.* By James L. Benedict. Washington, DC: GPO, 1875.

———. Treasury Department. Register of Employees, 1880, Port of New York. Records of the U.S. Customs Service, 1815–1942, Record Group 36, Federal Archives and Records Center, New York City.

———. Treasury Department. *Regulations for the Government of Officers of Customs, Under the Superintendence and Direction of the Surveyor of the Port of New York.* [By Alonzo B. Cornell.] Washington, DC: GPO, 1870.

———. Veterans Administration. Henry L. Potter Pension Application. Civil War Pension Application Files, Record Group 15. National Archives, Washington, DC.

———. War Department. Henry L. Potter Compiled Service Record. Records of the Record and Pension Office, 1784–1917. Records of the Adjutant-General's Office, 1780–1917, Record Group 94. National Archives, Washington, DC.

Whittier, John G. *The Letters of John Greenleaf Whittier.* Vol. 3. Ed. John B. Pickard. Cambridge, MA: Harvard UP, 1975.

Creation, Revision, and Edition:
Finding Melville's Text

14

Manuscript, Edition, Revision:
Reading *Typee* with Trifocals

JOHN BRYANT

Melville's first book is really three. Or rather one should say that 150 years after its publication one cannot read *Typee* thoroughly without reading it three ways. Or better, *Typee* is a book to be read with trifocals. And to do justice to Melville's rhetoric, we have to acquire a triple vision. This may sound painful, but it is instructive. And I'd like to suggest that this particular triple orientation may be helpful in establishing more effective and reliable ways of doing that form of criticism that falls under the general rubric of historicism, whether traditional or new.

As a textual document, *Typee* is unique in the Melville canon for three reasons. First, it is one of the few texts for which an extensive (although not complete) working manuscript exists. Second, it is the only Melville book to go through several significant editions during the author's life, so that we may, in comparing manuscript to first edition, infer changes that Melville either authorized or consented to under pressure from family or editors. And finally, a third peculiarity in *Typee* is that the novel's initial reception forced Melville to consent to an expurgated edition, which, despite its dubious textual authority, nevertheless allows us the opportunity to measure directly a significant interaction between author and audience. Taken together, all three phases of Melville's creation of this "fluid text" we call *Typee* constitute a single moment in Melville's lifelong dance with his readers; and therefore to read this text biographically, historically, or even as an organic whole, we must devise a methodology that permits us to read *Typee* three ways at once.

Discovered in a trunk in upstate New York in 1983, the *Typee* manuscript is a thirty-leaf "fragment" covering chapters 12–14. Melville may have begun the manuscript as a fair copy, but beginning a pattern of composition he would repeat thoughout his life, he revised the text as he copied and in fact invented, it seems, new material as he went along. By comparing the draft to its published form in the first British and American editions and by comparing that edition to the revised American edition with its expurgations, we can trace the full scope of Melville's artistic development at the anxious moment of his professional debut. In manuscript, we find the many additions and deletions, the Prufrockian decisions and indecisions of word choice that Melville entertained before going to print. We also find complete paragraphs fully recast or even deleted, never to appear in any published form. In short, we find evidence of Melville's modulations of humor and insight, his fabrications and transformations, his shaping of fictive elements, and his self-censorship. In revealing the choices Melville considered, the manuscript indicates the rhetorical choices the author made and the strategies he intended. Perhaps even more exciting are those passages the author labored over in manuscript to make right for his audience only to discover the very same passages cut a year later from his American revised edition.

What becomes clear to any eye that reads *Typee* trifocularly is that Melville made a good deal up as he wrote. Like anyone beginning to write, he learned his craft while performing it. Moreover, he developed his ideas compositionally. And even after he published, he continued to recast his ideas through revisions and expurgations. To read *Typee* as a document that expounds a finalized ideology, then, is to freeze a fluid process of thought into a single moment and to make that moment into a false, microcosmic representation of a larger, oceanic body of thought. This problem of reduction aside, we can also see, however, that a better way to ascertain Melville's ideology is to examine the way he created it from manuscript to first edition to revised.

I realize that what I am saying is likely to offend two critical camps that I fervently admire. On the one hand are those textual scholars intent upon establishing a single text of *Typee* that represents Melville's final intention as best we can ascertain it; these thinkers who are committed to the task of presenting a readable and reliable *Typee* are inclined toward a single rather than trifocular vision. After all, scholars and general readers can only read one word at a time.

Textual variants are displayed, of course, but only at the back of an edition along with the textual apparatus, and that is where readers with trifocals must go to reconstruct Melville's creative process. On the other hand, the second camp I am likely to offend is that of the New Historicists. I value this movement's agenda, which I take to be an attempt to free literature from the aridity of New Criticism and to challenge readers to discover new vitality in the way we relate works of art to culture. In actuality, I feel that what I am proposing here is a way of reading that enhances our understanding of the interaction of text and context. But because many New Historicists have shaped their approach to conform to the postmodern derogation of linear causality and of the author as agent, there is little room in their method for a notion of text that floats in meaning as it evolves. The problem for both camps is that the idea of reading *Typee* three ways at once assumes that Melville's text is a fixed product not a fluid process. Moreover, the New Historicism, especially in Wai Chee Dimock's *Empire for Liberty,* tends to allegorize Melville's author-audience relationship, making it, like the allegorized text itself, a frozen not evolutionary entity.

In assessing these two adverse responses to my approach, I find myself caught between a rock and a hard place—or as Melville might have put it, caught between the Tartarus of textual studies and the Paradise of historicism, between hard fact and cultural vision. But if we are to find a synthesis of these two approaches, we need to focus on the most lively arenas wherein individual talents may be found interacting with their audiences. For me that arena is the creative process, and to know this phenomenon we must draw upon a mixture of approaches. Not only sharp textual analysis of manuscripts and editions, not only a cultural analysis of the invisible forces of politics and the marketplace, but also a rhetorical approach that reveals the strategies inherent in an author's successive drafts and discarded language. This, too, is what I mean by reading *Typee* three ways.

To demonstrate my point I want to develop a few ideas that derive from the recently exposed textual crux that I have referred to elsewhere as Melville's "L-word." This crux, whether Melville intended to say "literally" or "liberally interpreted," occurs at a crucial moment in Tommo's search as an artist and cultural historian for a critical voice. Melville's dilemma is whether he shall transcribe, transform, or translate the language of his varied characters. It occurs toward the end of chapter 13.[1]

In this chapter, Tommo's companion Toby is wounded by several rival Happars and chased back to Typee Valley where he relates his adventure; Kory-

Kory responds with a remarkable oration against the Happar tribe that leaves Tommo exhausted and amused. In a sense, the two scenes (Toby's narrative and Kory-Kory's oratory) demonstrate different modes of rhetoric in telling a story. But the structural pairing of Toby's serious narrative and the native's comic harangue implicitly demeans Polynesian culture at the moment when Melville is attempting to deepen our respect for his captors. In its final printed version, Kory-Kory's speech gently trivializes the notion of Typee cannibalism, placing that burden on the more aggressive Happars. But the manuscript tells us more. Originally, Melville had planned a devastating lampoon of Kory-Kory, which if published would have seriously satirized Polynesian language and culture. The deletion of this burlesque along with other revisions provides intriguing glimpses of Melville's wrestling with the differences inherent in the transcription, transformation, and translation of experience into words.

Let's begin with Toby. The working draft manuscript reveals that Melville first transcribed Toby's narrative in a rather stiff, discursive tone and that in revising he transformed the literate prose into the rhythms of dramatic speech. For instance, Toby's phrase "Quite elated *at the close vicinity* of the Happars" as we find it in manuscript is changed in the printed text to "Quite elated at being so near the Happars" (*Typee* 101). The leaden pretense of "My first impulse was immediate flight" is happily transformed to Toby's impulse "to run for it." And so on.

Interestingly enough, two passages Melville labored over but then deleted altogether from any printed version record his apparent reluctance to conceal the obvious fact that these are not the actual words of one Tobias Greene that have been meticulously transcribed but Melville's own words revised for dramatic effect. Melville's first apologetic passage was clumsy: "As I cannot remember the words made use of by Toby in this occasion, I shall accordingly relate his adventure in my own language[,] tho' in the same[,] putting the words in his mouth" (leaf 8).[2] This Melville deleted. His second manuscript attempt is more fluid and revealing: "Though I cannot recall to mind anything like the precise phraseology employed on this occasion still for the sake of unity I shall permit my companion to rehearse his own adventures in the language that most readily occurs to me." Although this version is not canceled in manuscript like its predecessor, it, too, never made it into print; and with good reason: it unnecessarily diminishes the excitement of Toby's coming narrative while it calls attention to its fictionality. Nevertheless, the attention Melville paid in manuscript to some sort of apology reveals his serious concern not simply for his treatment of Toby but for his own role as a writer.

Both versions of Melville's apology register his desire to transcribe Toby's "precise phraseology," that is, to quote him directly. Both also plead that poor memory makes this impossible. The amiable rhetorical ploy resorted to is that Tommo will be more reliable because, while attuned to the larger matters of the heart, he (like us) forgets the little details. Ironically, the failure to recollect forces Melville to invent details or rather the words that create the facts. Failing to *transcribe* literally, then, he must *transform* Toby's experience into language. But here, the two versions of Melville's apology vary. Whereas the author first tells us he will use "my own words" to relate Toby's adventure; he subsequently allows Toby in the second version of the apology to "rehearse" his tale "in language that most readily occurs to me." The difference is subtle but important. In the first instance, Melville proposes simply to substitute his words for Toby's forgotten lines; in the second, he implies that he will devise language that is appropriate for a particular character in a particular circumstance. On the one hand, Melville is ventriloquizing for Toby; on the other, he becomes Toby. Thus, in shifting from indirect to direct dialogue, Melville must in fact endure a sea change, a momentary psychological transformation of himself.

Clearly, the manuscript shows us a young, untried writer stretching his muscles, testing the limits of his new profession and craft. His first instinct was to relate Toby's narrative in his voice, to maintain the tone of a genial reflective enthusiast that pervades the entire novel. But he quickly decides to invent a voice for Toby, to "permit [him] to rehearse his own adventures," and this readily explains the minor revisions from the prosy "immediate flight" to the more colloquial "run for it." But what is more exciting is the manuscript's revelation of Melville's urge to move beyond fact into fiction; it reveals as well both the tension and ease that accompany his slipping into a character. In scrutinizing his revisions, we can in effect see him do what he has his confidence man do: don a mask, assume a role, play a part.

Fascinating, too, is Melville's initial reticence in making his transformation. Initially, he feels a deep obligation to expose himself, to admit to readers that what they are about to read is in part a necessary fabrication. His assumption is that, unless apologized for, his fictionalizing will, if detected as such, seriously undermine his narrative reliability. To placate readers, he will make his transformation of reality, he argues, "for the sake of unity" suggesting that whatever is lost in terms of our faith in Melville's exact reportage of Toby's experience, he will regain in our appreciation of his creation of a voice commensurate with Toby's dramatic circumstances. The dilemma he was forced to recognize, of course, is that no unified rendering of experience can be literally factual; all narratives are fabrications; indeed, unity itself is a fiction. And yet readers who demand facts, like his skeptical publisher John Murray, also expect a unified narrative that requires aesthetic manipulations and inventions of fact. Realizing, then, that his apologetic passage would only call attention to his necessary fictionalizing of fact, Melville wisely dropped his apology altogether. As it now stands, Toby's narrative evolves seamlessly out of Tommo's, and readers are none the wiser of Melville's anxiety in supplying a fictive transformation rather than literal transcription.

Most certainly, Melville's deleted apology does not commemorate his first act of fictionalizing, but it is our earliest record of his self-awareness as a fiction writer and of his anxiety in addressing an audience. This little aesthetic epiphany takes on richer meaning in the second half of chapter 13 when in describing Kory-Kory's harangue, Tommo is obliged to do what he could not do with Toby: transcribe the native's words. What he attempts to do is "literally interpret" Kory-Kory, and his meticulous, word-for-word translation of Polynesian sounds into English equivalents suggests that Melville is true to the cause of precise linguistic renderings. Here he will report objectively and not fictionalize. But as the manuscript shows, Melville also experimented with a savage burlesque of Kory-Kory that would have seriously undercut his objectivity and respect for Polynesian life.

As it now stands in print, Kory-Kory's oratorical explosion is amusing enough, the outburst of an enthusiastic and loyal servant taking excessive pains to explain and repeat the obvious. He gesticulates wildly, running in and out of the hut, and at one point illustrates his warning of cannibalism by pretending to eat "the fleshy part of [Tommo's] arm." Such histrionics and "gibberish" give Tommo a headache, and the chapter ends. It is comic relief from Toby's more frightening version of the same incident.

In manuscript, however, Melville originally derided Kory-Kory as an "illiterate barbarian." This ethnic slur is surprising since Melville throughout his book refers to the Typees as "islanders" or "natives," carefully reserving the negative term "savage" for certain rare moments and never calling his friendly captors "barbarian." Melville's further criticism that "any millstone might have comprehended" the islander's meaning also violates the amiable stricture against ridiculing the harmless; it was later revised to the less graphic but more respectful line, "It was impossible not to comprehend [him]" (103).

Originally, Melville also wrote, past Tommo's headache, the following description of Kory-Kory's "gibberish":

he reminded me of a man with his mouthful of chub spluttering, choking, & spitting the bones out in every direction. Such a horrific [crucifying?]

merciless jargon never surely was heard before. [All these mad sounds seemed to be served up in a hasty kind of fricassee.] It might have been denominated a fricassee of vowels & consonants [dashed? coated?] with a spice of cayenne. Heaven defend me from such another infliction! It gave me rheumatic pains in every joint in my body. What it all meant I could not for the life of me conjecture without the speaker was [imploying?] the occasion to enlarge upon the transitory nature of all human enjoyments & the vanity of terrestrial expectations. (leaf 10)[3]

The image of language as a fricassee is appealing to an amiable mind drawn to gustatory joking and would be a palpable hit in any other book about pagan savages. (In fact, Melville saved the comic trope for use in *Omoo*.) But you will recall that in his preface, composed after his manuscript was completed, Melville had emphasized his fidelity to Polynesian, promising to render its "beautiful combinations of vocal sounds" far more accurately than had any other previous South Sea writer. Obviously, the "spluttering, choking, and spitting" of Melville's fricative fricassee would have to go. In toning down the burlesque, Melville preserves our growing regard for the island culture. If these "amiable epicures" are worth emulating socially and morally, then their language merits serious attention. It deserves objective translation, not ridicule. In his revisions and the final printed version of this section, Melville seems, in fact, to have forfeited broad humor for a treatment of Polynesian that is literal.

This last word, "literal," poses, however, significant problems in manuscript, first edition and revised edition, problems that require the ultimate in trifocular reading.

Because of the peculiarities of Melville's hand, it is impossible to determine flatly whether, in discussing Kory-Kory's harangue, the author wrote that he would supply a "literal" or "liberal" interpretation. The "L-word" that Melville actually wrote appears twice in manuscript, and in both cases the "t" (if that is what it is) is uncrossed and may be taken as a "b." You will instantly appreciate that the minute orthographic difference between the words "literal" and "liberal" results in two radically distinct readings, for in matters of interpretation, a liberal translation is worlds apart from one that is literal. In effect, the two possible readings are virtual antonyms. A gamesome Melville inspecting his own manuscript as we have done would have delighted in the confusion created by the simple omission of the crossing of a "t": a word intended to convey a precise meaning seems thwarted in that mission by the very nature of its orthographic form. Words are therefore hieroglyphic and inherently, inscrutably disposed to multiple meaning. But audiences do not read in manuscript; they read print, and these hermeneutic penetrations are lost on readers, for on a typeset page all "t's" are crossed and no "t" looks like a "b." Obviously, Melville intended no ambivalence when he wrote his "L-word"; he meant one word only at the moment of creation, and one would like to assume that printed versions of his "L-word" would clarify precisely what meaning he intended. The problem is that the authoritative first editions contain both readings.

Melville's first editors, both British and American, were the first to confront the problem. They printed Kory-Kory's Polynesian "gibberish" and followed it with Tommo's segue to his English translation: "—ah! nuee, nuee, nuee!" "Which, *literally* interpreted would imply, . . . ah Heaps, heaps, heaps etc." That is, they read the "L-word" as "literal." This, it would seem, would settle the matter, for in proofing galleys, Melville had every opportunity to get his "L-word" right in print. But in the revised American edition (also inspected by the author), the word has been changed to "liberally interpreted." Although the revised edition is known for its unwanted expurgations, it also contains legitimate and desirable authorial changes. Assuming that Melville, in fact, authorized this particular revision, modern editors of *Typee* have followed this last reading, printing "liberally" instead of "literally." This decision, however, was made fifteen years before the discovery of the *Typee* manuscript with its seemingly ambivalent hieroglyphic "L-word," and presumably editors will now want to reconsider their "liberal" reading in light of the "literal" evidence.

We can imagine at least three equally valid scenarios to explain the course of textual variation. Melville may have intended his "L-word" to be "liberally" in his working draft, but the word was misread by copyists and then typesetters as "literally" only to be *corrected* by Melville back to "liberally" in the revised edition. Or, Melville may have intended "literally" at all of the early stages, both in manuscript and print, only to change his mind in the revised edition and have the word *altered* to "liberally." Or, "literally" may have been intended all along, only to be *corrupted* to "liberally" through a typesetting mishap in the revised edition. Textually, then, "liberally" may be Melville's correction or alteration or a typesetter's corruption.

Today's Northwestern-Newberry editors have adopted "liberally" as their reading, taking it to be Melville's correction back to his original intention. Their argument rests on what we know about the way the American revised edition was set. Briefly, the revised edition used the plates from the first American edition; only those plates containing expurgations or Melville's authorized changes were actually reset. In resetting type to eliminate the space created by the expurgations, typesetters understandably created typos, and many small variations in the revised edition are of this nature. But "liberally" in the revised edition is not found within the range of an expurgation, and, accordingly, it seems more likely that the change was at Melville's request rather than a textual corruption. Hence, our modern editors feel that the change to "liberal" is the result of an authorial correction. It may too have been a change of mind.[4]

On the surface of it, the working draft manuscript evidence does not diminish the logic of this textual argument. It does, however, force us to consider more carefully the rhetorical strategies implied in the choice Melville had to make between "literally" and "liberally," for overall, if Melville intended a change to, or back to, "liberally," the decision would seem to be ill advised; "literally" is quite simply the better word.

To be sure, the case for "liberal" is appealing if only for its typically Melvillean ramifications. Consider the metaphysical nature of translation itself. Can one ever render one language into another literally, submitting one word as a precise equivalent of its foreign counterpart? Must not *translation* necessarily involve a careful *transformation* of words that can only approach but never fully achieve literal equivalency? Given that words in a Platonic or romantic framework are fated merely to represent, not create, reality, and given as well what Tommo finally discovers to be the seemingly unbridgeable chasm between the civilized and primitive mind, translation can only be a transformative not transcriptive act, a fictive process, a liberation, and hence something that must be done "liberally." Given, too, Melville's earlier wrestling in manuscript over Toby's narrative, we know that the author was particularly conscious of the inevitability of his own fictionalizing transformations. But we also know that his "liberal" fictionalizing of Kory-Kory's harangue had gone too far. Whereas Melville's transformation of himself into Toby succeeds as a flowering of the creative self beyond his actual being, his burlesquing of a native as an "illiterate barbarian" would suggest the writer's failure to transcend cultural barriers.

In cutting his too-liberal transformation of Kory-Kory, Melville reigned in his comic creation. Although the idea of "literal" interpretation may run counter to his growing metaphysical views, it squarely met his rhetorical need, at this point in the narrative, to render Typeean culture with respectful objectivity. To provide only liberal translations would be to suggest that Polynesian language is incomprehensibly silly and imprecise, meriting only the loosest of renderings into the Imperial Queen's more effective tongue. Melville surmised that a sign of a culture's relevance, in his reader's minds at any rate, lies in the degree of care taken in rendering its language "literally." In choosing to be literal with Kory-Kory's language, then, Melville not only made a further en-actment of aesthetic restraint, but he encouraged his readers to become more endeared to the inhabitants of his amiable Eden.

When read in manuscript, revision, and edition, *Typee* is no single text. It is three phases of development best understood not as a frozen end-product but as a fluid, variable experience, a creative process. Indeed, Melville's "L-word," shimmering on the manuscript in its structural ambivalence, mandates a three-way reading. Just before he died, Melville asked Arthur Stedman to change *Typee* once again. Among other things he authorized the changing of "Buggerry Island" to "Desolate Island." Perhaps late in life Melville regretted some of the bawdiness of his first book. Modern editors have not honored Melville's request; they have kept Buggerry Island. Whether this is a wise edito-rial decision or not is not at issue. The fact is that Melville never really finished *Typee*, and what we have is something to be read with trifocals. But clearly, the Buggerry Island problem presents a new dilemma: does the Melville of 1891 have the right to transcend time and rewrite the Melville of 1846? He tried. Should we?

I think I shall give up my trifocals. The new prescription calls for a pair of four-focals.

NOTES

1. See my *Melville and Repose: The Rhetoric of Humor in the American Renaissance* (New York: Oxford UP, 1993).

2. The *Typee* Manuscript consists of sixteen extant leaves and is located in the Gansevoort-Lansing Collection (Melville Family Papers), box 310, New York Public Library, New York City. Subsequent references are to individual manuscript leaves.

3. Compare Melville to the following notice in the *Minnesota Pioneer* description of Rev. Gideon H. Pond's periodical *The Dakota Friend,* which offered articles written in an English tran-scription of Lakotan. The transcription is done "imperfectly, but as well, probably, as our alphabet can be made to represent the hissing, sputtering, hawking, grunting, clucking, gutturals and *un-utterals* of the Dakota language, composed as it is, of words which fall upon the tympanum less like soft flakes than like a mingled tempest of tomahawks, hedgehogs and wild cats" (Rpt. *Nantucket Inquirer* [January 13, 1851], 2).

4. Since the presentation of this paper, continued inspection of the manuscript, under magni-fication, has revealed small but distinct dissimilarities between Melville's handwritten (uncrossed) *te* and *be* combinations (as evident in words like "obliterated" and "number"). Enlargements sug-gest a stronger likelihood that he initially wrote "liberally" and "liberal" in manuscript. Chances are he or his copyist (sister Augusta perhaps) misread the words as "literally" and "literal" and that typesetters perpetuated the "literal" version of the L-word into print.

15

Melville Revises "Art"

ROBERT C. RYAN

Art
In placid hours well pleased we dream
Of many a brave unbodied scheme.
But form to lend, pulsed life create,
What unlike things must meet and mate:
A flame to melt—a wind to freeze;   (5)
Sad patience—joyous energies;
Humility—yet pride and scorn;
Instinct and study; love and hate;
Audacity—reverence. These must mate,
And fuse with Jacob's mystic heart,   (10)
To wrestle with the angel—Art.

To understand as much as we may about how Melville revised "Art" and to
begin to make better sense of where and when he transformed the poem, it is
necessary to determine first the sequence in which he inscribed and altered
the surviving layers of the manuscript. This would seem elementary, and it is;
but so far not even those one must take to be serious readers of the poem—

readers who have looked at the manuscript—have cared or felt competent enough to figure out thoroughly the order of variants in it.

Willard Thorp claims the manuscript is "almost indecipherable" (427n18), and his "attempt . . . to reproduce" Melville's "rewritings" is incomplete and misleading. Similarly lacking and misrepresenting are the account and transcription offered by Howard P. Vincent in the "Textual Notes" (506–07) appended to volume 14 *(Collected Poems)* of the *Complete Works of Herman Melville.* Norman Jarrard (253, 386) does a clearer job of presenting the nature and sequence of local variants, but he, too, does not undertake to analyze the stages of inscription and revision visible in the manuscript, probably because he (like Vincent) is finally editing from a photofacsimile of some sort, not the original. For whatever reason, neither Thorp nor Vincent nor Jarrard notices at the top of the poem's mount or main leaf the canceled and covered-over (by a revision patch) two lines that were subsequently expanded and transformed into the four lines of "In a Garret." Curiously, neither does William H. Shurr notice those two lines in *The Mystery of Iniquity: Melville as Poet, 1857–1891,* though he is "tempted to make a connection" betwen the "grapple" of "In a Garret" and the "wrestle" of "Art" (243), and though he otherwise may pay at least some small attention to the successive, not just the final, readings in "Art" (242–43).[1] Among other notables who have looked over the manuscript in recent years, Robert Penn Warren does not venture to describe or analyze any of the variants in it but finds it "a very tangled work sheet," adding that "in spite of the struggle which this indicates," Melville does "not achieve the kind of sharp, epigrammatic economy and clarity at which the poem aims" (439). Figure 1 should suggest where Warren gets his "epigrammatic" impression, though his characterization of Melville's final aim and accomplishment in "Art" may appear off the mark. Visible in Figure 1 are inscription and revision from the poem's earliest surviving stages (here designated Bb and Bc, to indicate the possibility of at least one preceding stage), as well as pencil fair-copying ("Audacity—reverence . . . . more than") for a later stage (Bd). A common pin (see its horizontal traces just above "Humility,—") attaches a Stage Bb clip bearing the poem's earliest surviving inscription ("Sad patience . . . era meet") to the Stage Bc main leaf or mount where "Hard to grapple . . . freeze;" is inscribed. Rather than retranscribe legible text from a previous fair copy ("Sad patience . . . era meet"), text legible enough for the moment to serve in his next fair copy, Melville scissors (clips) it away from text we may infer is so revised as to require the sort of reinscription we find on the later-stage (Bc) main leaf here. That is, the initial inscription on the clip is earlier (Bb) than the initial inscription on the main leaf (Bc).

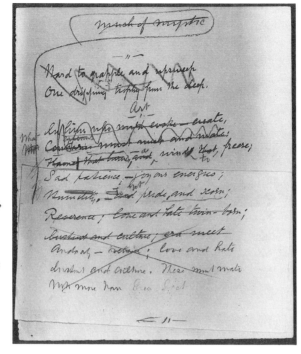

Stage
Bb
clip

Now missing,
Stage Ba (or
earlier) clip
was once
attached here
to Stage Bb
clip.

Figure 1. Melville's transcript of "Art," showing his later revision patches removed: his Stage Bc ink inscription is on the main leaf or mount ("Hard . . . freeze"), and his Stage Bb ink inscription is on the clip ("Sad patience . . . meet"); later, at Stage Bd, he penciled at the bottom of the clip "Audacity . . . more than" in a space earlier covered by a now-missing Stage Ba or earlier clip. *Reprinted with permission of the Houghton Library, Harvard University, Cambridge, Massachusetts.*

Not readily evident to anyone looking for the first time at the photofacsimile in Figure 1, but important to note, is that at the bottom of the clip, at Stage Bd, Melville penciled three fair-copy lines ("Audacity . . . . With more than" plus later erased "Even Jacob"[2]) just before Stage Bd ink-inscribing (and fair-copying) the poem's last four lines on a revision patch (see Figure 3). The Stage Bd penciled lines are later-inscribed than any of the inked lines on the Bb clip or Bc main leaf. Furthermore, and importantly, the space where the Stage Bd penciled lines now appear was earlier occupied by a nonextant Stage Ba or earlier clip attached to the bottom of the Stage Bb clip ("Sad patience . . . meet") and presumably bearing an earlier, substantially different version of the poem's ending. If that ending had not been substantially different, and subsequently much revised, Melville would not have judged it necessary to make a new fair copy at Stage Bd.

It may be doubted, of course, whether that Stage Ba (or earlier) ending was substantially different in one significant particular—its last line. Consider the evidence. Melville's pencil fair-copying into the space formerly occupied by the Stage Ba clip suggests: (1) that he is probably copying from that much-revised clip; and (2) that by the time he reaches "With more than" and / or erases the following "Even Jacob", he realizes both that he is satisfied with the revised text he has penciled in and that he need not go on with his pencil-transcription, since what follows on the Ba clip is either clearly enough revised or is largely if not completely unaltered, and he does not need to see in further pencil text that which already appears acceptable in Stage Ba ink (perhaps revised) on the clip he has been copying from. In fact, he inferably judges it time now to ink-inscribe his new fair-copy text onto a revision patch (and onto a revision patch rather than, perhaps, go to the further trouble of erasing his penciled lines and inscribing inked ones in their former place—that space previously occupied by the Stage Ba clip).

When properly analyzed, then, the mount and clip pictured in Figure 1 offer certain evidence of at least five revision stages—five episodes of altering that led to new fair-copying of significant portions of the evolving poem. For relational convenience, we may call the earliest implied stage A—that stage implied as preceding the one (Ba) represented by the nonsurviving clip once attached to the bottom of the extant Stage Bb clip. The other two stages are visible in the Bc ink inscription on the mount and in the Bd pencil transcription at the bottom of the Bb clip. There may have been other stages before or within A. Further, the stage designations stipulated here indicate only sequential relations—which inscribed text is earlier, which later—they indicate nothing about how much time passed between visible and inferable episodes of revision and fair-copying. Designating four of the "Art" stages as subsets of B rather than as, say, B, C, D, and E reflects only a considered hunch—based largely on ink and paper evidence—that these revision and reinscription episodes occurred within a relatively short period of time—say, within a month or so. But Stage A might have occurred in that short period, too.

In considering the substance of what changed from stage to stage, of most initial interest might be what happened—or may appear to have happened—at Stage Bc, when Melville inscribed the first two lines ("Hard . . . deep.") on the main leaf. It could be these two lines that mainly induced Robert Penn

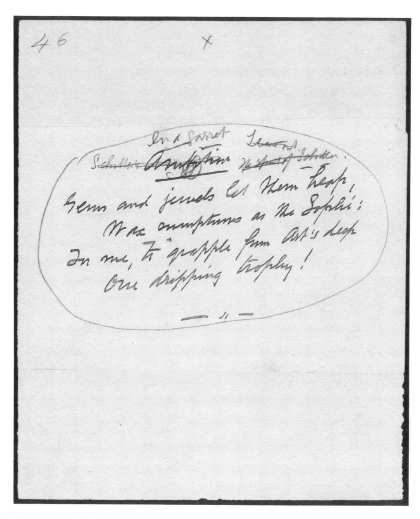

Figure 2. Melville's transcript of "In a Garret." *Reprinted with permission of the Houghton Library.*

Warren to think Melville aiming in "Art" at the "epigrammatic." As already noted above (though not noticed by Warren and others), Melville eventually, perhaps even soon, turned the indeed epigrammatic lines into "In a Garret" (see Figure 2). What further, however, may be made of these lines as they seem, at Stage Bc, to begin the poem later titled "Art"? The physical and contextual evidence suggests several possibilities.

First, it may be that at Stage Bc Melville—ever willing to vary the length of verse paragraphs—thought to begin his poem with a punchy two-line stanza, the disparate but nonetheless apposite figure and form of which he imagined he might indicate with a wide line-space, the two-liner functioning then both epigrammatically and epigraphically, as well as with apt indirection, to introduce the art topic. (Look again at Figure 1 and visualize that wide space before it was later filled by his penciled "Art" and device.) Further supporting this conjecture may be Melville's characteristic beginning (and ending) device inked in preceding the two lines in question. That is, these two lines are indicated as beginning some poem (why not the obvious candidate—"Art"?), and the absence of an ending device (in the wide space, say) implies that they are not the only two lines in that poem.

Secondly, however, we can speculate that such an ending device could have been inscribed on the top portion of the Stage Bb clip—the top portion that was scissored away at Stage Bc. That is, Melville might always have imagined the two-liner as a separate poem, the first in a series of brief takes on the topic of art and art-making, the group's title as yet undetermined, but the strung-together collection of poems conceived according to a notion similar to that which informs the gathering of seven under the heading of "Pebbles" in *John Marr* and three as "Rosary Beads" in *Weeds and Wildings*.

Thirdly, though, we could notice the possibly significant fact that Melville canceled these two lines with blue pencil. It is hard to say what that blue pencil may signify, for our present purpose, other than an intention to cancel finally, as perhaps distinguishable from an intention to revise that is expressed elsewhere in the manuscript by black pencil. But such a distinction—if it amount to one—would seem to tell us little that we want to know.

Fourthly, then, we might speculate that Melville canceled his first two lines in mid-draft, at Stage Bc, and, in fact or in effect, began over again with "In him who would evoke—create, / Contraries must meet and mate".[3] He might be imagined as canceling thus in mid-draft if (choose one or more): (1) he decided to expand "Hard . . . deep" into the explicitly separate poem it became in "In a Garret"; (2) he gave over his earlier plan (if it was such) to group together under one title (say, "Art") a group of epigrammatic poems, especially when he saw that the then-second poem had turned into something other than epigram; (3) he judged that, figurally and rhetorically, as well as otherwise, too considerable a disparity existed or had developed between his first two lines' artworks as trophies, to be dived for as pearls or wreck-treasures, and his subsequent lines' inquiry into the complex process of art-making. (On the basis of available evidence, it is difficult or impossible to conceive of a nonsurviving line or two that could suffice to meld "Hard . . . deep" and "In him . . . mate" and subsequent lines into a unified and coherent poem.)

Other suppositions about "Hard . . . deep" might suggest themselves; but having laid out a few of the likely more relevant, we may move on. What else of some substance is revealed by the Stage Bc main leaf and Stage Bb clip? First, that Stage Bc's first three lines ("In him . . . freeze") constitute a revised opening for the poem eventually titled "Art," though what the Stage Bb version(s) of those lines may have been we cannot tell, since they were scissored away from the top of the Bb clip at Stage Bc. Secondly, the earliest inscribed surviving lines in the final poem are Stage Bb's "Sad patience . . . scorn". Thirdly, Melville alters wording, word order, and rhyme scheme in arriving at the final versions of his last four lines.

For lack of surviving evidence, we cannot tell whether, at Stages Ba or Bb, either Jacob's heart or wrestling with the "angel—Art" were present. Maybe not. But a plausible hunch would be that of all the elements in the poem's varying avatars, that heart and Art are likely survivors from its earliest version. Whatever the earlier case, though, as Melville revises the text on his Stage Bd revision patch (see both Figures 3 and 1), we can watch as he moves and improves from "With more than even Jacob's heart" to "With much of mystic Jacob's heart" to "Must fuse with Jacob's mystic heart" to "And fuse with Jacob's mystic heart". A given reader might prefer the penultimate "Must" to "And" for its assonantal and consonantal as well as semantic force, but "And" may be granted as inferentially more exact, and no disagreement is likely over the superiority of "Jacob's mystic heart" or the manifold suggestiveness of "fuse".

Further, and finally, for present purposes of clarifying the significance, nature, and revisionary implications of Melville's alterings, his penciled, circled, and guide-lined "much of mystic" at the top of the mount (see Figure 1) not only constitutes post–Stage Bd revision of the poem's next-to-last line, but also indicates he inscribed the Stage Be patch ("In placid . . . . mate") later than that post-Bd revision it covers over. Why remark this (once it is pointed out) obviousness? Because the sequence of revisions thereby established suggests also the closeness in time, if not necessarily the exact succession, of some of Melville's more significant recastings of his poem. Not until post-Bd revision does either Jacob or his heart become (explicitly) "mystic". Not until post-Bd revision does "dream" appear in the poem's first line. Did Jacob the dreamer as well as thigh-touched angel-wrestler (Genesis 28:31, 32) suggest the explicit

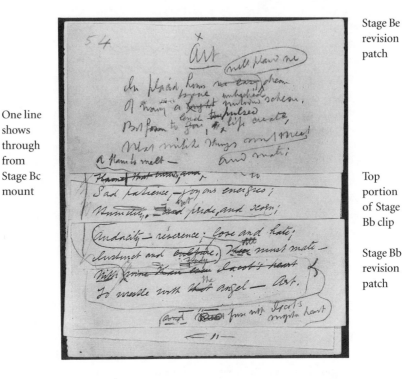

Stage Be
revision
patch

One line
shows
through
from
Stage Bc
mount

Top
portion
of Stage
Bb clip

Stage Bb
revision
patch

Figure 3. Melville's transcript of "Art," showing revision patches attached, below, at Stage Bb ("Audacity . . . Art") and, above, at Stage Be ("Art / In placid . . . mate"). (The reader may find it useful to devise a rough facsimile of Melville's transcript by photocopying Figures 1 and 3, scissoring apart the representations of clips and patches, and pinning them as he did.) *Reprinted with permission of the Houghton Library.*

figure of the dreaming artist in line 1, or did Melville's transforming his creater from the impersonal "him" of Stage Bc to the more personal "we" of Stage Be somehow enable the enlivening transfiguration in "Jacob's mystic heart"? There is no way to tell. But one or the other possibility is certainly to be made something of in any full account of what the revised poem does and is as narratized-dramatized supposing about the art-making process "we" enter through "dream" and "scheme"—only to discover that if we would "lend" form and create "pulsed life," we must do more than passively attend the otherwise unassisted meeting and mating of contraries; must do other than dive, discover and seize; must have or appropriate "Jacob's mystic heart" in order to wrestle effectually with that angel which, agent or principal, may

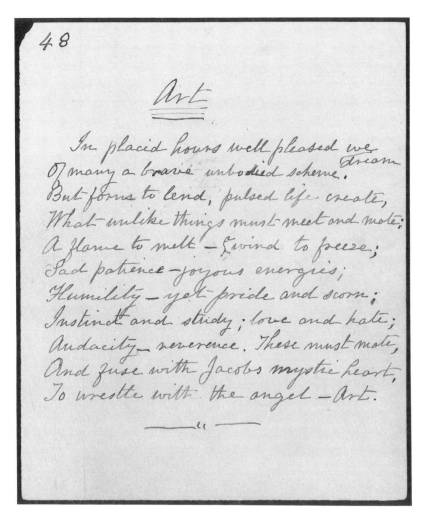

Figure 4. Elizabeth Shaw Melville's transcript of "Art." *Reprinted with permission of the Houghton Library.*

injure but is nonetheless godlike and therefore most worth trying to get a headlock on.

Melville's latest revisions of "Art" appear in his wife's transcript (see Figure 4), which became printer's copy for the poem in *Timoleon Etc.* (1891). Impossible to see in a photofacsimile but necessary to know is that it is he, not she, who is the source of advertent variants in her transcript. In line 2, for example, he pencil-cancels the "bright" that she has copied from his transcript and inserts "brave" above her inscription line, which "brave" she erases after she has inked his revision in over the scratched-out last four letters of her earlier "bright"; she also copies "brave" back into his transcript, presumably to ensure they will have a revised text on hand if her transcript gets lost or marred at the print shop. Similarly, in line 3, he pencil-alters her "give" to "lend"; then she scratches out her "give" and inks in "lend" and copies "lend" back into his transcript. The "unbodied" she pencils into his transcript just above his penciled "unbodied" is not a revision but a clarification, for her purposes, of the word he intends, space for the "odie" letters in which she initially leaves blank in her own transcript. In line 3 she mends (for clarity) his "form"; in her transcript he pencil-alters the word to "forms"; in *Timoleon Etc.* the reading reverts to "form", presumably a restoration of his earlier choice.

Specifying this much should indicate the hazards of describing or interpreting from photofacsimiles. But the interested reader will also want to know that the apostrophe missing from Mrs. Melville's "Jacobs" is Melville's responsibility; that is, the pointing in Mrs. Melville's transcript is to be understood as Melville's own, she having been directed to transcribe without punctuation, then to ink in only the pointing he subsequently pencils in. The reader will want to notice as well that Mrs. Melville's inscriptions of "lend" and "unbodied" in Melville's transcript (Figure 3) show how she can sometimes mime his hand closely enough that even the expert may be wisely unsure till a closer look reveals significant differences—here, in the beginning of her "u" as well as in her distinguishable "d", both terminal and medial.

Some think—or affect to think—that only the truly masochistic may be compelled to venture further into the wilds of revisionary description. The attentive will have learned by now, however, that though the "Art" situation is complex, Melville's manuscript changes are by no means "almost indecipherable" and can even be tolerably interesting. A few, then, will be curious enough to try the maze—if enough thread be supplied. The more competitive may wish to imagine themselves going to the mat for Art's sake. Whatever the motive or figure, the following interpreted account of variants in Melville's and his wife's transcripts of "Art" should enable anyone to get closer to the details of his altering visions and revisions. If some be moved by the evidence to re-figure whether and how much the poem may directly or indirectly derive from, say, Kant, Goethe, Schiller, Akenside, Wordsworth, Coleridge, Emerson, so much the better.

In the Northwestern-Newberry *Published Poems* volume may be found the further specification of any assumptions and conventions of variants-reporting here left tacit. For present purposes, though, a few definitions and explanations of symbols and terms will help the intrepid find their way.

HM	Herman Melville's hand or transcript
EM	Elizabeth Shaw Melville's hand or transcript
EM\HM	EM's transcript\HM's hand
1, 2, . . .	a variant numeral following HM, EM, EM\HM indicates where in the inscription and revision sequence the specified variant occurs
→	an arrow preceding a variant numeral means the variant indicated was immediately superseded at the original time of inscription
T	*Timoleon Etc.* (1891)
substantive variant	a different wording
nonsubstantive variant	a different punctuation or pointing: spelling, capitalization, indention, spacing, etc.—what Sir Walter Greg calls the "accidentals" of a text
~	in the account of nonsubstantive variants, a similar sign indicates that the word did not change though the specified punctuation did
∧	in the account of nonsubstantive variants, a caret indicates the location of absent punctuation
mount	a manuscript leaf to which a clip from an earlier inscription stage has been attached
clip	a partial leaf scissored (clipped) from an earlier inscription stage than the mount to which it is attached
patch	a partial leaf inscribed at a later stage than the leaf to which it is attached as a revision

Below, entries are keyed to line numbers in the final text of "Art" reprinted at the beginning of this chapter. All italicized description is editorial.

ART

SUBSTANTIVE VARIANTS

[the first entry here designates each leaf and part-leaf of the "Art" manuscript, each identified by specification of its head- and end-words]

1–11   In . . . . Art] [*HM Leaf 1(Bc)* a wind to freeze *{only uncanceled inscrip-tion} HM Leaf 1.patch 1(Be)* In . . . . melt *HM Leaf 1.clip(Bb)* Sad . . . scorn *HM Leaf 1.patch 2(Bd)* Audacity . . . . Art *EM Leaf 1* In . . . . Art]

1–4   In . . . . mate] HM2(Be); [*see following description of superseded Stage Bc matter inscribed in ink on HM Leaf 1*]

———‖———[*beginning device*]

Hard to grapple and upsweep
One dripping trophy from the deep.

[*wide line-space*]
[*then cancel* Hard. . . deep *with blue pencil*]
[*after ink inscription of following Stage Bc lines, insert, in pencil, the title*

Art
and   ———‖———*{beginning device}*]
[*the following is Stage Bc ink inscription*]
In him who would evoke—create,
Contraries [*then* What extremes *then* Contraries *then* What contraries] must meet and mate:
[*then pencil-cancel* In . . . mate *and supersede by covering over with Stage Be patch*] HM1(Bc)

1   well pleased we] HM2; we easy HM1
2   brave] EM\HM; bright HM
3   form] HM,T; forms EM\HM
3   lend] EM\HM; give HM
3   pulsed] HM3; a HM1; true HM2
5   A flame to melt—] HM3(Bc); Flames that burn, HM1(Bc); Flame that burns, HM2(Bc)
5   a wind] HM2,EM,EM\HM2; and winds HM1; winds EM\HM1
5   to] HM2; that HM1
7   Humility—yet pride^] HM3; Humility—and pride^ HM1; Humility, pride, HM2
8–10   Instinct . . . Jacob's] [*see following description of superseded Stage Bb matter on clip*]

Reverence; love and hate twin-born;
Instinct and culture; era meet
[*then pencil-cancel* Reverence . . . meet *and pencil-add*]
Audacity—reverence; love and hate

Instinct and culture. These must mate

With more than Even Jacob

[*then erase* Even Jacob *and pencil-cancel* Audacity . . . more than *and cover over with Stage Bd patch*] HM1(Bb)

8–9   Instinct and study . . . Audacity—reverence] HM2; Audacity—rever-
        ence . . . Instinct and study HM1

8   study] HM2; culture HM1

9   These] HM1,HM3; All HM2

10–11   And . . . Art] [*HM pencil-circles these lines for attention and only partly
        erases the circling*]

10   And . . . mystic] HM→4,HM6; With more than even Jacob's HM1;
        With much of mystic Jacob's HM2; Must fuse with Jacob's mystic
        HM3; [*no variant evidently inscribed for* And] fuse with Jacob's mystic
        HM→5

11   the] HM2; that HM1

NONSUBSTANTIVE VARIANTS

4   mate:] HM1,EM\HM; ~ ; HM2

5   melt—a wind] HM,EM\HM; melt a EM→1 [*a first mistranscription
        caused by the much-revised state of HM's transcript*]; melt—[*or a wide-
        space left for later insertion of a possible dash*]winds EM2 [*a second
        mistranscription*]

6   patience—] EM\HM2; ~ ,— HM [*though the comma and dash may
        have been inscribed at different times, neither is canceled in favor of the
        other*]; ~ , EM\HM1

7   Humility—yet pride^] [*see substantive note*]

7   and scorn] [*not underlined*] HM1,EM; [*pencil-underlined, probably as
        part of HM's considering how to revise the line*] HM2

7   scorn;] HM, EM\HM2; ~ : EM\HM1

8–9   study; . . . reverence.] HM2; reverence; . . .study. HM1 [*in revising, HM
        transposes phrases but not (explicitly) punctuation*]

9   mate,] EM\HM; ~ ^ HM1[*in superseded text; see substantive note on
        lines 8– 10*]; ~ — HM2

10   Jacob's] HM,T; Jacobs EM

10   heart,] EM\HM; ~ ^ HM

NOTES

1. Even if not consciously, Shurr may need to overlook both the art-as-trophy orientation of the canceled lines and the potentially instructive connection between the "wrestle" in "Art" and the "grapple" in "In a Garret," since he is inclined to make the latter evoke "grappling hooks and dragging operations" that "are likely to bring up some ultimate horror" (243–44), thereby supporting his overall argument about Melville as deep-fisher forever dredging up iniquity and the profound mysteries thereof.

2. The capital "E" on "Even" is inferably an anticipatory slip of the hand as his mind looks forward to the capitalized "Jacob".

3. Those who do not know his transcriptional habits might speculate that in making his Stage Bc fair copy of "Art," Melville is merely reusing a leaf, the only previously inscribed two lines on which he has already canceled as he expanded them into "In a Garret." In recycling superseded leaves, however, Melville's nearly invariable habit is to use their blank, completely uninscribed versos, and the verso of this Stage Bc main leaf is blank, implying that when he began inscribing on it, its recto was also blank.

WORKS CITED

Jarrard, Norman. "Poems by Herman Melville: A Critical Edition of the Published Verse." Ph.D. diss. University of Texas, 1960.

Shurr, William H. *The Mystery of Iniquity: Melville as Poet, 1857–1891*. Lexington: UP of Kentucky, 1972.

Thorp, Willard, ed. *Herman Melville: Representative Selections*. New York: American Book, 1938.

Vincent, Howard P., ed. *Collected Poems*. Vol. 14: *Complete Works of Herman Melville*. Chicago: Packard, 1947.

Warren, Robert Penn, ed. *Selected Poems of Herman Melville: A Reader's Edition*. New York: Random House, 1970.

16

Imagining *Pierre:*
Reading the Extra-Illustrated Melville

JEAN ASHTON

One of the pleasures to be had from working as the custodian of a library collection that owes its shape to the interests and ambitions of the great nineteenth-century collectors is the opportunity to follow byways of the past that are seldom discovered by researchers who pursue the direct and straight-forward paths of conventional literary or historical scholarship. A volume tucked away in the recess of a shelf and stumbled upon serendipitously by the earnest librarian seeking to reorder a shelf of nineteenth-century pamphlets may lead the way to whole new areas of knowledge or speculation. When I was Librarian of the New-York Historical Society, an event of this sort, a chance encounter with two massive extra-illustrated editions of a published memoir of old New York, coming on the heels of a request to think about the rele-vance of New York history to Herman Melville's *Pierre,* led me to wonder what might be learned if similar versions of that complex, problematic novel had been created by one of the author's contemporaries and had survived into the twentieth century. Would they be dismissed today as glorified scrapbooks con-structed out of the ruins of the early edition, of interest mainly to collectors of historical prints? Or might they not be used instead as visual guides to the historical reality that surrounded the contemporary reader of Melville's novels, marking out pathways through the common ground of language and imagery shared by audience and author?

The practice of "extra-illustrating" or "Grangerising" contemporary editions of favorite texts was well known in the nineteenth century as one of the more eccentric forms of that obsessive love of books and book collecting dubbed "bibliomania" by the nineteenth-century bibliographer Thomas Frognall Dibdin. The process was named after the Reverend James Granger, an English clergymen who produced in 1769 a *Biographical History of England* that included blank leaves designed to be filled with portraits chosen by readers from outside sources. As the idea spread, collectors touched by the mania plundered shops and cannibalized published books, often cutting apart and destroying rare editions for the sake of a single image. They cut and pasted with abandon, creating eccentric, highly personal volumes that in later generations tended to languish in the recesses of the library, where they might be discovered from time to time by art historians or dealers interested in the prints or manuscripts within.[1]

The texts most commonly chosen for such elaboration were, like Granger's, biographical or historical in nature. In America, the vogue for extra-illustration lasted from about 1850 until 1900, a period marked by a general fascination with the local or national past, and the images used were as likely to be depictions of historical events or famous places as portraits of notable figures. Items chosen to illustrate a particular passage in the text, or in some cases a word, a phrase, or a figure of speech, were often lithographs or other prints produced as multiples, but might just as well be broadsides, photographs, cartes-de-visite, newspaper clippings, sheet music, watercolor paintings, pencil sketches, letters, trade cards, or even coins—any objects that could be folded or mounted onto pages of uniform size. The original book was customarily disbound and split apart. In many cases the individual pages were pasted or mounted within larger leaves; the illustrations in their various forms were inserted in the appropriate location and the whole rebound, often with great care and considerable expense. The augmented text was, of necessity, much larger than the original. In England, a Mr. Sutherland extended the Earl of Clarendon's one-volume *History of the Rebellion and Civil Wars in England* (1702–04) into a 270-volume set by the addition of more than nineteen thousand illustrations.

Connecting *Pierre* with Grangerising and bibliomania is not as farfetched as it might first seem. Throughout *Pierre* there is ample evidence that the novelist is aware of the book as an independent and symbolic object, distinct from its content. This is made particularly clear in the final third of the novel (Books 16–26), where the action takes place in the fictionalized city of New York. A discussion of the physical formats that are associated with popular success provides the main substance of Book 7, "Young America in Literature." Pierre Glendinning notes the contrast between worthless or mundane texts and the gilded covers and lavish illustrations the commercial world uses to encase and embellish them; these gaudy and frivolous volumes are in turn implicitly contrasted not only with the Plotinus Plimlimmon pamphlet, "Chronometricals & Horologicals"—"a thin, tattered, dried-fish-like thing; printed with blurred ink upon mean sleazy paper" (206)—but also with Pierre's own masterpiece, which, of course, never becomes a published book at all.

Moving as he did on the fringes of New York literary circles, Melville is likely to have been aware that his editor and sometime-friend Evert Duykinck was both a book collector and a committed extra-illustrator. Duykinck's Granger-ised copy of Washington Irving's *A Knickerbocker History of New York* is now in the collection of the New York Public Library. James Lenox, another of Melville's contemporaries and a founding member of that library, was also an extra-illustrator whose editions survive (see Tredwell). Melville may not, however, have known that one of the favorite texts for Grangerising in the 1860s and 1870s would be a memoir of city life that mentioned his own "romances" as having "met with a reception flattering to the most inspiring author" (see Miller 19). This latter work, *Old New York,* by John Wakefield Francis, is the foundation of the two multivolume extra-illustrated editions in the New-York Historical Society collections that provide a model for my similar but imaginary edition of *Pierre.*

Dr. Francis may be familiar to Melville scholars as a central figure in the salon life of Manhattan literati, a raconteur and man-about-town who, according to Perry Miller, was a leading candidate for the title "foremost citizen" of midcentury New York. Although not an intimate friend of the novelist, John Francis attended the wedding of Herman's brother Allan Melville in 1847, and Herman himself is reported to have joined parties at the doctor's Bond Street home (see Miller 19). In 1857 Francis, whose wit was described as "Rabelaisian," gave a speech before the New-York Historical Society in which he recounted at length the history of the city's institutions and recalled to the consciousness of his audiences the stalwart personalities who had founded them. The content of the speech is worth passing attention since, like the many pictorial explorations of the city that appeared in the 1850s (for example, the enormously popular illustrated editions of the *Manual of the Corporation of the City of New York* [1841–70] and the sensational tours of the popular society and the underworld written by journalists like George Foster, *New York in Slices, New York by Gaslight,* and *New York Naked,* among others)—*Old New York: or, Reminiscences of the Past Sixty Years* (as Francis's lecture was entitled upon publication in 1858) articulated a growing self-consciousness about urban life and a certain ambivalence about growth and change, feelings that are recognizable also in the far more pessimistic urban passages of *Pierre* as well as in Melville's many other descriptions of his native city. "In the old world," Francis reminded his audience,

> we are called a fast people, and the history of no sort in our vast confederacy, is more impressed with the change that seems a normal condition of our republican life, than this city. Its original land-marks are scarcely to be recognized; its population is utterly transformed; its resources indefinitely enlarged; nay, to the backward and loving gaze of a venerable Knickerbocker, its individuality is almost lost. (376)

After Dr. Francis's death in 1862, the book was reissued in a limited edition with an added memoir of the author's life written by the critic H. T. Tuckerman, another member of the New York world of publishers, editors, and literary men-about-town. Shortly thereafter, a local rare book dealer, T. H. Morrell, purchased and disbound the expanded text, enlarged the pages to folio size, and extended the work to nine volumes by adding approximately three thousand manuscripts, maps, and prints. A later collector, Lucy W. Drexel, added a tenth volume to the Morrell set in 1892. A second Grangerised edition, in quarto, was prepared by Ogden Goelet. This version comprises thirteen volumes, and contains, along with the usual prints and manuscripts, a number of rare broadsides and over 160 original drawings and watercolors of New York scenes. In the words of the 1935 catalog of the Goelet sale, in this set, "practically every name or place mentioned by Dr. Francis is represented by a portrait, autograph, or view" (American Art Assoc. 96).

What might be learned had a similar edition of *Pierre* been created from it? To begin with, extra-illustrated books provide a unique opportunity to study the relationship between reader and text. The desire to expand a particular work by the addition of pictures and works of art may be attributed in part, as critics of the practice have at times accused, and its practitioners have confessed, to a passion for collecting and owning that is of more interest to the psychologist than the literary critic or historian. In some cases, however, it may also be seen as the product of an effort to extend the experience of reading in time and to create from a fixed and common text a new work that is different from all other versions of that text—that is, to make or "write" a book of one's own. An extra-illustrated book includes both the printed version of the author's words and a concrete embodiment of the reader's interpretation of those words as it appears in an illustration or document. It thus records a response to the text that juxtaposes the reader's experience with the writer's inspiration or intention.

Thus, an extra-illustrated version of *Pierre,* should one exist, would be a key to the hidden pictorial vocabulary of the book that could suggest common meanings and reference points that have now been lost or turn up only fleetingly in the historical record. The twentieth-century reader, for example, learning in Book 16 of *Pierre* of the stagecoach's descent into the "vast, triangular town," is likely to be unfamiliar with the widely published views of New York of Melville's period that show the city truncated at its broadest point, in midtown, and reaching down toward the pointed shores of the Battery. Similarly, the description of a statue on a revolving pedestal, described in section 3 of Book 25, an image that might mystify a reader today, might well have evoked in the mind of a contemporary reader not only the real practice of contemporary museums of Melville's day but also the perversion of that display in the phony "galleries" described in Foster's *New York Naked,* where prostitutes or "models" were posed on similar pedestals in various states of undress.

The illustrations of an extra-illustrated book act, in effect, like visual footnotes. Because they are added privately, without the pretense of being authoritative, and are, or may be, added within the period in which the book was produced, they may act as clues to contemporary reader response and may also open pathways into the text that have long been closed. The language of popular culture and the common vocabulary of the built environment becomes indecipherable sooner than literary language exactly because both are common and popular and thus are either effectively beneath the level of day-to-day consciousness or are thought to need little explanation. Enough clues to this can be discerned in reading guidebooks and descriptions of midcentury New York to make it clear that many of Melville's references and hidden allusions would evoke scenes that were part of the everyday life of the Manhattanite of the period; an extra-illustrated edition created at the time could surely expand our knowledge of the historical reality that lay beneath or behind the fictive structure and deepen our understanding of the novel.

Although, for example, *Pierre* is a work of the imagination and presumably different in intent from Dr. Francis's rather pedestrian memoir, nostalgia and fascination with the past provide the shape and, to some degree, determine the tone of both works. The city of New York is never mentioned by name in the novel, but it is clearly the scene of the action in the last part of the work, a place where the changes described by Dr. Francis had often obliterated the lineaments of earlier times and where only tantalizing glimpses of what once was could be discerned from time to time beneath the complexities of the busy present. Pierre's New York, like John Francis's, is a place where present reality is informed by memories or relics of a time when things were different, of odd survivals and incongruous expectations based on a half-remembered and incompletely documented past where symbolic and real change were closely intertwined.

Consider, to begin with, the dwelling of the Apostles, the converted church that forms so resonant a symbol in the history of Pierre Glendinning. It had a number of real counterparts in Manhattan: the repeated transformations of these sometime houses of worship might indeed have propelled any city dweller of the middle decades of the century to a contemplation of the nature of change, if not to more metaphysical speculations. The Huguenot Church on Pine Street, for example, sometimes identified as the prototype of the fictional hostel, was one of several downtown churches that had been overtaken by the commercial development of the city and used for secular purposes. The most impressive conversion was that undergone by the Dutch church on Broadway, which in 1845 had been expensively fitted up as the city's main post office, a transformation so Melvillean that it is hard to believe it was not invented by the author. The South Baptist (earlier the German) Reformed Church has also been suggested as the original of the Apostles (see Murray xxi, ii). By 1840 this structure, in the New York City directory at 64–66 Nassau Street (although it appears as 82 Nassau in the 1852 Perris map), had become "Gosling's Dining Saloon," a thriving establishment that fed upwards of a thousand people a day.[2] Similar transformations had overtaken many of the decaying frame houses of lower Manhattan in the same period as the respectable population moved uptown to the new genteel areas of Gramercy Park and Chelsea. Like the brownstone row houses of today's Madison or Lexington Avenues, almost invisible behind the glossy facades of shopfronts, the surviving buildings of the federal period had by the 1850s either been put to commercial use or abandoned to those who out of necessity or desire clung to the past, becoming architectural "spinsters" like those described in *Pierre*, embodying qualities of sterility and impotence.

The speed of change in New York City mentioned by Francis in the passage cited above has been a feature of the metropolis since its founding. In Melville's middle years, the pace of change had increased dramatically as the tide of new inhabitants from Ireland, from Germany, from the small towns and villages of the American countryside swept in, drawn by the vitality that new industries and newly expanded forms of communication, particularly newspapers, had helped to create. The city, where 35,000 had lived at the time of the American Revolution, had grown to 300,000 by 1840 to 500,000 by 1850 to more than 800,000 by 1860—all largely below the current boundaries of Central Park. If the nearby suburbs of Brooklyn and Westchester are included, the metropolitan population by the time of the Civil War was more than a million and a half. George Foster, the peripatetic journalist whose newspaper sketches in the late 1840s captured the seediness and variety of urban life, noted that in 1848 alone 38,000 people took up residence in Manhattan. The traffic, the noise, and the chaos of the place were overwhelming (see Spann). No wonder men like Dr. Francis were bemused and nostalgic. The eerie isolation of Pierre and his household, like the corresponding spiritual isolation of Bartleby, in Melville's story of this same period, stands in mute contrast to the tumultuous and ever-growing metropolis that extended in every direction around him.

Pictorial images still available in pamphlets and periodicals give some indication of the kinds of illustrations that might have been chosen by contemporaries to depict the chaos of downtown streets and the uneven pace of development. The violence and danger of the streets encountered by Isabel and Dolly when they first enter the city, well documented by modern social historians (most recently by Guilfoyle), can still be discerned in trial reports, printed song sheets, medical records, and sketches from the more sensational newspapers that attempted to inflate them for their readers. A published 1859 guide to the bordellos of the city, *The Seraglios of New York,* survives in the New-York Historical Society Collections to testify both to the omnipresence of prostitution and to the fine line that might separate the respectable girl from her fallen sister, making plausible the outraged reaction that Pierre's relationship with his household of otherwise unprotected females evokes and explaining to some degree the sense of desperation that hangs over them all.

Other themes that seem to be quintessentially Melvillean reflect with equal clarity common perspectives on the peculiarities of city life in the 1850s. The contrast and dualities that abound in the novel correspond to a sense of disjunction that often affected New Yorkers of the period who were younger and less sentimental than Dr. Francis. Pierre notices, for example, that the rich and poor meet on Broadway, a street that, although open to all without constraint in the daytime, in the evening separates the rich from the poor—the wealthy and respectable walking only on the east side (still considered the more socially desirable side of New York), leaving the west or "shilling side" to those who did not care about their reputations. This was, in fact, a real phenomenon, noted once more by George Foster: "In the morning, or at midday, if absolutely forced to go through Broadway, you may take the sidewalk most shady or convenient without positive loss of character. But at the grand promenade hour, wo [*sic*] be to the unhappy wight or distressed damsel who should be seen plodding along the shilling pavement" (*NY in Slices* 9).

Similarly, the moral ambiguity that entraps Pierre is found throughout Melville's work, also corresponds to a widely reported conviction at the time that one's eyes and ears could not be trusted in the city, that a confusion between appearances and reality was both dangerous and endemic in a modern business community. Confidence men—to use a descriptive period term that would be explored to such brilliant effect by the author a few years later—were as common as "panel girls," prostitutes who arranged for the clients to be robbed through sliding wall panels in their rooms. The popular press was filled with warnings that society ladies and respectable gentlemen were often not what they seemed (see Kasson 70–111). And the criminal deceptions that lurked in the streets had their counterpart in the commercial tom-foolery of entrepreneurial self-promotion. Pierre's fictitious dwelling was down the street from newspaper row, the home of modern advertising, and around the corner from the spot where the greatest genius of that field, P. T. Barnum, had established his museum on the corner of Broadway and Ann Street. It might be argued that Barnum, whose gloriously fraudulent attractions like the "Fejee Mermaid" and "Fremont's Woolly Horse" attracted thousands of visitors each year and who was perhaps the best-known American of his day, is as vivid a presence in *Pierre* as in *The Confidence-Man*, though he is not mentioned in either. Certainly, his family museum, which raised illusion and deception to the status of family entertainment, was viewed by contemporaries with a skepticism and ambivalence that would not have been lost on Melville.[3]

An extra-illustrated edition of *Pierre,* had one been created, might thus have added not only to our sense of the visual and tactile world that surrounded the author but to our understanding of what might be called his transformative skill: his ability to use places and events that were already loaded with meaning for his contemporaries as elements in a work of fiction that both enhanced that meaning and used it as part of a larger metaphysical structure. Indeed, the more carefully grounded in historical reality Melville's scenes and references prove to be, the more complex and subtle the author's skill may seem to the modern reader. New Year's Day visiting cards; a reproduction of Guido's "Cenci" displayed in a downtown art gallery in 1850; pages from the city directory; sample gift-annuals with gilded bindings; leaves from young ladies' albums, like those proffered to the young author for his signature and "by-and-by monopolized an entire shelf in his chamber"; lecture invitations coming from "venerable gray-headed metropolitan Societies"[4]—a copy of the novel expanded to include these and other bits of ephemera and memorabilia selected at the time the book first appeared would allow a more detailed analysis of Melville's skill in converting experience into art than has hitherto been possible and provide additional insights into the nature of his perception of the material world.

Henry Murray, in his introduction to the 1949 edition of *Pierre,* explicitly turns away from the kind of visualization the extra-illustrator pursues: "Highly probable originals for all the natural objects [in *Pierre*] have been found," he notes. "Had it been desirable, this volume could have been illustrated with photographs of the Glendinning manor-house" as well as "the main thoroughfare of the city" and "the Church of the Apostles." From his point of view, it was clearly not "desirable" to do so; however, it should be evident by now that views, maps, and other illustrations that have been brought together by a contemporary reader at the time of the book's initial appearance can create a useful visual subtext, a vademecum for the universe of the reader who lived in close proximity in time and space to the author's fictional world. That this universe must ultimately prove to be a private one should come as no surprise. If every reader does indeed bring a cluster of private meanings to the language and structure of every text, the extra-illustrated book might then be described as an attempt to extend these private meanings into the world of historical reality—or, obversely, as an effort to use images of this world to entrap the fleeting emotions and personal memories evoked by words.

And yet, perhaps it is wise not to expect too much.

At the heart of *Pierre,* after all, lies the question "how can we know the past?" The book is, in a very real sense, about history, its representation and interpretation. How trustworthy are the fragments of the past that have come to us—the portraits, the family stories, the shadowy memories and dreams? And upon whose interpretations of them, whose histories, would we rely if not our own? Pierre's search for self, a search that ended in the destruction of nearly every fictive character whose life had touched his own, depended on a willful interpretation of just those kinds of images an extra-illustrator might pursue.

Which portrait of the senior Glendinning shows the "real" man? The heroic painting in the parlor? The studio sketch of the lover? The "Italianate" image in the gallery that fascinates both Isabel and Pierre? It is instructive to think that at the very moment when Melville's friends and bookish fellow citizens were reading and writing popular histories like *Old New York* and beginning to amass portraits and autographs to document their own versions of the past in Grangerised editions, the author of *Pierre* should hold up to scorn the reliability of such documentation and the problems that surround its interpretation. Pierre, the bookmaker, the writer, creates in a sense an extra-illustrated version of his own biography, an extended folio of his own past. Although I have just argued that for the modern reader such editions, despite their subjectivity, can lend an essential dimension of historical reality to the reading experience, for *Pierre,* turning the pages leads not to illumination but to a welter of ambiguity and confusion.[5]

NOTES

1. A useful description of extra-illustration by an avid practitioner can be found in Tredwell; see also Andrews. A modern appreciation of one collector can be found in Rosenblum.

2. See Stokes 1832, who suggests that the original structure may have been torn down by the time Melville was writing Pierre. Further transformations of the old church buildings are described in Greenleaf.

3. Foster, in *New York by Gaslight,* exaggerates the horrors of the city to create the appropriate gothic effect. Nonetheless, the following passage from the chapter "Broadway at Evening" is suggestive: "Here we are at the American Museum, crowned with is Drummond Light, sending a livid, ghastly glare for a mile up the street, and pushing the shadows of the omnibuses well-nigh to Niblo's. From the balcony of the third-story windows a cascade of horrent harmony . . . is tumbling down upon the up-turned faces of the boys and negro-women on the opposite walk—while that untiring chromatic wheel goes every round and round, twining and untwining its blue, red and yellow wreaths of lights in unvarying variety. Although it cannot strictly be said of it that it is without change, yet the shadow of its turning is painfully perceptible" (7).

4. Melville spoke on *Typee* at the New-York Historical Society on February 7, 1859, as part of a public series. No copy of his lecture survives.

5. This paper was delivered as a slide-lecture at the New-York Historical Society in 1991. The rapid development of inexpensive digital scanning equipment since that time makes it clear that a new era of extra-illustration may be dawning.

WORKS CITED

American Art Association. *Catalog, Sale #4148. The Library of the Late Ogden Goelet of New York, Part Two.* New York: Anderson Galleries, 1935.

Andrews, William Loring. *Of the Extra-Illustration of Books*. London: Zaehnsdorf, 1900.

Foster, George. *New York by Gas-Light, With Here and There a Streak of Sunshine*. New York: DeWitt and Davenport, 1850.

———. *New York Naked*. New York: DeWitt and Davenport, 185?.

———. *New York in Slices, By an Experienced Carver*. New York: W. F. Burgess, 1849.

Francis, John Wakefield. *Old New York: or, Reminiscences of the Past Sixty Years*. New York: The New-York Historical Society, 1858.

Greenleaf, Jonathan. *A History of the Churches of All Denominations in the City of New York from the Final Settlement to the Year 1846*. New York: E. French, 1846.

Guilfoyle, Timothy. *City of Eros: New York City, Prostitution, and the Commercialization of Sex 1790–1920*. New York: W. W. Norton, 1992.

Kasson, John F. "Reading the City: The Semiotics of Everyday Life." In *Rudeness and Civility: Manners in Nineteenth-Century Urban America*. New York: Hill and Wang, 1990.

Miller, Perry. *The Raven and the Whale: The War of Words and Wits in the Era of Poe and Melville*. New York: Harcourt, Brace, 1956.

Murray, Henry. Introduction to *Pierre: or, The Ambiguities*. New York: Farrar Straus, 1949.

Rosenblum, Joseph. "Irving Browne and the Extra-Illustrated Book." *Antiquarian Bookman* (November 25, 1991): 2097–108.

Spann, Edward K. *The New Metropolis: New York City, 1840–1857*. New York: Columbia UP, 1981.

Stokes, Isaac Newton Phelps. *The Iconography of Manhattan Island, 1498–1909*. New York: Robert H. Dodd, 1928.

Tredwell, Daniel. *A Monograph on Privately-Illustrated Books: A Plea for Bibliomania*. 2d ed. New York, 1892.

17

The Text of Melville
in the Twenty-First Century

G. THOMAS TANSELLE

A hundred years ago, at the time of Melville's death, most of his books were out of print. In the United States, Harper's had a small stock of a few of them but had no plans for reprinting, and in England only *Typee* and *Omoo* were still available from a publisher (the original one, John Murray). Whether there would be any accessible texts of Melville's works in the coming century was a matter of intense concern to Arthur Stedman, who assisted Melville's widow as literary executor, and he immediately set about arranging for a new edition of some of them. Just a year later, in September 1892, the United States Book Company brought out Stedman's editions of *Typee* and *Omoo,* followed a few weeks later by *White-Jacket* and *Moby-Dick.* When the twentieth century began, these editions were still in print (from a different publisher), along with another edition of *Moby-Dick,* published by Scribner's in 1899. We are now about to enter the twenty-first century, and one symbol of what has happened to Melville studies in the interval is the presence of the Northwestern-Newberry Edition, with thirteen of its fifteen volumes published. Predicting what position it will occupy in Melville study of the next century is a two-stranded undertaking that combines some of the dominant issues of literary criticism in the late twentieth century. The first strand is a consideration of authorial intention; the second, of literature as a collaborative effort, a concept that has been offered as a challenge to intentionality in recent decades.

The aim of the Northwestern-Newberry Edition is to present texts that reflect Melville's intentions as closely as extant evidence permits. What distinguishes it from earlier editions is not its focus on intention but its conception of intention (as well as its thoroughness in analyzing and recording the surviving evidence). Previous editions of Melville were concerned, explicitly or implicitly, with Melville's intention—indeed, nearly all textual criticism from antiquity to the middle of the twentieth century was directed toward the establishment of texts as intended by their authors. But intention was generally not defined so precisely as to distinguish it from expectation, and thus what authors expected to happen to the texts of their works during the process of publication—and in this way tacitly approved—was considered to be intended. Some such rationale presumably underlies the readiness of earlier editors to accept publishers' punctuation and to make further changes in spelling and punctuation aimed at bringing about consistency or adherence to an established convention. Of course, editors—like many other people over the years—have often believed that spelling and punctuation do not, by and large, affect meaning and that they can be regularized or modernized without violating authors' intended meanings. But this practical argument must ultimately rest, for those concerned with authorially intended texts, on the idea that such changes were expected, and thus in effect intended, by the authors.

Stedman, for instance, certainly wished—as Melville's friend—to follow Melville's intention: he therefore used the text of the English edition of *Typee* because it contained passages Melville had been asked to excise by the American publishers; he made some changes that he said followed the "written direction of the author"; and he emended many words to what he thought Melville intended. But he also made changes in punctuation and asked Titus Munson Coan to help him "harmonise" the spelling of Polynesian words.[1] Similarly, Michael Sadleir, the great bibliographer and an English admirer of Melville, did not imagine that he was altering Melville's intention when he allowed the texts of the Constable Edition (1922–24) to be extensively repunctuated and to incorporate British spellings. And the Hendricks House Edition (1947–), which takes for granted that a scholarly edition concentrates on authorially intended texts, often makes emendations in spelling and punctuation to secure consistency.[2]

The Northwestern-Newberry Edition, in contrast, separates intention from expectation: it attempts to approach Melville's artistic intention, held in the privacy of his own study, before that intention got entangled with the intentions of other persons involved in the publication process (however much Melville may have expected those persons to alter his texts). Like all other human projects, this edition is a product of its time and is one of many editions that in the last four decades have followed an approach deriving from W. W. Greg's "The Rationale of Copy-Text" (1949).[3] Greg believed that spelling and punctuation are important reflections of authors' artistic intentions; and he therefore encouraged editors, as a general rule, to follow texts that were as close in descent as possible to those of authors' manuscripts, as a way of maximizing the preservation of these features of authors' writing (even when later texts contain authorial revisions of wording, for those revisions can then be incorporated into the early texts). Although Greg was specifically thinking of English Renaissance drama, for which there are practically no surviving manuscripts, the drift of his rationale is clearly toward the choice of a final manuscript as copy-text when such a manuscript does exist (as is frequently the case for works written in the nineteenth and twentieth centuries).

As it happens, very few fair-copy manuscripts of Melville's published writings survive, but those that do (for his contributions to the *Literary World* and for *John Marr* and *Timoleon*) are used as copy-texts by the Northwestern-Newberry editors. And neither for these works nor for all the others, where the copy-texts are the first printings based on the manuscripts Melville provided the publishers, do the editors attempt to bring about consistency in spelling and punctuation or to make the texts conform to a presumed standard. The manuscripts that survive offer no basis for thinking that Melville himself strove for consistency in these matters, and Melville's own wishes—as deduced from his practice—is all that the Northwestern-Newberry editors regard as relevant. Even if Melville expected his publishers to make his spelling and punctuation consistent (a questionable assumption in any case), the way he in fact wrote can be assumed to reveal nuances of meaning that could be lost through alteration; and although printed copy-texts already incorporate departures from the manuscripts, the editors try to guard against making emendations that would in fact be further departures. In their view, reconciling inconsistencies would in most instances run the risk of moving the text away from what Melville wrote (and intended to write). The focus of the Northwestern-Newberry Edition is clearly on the private Melville, on Melville's writings as they existed independently of the modifications imposed on them by the exigencies of publication. Surviving materials do not permit the editors to eliminate all such modifications, but their aim is to move in that direction.

This aim is of course reflected in the treatment of wording as well as of spelling and punctuation, and nowhere better than in the restoration of the cuts in *Typee*. Melville made the changes himself and even claimed that they improved the work; because they were instigated by outside pressure, however, and because Melville's next book contained passages similar to those he was asked to eliminate from *Typee*, the editors argue that the cuts do not stem from Melville's artistic intention. But Stedman, after all, restored the cut passages to *Typee* also; and the distinctive point of view of the Northwestern-Newberry Edition—and of a number of similar editions from the last third of the twentieth century—lies not so much in favoring the author's intention over the publisher's as in recognizing that such an approach is inconsistent if it is not applied to the spelling and punctuation along with the wording.

Nevertheless, another aspect of the treatment of wording in the Northwestern-Newberry Edition does call attention to an issue that has been prominent in recent editorial debates: how to choose among shifting authorial intentions, as reflected in successive revisions. The cuts in *Typee* are not an example if they are defined as not reflecting Melville's intention. But some of the differences between the American and English editions of *Moby-Dick*, for instance—or between the magazine and book texts of the pieces collected in *The Piazza Tales*—do represent Melville's revision of his own previous wording and thus his change of intention at those points (see NN *MD* 781–91; NN *PT* 551–56). Some authors continue to revise their works after initial publication, sometimes creating in the process what can be considered different works, but the only known examples of what are possibly Melville's late revisions are trivial—the "Memoranda" in Melville's wife's hand stating that four changes were requested by Melville "for re-issue of 'Typee'" and the four-stanza lyric that Melville copied out from *Clarel* in 1888 (under the title "Ditty of Aristippus") with two differences of punctuation (see NN *Typee* 312–13; NN *Clarel* 698–99, 867–70). The Northwestern-Newberry editors accept Melville's revisions of *Moby-Dick* and the pieces in *The Piazza Tales* as reflecting his final intention, but the late changes in *Typee* and *Clarel* are not adopted. Although the uncertain status of these late changes is sufficient in itself to result in their rejection, the editors add in each case that the changes are examples of isolated alterations far removed in time from the original composition and not springing from the same process of thought that underlay it. Their editorial focus is thus not simply on the author's private, artistic intention but on the final such intention that emerged from a full engagement with the original conception of a work.

This position supplies one set of answers to the two questions that all editors must take a stand on: what agent or agents are to be emphasized as the producers of a work, and what stage in the evolution of a work is to be the focus of attention? Another set of answers has in recent years been forcefully proposed. According to this view, literature is a collaborative art, because what is released to the public has generally been affected by a number of persons besides the nominal author—whether friends or publishers' editors or scribes or printers. A literary work is thus a social construct, the result of a group effort, and the product so formed is what readers encounter and respond to. Such observations have led some textual critics to feel that scholarly attention should be directed to the texts that emerged from the publishing circumstances of a given moment, not to the texts envisaged by authors working alone at their desks. The former approach is seen as recognizing historical realities, whereas the latter is regarded as focusing on an artificial goal, just as unrealizable now as it was in the author's own time. One should not be surprised that this point of view has become prominent in an age when the most publicized literary theories have been concerned with ways in which language subverts attempts at individual expression and with the responses of readers to clusters of language rather than with the intentions of creators in assembling those clusters. In literary studies, as in other fields, an emphasis on social forces inevitably alternates with an emphasis on the formative influence of individuals, and in the late twentieth century the social approach has been in the ascendant.

Such cycles, however, have not previously had a major effect on the practice of textual criticism, and the last two decades or so have been the first time in the two millennia of Western textual criticism when there has been substantial support for the scholarly production of texts that reflect intentions other than those of authors. In the past, textual theory alternated between the poles of maximizing or minimizing the role of editors' judgment; but even those who wished to minimize the place of judgment (and therefore advocated minimal alteration of inherited texts) did so because they believed that the result would best approximate authorial intentions (or expectations), not because they welcomed the nonauthorial elements that were embedded in documentary texts. The contribution of recent discussion has been to elaborate the reasons for being interested in texts that result from the combined efforts of authors and of others involved in the production process—to show, indeed, why those texts are valuable in their own right and not simply as a means to something else. Obviously some kinds of historical study—such as the examination of contemporary responses to a work—must be based on the texts that were made available at particular past moments, however widely they may have diverged from the texts desired by their authors; and it is salutary to have the claims of socially produced texts emphasized in the face of the longstanding attention to authorially intended texts. What is less helpful, however, is the tendency on the part of some writers who make these points to denigrate the study of authorial intention, as if a recognition of the collaborative aspect of literary production invalidated a concern with the intentions of authors alone. Although authors' intentions are not directly locatable in documents and must be reconstructed through editorial judgment (and are therefore always subject to question), they do constitute past events, just as the activities that produce texts for public dissemination do. The two scholarly approaches are complementary, concentrating on different past moments.

If the social approach to texts does not eliminate the need for research into authors' intentions, it must nevertheless be taken seriously. How, one may ask, would the text of Melville edited according to this approach be different from the Northwestern-Newberry text? It would, for example, include the expurgated *Typee* and the text of *The Piazza Tales* containing the softenings introduced by the editorial staff of Dix and Edwards (see NN *PT* 554). For "Hawthorne and His Mosses," the text as printed in *The Literary World,* containing the revisions Melville apparently made under pressure from the editor, would be preferred over the unrevised text recoverable from the surviving manuscript (see NN *PT* 655–56). Two texts of *Moby-Dick* would be included, because the alterations made by the cautious editors in Bentley's office created a version so different in its effect from the American as to require its separate presentation, since it is the product of a discrete set of social forces. Even in those cases where the differences between the American and English texts are far less dramatic, as with *Mardi* and *Redburn,* such differences as there are (largely in spelling and punctuation) do reflect distinct cultural settings, and a case can be made that each published text deserves individual treatment, for each one emerged from a separate collaborative action and was directed at a particular audience.

The primary question that would arise in such an undertaking is whether each text should be a critical reconstruction (that is, incorporating emendations that result from editorial judgment) or an unaltered reproduction of an existing text. In effect, this question asks whether or not the focus is still on intentions, even if not now entirely on those of the author. If the aim is to represent the collaborative intentions of the persons involved in the production of texts, that goal cannot be accommodated by the mere reproduction of texts as published any more than the presentation of authorial intentions can. Obviously what gets published does not necessarily correspond in every respect to what those responsible for its publication intended. The principal classes of corruption from this point of view are misreadings of copy, by publishers' copyists or compositors, and so-called typographical errors. Such mistakes are not always obvious, and their detection and correction require editorial judgment. The same corrections would of course also be made by editors interested in authorial intention; but once those corrections are taken care of, editors concerned with collaborative intention would generally have fewer further emendations to consider than editors concerned with authorial intention. That the former, however, do sometimes face serious additional problems can be illustrated by the absence of the Epilogue in the Bentley text of *Moby-Dick*. A strong argument can be made that the Epilogue is missing because it was lost, misplaced, or overlooked in Bentley's office, rather than because it was never sent to Bentley or because he rejected it (see NN *MD* 678–80); and an editor might therefore take the position that a text reflecting the publisher's intention would have to include the Epilogue. Furthermore, the pattern of differences between the American and English texts shows clearly that Bentley's office wished to tone down statements that seemed too outspoken on religious, political, and sexual matters; a critical editor focusing on the publisher's intention—and carrying this position to its logical conclusion—might have to consider the possibility of altering other statements of the same kind if a case could be made that they were missed through negligence.

Establishing the publisher's intended text can therefore be just as problematical as establishing the author's intended text (even aside from the question of how intention in either case is to be defined). Nevertheless, in most instances the result of attempting to establish a publisher's intended text would not be very different from an unaltered reprint of what the publisher in fact did publish. And since what was actually published has its own interest and importance—for it (misprints and all) was what contemporary readers had in front of them—one must ask whether the photographic or digitized reproduction of original editions might not have a greater usefulness for social textual criticism than editorially emended texts. Facsimiles are, of course, an established genre of scholarly edition, especially for manuscript material; but the recent interest in the social production and reception of texts has provided new reasons for the value of facsimiles (at least reasons that were not generally uppermost in the minds of those who prepared facsimiles in the past). A set of volumes or CD-ROMs containing reproduced images of the original American and English typesettings of Melville's books and the original appearances of his shorter pieces would indeed be useful: it would be a convenient supplement to the Northwestern-Newberry Edition, presenting evidence not recorded there, and it would make more widely available, in easily readable form, the texts of Melville's works as they emerged from the publication process and were offered to readers. Substantive variants in those texts are listed in the apparatus of the Northwestern-Newberry volumes, along with the spelling and punctuation of the texts chosen as copy-texts; but the spelling and punctuation of the texts of the other authorized editions are not recoverable from the Northwestern-Newberry lists, nor are most of the details of the typographic design of any of the editions. Reproductions cannot, of course, be adequate substitutes for originals in every respect, but when properly prepared they can serve the scholarly, and the more general, public well by complementing critical editions.

Proper preparation requires the collation of multiple copies of each edition (a process already completed for the Northwestern-Newberry Edition) in order to identify variants—both intentional alterations, all of which should ideally be reproduced, and typographical eccentricities (such as faulty inking and shifting type), which might affect the selection of a copy (or copies) for reproduction.[4] Furthermore, the reproduced images must be proofread against the originals as carefully as if the text had been reset, so that any places where the reproductions are misleading can be located and new reproductions can be made. If it is impossible to secure reproductions that accurately reflect the original, notes must be provided to explain the situation; and notes must in any case record the details of such unreproducible features as the paper of the original.

Prepared in this way, a set of facsimiles would be a valuable resource for Melville studies, supplementing the Northwestern-Newberry Edition by completing its documentation and by providing a fuller basis for the social study of Melville's texts. Collections of printed facsimiles relating to a single author have in the past been thought of primarily in terms of manuscript (or typescript or proof) materials, as in *The James Joyce Archive* or *F. Scott Fitzgerald Manuscripts*. But published editions are important historical documents also, a fact being recognized in recent projects for collecting electronic texts and images into "hypertext" or "hypermedia" archives, such as *The Complete Writings and Pictures of Dante Gabriel Rossetti* (see McGann's report in *Text*). Melville offers an ideal opportunity for publicizing the usefulness of a published collection of reproductions of printed items: his writings are widely studied; printed editions are the primary documents for approaching them, since very little manuscript material survives for the writings published during his lifetime; and the size of the undertaking would be manageable, since the number of his book-length works is not large, none of them had more than two authorized editions during his lifetime (though *Typee,* with two versions of its American edition, would require being reproduced in three texts), and there were only six unauthorized editions.

Such a Melville archive should also contain reproductions of what manuscript material there is. Although it will never be possible to study Melville's process of composition in the detail available for many nineteenth- and twentieth-century writers, enough survives to provide samplings of the process at various times in his life. There are draft versions in Melville's hand of a chapter of *Typee,* two paragraphs of *Mardi,* the preface to the English edition of *White-Jacket,* and several passages (mostly in one chapter) of *The Confidence-Man,* as well as a draft version of a few lines of "Bartleby, the Scrivener" in his sister Augusta's hand; there are final (printer's-copy) manuscripts in his hand for four of his five *Literary World* pieces and a final copy of the other one ("Hawthorne and His Mosses") in his wife's hand but revised by him, thus allowing in five instances a comparison of published texts with printer's copies; there is a final manuscript, in Augusta's hand and revised by Melville, for an unpublished piece ("The Two Temples"); there are drafts of many poems and prose pieces (including *Billy Budd, Sailor*) from late in Melville's life (as well as marked proofs of some poems); and there are some three hundred pages of journals and some three hundred letters, along with a considerable quantity of marginalia, all of which further show his writing habits. Many of the shorter manuscripts and portions of some of the longer ones are reproduced in the Northwestern-Newberry Edition, but it would be a great convenience to have a compact gathering of reproductions of all the surviving manuscripts in their entirety.

Although manuscript texts have of course always been of interest to historically minded scholars, the recent reaction against studying final authorial intention has led, not surprisingly, to an increased concentration on earlier intentions—or, more precisely, on textual genesis and development as reflected in successive drafts and revisions. Even the concern with published writings as social products has had its effect on the way manuscripts are approached: in this context manuscripts are seen as providing evidence of social accommodation, the process whereby writers altered their private thoughts to a form more in line with the public image they wished to project to the world. Editorial focus on the texts of documents as they exist is also a way of showing disaffection with the longstanding dominance—at least in the literary field—of critical editing, in which eclectic texts are produced through the exercise of judgment. Editions emphasizing textual genesis, stressing process rather than stasis, are in tune with the temper of the times; and a European movement sometimes called *critique génétique* now underlies a number of editions of European writers (see my "Textual Criticism and Literary Sociology" 112–18). This cluster of attitudes reinforces the desirability of making reproductions of Melville's manuscripts readily available. The Northwestern-Newberry Edition does report the variant readings and the alterations in these manuscripts, but its lists (and occasional photographs) do not, and were not intended to, eliminate the need for full facsimiles that show as much of the physical evidence as can be reproduced.

In suggesting the value of a "Melville archive" of printed and manuscript documents—or, indeed, a similar "archive" of any author—I wish to emphasize the relation of documents to literary works. I have said that such a collection of reproductions would complement the Northwestern-Newberry Edition, not that it would supplant it, and the reasons do not imply a judgment of the Northwestern-Newberry Edition but are entirely connected with the fact that it is a *critical* edition. Those scholars who in the 1940s and 1950s laid the groundwork for the organized production of editions of American authors could not have imagined that by the time some of those editorial projects were in their final stages there would be reviewers complaining about the concern with authorial intention in them and their "privileging" of a single reconstructed text of each work. The vision of those earlier scholars can in retrospect be regarded as partially flawed because it did not encompass the claims of other textual goals than authorial intention; but recent textual critics who have belittled the search for authorial intention are equally to be blamed for failing to acknowledge that this search is one of the natural and inevitable approaches to the experiencing of verbal works, arising from the essential nature of the medium.

When those critics claim, as they are inclined to do, that the physical features of the presentation of texts, such as typography and book design, are elements of literary works, they are (rather surprisingly) diminishing the gap between reader response and authorial intention and are not thinking through the relationship between physical texts and intangible media (such as language). There is no question that readers' responses are frequently affected by the layout and design of texts on paper and that scholars examining the reception accorded to particular writings over the years must take these visual elements into account. But it is also true that most writers have not regarded the typographical presentation of their works as an integral part of the works themselves; there are exceptions, of course, but for the most part writers conceive of their work as verbal, not as a combination of the verbal and the visual. Because the medium of verbal work is language, and language in intangible, it follows that a printed or handwritten text of a verbal work cannot be the intended work itself but only the means for transmitting in tangible form the instructions for recreating an intangible work. (A traditional musical score is another example of a physical object produced for the same purpose.) Anyone interested in intended *works*—as opposed to particular *texts* that appear in individual documents—must nevertheless study those documents with great care, for there is no physical feature of documents or the notations on them that may not play a role in evaluating the authority of those notations. (See my *A Rationale of Textual Criticism* and *Libraries, Museums, and Reading.*) The publication of responsibly prepared facsimiles—of both printed and manuscript materials—therefore assists scholars of varying interests, not only those concerned with *texts* as they were produced but also those concerned with *works* as they were intended.

These two approaches must always be with us, reflecting, as they do, two fundamental ways of recovering the past, each one telling only a part of the story. We must all start with the documents, and they can be an end in themselves; but some people will always wish to look behind them to the intended works for which the documents supply the evidence. It is in the nature of all works in intangible media that their intended form (or forms) can never be precisely known and must be continually reconstructed. The process of reading always requires making judgments about the constitution of the text—about whether or not to accept each element in any given documentary text. Some readings find their way into print as essays, book-length writings, or editions; but every act of reading is also an editorial act. Any critical edition, such as the Northwestern-Newberry Edition, offers one reading of the evidence, but no single reading can ever be the only justifiable reading. The Northwestern-Newberry editors specifically encourage readers to engage in a reconsideration of their textual decisions, using the evidence provided; and the publication of reproductions would significantly augment that evidence.

The likeliest form for such publication has changed in recent years from photographs to electronically scanned images. Although high-quality photographic facsimiles in original size will always be useful, electronic texts have the advantage of greater manipulability. It is possible for digitized images to be enlarged at will by readers (a particularly useful feature for studying manuscripts); and the scanned images of all relevant documentary texts can be linked to searchable and interlinked transcriptions of those texts, with the result that readers can easily find any given word, see it in its original paleographic or typographic setting, and move to its variant in another text or read parallel texts on the screen simultaneously. The accessibility to documentary texts afforded by such hypertext editions certainly marks an improvement over the traditional apparatus in printed form; but it does not eliminate the need for critical texts, reflecting scholars' judgments as to what was intended at particular times. Indeed, one of the advantages of electronic presentation is that more than one critical text can feasibly be offered, reflecting different persons' intentions at different times (as well as different editors' reconstructions of these versions). Hypertext editions have often been discussed only as archives of documentary texts; but archives that also include critical reconstructions will be more useful, since some readers—in the future as in the past—will wish to have access to the judgments of specialists as they think about the texts they are reading.[5] The Northwestern-Newberry Edition, as well as other significant critical editions, should therefore be included in a comprehensive hypertext edition of Melville. The twenty-first century, like the twentieth, will have need both for critical texts with apparatus and for reproductions of documentary texts, regardless of the forms in which they appear, because both are required for the most productive thinking about texts.

At the end of *The Melville Log*, Jay Leyda listed some of the tasks he had not completed, entitling his list "The Endless Study." Every subject can be studied endlessly, if it interests us enough, for we never capture the whole truth or know with certainty that we have caught part of it; and the indeterminacy of the texts of verbal works is a perfect illustration of the necessity for endless reconsideration. For a century now Melville's texts have repaid such scrutiny; if his works continue to attract readers in the next century—and there seems no reason to doubt that they will—the texts of those works must continually be reexamined by every reader. If readers of Melville are in a better position to enter the twenty-first century than they were to enter the twentieth, it is not because the textual problems have been settled for all time but because the textual scholarship of the twentieth century has given readers a sounder basis for confronting those problems, and perhaps a firmer understanding of the precarious existence of verbal art.

NOTES

1. For brief discussions of Stedman's edition, see NN *Typee* 312–14. Comments on his other three volumes appear in NN *Omoo* 352–53; NN *WJ* 448–49; and NN *MD* 775–76. See also my "Melville and the World of Books" 806–08. The most thorough discussion of Stedman's activities is provided in Sealts, *The Early Lives of Melville* 47–64 (with Stedman's introduction to *Typee* reprinted on 154–66).

2. Some discussion of the texts of the Constable Edition and the Hendricks House Edition occurs in each relevant NN volume (in each "Note on the Text," near the end of the section entitled "The Texts"). See also my "Melville and the World of Books" 808–09, 811–13.

3. For a survey and examination of this period, see my *Textual Criticism since Greg*, "Textual Criticism and Literary Sociology," and "Textual Instability and Editorial Idealism."

4. Two landmark facsimiles that illustrate a responsible approach are Charlton Hinman's of the Shakespeare First Folio and David L. Vander Meulen's of Pope's 1728 *Dunciad*. For further discussion of the limitations and uses of reproductions, see my "Reproductions and Scholarship" and "The Future of Primary Records."

5. I have discussed this point in more detail in "Critical Editions, Hypertexts, and Genetic Criticism" and in the last section of "Textual Instability and Editorial Idealism."

WORKS CITED

Fitzgerald, F. Scott. *F. Scott Fitzgerald Manuscripts.* 18 vols. Ed. M. J. Bruccoli, with Alan Margolies. New York: Garland, 1990–.

McGann, Jerome. "The Complete Writings and Pictures of Dante Gabriel Rossetti: A Hypermedia Research Archive." *Text* 7 (1994): 95–105.

Joyce, James. *The James Joyce Archive.* 63 vols. Ed. Michael Groden, with Hans Walter Gabler, David Hayman, A. Walton Litz, and Denis Rose. New York: Garland, 1977–79.

Melville, Herman. *The Complete Works of Herman Melville.* Gen ed. Howard P. Vincent. 8 vols. to date. Chicago: Hendricks House, 1947–.

———. *Typee, Omoo, White-Jacket, Moby-Dick.* 4 vols. Ed. Arthur Stedman. New York: United States Book Co., 1892.

———. *The Works of Herman Melville.* 16 vols. London: Constable, 1922–24.

Sealts, Merton M., Jr. *The Early Lives of Melville: Nineteenth-Century Biographical Sketches and Their Authors.* Madison: U of Wisconsin P, 1974.

Shakespeare, William. *The Norton Facsimile: The First Folio of Shakespeare.* Ed. Charlton Hinman. New York: Norton, 1968.

Tanselle, G. Thomas. "Critical Editions, Hypertexts, and Genetic Criticism." *Romantic Review* 86 (1995): 581–93.

———. "The Future of Primary Records." *Encyclopedia of Library and Information Science.* Vol. 58. Ed. Allen Kent. New York: Dekker, 1996. 53–73.

———. *Libraries, Museums, and Reading.* New York: Book Arts Press, Columbia U School of Library Service, 1991.

———. "Melville and the World of Books." *A Companion to Melville Studies.* Ed. John Bryant. New York: Greenwood, 1986. 781–835.

————. *A Rationale of Textual Criticism*. Philadelphia: U of Pennsylvania P, 1989.

————. "Reproductions and Scholarship." *Studies in Bibliography* 42 (1989): 25–54.

————. "Textual Criticism and Literary Sociology." *Studies in Bibliography* 44 (1991): 83–143.

————. *Textual Criticism since Greg: A Chronicle, 1950–1985*. Charlottesville: UP of Virginia for the Bibliographical Society of the University of Virginia, 1987.

————. "Textual Instability and Editorial Idealism." *Studies in Bibliography* 49 (1996): 1–60.

Vander Meulen, David L. *Pope's* Dunciad *of 1728: A History and Facsimile*. Charlottesville: UP of Virginia for the Bibliographical Society of the University of Virginia, 1991.

Reading Melville:
The Example of *Pierre*

18

The Overwrought Landscape of *Pierre*

SAMUEL OTTER

At the start of Herman Melville's *Pierre; or, The Ambiguities* (1852), the reader is placed in the conventional position of urban visitor embarking on a rejuvenating picturesque stroll in the country:

> There are some strange summer mornings in the country, when he who is but a sojourner from the city shall early walk forth into the fields, and be wonder-smitten with the trance-like aspect of the green and golden world. Not a flower stirs; the trees forget to wave; the grass itself seems to have ceased to grow; and all Nature, as if suddenly become conscious of her own profound mystery, and feeling no refuge from it but silence, sinks into this wonderful and indescribable repose. (3)

Yet the prospect offered in the first books of *Pierre* is not what the picturesque viewer has been taught to expect. Instead of the pleasures of manipulated perspective and the satisfactions of distanced contemplation, the viewer in *Pierre* is drawn into the picture. Despite the assurance of the opening lines that the

Portions of this essay have appeared in Samuel Otter, "The Eden of Saddle Meadows: Landscape and Ideology in *Pierre*." *American Literature* 66 (March 1994): 55–81. © 1994 by Duke University Press. Reprinted with permission.

personification of natural features will be held in check, over the course of the first books the grass and flowers of Saddle Meadows throb with ominous intensity. The trees of Saddle Meadows resemble less the signature blasted trunks of the contemporary landscape painter Thomas Cole and more the sinuous, entwining limbs of, say, the late nineteenth-century artist Edvard Munch. Trained to frame, compose, and interpret country views, the sojourner from the city finds himself at the mercy of a recalcitrant, vengeful landscape. Strolling forth into the fields of *Pierre,* the reader is greeted with a very strange summer morning in the country indeed.

Saddle Meadows is not the site of innocence but the intersection of intense political, patriarchal, and sexual anxieties.[1] The explicit rhetoric of rural paradise in the opening sections is repeatedly challenged by displacements, overstatements, anticlimaxes, and the mingling of categories. In the first of a series of excessively developed, strangely literalized metaphors, in which figures are inflated, inverted, and examined, Melville gives us a sense of Pierre's deforming inheritance through a distended version of the romantic cliché of Nature's inspiration:

> [Nature] blew her wind-clarion from the blue hills, and Pierre neighed out lyrical thoughts, as at the trumpet-blast, a war-horse paws himself into a lyric of foam. She whispered through her deep groves at eve, and gentle whispers of humanness, and sweet whispers of love, ran through Pierre's thought-veins, musical as water over pebbles. She lifted her spangled crest of a thickly-starred night, and forth at that glimpse of their divine Captain and Lord, ten thousand mailed thoughts of heroicness started up in Pierre's soul, and glared round for some insulted good cause to defend. (14)

Clearly, this is one part joke—we can almost hear the straining of Nature's lungs—but it is also play with a purpose: the rhetoric molds the character's thoughts and provides the contours for his actions. Pierre doesn't simply have a mind stirred by Nature's call; in Melville's revealing neologism, he has "thought-veins," channels through which ideas flow.[2] Like the conventional figures of English and American Romanticism, Melville's natural metaphors exalt in the aesthetic realm a relation to nature that had become debased in the economic sphere by the early nineteenth century. Yet Melville's excess here verges on distortion, and his metaphor threatens to collapse under the weight of its elaborate figurative contortions. Melville's "aeolian harp" is too leaden (with such nominalizations as "humanness" and "heroicness"), too literal (Pierre seems practically metamorphosed, half-man and half-horse, as he "neighs" out his "lyrical" thoughts, and his "soul" seems overpopulated, not to mention overdressed, with all those "mailed thoughts of heroicness" milling about), and too mixed (with war horses, foaming lyrics, deep groves, musical water rushing over pebbles, spangled crests, and massed armies all occupying the same ground). Melville's excess does not simply subvert the Romantic convention; the excess breathes new life into it, conveys its particularly intense antebellum American invocation. The figures Melville uses do not merely describe transmission; they are vehicles for transmission, shaping the reception and expression of thought. Throughout the Saddle Meadows sections of *Pierre*, the descriptions of Pierre's rural inheritance are marked by such excess, dissonance, and literalness.[3] The exorbitance of Melville's representations of Saddle Meadows—the repetitions with a difference, the hyperbole that insists to the point of queasiness, the unsettling juxtapositions, and especially the emphatic, insinuating allusion to the struggles that mark the American landscape—is a response to the antebellum "picturesque project," the effort to construct and empower the American difference through representations of the land, to, as the painter Thomas Cole put it, "cultivate a taste for scenery" (98, 109).

Over the past two decades, critics of British culture have delineated a politics of the picturesque, exploring the relations between landscape and ideology. Treating materials from oil paintings to graphic prints to topographical prospect poems to landscape gardening, they have described in British culture the imposition of a new order on nature, beginning in the middle of the eighteenth century and linked to the revolution in agricultural practices. John Barrell and Ann Bermingham have traced the ideological operations of the pastoral and picturesque gaze: the aesthetic detachment, the composition of a synthetic landscape, the subordination of individual elements to a unified whole, the refinement of vision at the expense of objects within the frame, the evasion of historical processes and conflicts, the aestheticization of poverty, the acts of appropriative nostalgia and visual possession.[4]

Critics of American culture have analyzed a particularly intimate ideological bond between landscape and nation during the political and economic transformations of the early nineteenth century. While the British public's interest in the picturesque reached its peak at the turn of the nineteenth century, the American fascination was most intense from the 1830s to the 1860s, as evidenced in aesthetic and political debates, in the market for paintings and prints, and in the popularity of prose sketches and landscape gift books. During these years, writers and artists articulated an "American picturesque," in which British perspectives were appropriated and revaluated. In obsessive comparisons with the European scene and relentless exchanges with European critics, Americans presented a grandiloquent case against charges of national inferiority and for United States superiority to the old, exhausted, sterile landscapes of Europe. In the northeastern United States, particularly, there was a call for American viewers to turn their attention to the distinctive and unique qualities of American scenery. In the redemptive Edenic landscape was written not the burden of the past but the divine assurance of the nation's glorious future. In these nationalistic visions, aesthetics, religion, and politics were conflated, and the sublime promise of the United States was seen as fulfilled in the cultivated scenery of picturesque America.[5]

The writers and artists of the New York City cultural establishment— "sojourners from the city"—were crucial in shaping and popularizing the new perceptions. Their verbal and visual depictions of American "scenery" and its "associations" focused on northeastern landscapes, and particularly on the Hudson River and its environs. Such efforts included Irving's *Sketch Book* (1819–20), Bryant's poetry, the paintings of Thomas Cole and Asher B. Durand, aesthetic treatises such as Cole's "Essay on American Scenery" (1835), and landscape gift books such as Nathaniel Parker Willis's popular *American Scenery* (1840) and the anonymously edited *Home Book of the Picturesque* (1852), the culminating antebellum reflection on the American picturesque, published in the same year as *Pierre*.[6] In the sentimental education outlined by these literary and visual artists, American viewers were trained to see the difference between American and European prospects. They were taught to feel through their eyes, to perceive American scenery with emotion and appetite. The American land was represented not as the site of historical struggle between competing interests, not as the arena in which entire populations had been and continued to be displaced and enslaved, but as an Eden paradoxically urging its own manipulation and destruction. By contrast, the fraught landscape of *Pierre* presents a hyperbolic version of the "picturesque project," in which the American boast is turned inside out, allusions proliferate to the struggles that mark the history of the American land, and the tropes of visual possession are pressed to revealing and rupturing limits.

In both British and American discussions of the picturesque, the issue of "associations" was crucial. Using Lockean psychology as a model, British aesthetic theorists such as Uvedale Price and Richard Payne Knight argued that aesthetic ideas resulted from the transformation of sensory data through mental associations. Theorists disputed the origin and quality of these associations. Agreeing on the predominant role of abstract visual qualities in shaping aesthetic response, Price argued that associations with line and color had their source in human feelings, while Knight maintained that associations with light and color were defined and sharpened by the viewer's experience of the art of painting. In contrast to Price and Knight, the landscape gardener Humphrey Repton stressed the role of associations with concrete personal or historical circumstances in determining aesthetic response. These theorists of the picturesque were interested in visual training: the interplay of scenery and mind and the dynamic relationship of form and response in shaping meaning and value. In a resonant passage, Knight described the complex act of perception that was his object of study: "The spectator, having his mind enriched with the embellishments of the painter and poet, applies them, by the spontaneous association of ideas, to the natural objects presented to the eye, which thus acquire ideal and imaginary beauties; that is, beauties that are not felt by the organic sense of vision, but by the intellect and the imagination through that sense." Knight sought to chart the structure and function of the mind's eye, to analyze the apprehension of the natural and the operation of the organic.[7]

Melville shares with the American and British picturesque theoreticians a fascination with form and response, with the shaping of views. While accepting the analysis of consciousness as being composed of ideas linked by associations, Melville historicizes and denaturalizes these mental contents and rearticulates the terms and principles of connection. In Melville's Saddle Meadows, the associations are not absent in American scenery but hauntingly present. In place of the divine associations ascribed to American scenery, Melville provides historical allusions to the centuries-long struggle for literal and figurative possession of the American land. He examines the complex acts of perception in which these associations are erased or obscured and the landscape is transformed and animated. In addition to the established associative principles of temporal contiguity, similarity, and frequency, Melville suggests the principle of historical contiguity: the intimate, tenacious bond between present and past. In Melville's prose, associationist psychology becomes both the object of ideological investigation and the technique for exposure and retrieval, as he analyzes sources, structures, contents, and effects of consciousness.

In *Pierre*, Melville demonstrates the crucial role played by "association" and its rhetorical analogue "allusion" in the antebellum debate over the nature of the American arena: the construction of the country's past, the justification for removal and slavery, and the description of possibilities for action in the present and future. Does America have a past? Do its citizens bear the weight of history? Who "owns" the land? Is there a divine sanction for American internal colonization? Is there an American "difference," and what difference does that difference make? In this debate, the control over "association" or "allusion" is the control over American absences and presences, the ability to mask and to invigorate. Melville tells us that the scenery at Saddle Meadows was "the perfect mould" (5) for Pierre's mind, and he shows how such "moulding" operated: how the antebellum ideology of the unmarred, apotheosized, imperative American landscape both compelled and incarcerated.[8]

In the opening sections of *Pierre*, we are presented with Pierre as young heir to the estate of Saddle Meadows, "the only surnamed male Glendinning extant," as we are told twice in the same paragraph (7–8). Pierre is the sole bearer of the precious Glendinning legacy, shaped by its rural and sentimental entailments: "It had been his choice fate to have been born and nurtured in the country, surrounded by scenery whose uncommon loveliness was the perfect mould of a delicate and poetic mind; while the popular names of its finest features appealed to the proudest patriotic and family associations of the historic line of Glendinning" (5). Here, at first glance, Melville apparently celebrates the glories of the family line and of rural education, particularly the education through landscape championed by antebellum painters and theorists. (The narrator repeats his assertion—"it had been the choice fate of Pierre to have been born and bred in the country"—a few pages later.) The representation of Saddle Meadows seems merely picturesque, in the tradition of Irving's sketches, Cole's oil panoramas, and Willis's views. The conventional terms are introduced—"scenery," "associations," and "a delicate and poetic mind"—but over the course of the first two books these key antebellum terms for framing the American land are anatomized and revised so that "choice fate" also becomes a historical curse; "the perfect mould" also describes a process of deformation; "a delicate and poetic mind" is represented as divided, dependent, and guilty; the proliferation of "popular names" and "family associations" not only inspire but also occlude; and "the historic line of Glendinning" becomes a garrote.

The landscape of Saddle Meadows is repeatedly described as sentimentalized and owned by Pierre: "But not only through the mere chances of things, had that fine country become ennobled by the deeds of his sires, but in Pierre's eyes, all its hills and swales seemed as sanctified through their very long uninterrupted possession by his race. . . . Pierre deemed all that part of the earth a love-token; so that his very horizon was to him as a memorial ring" (8). Here, through diction and juxtaposition, the terms of representation are not simply inverted or reversed but are pressed to revealing limits. Connotations invoke repressed significances. Etymologies restore forgotten histories. "Sires" and "swales," words ostensibly alien to the democratic American landscape, suggest anachronism and privilege. Sanctification here is conferred not only through the divine mandate often invoked in nineteenth-century American civil religion but also by right of "possession." And "possession" is asserted in the name of "race," evoking not only the legacy of Pierre's great-grandfather, the Dutch patroon ("race" in the older sense of a group of persons descended from a common ancestor) but also evoking Anglo-Saxon authority in the struggle over the American land ("race" as defining the natures and places of different human types, a meaning with particular force in the context of nineteenth-century justifications of racial slavery and displacement).[9]

The emphasis on "race" in the opening pages of *Pierre*—in addition to being told that the landscape is "possessed by his race," we are told that Pierre views Saddle Meadows as "the background of his race" and that he has descended from a "martial race" (6)—reminds us that Saddle Meadows has been "sanctified" through blood, particularly the blood of Indian battles, and that the Glendinning possession of the land has not exactly been "uninterrupted," that is, undisputed. We are told that the blood of Pierre's great-grandfather had seeped into the grass of the sloping meadows, as he exerted his claim against Native Americans during the colonial period, and that Pierre's grandfather had spilled the blood of the Iroquois in his effort to retain control over the region during the Revolutionary War, in a battle that echoes Melville's own maternal grandfather Peter Gansevoort's successful and much-celebrated efforts to hold Fort Stanwix, near present-day Rome, New York, in 1777.[10]

In an extended digression on the "large estates" and "long pedigrees" of England and America, Melville manipulates the rhetoric of American exceptionalism, the conventional statement of America's lack of antiquity and aristocracy. The narrator insists that America surpasses the mother country in the natural power of its political institutions and the strength of its ruling class, finding an "apt analogy" between "the democratic element" and the "subtile acid" that produces "verdigris":

> For indeed the democratic element operates as a subtile acid among us; forever producing new things by corroding the old; as in the south of France verdigris, the primitive material of one kind of green paint, is produced by grape-vinegar poured upon copper plates. Now in general nothing can be

more significant of decay than the idea of corrosion; yet on the other hand, nothing can more vividly suggest luxuriance of life, than the idea of green as a color; for green is the peculiar signet of all-fertile Nature herself. Herein by apt analogy we behold the marked anomalousness of America; whose character abroad, we need not be surprised, is misconceived, when we consider how strangely she contradicts all prior notions of human things; and how wonderfully to her, Death itself becomes transmuted into Life. So that political institutions, which in other lands seem above all things intensely artificial, with America seem to possess the divine virtue of a natural law; for the most mighty of nature's laws is this, that out of Death she brings Life. (9)

Both "the democratic element" and "the subtile acid" appear to corrode original structures but actually reinvigorate them in a new form. Here, in an argument for America's equality in the family of nations, Melville unravels the progress and originality that structure the American narrative. America is not different from England in its lack of the burdens of history or class; in fact, America out-Englands England, managing to transmute its structures of property and class into more potent elements through the agency of its difference, thus rendering them "natural" and invisible, in contrast with the "artificial" and so more fragile structures of England. The "aptness" of the analogy between "the democratic element" and "a subtile acid" lies in its apparent incongruity yet functional success. Progress is linked with corrosion in a narrative of "natural law." Out of Revolutionary "Death" comes new "Life" for old institutions. *Pierre* is steeped in the language of such antebellum alchemy. Yet there is also something not quite right about the analogy—as there is often something jarring or excessive about the rhetorical constructions in *Pierre*. Here "new" democracy is associated with the antique aura of a patina, and the process described, despite Melville's winking assurance at the climax of the paragraph, is not natural but explicitly artificial: the French, he explains, induce verdigris by pouring grape-vinegar on copper plates. And there is at least a slight mocking of early American Athenian pretensions in the comparison of democracy to vert-de-Grice, literally the green crust of Grecian artifacts.[11]

Melville ends his digression not with a paean to absence but with a figure of salience. The "Revolutionary flood," he writes, did not clear the land but receded to reveal the "mighty lordships" fortified and defended by the state militia, surviving the deluge like "Indian mounds" (11). Hudson River estates are associated with Ohio and Mississippi Valley earthworks, Dutch manors with Native American burial mounds. Unlike the observers in Bryant's "The Prairies," Cole's "Essay on American Scenery," or Willis's *American Scenery,* the narrator-observer in *Pierre* perceives a network of historical associations linking conspicuous landscape features, which here serve as enduring monuments to the tenacity of privilege and the death of civilizations. Melville's insistence on America's greatness leaves the reader with a queasy feeling. It is a boast in the tradition of American swagger, but one that is turned inside out, its structure and its costs exposed. The reader is more dizzied than captivated by the twists of an argument for American equivalence that becomes an argument for American exceptionalism by transforming the American difference from a badge of inferiority to a mark of efficiency.

We are further reminded of the violent struggle necessary for the appropriation and retention of land in America's first three centuries in Melville's strangely oblique allusion to the fierce, prolonged Anti-Renter Wars in the Hudson River Valley from 1839 to 1846, during which tenants rioted against the feudal practices of their landlords and were, in turn, suppressed by the state militia: ". . . regular armies, with staffs of officers, crossing rivers with artillery, and marching through primeval woods, and threading vast rocky defiles, have been sent out to distrain upon three thousand farmer-tenants of one landlord, at a blow. A fact most suggestive two ways; both whereof shall be nameless here" (11). Melville's archaic irony ("primeval woods," "vast rocky defiles," "to distrain upon") does not simply subvert the feudal pretensions of the Hudson Valley landlords, although certainly one effect of the diction and the syntax is to distance the events as reactionary. Coming at the climax of the digression on the creation of "mighty lordships in the heart of a republic," the inflated diction and antiquated syntax indicate the success of the retrogressive venture, as classes contend and landlords supported by armies suppress their tenants against an epic backdrop—an anachronistic venture in supposedly new and democratic nineteenth-century America, to be sure, but an anachronism that seems to work. The irony in this passage illuminates and amplifies the effectiveness of antebellum social practice: the archaic language seems appropriate and commensurate as a description of the landowners' imposition of their feudal will on their Hudson Valley tenants in the early nineteenth century. When Melville represents Saddle Meadows as a "manor," the portrayal is charged with a mid-nineteenth-century political meaning. The term was animated, not antiquated, in contemporary discourse.[12]

Melville alludes to the landlord-tenant class structure of Saddle Meadows specifically in Book 20, when he describes the "povertiresque" lives of the Millthorpes, the Glendinnings' tenants, who must abandon their farm because they cannot pay the manorial rent. The irony is much easier to track here, as Melville attacks the violent complacency of those writers and artists who employ "poverty" as a piquant element in their compositions. (Possible targets might include male sentimentalists such as Irving, Willis, and Donald Grant Mitchell.) Melville had made a similar point in the "Launcelott's Hey" section of *Redburn* (1849), in which the young narrator strolls down a narrow Liverpool street and discovers not one of Irving's insulated urban retreats but a cellar offering a still life of fatal poverty, a view unheralded in his picturesque old guidebook. In "Poor Man's Pudding and Rich Man's Crumbs" (1854), Melville depicts the ways in which poverty ruptures the verbal and visual frames of its representations. This diptych represents the inability of euphemism to contain its object and climaxes with a spectacle of charity that is rent by scorn. In *Pierre*, the mention of the penurious Millthorpes in Book 20 is not a dark revelation about the golden Saddle Meadows of Books 1 and 2. It serves more as a redundant reminder of the fraught landscape of the first sections, an afterthought that materializes in the plot the social violence and historical burdens that already have been in the rhetorical emphases, repetitions, counteractions, and allusions of the opening.[13]

Some of the ways in which the "fact" of the landlords summoning troops against their tenants might have seemed suggestive to Melville are personal: the descendants of his Dutch ancestors on his mother's side, the Van Rensselaers, were the largest and wealthiest landowners in the Hudson Valley, the only retainers of a patroonship (or, we might say, a "mighty lordship") after the Revolutionary "flood." They were the family most centrally involved in the struggle between owners and tenants over the restrictive clauses in land leases and the payment of "rents," or feudal returns, a struggle that simmered to violent climaxes during the 1750s and 1760s and during the 1830s and 1840s. Living in Albany or the Albany area from 1830 until 1840, Melville would have known firsthand of the conflict. In waging their guerilla attacks on the legal authorities, the Anti-Renters assumed a calico "Indian" disguise, allying themselves explicitly with the savage "Indians" of Boston Harbor in 1773 and also, by association if not intent, with the displaced Native Americans and the centuries of struggle over the American land involving the competing interests of federal and state governments, middle-class entrepreneurs, Native Americans, large estate holders, and poor whites.

When Melville alludes in Book 1 to the regular armies sent out to subdue masses of farmers, the remark suggests not only the Anti-Renter Wars of the 1830s and 1840s but also the most notorious class revolt in the early years of the United States: Shays' Rebellion, the 1786–87 civil and military resistance of small farmers in western Massachusetts to the severe economic measures taken by the state during the postwar depression. In the wake of the unfinished American Revolution, both Berkshire County and the Hudson Valley were arenas for struggle over economic justice and land ownership. Across Massachusetts in the 1780s, but particularly in the western counties and in Berkshire County with a notable violence, small farmers protested the increasing imprisonment for debt, the spread of peonage, and the levying of heavy taxes. The poor farmers of western Massachusetts, like the tenant farmers of New York, were associated by their enemies with Native Americans. In October 1786, Secretary of War Henry Knox requisitioned federal troops on the pretense that they would be used against Indians in the northwest but stationed them in Massachusetts in order to quell a different kind of native revolt. As in the case of New York State resistance, in Massachusetts military defeat was followed by legislative victory. Shaysites in the state legislature reformed debt collection and court procedure and reduced the tax burden.[14]

The Berkshires retained personal, as well as historical, associations for Melville. He wrote *Pierre* while living on his farm, Arrowhead (named for the Indian relics found on the land), in Pittsfield, Massachusetts. *Pierre* is dedicated to the Berkshire Mount Greylock, which was also known as Mount Saddleback or Saddle Mountain, and Melville used other local features, such as Balance Rock (the "Memnon Stone" in *Pierre*), as models for the topography of Saddle Meadows.[15] Like the Hudson River Valley, the Berkshires were a mecca during the antebellum period for travelers in search of the picturesque combination of wilderness, pastoral, and civilization. The pleasures of viewing the Berkshires were bound up with acts of framing, veiling, and erasure. Despite the industrial development in the Housatonic River Valley, especially the development of paper mills (one of which Melville would visit at Dalton, Massachusetts, in 1851 and use as a model for "The Tartarus of Maids"), Berkshire observers praised the invisibility of local industry, the ways in which the sloping topography hid mills and factory villages from view. Both the Berkshires and the Hudson River Valley were sites for a developing tourist industry and for a community of writers and artists who shaped and marketed their views. Around Stockbridge and Lenox clustered such figures as Bryant, Sedgwick, Holmes, and Longfellow. Bryant, the poet laureate of the Berkshires, proclaimed that the region offered the security of traditional class relations and a retreat from the contaminations of industry. The painters Cole, Church, Durand, and Kensett all visited the region and produced Berkshire canvases.

Melville's Saddle Meadows is a composite landscape, alluding repeatedly to the manors, landlords, and tenants of the Hudson River Valley, to the visual and verbal lessons of the Hudson River School, and also to the contested picturesque terrain of the Berkshires.[16]

As did those involved in the rebellions in western Massachusetts and eastern New York, Melville associates the possession of land with the exploitation of poor whites and Native Americans. In describing the terms of the rent-deeds offered to the tenant farmers by the Hudson Valley patriarchs, he twice uses the notorious phrases of President Jackson's 1829 "Message" to the Creek Nation, in which the "Great Father" promised that the Creeks would be able to occupy the Oklahoma land to which they were being transported "as long as grass grows or water runs":

> . . . consider those most ancient and magnificent Dutch Manors at the North, whose perches are miles—whose meadows overspread adjacent counties—and whose haughty rent-deeds are held by their thousand farmer tenants, so long as grass grows and water runs; which hints of a surprising eternity for a deed, and seems to make lawyer's ink unobliterable as the sea. . . .
>
> These far-descended Dutch meadows lie steeped in a Hindooish haze; an eastern patriarchalness sways its mild crook over pastures, whose tenant flocks shall there feed, long as their own grass grows, long as their own water shall run. (10–11)

The Jackson allusion links the federal displacement of Native American groups in the southeast with the state-supported exploitation of the tenant farmers in the northeast: both Native Americans and farmers are subject to the promises and sway of the Great Father. Here Manifest Destiny is ironically given a legal formula ("fee simples cotemporized with eternity"), and the Native American account of the different white and Indian claims to the American land is echoed (spiritual claim as vastly more enduring than legal deed). Jackson's guarantee to the Creeks that they may live on the Oklahoma land "as long as grass grows or water runs"—sentimental, hypocritical, poetic, an appropriation of natural metaphor to sanction the severance of a people from their environment, an assurance inscribed in the landscape, a metonymy backed by the full faith of the U.S. government—was fixed upon and turned back against its owner in several contemporary responses: by the Creek chief Speckled Snake, who, in a speech to his people, sarcastically translated Jackson's words into "Get a little farther; you are too near me" (1829); by Thoreau, several times in his *A Week on the Concord and Merrimack Rivers* (1849); by Melville, not only in the opening pages of *Pierre* but also in chapter 27 of *Typee* (1846), where he uses it to criticize the French colonial seizure of Marquesan natural inheritance; and, implicitly, by a long line of Native American orators, who repeatedly directed their auditors' attention to the discrepancy between American words and actions.[17]

The landscape of Saddle Meadows, then, is not merely embellished with images of Pierre's ancestors—"on those hills his own fine fathers had gazed; through those woods, over these lawns, by that stream, along these tangled paths, many a grand-dame of his had merrily strolled when a girl" (8)—nor simply infused with the qualities of "this new Canaan" (33) but saturated with reminders of those who were dispossessed. Melville's Saddle Meadows is Washington Irving's storied landscape represented with a vengeance. "Associations," excessive and violent, circulate through Melville's Saddle Meadow scenes. Melville takes the vaunted American difference and turns it inside out and then back upon itself. Melville provides in his American landscape "the shadowy grandeurs of the past" and "the accumulated treasures of the age" that Irving's Geoffrey Crayon sought in Europe, but in Saddle Meadows the shadows compete with the grandeurs and the accumulation of treasure encumbers the view. In the opening pages of *Pierre,* the references to the violent struggles for possession of the American landscape accumulate: the colonial wars between European colonists and Native Americans; the Revolutionary War battle of Fort Stanwix, pitting the American rebels against the English and the Iroquois; the postrevolutionary skirmishes against courts and banks waged by debtor farmers; the Anti-Renter Wars between landlords and tenants; and Jackson's forced removal of the Creeks. These associations thicken the atmosphere of Saddle Meadows; they seep into its soil. The trajectory of associations points toward the past and not the future. Pierre does not possess the landscape; rather, the landscape itself is possessed by the specters of the displaced, made intractable by the weight of their stories. Allusion in *Pierre* is a conduit for the historical memory so often erased from representations of the American land, a pathway for the reentry of ghosts. Thus we might view *Pierre* as a key text in the literature of insistent memory, an example of an emphatically American gothic.[18]

In Book 2, "Love, Delight, and Alarm," Pierre takes his betrothed Lucy on a phaeton ride over the fields and into the hills that ring Saddle Meadows. An extended pun governs this journey: as the ancestral vehicle rolls over the ground of Saddle Meadows, Melville examines the vehicles, tenors, and grounds of the metaphors that shape antebellum views. During this literal and figurative ride on a strange summer morning in the country, sensory metaphors are inflated and stretched to the breaking point. In these extended figures, Melville makes visible the formations and deformations of picturesque perception. The terms of the book's title—"Love," "Delight," and "Alarm"—are not merely items in a series. They augur the alarming results of the loving and delightful associations invoked during Pierre and Lucy's sightseeing trip, and they suggest the rhetorical technique of unsettling excess that marks the Saddle Meadows books of *Pierre*.

Pierre and Lucy embark on their excursion on a particularly liquid morning: "That morning was the choicest drop that Time had in his vase. Ineffable distillations of a soft delight were wafted from the fields and hills" (32). As the morning unfolds, effusions of a more unsavory sort fill the air: "high in heaven you heard the neighing of the horses of the sun; and down dropt their nostrils' froth in many a fleecy vapor from the hills" (35). Toward the end of the outing, warm tears flow from Lucy's "over-charged lids" (36). It is a morning that begins with choice drops and ineffable distillations and ends in nasal excretions and seeping eyelids. Like the morning's air, the language used to describe Saddle Meadows is oversaturated.

During the phaeton ride, the narrator delivers a piercing tribute to Nature and Love. Two successive paragraphs begin with the apostrophe "Oh, praised be the beauty of this earth, the beauty, and the bloom, and the mirthfulness thereof" (32). In Saddle Meadows, to bend one's ear to the music of Nature is to risk rupturing the eardrum: "Love has not hands, but cymbals; Love's mouth is chambered like a bugle, and the instinctive breathings of his life breathe jubilee notes of joy!" (33). Melville's narrator continues, breathlessly: "So on all sides Love allures; can contain himself what youth who views the wonders of the beauteous woman-world?" (34). This cacophonous paean to the "new Canaan" (33), in the course of which neither observer nor landscape can contain themselves, is delivered in the isocolon, antithesis, and syntax of a sermon and emphasizes how the American landscape is gendered, sentimentalized, and sanctified. It is as if the volume in Cole or Willis were turned up to the point of distortion.

Yet it is not only the faculty of hearing that is strained and tested on that green and golden morning but also the sense of smell. In a tender exchange that is much stranger than it seems at first, Pierre and Lucy trade compliments:

Wondrous fair of face, blue-eyed, and golden-haired, the bright blonde, Lucy, was arrayed in colors harmonious with the heavens. Light blue be thy perpetual color, Lucy; light blue becomes thee best—such the repeated azure counsel of Lucy Tartan's mother. On both sides, from the hedges, came to Pierre the clover bloom of Saddle Meadows, and from Lucy's mouth and cheek came the fresh fragrance of her violet young being.

"Smell I the flowers, or thee?" cried Pierre.

"See I lakes, or eyes?" cried Lucy, her own gazing down into his soul, as two stars gaze down into a tarn. (33)

Pierre's inverted syntax and unfortunate apposition raise the possibility that the "smell" of Lucy might be a stench ("Smell I thee?"), and Lucy's metaphoric rejoinder conjures the spectacle of huge volumes of water having been pumped into Pierre's eyes. Such an optic inundation is invoked again when, a couple of pages later, Pierre risks drowning after he "dives deep down into the Adriatic" of Lucy's eyes (35).

The analogies between sensory organs and landscape features are not accidental or occasional in these sections of *Pierre*. Such analogies structure the representation of character. Lightning forks upward from Pierre's brow. Pierre sees stars and clouds in Lucy's eyes and the seasons in her face. Lucy's eyes contain unparalleled natural multitudes: "All the waves in Lucy's eyes seemed waves of infinite glee to him. And as if, like veritable seas, they did indeed catch the reflected irradiations of that pellucid azure morning; in Lucy's eye's, there seemed to shine all the blue glory of the general day, and all the sweet inscrutableness of the sky" (35). Lucy is a walking encyclopedia of scenic features— clouds, seasons, waves, seas, lakes, skies. In Melville's picturesque twist on the sentimental efficio, or "fashioning" of a female figure, Lucy is an animated and overstocked embodiment of individual, natural, and national character. The land does not merely lie before Pierre; it rises up and embraces him in the form of an inordinate, geomorphic angel. Pierre declares that a god has decreed his "unchallenged possession" of Lucy. She will be his "inalienable fief" (36).

When Pierre observes the atmospheric effects in Lucy's eyes, he cannot contain himself, or, to be more precise, he cannot contain his eyes, or, to be even more precise, his eyes cannot contain their pupils: "Then would Pierre burst forth in some screaming shout of joy; and the striped tigers of his chestnut eyes leaped in their lashed cages with a fierce delight. Lucy shrank from him in extreme love; for the extremest top of love, is Fear and Wonder" (35). Here the pleasures of perception are rendered disturbing through the insinuating, unsettling juxtapositions of adjective and noun ("screaming shout of joy," "fierce delight," "extreme love"). The love in Pierre's eyes is given a savage shape and a ravenous appetite. Melville represents the blinding fulfillment of the picturesque goal of feeling through the eyes, as Pierre's eager pupils threaten to rupture the aqueous humor, to tear through the lashes, break out of their ocular confinement, and pounce upon the victim of their gaze. Perception here is conjoined with desire, excess, and violence. The extremes are taken to their extremity, as Melville maps the contours of the sublime and ambivalent peaks of Love.

The sensory mechanisms of sight are the principal objects of study in Melville's anatomy of picturesque perception, and he presents his most telling visual figure immediately after Pierre and Lucy gaze into one another's eyes. In contrast to such observers as Cole and Willis, who link sight and desire in a metaphorics of possession, Melville offers the catachrestic "lovers' eyes" of Book 2. In these eyes the hypnotic transaction between viewer and object—what Melville calls at the beginning of *Pierre* "the verdant trance" and "the trance-like aspect of the green and golden world [of Saddle Meadows]"(3)—is broken and the picturesque optics are strained and literalized. As in Cole, Willis, and Bryant, topographia in *Pierre* is linked with "optigraphia," praise of landscape with power of vision, but in Melville's "eyes" the visualization of desire leads to metaphorical overextension and collapse. "'See I lakes, or eyes?'" asks Lucy, as she gazes down into Pierre's soul, and the answer Melville gives is neither:

> No Cornwall miner ever sunk so deep a shaft beneath the sea, as Love will sink beneath the floatings of the eyes. Love sees ten million fathoms down, till dazzled by the floor of pearls. The eye is Love's own magic glass, where all things that are not of earth, glide in supernatural light. There are not so many fishes in the sea, as there are sweet images in lovers' eyes. In those miraculous translucencies swim the strange eye-fish with wings, that sometimes leap out, instinct with joy; moist fish-wings wet the lover's cheek. Love's eyes are holy things; therein the mysteries of life are lodged; looking in each other's eyes, lovers see the ultimate secret of the worlds; and with thrills eternally untranslatable, feel that Love is god of all. (33)

The pastoral is ruptured by the intrusion of Cornwall miners. In terms of nationality, class, and trade, the Cornwall miners would seem to have no place in the literal or figurative landscape of Saddle Meadows. Yet Melville represents them as a constitutive and revealing part of the scene. Entering a landscape constructed by excluding transatlantic connections, veiling acts of labor, and avoiding the excavation of grounds, the Cornwall miners come to tear the canvas.

As eyes look into eyes in Melville's defamiliarizing passage, the intervening medium is filled with ridiculous creatures. In this heightened and revealing version of the loving gaze, the eye is not at all a receptive organ but becomes an active, projecting, violating force, and its projections are absurdly literalized. Neither particle nor wave, the "light" from the lover's eye is composed of "strange eye-fish with wings." The mood of the loving gaze is figuratively broken here. The mystifications are materialized. The violence is made explicit. Love's eyes are "holy things," Melville insists, after representing them as profane fish ponds. The eye is Love's own "magic glass," Melville proclaims, and then he shatters the delicate vessel. Visual penetration is compared to the sinking of mine shafts, and visual transaction threatens to become a literal "driving through": when eyes bore into eyes, the shaft, one assumes, must be sunk through the cornea.

As Melville's allusive linking of the Glendinning phaeton with the chariot of the ill-starred Phaeton implies, Pierre and Lucy's carriage offers an exhilarating, dangerous ride. During the ride, the lovers' conversation and the writer's figures center on the mechanisms and effects of perception, and especially on the sense of vision. During the ride, Melville heightens the senses of his characters and extends the figures of perception. Noses fill with liquid or with malodor. Eardrums distend and rupture. Eyes blind. Figures are specified, literalized, and drawn to the verge of collapse, a perspective from which we can trace their contours, track their relations, and chart how meanings are shaped and distorted. The literal ground of Saddle Meadows becomes the stage upon which Melville mines the grounds of picturesque perception, the network of figures and associations in which individual, nature, and nation are bound. During the wild phaeton ride, metaphorical vehicles unsettle their tenors and the reader feels the force of the impact: the crash of the striped tigers of Pierre's eyes against their lashed cages, the thud and splash of the Cornwall miners performing their ocular excavations, the slap of strange eye-fish with wings against the lover's cheek.

In the first section of "Nature" (1836), Emerson, too, conjoins an absurdly literalized visual figure with praise of the natural landscape. "Nature" was published in the same year as Cole's "Essay on American Scenery," and the two essays climax the confident early phase of the American picturesque. In "Nature," after an exalted account of the poetic possession of the land ("There is a property in the horizon which no man has but he whose eye can integrate all the parts, that is, the poet") and immediately following the assertion that the visual faculty is the sine qua non of human existence ("In the woods . . . I feel that nothing can befall me in life,—no disgrace, no calamity [leaving me my eyes], which nature cannot repair"), Emerson offers his famous catachresis: "I become a transparent eyeball; I am nothing; I see all; the currents of the Universal Being circulate through me; I am part or parcel of God." Yet the bizarre physicality of Emerson's "eyeball" does not interfere with the metaphorical operations of the passage. The "transparent eyeball" stands as a desire for all-encompassing vision, for the removal of barriers to visual participation in the world, for the ultimate "integrity of impression made by manifold natural objects." It is the strategically preposterous epiphany of Emerson's "occult relation between man and the vegetable." In Melville's figure of the "strange eye-fish," such an "integrity of impression" is fractured; the magic of the "occult relation" is materialized and specified to the point of absurdity; and the correspondence between viewer and landscape is converted to narcissistic projection. In *Pierre,* the metaphorical distortions of antebellum "eyes" are foregrounded in strained and viscous images. In *Pierre,* there is no antebellum Pisgah prospect, no empowering and consuming aerial view, as there is in Emerson, Cole, Willis, and Bryant. The most striking visual metaphor in *Pierre* describes eyes looking into eyes, in a twisted visual tautology.[19]

In a spectacular passage in "The Ponds" chapter of *Walden* (1854), Thoreau describes the erotic charge of eyes looking into eyes. In his "mind's eye," Thoreau recalls being seated in a boat on the pond and marveling at the natural composition of the scene before him: the reflective foreground of the water, the western shore indented with deep bays, the bold northern shore, the beautifully scalloped southern shore, the subtle gradations guiding the eye from the low shrubs at the water's edge back and up to the highest trees. For Thoreau, this is a remarkably intimate moment: "A lake is the landscape's most beautiful and expressive feature. It is earth's eye; looking into which the beholder measures the depth of his own nature. The fluviatile trees next the shore are the slender eyelashes which fringe it, and the wooded hills and cliffs around are its overhanging brows." In *Walden,* when the "mind's eye" looks into "earth's eye," neither party blinks. There is mutual recognition. When the "mind's eye" looks into "earth's eye," it's love at first sight. When Lucy and Pierre look into each others "lakes, or eyes," the scene is not composed in graded recessional planes but is swarming with strange figures. It is a scene not of self-recognition but of self-projection and mutilation. In the ocular waters of *Pierre,* not fringed but caged by lashes, there swim and leap strange eye-fish with wings. In Melville's American scenery, the observer's reverie may be interrupted by a moist touch extending out from the view.[20]

The phaeton ride ends abruptly, when Pierre and Lucy flee the hills surrounding Saddle Meadows to the level safety of the plains. Fearing that "too wide a prospect" meets them on the slopes, Lucy insists they descend (38). Lucy's prospective anxieties are spurred by her recollection of Pierre's story about the mysterious face he saw at the Pennie sisters' sewing circle, the face whose lineaments persist on both their retinas. This is the first of Melville's many allusions to the "riddle" of Isabel's face (37). Remembering, Lucy loses the inspiration of the morning and sheds some tears. The memory of Isabel's face interposes between Pierre and his view of the glorious and golden Saddle Meadows. Associated in Melville's narrative with Europe, with the lordly sins of the fathers, and with illegitimate acts of possession and dispossession, the features of Isabel's face haunt the prospects of Saddle Meadows. Under the pressure of this image on Pierre's eyes and the force of its associations on his mind, the enamel of Saddle Meadows cracks to reveal past violation and present injustice. Pierre's views are reconfigured, and his inheritance appears in a new light and an altered frame. He loses title to the "inalienable fief" of Lucy and becomes burdened by the alienating terrain of Isabel and seared by "the charred landscape within him" (86). In the picturesque plot of the opening books of *Pierre,* Isabel personifies a set of excluded, insistent "associations" whose presence transforms the content of Pierre's consciousness and propels the narrative toward renunciation, flight, incarceration, and death.

Melville's Saddle Meadows is a Hudson River landscape with a twist, or rather a tilt. From one angle, that is, read from the perspective of explicit statement, it seems simply to celebrate the sentimentalized, apotheosized American Eden. However, read with attention to the strange stylistic motions, the topography of Saddle Meadows looks quite different from the cultivated prospects in Cole's oil paintings or the pliant vistas in Willis's *American Scenery.*[21] The redefining repetitions, the illuminating juxtapositions, the disconcerting hyperbole, the eye-opening literalizations, and the insinuating allusions—these gestures expose the forms and deformations of the antebellum ideology bequeathed to Pierre exalting the unscarred, apotheosized, imperative American landscape. *Pierre* is not the story of a fall from the golden age to the age of lead, from city to country, from Eden to Tartarus. Rather than a jeremiad about how the contemporary generation has squandered its noble inheritance, it is an intimate, excessive portrayal of how the past suffuses and encumbers the present, how the present is scored over and over with the lines of the past. Pierre is both the heir of the first part of the book and the victim of the second part—the victim, we should say, of his inheritance. And *Pierre* is the anatomy of that inheritance, an exposure of the seams in the construction of Saddle Meadows.

NOTES

I am grateful for the keen advice of Phillip Barrish, Mitchell Breitwieser, Dorothy Hale, Robert Milder, Nancy Ruttenburg, Mark Seltzer, Lynn Wardley, and Hertha Wong.

1. For modern views of Saddle Meadows as an untroubled Edenic landscape, see Murray xxxiii–xliv; Lewis 148–49; and Jehlen 186, 198–99, 206. Brodhead suggests that Saddle Meadows is an "overripe" Eden, "its very lushness a symptom of unresolved and unrecognized problems" (167).

2. At the end of Book 4, when the narrator describes Pierre's resistance to the innuendo of father Glendinning's "chair portrait," he repeats and extends the "thought-channels" metaphor, with an emphasis on fluid mechanics: "Nor did the streams of these reveries seem to leave any conscious sediment in his mind; they were so light and so rapid, that they rolled their own alluvial along; and seemed to leave all Pierre's thought-channels as clean and dry as though never any alluvial stream had rolled there at all" (85).

3. For examples from *Pierre,* see the extended and interrupted account of Pierre and Lucy's phaeton ride through Saddle Meadows on a lovely June afternoon, including a digression on the "acoustics" of Love (33) and a description of the effusions of the celestial "horses" (35). Groh and Sieferle argue that representations of nature became strained—more "literal" and less metaphorical and allegorical—through a kind of bourgeois compensatory urgency, as the natural world became the object of increasing exploitation under the pressures of advancing capitalism.

4. See Barrell and Bermingham. Hipple outlines the ideas of William Gilpin, Uvedale Price, Humphrey Repton, Richard Payne Knight, and Dugald Stewart, the theorists of the picturesque (185–302). Michasiw challenges critical assumptions about the relations between discourse and action and argues for the recognition of differences within the picturesque tradition. According to Michasiw, the first phase of the picturesque, represented by the work of Gilpin, articulated a freer, contingent sense of the relations between subject and object, an anti-aesthetic alternative to the imperialist eye of the second phase governed by Price and Knight.

5. On the ideology of the American landscape, see Kolodny, Jehlen, and Angela Miller. Kolodny writes about male fantasies of the American frontier land as "essentially female" and about women's images of the frontier as cultivated garden. She describes the unique historical circumstances of the American "pastoral impulse," how the figurative paradise became literal with the discovery of the continent. Jehlen sharply analyzes the fusing of the political and the natural

in this American "incarnation." She devotes a chapter to *Pierre* (185–226); her conclusions differ from mine. Rather than fold Melville's treatment of the landscape into a general notion of "American" ideology (Jehlen's "monochrome, unisex, and one-class society"), I suggest that Melville's exorbitant rhetoric delineates a more complicated landscape, in which the antebellum acts of exclusion and manipulation are foregrounded and contested. Miller details the complex relationships between the dilemmas of landscape representation and those of nation-building in the decades before the Civil War and the consolidation of a specifically Northern nationalism in landscape imagery in the 1850s. Efforts to analyze an "American picturesque" include Powell; Moore 1–58; Berthold; and Sweet 79–106, 138–64.

6. See Irving's *Sketchbook,* and especially "The Author's Account of Himself" (743–45); Bryant, "The Ages," "Monument Mountain," "To Cole, the Painter, Departing for Europe," "The Prairies," in *Poetical Works* 1:53–67, 102–07, 219, 228–32, and "Funeral Oration on the Death of Thomas Cole, 1848," excerpted in McCoubrey 96–97; Cole, "Essay on American Scenery" 98–110; Willis, *American Scenery;* and *The Home Book of the Picturesque,* especially Susan Cooper, "A Dissolving View" 79–94. See also Cole's influential oil painting "View from Mount Holyoke, Northampton, Massachusetts, after a Thunderstorm (The Oxbow)" and Asher Durand's picturesque commemoration of Cole and appreciation of Bryant in his famous "Kindred Spirits," reproduced in *American Paradise* 125, 109. Callow discusses the New York City group of artists and writers who helped to shape American views (3–38). The sights of the Hudson River Valley were at the center of interest for antebellum painters, tourists, and aesthetic theorists. See the exhibition catalogs and accompanying essays in *American Paradise;* Myers; and Anderson. In an earlier version of this essay, "The Eden of Saddle Meadows," I analyzed the picturesque contributions of Cole and Willis.

7. Knight 151, quoted in Moore 28. Hipple discusses the associationist debate among Price, Knight, and Repton (206–08, 235–37, 239–40, 261–70). On associationism, see also Powell, "Cole and Associationism"; Moore 17–20, 23–25; and Angela Miller 79–82, 101–05. Hussey 1–17 discusses the picturesque link between emotion and vision.

8. While *Pierre* is Melville's most intimate, material, and extended investigation of the American picturesque, he continued to be concerned with issues of the picturesque throughout his writing career. The aesthetic scrutiny in *Pierre* seems to have set in motion the meticulous construction of frame, manipulation of perspective, and density of allusion in the sketches of the mid-1850s: the walled views of "Bartleby" (1853); the cindered prospects and ocular deceptions seen from Rock Rodondo in the fourth sketch of "The Encantadas" (1854) and the oval frame of branches that renders the stranded Hunilla a helpless witness to the beautiful deaths upon the water of her husband and brother in the eighth sketch; the calibrated orientations and disorientations of perspective in "Benito Cereno" (1855); the overlapping borders of the diptychs—"Poor Man's Pudding and Rich Man's Crumbs" (1854), "The Paradise of Bachelors and the Tartarus of Maids" (1855), and the unpublished "The Two Temples"—that associatively implicate America with England, male with female, and rich with poor; the disturbing, sexually charged landscape of "The Tartarus of Maids"; and Melville's culminating treatment of the picturesque in the short fiction "The Piazza" (1856), in which the narrator enters the magical view he has framed and returns disenchanted, haunted like Pierre by the face and the story of a strange, distressed woman he encounters. See also the picturesque representations and meditations in the poetry: the aftermaths and epitaphs of "Shiloh" and "Malvern Hill" in *Battle-Pieces* (1866); the melancholy, barren scenes of "Jerusalem" and "The Wilderness" in *Clarel* (1866); the dialogue among famous painters about the meaning of the term "picturesque" in "At the Hostelry," part of the unfinished *Burgundy Club;* and the nostalgic scenes of "A Dutch Christmas up the Hudson in the Time of the Patroons" and "Rip Van Winkle's Lilac," both part of *Weeds and Wildings, with A Rose or Two* (unpublished in

Melville's lifetime). "At the Hostelry," "Dutch Christmas up the Hudson," and "Rip Van Winkle's Lilac" may be found in Vincent, ed., *Collected Poems* 313–38, 271–72, 281–94. For a collection of essays examining Melville's aesthetic concerns, see Sten, especially John Bryant's "Toning Down the Green: Melville's Picturesque" 145–61. Bryant expands his analysis of Melville's interest in the fusions and mediations of the "picturesque" in *Melville and Repose* 16–19, 139–40, 200–204.

9. For a discussion of the historical shift in the meaning of the word "race," focusing on its nineteenth-century mutations, see Williams 148–50.

10. For the parallels between Melville's family history and his fictional representations in *Pierre,* see Murray 430, 432, 440, and Rogin, *Subversive Genealogy* 159–86. See also Parker.

11. There is a similar trajectory to Melville's justification for his digression on family names, when he asserts "the great genealogical and real-estate dignity of some families in America" (12). The phrase looks fine at first glance, when the emphasis falls on the eminently acceptable "genealogical dignity," but the material implications of "*real-estate* dignity" are more difficult to assimilate.

12. The Anti-Renter Wars involved the rebellion of tenant farmers against the feudal practices of the great Hudson Valley landlords, in particular the collection of yearly tributes in produce, labor, or money and the levying of huge share payments, either a quarter or a third, on the sale of a leasehold. The struggle was a critical event in New York history with broad political implications, including the adoption of a new state constitution in 1846 that finally abolished the feudal system. Christman describes the "Wars." See also the July 4, 1839, "Anti-Renter's Declaration of Independence," reprinted in Foner 59–63. James Fenimore Cooper referred to the conflict in the 1840s as "the great American question of the day." Cooper justified the class and economic structure in the Hudson River Valley in a trilogy of historical novels, beginning with colonial times in *Satanstoe* (1845), continuing through the Revolution in *The Chainbearers* (1845), and climaxing with *The Redskins* (1846) and its contemptuous portrayal of the tenant rebels. For a brief discussion of the events of the Anti-Renter Wars and their relation to *Pierre,* see Murray 435–36.

13. Royster argues that in the Mount of Titans sequence (Book 25) Melville represents the "mythically disguised social landscape" of Saddle Meadows, in which unequal class structure is depicted as part of the natural order (329–35). For a nonfictional account of poverty in the midst of New York State plenty in the 1830s and 1840s, see Conklin's autobiographical *Through Poverty's Vale.*

14. Morris describes the context, evolution, climax, and aftermath of Shays' Rebellion. I am grateful to Jeanne C. Howe for suggesting the significance in *Pierre* of the analogy between Shays' Rebellion and the Anti-Renter Wars.

15. Murray discusses the correspondences in *Pierre* between autobiography, topography, and fiction (429–32, 462). Moore interprets "The Piazza" as a mediation on Berkshire scenery and a critique of picturesque trust in sensation and glorifying of American nature (48–53). See also Vincent, ed., *Melville and Hawthorne in the Berkshires.*

16. On picturesque interest in Berkshire county, see Hickey and Oedel 7–53.

17. For Jackson's "Message," see Remini: "Say to [the Creeks] where they now are, they and my white children are too near to each other to live in harmony and peace. Their game is destroyed, & many of their people will not work, & till the earth. Beyond the great river Mississippi where a part of their nation have gone, their father has provided a country, large enough for them all, and he advises them to remove to it. There, their white brethren will not trouble them . . . and they can live upon it, they and all their children as long as grass grows or water runs in peace and plenty. It will be theirs forever" (128). Jackson's formulation was masterful, transmuting expulsion into promise, displacement and extermination into parental benevolence. Rogin offers an ex-

tended account of Jackson as national patriarch in *Fathers and Children*. Melville alludes to Jackson's "long as grass grows or water runs" in *Typee* 202.

For representative examples of Native American argument about contrasting land claims, as transcribed by European interpreters, see the speeches by the Shawnee chief Tecumseh (1810) in Armstrong 43–44; by the Suquamish and Duwamish chief Seattle (1854) in Swann and Krupat 518–21; and by the Sioux leader Sitting Bull (1877) in Turner 254–55. The quotation from Speckled Snake is in Armstrong 57. For a particularly sharp attack on American duplicity, see the speech of the Flathead chief Charlot to his people in 1876, when they were being pressured to leave their lands in Montana, in Armstrong 99.

18. Irving 744. The insistent allusion in *Pierre* seems a more urgent and palpable representation than Melville's earlier conventional call for a historical memory in the scroll of Vivenza in *Mardi* (1849), which the voyagers encounter during the extended allegory of America in 1848 (chapters 145–68). Against the dominant ideology, which employs allusion to efface or sanctify or naturalize, there have been voices in American literature that insist on acknowledging the haunted dimension of the supposedly Edenic American land. See, for example, the ancestral vision of Chief Seattle (1854), in Swann and Krupat 521, and the specter-ridden Reconstruction Ohio of Toni Morrison's *Beloved* (1987).

19. Emerson 9–10. Jehlen argues that the "axis" of the American landscape is pivoted in *Pierre*. Instead of the characteristic horizontal and open-ended perspective found most famously in Jefferson's expanding Blue Ridge horizons in *Notes on the State of Virginia,* the view in *Pierre* is vertically blocked by the mountains surrounding Saddle Meadows, the walls of New York City, and the impassable terrain of Enceladus (219–25).

20. Thoreau 470–71. In another extraordinary antebellum ocular encounter, Dickinson frames a face-to-face meeting in landscape terms in her poem "Like Eyes that looked on Wastes—" (Johnson no. 458; ca. 1862). Unlike the loving recognition in "The Ponds" or the swarming impact in *Pierre,* when eyes look into eyes in this Dickinson poem they see nothing: "Just Infinities of Nought—."

21. Melville's landscape in the opening pages of *Pierre* is stylistically closer to the hyperbolic, haunted "Meadows" of the late Hudson River painter Martin Johnson Heade. See, for example, the reproductions of Heade's paintings in *American Paradise* 163–78 and in Wilmerding.

WORKS CITED

American Paradise: The World of the Hudson River School. New York: Metropolitan Museum of Art, 1987.

Anderson, Patricia. *The Course of Empire: The Erie Canal and the New York Landscape, 1825–75.* Rochester, NY: Memorial Art Gallery of the University of Rochester, 1984.

Armstrong, Virginia Irving, ed. *I Have Spoken: American History Through the Voices of Indians.* Chicago: Swallow Press, 1971.

Barrell, John. *The Dark Side of the Landscape: The Rural Poor in English Painting, 1730–1840.* Cambridge: Cambridge UP, 1980.

———. *The Idea of Landscape and the Sense of Place, 1730–1840.* Cambridge: Cambridge UP, 1972.

Bermingham, Ann. *Landscape and Ideology: The English Rustic Tradition, 1740–1860.* Berkeley: U of California P, 1986.

Berthold, Dennis. "Charles Brockden Brown, *Edgar Huntly*, and the Origins of American Picturesque." *William and Mary Quarterly* 41 (January 1984): 62–84.

Brodhead, Richard. *Hawthorne, Melville, and the Novel*. Chicago: U of Chicago P, 1976.

Bryant, John. *Melville and Repose: The Rhetoric of Humor in the American Renaissance*. New York: Oxford UP, 1993.

Bryant, William Cullen. *The Poetical Works of William Cullen Bryant*. 2 vols. Ed. Parke Godwin. New York: D. Appleton, 1883.

Callow, James T. *Kindred Spirits: Knickerbocker Writers and American Artists, 1807–55*. Chapel Hill: U of North Carolina P, 1967.

Christman, Henry. *Tin Horns and Calico: A Decisive Episode in the Emergence of Democracy*. New York: Holt, 1945.

Cole, Thomas. "Essay on American Scenery." *The American Monthly Magazine* n.s. 1 (January 1836). Rpt. in *American Art 1700–1960: Sources and Documents*. Ed. John W. McCoubrey. Englewood Cliffs, NJ: Prentice-Hall, 1965. 98–110.

Conklin, Henry. *Through Poverty's Vale: A Hardscrabble Boyhood in Upstate New York, 1832–1862*. Ed. Wendell Tripp. New York: Syracuse UP, 1974.

Emerson, Ralph Waldo. *Essays and Lectures*. New York: Library of America, 1983.

Foner, Philip S., ed. *We, the Other People: Alternative Declarations of Independence by Labor Groups, Farmers, Woman's Rights Advocates, Socialists, and Blacks, 1829–1975*. Urbana: U of Illinois P, 1976.

Groh, Dieter, and Rolf-Peter Sieferle. "Experience of Nature in Bourgeois Society and Economic Theory: Outlines of an Interdisciplinary Research Project." *Social Research* 47 (Autumn 1980): 557–81.

Hickey, Maureen Johnson, and William T. Oedel. *A Return to Arcadia: Nineteenth Century Berkshire County Landscapes*. Pittsfield, MA: The Berkshire Museum, 1990.

Hipple, Walter John, Jr. *The Beautiful, the Sublime, and the Picturesque in Eighteenth-Century British Aesthetic Theory*. Carbondale: Southern Illinois UP, 1957.

The Home Book of the Picturesque: or American Scenery, Art, and Literature. 1852. Gainesville: Scholars' Facsimiles and Reprints, 1967.

Hussey, Christopher. *The Picturesque: Studies in a Point of View*. London: Putnam, 1927.

Irving, Washington. *The Sketchbook of Geoffrey Crayon, Gent*. 1819–20. In *Washington Irving: History, Tales, and Sketches*. Ed. James W. Tuttleton. New York: Library of America, 1983. 731–1091.

Jehlen, Myra. *American Incarnation: The Individual, the Nation, and the Continent*. Cambridge: Harvard UP, 1986.

Johnson, Thomas H., ed. *The Poems of Emily Dickinson*. 3 vols. Cambridge, MA: Harvard UP, 1955.

Knight, Richard Payne. *An Analytical Inquiry Into the Principles of Taste*. London: T. Payne and J. White, 1805.

Kolodny, Annette. *The Lay of the Land: Metaphor as Experience and History in American Life and Letters*. Chapel Hill: U of North Carolina P, 1975.

Lewis, R. W. B. *The American Adam: Innocence, Tragedy, and Tradition in the Nineteenth Century*. Chicago: U of Chicago P, 1955.

McCoubrey, John W., ed. *American Art 1700–1960: Sources and Documents*. Englewood Cliffs, NJ: Prentice-Hall, 1965.

Michasiw, Kim Ian. "Nine Revisionist Theses on the Picturesque." *Representations* 38 (Spring 1992): 76–100.

Miller, Angela. *The Empire of the Eye: Representation and American Cultural Politics, 1825–1875.* Ithaca: Cornell UP, 1993.

Moore, Richard S. *That Cunning Alphabet: Melville's Aesthetics of Nature.* Amsterdam: Rodopi, 1982.

Morris, Richard B. "Insurrection in Massachusetts." In *America in Crisis: Fourteen Crucial Episodes in American History.* Ed. Daniel Aaron. New York: Knopf, 1952. 21–49.

Myers, Kenneth. *The Catskills: Painters, Writers, and Tourists in the Mountains, 1820–95.* Yonkers, NY: The Hudson River Museum of Westchester, 1987.

Murray, Henry. Introduction and Explanatory Notes. *Pierre; or, The Ambiguities.* By Herman Melville. New York: Hendricks House, 1949. xiii–ciii, 429–503.

Otter, Samuel. "The Eden of Saddle Meadows: Landscape and Ideology in *Pierre.*" *American Literature* 66 (March 1994): 55–81.

Parker, Hershel. "Melville and Politics: A Scrutiny of the Political Milieux of Herman Melville's Life and Works." Ph.D. diss. Northwestern University, 1963.

Powell, Earl A., III. "Thomas Cole and the Landscape Tradition: Associationism." *Arts Magazine* 52 (April 1978): 113–17.

———. "Thomas Cole and the Landscape Tradition: The Picturesque." *Arts Magazine* 52 (March 1978): 110–17.

Remini, Robert V. *Andrew Jackson.* New York: Twayne, 1966.

Rogin, Michael Paul. *Fathers and Children: Andrew Jackson and the Subjugation of the American Indian.* New York: Random House, 1975.

———. *Subversive Genealogy: The Politics and Art of Herman Melville.* Berkeley: U of California P, 1983.

Royster, Paul. "Melville's Economy of Language." In *Ideology and Classic American Literature.* Ed. Sacvan Bercovitch and Myra Jehlen. New York: Cambridge UP, 1986. 313–36.

Sten, Christopher, ed. *Savage Eye: Melville and the Visual Arts.* Kent, Ohio: Kent State UP, 1991.

Swann, Brian, and Arnold Krupat, eds. *Recovering the Word: Essays on Native American Literature.* Berkeley: U of California P, 1987.

Sweet, Timothy. *Traces of War: Poetry, Photography, and the Crisis of the Union.* Baltimore: Johns Hopkins UP, 1990.

Thoreau, Henry David. *A Week on the Concord and Merrimack Rivers; Walden, or Life in the Woods; The Maine Woods; Cape Cod.* Ed. Robert F. Sayre. New York: Library of America, 1985.

Turner, Frederick W., ed. *The Portable North American Indian Reader.* New York: Penguin, 1974.

Vincent, Howard P., ed. *Collected Poems of Herman Melville.* Chicago: Hendricks House, 1947.

———. *Melville and Hawthorne in the Berkshires.* Kent, Ohio: Kent State UP, 1968.

Williams, Raymond. *Keywords: A Vocabulary of Culture and Society.* 1976. New York: Oxford UP, 1985.

Willis, Nathaniel Parker. *American Scenery; or Land, Lake, and River: Illustrations of Transatlantic Nature.* Illus. W. H. Bartlett. 1840. Barre, MA: Imprint Society, 1971.
Wilmerding, John. *American Light: The Luminist Movement, 1850–1875.* 1980. Princeton: Princeton UP, 1989.

19

Pierre, Kavanagh, and the Unitarian Perplex

JOHN SEELYE

Sometimes I live in the country,
Sometimes I live in town;
Sometimes I take a great notion
To jump in the river and drown.

I begin with the assumption that *Pierre* is a problematic text, not because, like *Moby-Dick* and *Huckleberry Finn,* it contains inherent indeterminacies— we have little doubt as the "meaning" of the story, nor are we like the hero done in by its "ambiguities"—but because a significant number of readers have dismissed the novel as a failure of form, an aesthetic botch. Even critics who admire Pierre generally feel called upon to mount a rhetoric of apologetics, acknowledging the large body of negative opinion but expressing the certainty that this or that particular "reading" will set things right. One of the problems vexing those readers who care enough to care is the apparent disjunction in style and subject matter between the opening chapters, set in the pastoral "Saddle Meadows," and those that follow, which have the dark underworld of New York for a backdrop. This jarring transition, explained by Pierre's sudden fall from his mother's favor—and fortune—is made even more difficult to accept by the equally sudden intelligence that the young hero intends to support himself and his growing entourage by his pen. Nothing has been said earlier of his creative talents, requiring Melville to provide a belated account of Pierre's modest literary gifts and their overblown reception by the sentimentally inclined venues of the day.

Something similar happens in *Moby-Dick,* when in the Epilogue Ishmael bobs into view like a long-forgotten friend suddenly remembered, the narration having increasingly been in the care of an omniscient point of view, not a first-person narrator. We forgive Melville this particular sin of literary omission because it is a relatively minor flaw in a mighty book, a book moreover of such a self-consciously contrived kind as to pass muster as an early instance of postmodernism, a mode that allows for absolute freedom to abuse literary conventions. *Pierre* has its postmodernist moments also, with a busy stage-managerish presence interposing itself between scenes, many of which are so heightened by theatrical language as to dispel any illusion of reality. But when the author has to stop part way into the narrative and provide us with information that should have been available at the start, then we are likely to suspect we are in the presence of ineptitude, not a dazzling display of surreal juggling. Characters in search of an author is one thing, but the author running down the street trying to catch up with his characters is another. We are apt to lose confidence in such a person, the kind of trust essential to a literary transaction, and wonder if we should continue following him along the paper trail he leaves scattered behind as he runs.

I do not intend to resolve these aesthetic problems. In my opinion *Pierre* is a book that could not make up its mind, and in place of the grand opposing complexities of *Moby-Dick,* it provides a broken line, not a circle. Melville's whaling story is many books in one, a planetary scheme of satellites revolving around the romantic narrative of Ahab's hunt for Moby Dick. *Pierre* is two books in one, and though we can (and shall) reconcile those parts to a larger gender-defined whole, the result is a fabric so transparently constructed that you can view (as with Pip) the foot of the author upon the treadle of the loom, not because the water is so deep but because it is so shallow. Gathering the materials for *Moby-Dick,* Melville as Ishmael claims to have swum through libraries, and there is a long shelf of books and monographs that have been devoted to retracing his watery path. But for *Pierre* his preparatory reach was much less ambitious, as befitting perhaps a work of fiction intended to attract a popular audience. Shakespeare and Dante are the obvious window dressing, but Melville's thickest intertextual dependance is on fiction generally deemed subliterary, the *sans-culottes* of a democratic culture.

David Reynolds in *Beneath the American Renaissance* (1988) has demonstrated the extent to which *Pierre* belongs to the "city-mysteries" genre, exemplified by the works of Eugene Sue in France and George Lippard in America (to which we may add aspects of Dickens's London novels as well). Lippard's *Quaker City* (1844) especially shares in common with Melville's novel an urban setting and the sensational themes of incest and criminal passions. While giving credit due to Reynolds, I would like to go on to suggest that the "city-mysteries" genre is but half of the whole and emphasize that there is yet another tradition that lies back of both Lippard's and Melville's tales of error, contextual matters that will do nothing to resolve the aesthetic problems of *Pierre* but give us something to talk about while maintaining a discrete silence regarding matters that, not being curable, had best be ignored.

Reynolds, who was anticipated by Leslie Fiedler's *What Was Literature* (1982), goes much farther than Fiedler in drawing out convincing analogues between *Pierre* and the city-mysteries novel (though "romance" might be a more accurate label). Indeed, Reynolds attributes the failure of Melville's book to intertextual overload: "*Pierre* was *too* broadly representative of antebellum popular culture—with all its crippling moral paradoxes—to have wide appeal" (159). It may be difficult to imagine the American public getting too much of what it says it wants, but then we should perhaps not make assumptions about taste in Melville's time based on modern experience. The important point to be made, moreover, is that Reynolds reads *Pierre* as a virtual repository of current popular modes: "The first half of the novel portrays the Conventional world of pastoralism, domesticity, the angelic exemplar, hopeful religion, military heroism, and innocence. The second half of the novel plunges us into the Subversive world of dark city mysteries, shattered homes, illicit love, social and philosophical radicalism, and bloody crime" (159). In sum, *Pierre* is both too Conventional and too Subversive, and like a joint conference of Young Republicans and the PLO, it fails to find common ground.

A similar aesthetic dysfunctionalism plagues *Mardi* as well, with an opening series of chapters promising a realistic adventure novel that disappears into a fantastic voyage *cum* philosophical symposium. Nor is *Moby-Dick* free of these faults, either; it fell far short of the popularity both author and publisher had hoped for. Melville's strategy, inspired by Coleridge's account of Shakespeare's binarism, was to write a double-layered text aimed at two audiences—one popular, the other an elite cognoscente or illuminati—and the result was rarely fortunate. But then Melville's situation is typical—only extreme—of authorship in the United States at midcentury, as writers of genius found themselves competing against a rising tide of pulp, identified by Hawthorne with "scribbling women" but hardly gender-limited. Thus the Conventional literary output may in general be credited to women while the Subversive stuff was largely written by men (but "cross-dressing" was inevitable, as we shall soon see).

Again, Leslie Fiedler has been a pioneer in asserting that popularity is a criterion of literary excellence not inferiority, and feminist critics like Mary Kelley and Jane Tompkins have further warmed the climate of interest that made Reynolds's study possible. William Spengemann long ago divided American literature into categories of Adventure (male) and Domestic (female), since which time the latter has increasingly improved in status and canonical respectability while the former has been attacked for its imperialistic tendencies and intolerably high levels of testosterone. Reynolds's own bifoldism is of a similar kind as Spengemann's, but without connotations of value, save when assessing the success of writers like Melville when they attempt to utilize the materials of writers like Lippard. These also are matters I do not wish to discuss further, the mysteries of popular success and literary "genius" being akin to the complexities of the stock market and pork futures, and like Sue's "Mysteries de Paris," they are the kind into which fools stroll only to take flight as angels at the far end. But I would like to take this opportunity to supplement Reynolds's discussion of the intertextual elements in *Pierre,* bringing in another work of fiction that opens Melville's romance to a discussion that entirely avoids aesthetic considerations but does bring up biographical and ideological material of some interest, I hope, as well as matters of genre.

Reynolds, who has previously published important studies of George Lippard's fiction, concentrates on the Lippard spots in *Pierre* and pretty much lets the Conventional aspects stand unsubstantiated by analogous texts. With no ambition to match Reynolds's erudition in popular literature, I would like to suggest that a comparison of *Pierre* with what might appear at first to be an unlikely text for that purpose, Longfellow's *Kavanagh,* provides another avenue of access to Melville's problematics of form. Reynolds does mention *Kavanagh* but only in an anecdote about how Emily Dickinson's brother Austin was forced to smuggle Longfellow's novel into the house, not because the story involved incest (it does not) or illicit sex (it does) but because the book was considered doctrinally subversive, dramatizing as it did "the collapse of theological preaching . . . and the ascendancy of imaginative religion," a subject that was anathema in the home of the conservative bursar of Amherst College (31). Reynolds tells us that Emily "felt a special kinship with the novel's heroine, Alice Archer, a gloomy, dreamy girl who sublimates her hopeless infatuation for Kavanagh in poetic visions." Longfellow thereby provided the Belle of Amherst with a role model in the Domestic range, Subversively salted with doctrinal matters, complementing her infatuation with Charlotte Brontë's morbidly self-sacrificing heroines. Melville of course was not seeking subversive role models—he was too busy creating them—but in that theological tension between the Good Old Way of Trinitarian Congregationalism and the New Way of Unitarianism that Longfellow's novel is concerned with, there was hidden an ethical dilemma similar to the tragic trap that Pierre stumbles into.

But *Kavanagh* is about much more than sermon techniques and forlorn, doomed maidens. Like *Pierre*, it is about the problems of authorship in America and the changeover in ministers with which the story begins resonates also with the emergence of transcendentalism through the fissure provided by the schism in the Congregational Church. Longfellow's little book is a serious attempt to come to terms with a number of cultural issues troubling American intellectuals of the day and as such establishes tangents with Pierre that may be merely coincidental but that yield a modest sum of comparable parts. That Longfellow was himself able to combine with relative success elements of both Domestic and Subversive fiction is in itself suggestive—the novel, although not popular, had respectable sales. But significant differences remain between Longfellow's attempt to write in a genre identified with female authorship chiefly and Melville's *Pierre* to provide a basis for a useful comparison.

An added dimension of interest derives from the appearance in both works of characters at least in part inspired by Nathaniel Hawthorne. In his notes to the Hendricks House edition of *Pierre,* Henry Murray pointed out that the tower inhabited by the inscrutable Plotinus Plinlimmon has an analog, if not a source, in *Kavanagh,* where the eponymous hero maintains a study in a steeple, from which he can catch vicarious glimpses of the village below. And Longfellow's steeple is patently borrowed from Hawthorne, whose "Sights from a Steeple" virtually identified the self-styled reclusive author with elevated voyeurism. And "Kavanagh," as the introduction to the old Riverside Edition of Longfellow's novel indicates, is a name associated, like Hawthorne's boyhood years, with Maine. Though Longfellow's minister-hero owes something to Emerson—he is a Unitarian searching for a larger canvas than a parish for his talents—in the contrast between the clearly autobiographical alternative hero—a schoolteacher named Churchill, who entertains literary ambitions—and the dynamic, mysterious, and romantically handsome Kavanagh, we can detect deflections from Longfellow's pen envy of his Bowdoin classmate and long-time literary friend.

Counterpart to young Kavanagh in *Pierre* is old Plotinus Plinlimmon, identified by Murray with Emerson, with his transcendental philosophy, blue eyes, and bland features. But there is a hint of Hawthorne in Plinlimmon's presumed scorn of Pierre's idealism—of Melville's Hawthorne, let me add—an expression of that "darkness" Melville detected in his writing, coefficient of the "mystery" he identified with the man. But Hawthorne can be detected in *Pierre* in another guise as well, as I sought thirty years ago to demonstrate, with a reaction similar to that attending Pierre's decision to give a name to his relationship with Isabel by marrying her, for it was my thesis then (and now) that Melville's dark, mysterious, and beautiful heroine was as much inspired by Hawthorne as was Longfellow's Kavanagh. Since Melville's homosexuality and the consequent need to express it covertly (if not Subversively) is no longer a novelty, and since I have already had my say about Melville's problem in that regard with Hawthorne, let me turn instead to Longfellow's problem, which seems to have had no psychosexual undertow but was purely professional—if anything is pure, if anything is professional.

In 1849, Hawthorne's literary career was still short of the fame brought by *The Scarlet Letter,* but that did not prevent a certain quality of envy from creeping into Longfellow's journal entries about his friend. Where the poet was forced to keep himself and his growing family from want by teaching foreign languages to Harvard undergraduates, thereby taking time away from his poetry and other creative pursuits, Hawthorne seemed the very picture of an independent author. We of course know that Hawthorne had his unpleasant chores to do, also, from hack work for periodicals to his stultifying stint in the Salem Custom House, but in Longfellow's eyes he seemed an admirable instance of an author able to sustain himself through his writings; nor did Hawthorne help much when he cheerfully urged Longfellow to give up his secure post at Harvard for the dangerous, impecuniary life of the freelance man of letters. Whatever the reality, Hawthorne was for Longfellow the symbol of artistic freedom, much as the young bachelor Kavanagh seems to the married Churchill to be a paragon of intellectual independence. He is, as well, a figure of considerable erotic potential, judging from his effect on the village maidens, while Churchill has not only a wife but children, not counting his students in school.

The course of literary relationships seldom runs smooth, and—at least from Hawthorne's viewpoint—the matter of *Evangeline* put a serious strain on the friendship, Longfellow having appropriated material that Hawthorne had assumed was his own. But regarded from Longfellow's side of the table, as revealed by his references and letters from Hawthorne, the indebtedness was more than fairly balanced. The two men had been only acquaintances at college, and the literary friendship began in 1837 with a letter from Hawthorne acknowledging his classmate's rise to literary prominence in terms bordering on obsequiousness, a letter that also informed Longfellow he would soon be receiving a copy of *Twice-Told Tales*. The gift was a hint the poet was quick to take, for he placed a favorable notice of the book in the *North American Review*. This good turn brought another admiring letter from Hawthorne, epistolary bread well buttered with thanks. If, as Jane Tompkins and others have maintained, Hawthorne's literary fame was sustained by a network of male friends, his early letters to Longfellow suggest that every warp must have a woof so that a literary dog may have his day.

Thus the two writers were drawn together by a kind of literary necessity, resulting in a friendship of mutual advantage lasting from 1837 until Hawthorne left for England in 1853. Longfellow was on friendly terms with other writers, including Emerson, references to whom in his journals are frequently of a mildly sarcastic sort, dismissive of the author of *Nature* as a dreamer and an obscurantist. The skeptical Hawthorne was much closer to Longfellow's own essential conservatism, and he regarded his friend as a compatriot in the struggle to achieve popular recognition and professional standing for America's native-born writers. The exchange of letters was matched by friendly visits and companionable conversations between the two men, so that by 1850 the cozy relationship Melville sought with Hawthorne had long since been enjoyed by Longfellow, albeit on somewhat less intense grounds. Whatever may have been Hawthorne's assessment of his friend's literary genius (it does not seem to have been very high), he certainly enjoyed his company, which came without the demands made by Melville, who sought a degree of intimacy Hawthorne could hardly provide.

On the receipt of the book of Longfellow's poems, Emerson wrote the author a marvelously qualified appreciation, in which he said that he felt "safe" in the hands of such a poet. Nobody ever felt safe in Melville's hands, most certainly not Hawthorne. Melville was a risk taker, pirouetting on the brink of an abyss, and Hawthorne declined the dance, much preferring the safety network provided by the prestigious, undemanding company of Longfellow, which had the comfort and drape of a hammock. Longfellow, in turn, though intrigued by Hawthorne's quietly mysterious yet attractive manner (as were many of his friends), did not push his advantage and attempt to worm out his friend's "secret." Both men inherited a Puritan restraint, after all, with an appreciation of fences and walls. Thus when Longfellow wrote his friend into *Kavanagh,* the portrait is similarly discrete, even demure, blended with equal parts of Emersonian idealism, properly seasoned with transcendental elements imported from Europe. At the end of the story, Kavanagh and his wealthy bride have dedicated themselves to organizing Christians into one worldwide sect, hardly a Hawthornean errand and Emersonian only in its emphasis on transcendent unity.

Nor is this, for that matter, an errand we can associate with Melville's Plinlimmon, whose remnant pamphlet has a decidedly skeptical, even cynical cast, promoting a relativism that encourages an airy disdain of good works or indeed of any earthly endeavor inspired by heavenly motives. Although completely in accord with Melville's blighted view of transcendentalism, Plinlimmonism is antithetical to Longfellow's much more positive—if somewhat qualified—Kavanaghism, a project the poet associated with a crack-brain enthusiast he had encountered in Europe. But what I am attempting to demonstrate here is not that *Pierre* is a response to Longfellow's novel in terms of particulars, only that in terms of inspiration and theme it shares common ground. The ground, moreover, is located in the vicinity of Pittsfield, Massachusetts, where Longfellow's second wife had close family ties and where the poet and his family occasionally spent the summer months escaping the Cambridge heat. Longfellow's diary actually records a visit paid to the Melvilles of Broadhall in 1848, with a reference to having met "Fayaway," for Longfellow was an early admirer of *Typee,* but with perhaps an imperfect recollection of the names and genders of its characters—unless we are to credit him with powers of perception even greater than Hawthorne's regarding Melville's sexual identity. The village called "Fairmeadow" in *Kavanagh* is a nicely pastoral adaptation of "Pittsfield," a terrain dominated likewise by the crow-haunted height of Mount Greylock, establishing a connection of which Melville could hardly have been unaware.

More important than this tenuous personal connection is the literary context from which both *Kavanagh* and *Pierre* take much of their meaning. Like Melville's Pierre, Longfellow's Mr. Churchill is an autobiographical projection, author and character being schoolteachers ambitious to become authors but whose school room and other responsibilities continually interfere with their literary pursuits. Like Longfellow, Churchill has some at least local fame and is besieged by younger poets for advice and counsel, a problem Longfellow also had to contend with. Like Longfellow, he has a growing family that also drags him down from Parnassus, and like him he regards the chauvinistic, nationalistic Young America movement with disdain. In one memorable chapter, Churchill is visited by an advocate of American literary nationalism, a Cornelius Matthews–like character who spouts rhetoric about Niagara Falls while Churchill quietly rebuffs him with references to literary universality and European continuities, a cosmopolitanism similar to Pierre's youthful eclecticism. Like Pierre, Churchill is "at work" on an extended romance, and one of the main points of Longfellow's novel is established by Churchill's failure to see that he has had the materials for a novel of real life happening all around him. He need not, counsels his friend Kavanagh, have sought out exotic locales or romantic characters, a Domestic emphasis that connects the novel with the emerging regional literature identified with the New England muse—if not exactly with Hawthorne, who with Melville continued to pursue the romantic ideal in fiction.

This regional aspect of *Kavanagh* is acknowledged by Lawrence Buell in his magisterial study of New England culture, but the novel is more than an early demonstration of nativist realism. It is, as well, a book animated throughout by the Unitarian ideology that Buell identifies as a powerful motivating force permeating New England thought and political action, the very qualities that added the subversive dimension emphasized by Reynolds. *Kavanagh* is also an early draft of Longfellow's ambition to frame a work that would embrace the whole history of Christianity, an ambition that resulted in the slow and at times painful creation of his three-part poem, *Christus,* somewhat foreshadowed by Kavanagh's vision of Christian unity. The connection between the early and late works is established in the novel's eighteenth chapter, which Longfellow added after the book was finished and which he regarded as the "keystone" to the ideological "plot" of the several-stranded text. There he traces Kavanagh's spiritual biography, his progress from Catholicism to Protestantism in its most liberal form, an epitome in small of the drift (as Longfellow saw it) of Christianity in general. A Unitarian finally, Kavanagh is necessarily an advocate of good works, an ideal common with Catholic doctrine but a Socinian heresy in the eyes of traditional Calvinists. It is he, once again, who urges his friend Churchill to stop dreaming up impossible romances and use the simple rural world around him, linking literary realism to the Unitarian commitment to social reforms. As if to drive this nail home, Longfellow stages one of their conversations on a bridge at night, as the distraught and betrayed Lucy, Churchill's former housemaid who has been seduced and abandoned, quietly slips into the river and drowns.

Another of Churchill's perpetually unfinished projects is a history of suffering womankind that concentrates on the martyrs of the early Christian church, while Kavanagh points out to him the prevalence of contemporary female suffering. As with the episode at the bridge, there is some suggestion that Longfellow is capable of a certain quiet irony: it is the handsome young minister who is chiefly (if innocently) responsible for much of the female suffering in the story. The major victim is Emily Dickinson's favorite, the pale, unhealthy maiden named Alice Archer, who, having fallen in love with the charismatic young preacher, must accept the fact that he loves another, her best friend and confidante, Cecilia Vaughn. In the manner of many sentimental martyrs, Alice falls convenient victim to consumption and fades obligingly away before the second year that makes up the novel's chronology is out. And like many sentimental novels, *Kavanagh* is a text that is seriously engaged with contemporary cultural and ideological issues, thereby providing a substantive counterpart to *Pierre*, even to the point of failing to propose specific reforms— if for entirely different motives.

Here again, *Pierre* must be chiefly measured in terms of difference. Melville was, if only tangentially, a member of the Young American movement that Longfellow attacked, and his fiction is not associated with the regional muse. Where we can recognize in *Kavanagh* telltale features of the Pittsfield landscape, *Pierre* is set deep in Melvilleland—a territory, like Poe's, chiefly of the mind, with occasional depths reaching into the darkness of the psyche. Melville's was a romantic sensibility, interested in extreme contrasts of character to the point of melodrama and, most characteristically, seeking out or manufacturing exotic locales. Nor are the Domestic aspects of *Pierre* the usual kind of thing. Notably, where Longfellow's Churchill is a humble schoolteacher and a family man, Pierre is a handsome young aristocrat, a potential heir to hundreds of acres and a collector of land rents. Much is made of his high-born lineage and his haughty, elitist, even queenlike mother is a virtual caricature of privilege. Longfellow emphasizes the quiet routines (and silent tragedies) of village life; Melville—at the start—stresses life at the Glendinning manor house where servants hover to assist and the mother and son seem characters in a high drama of their own composition. Like Pierre, Churchill is surrounded by women, but with no erotic overtones—he is also surrounded by children—and Kavanagh may be the cynosure of female parishioner's eyes, but marriage, not seduction, is the goal, a social norm not a mask for incest. Even the seducer of Lucy is a rascally vendor of secondhand clothes, not the usual rake of sensational literature. Where Lucy yields to the sentimental tradition and dies an Ophelia-like death, Melville's Delly Ulver, her dishonored counterpart in *Pierre,* is made of much tougher, if not nobler, stuff and like Horatio survives the deaths of Pierre and Isabel.

These differences, though indicative of the disparate qualities of the two books—in *Pierre,* after all, the Conventional is overtaken by the Subversive fairly early on, while Longfellow maintains a nice balance between the two elements—must yield to the main distinction: *Kavanagh,* once again, is a major document of New England Unitarianism, having been written to demonstrate, even illustrate, its sectarian commitment to charity in all its complex manifestations; *Pierre* is not. The subversiveness of Longfellow's novel was contingent on a passing manifestation of sectarian differences and is hardly detectable to a modern reader innocent of the great Unitarian-Trinitarian debate, while *Pierre,* with its sexual and social abnorms, is still subversive of middle-class conventions. Indeed, to read Melville's novel in a Unitarian context—hardly a common exercise—is to read it as a refutation of the Unitarian idealism Longfellow championed even as Emerson preferred a higher, transcendental plane and scorned reformational particulars. As "read" by the Emersonian Plinlimmon, Pierre, as a fool of virtue, is something of a Unitarian clown. When he attempts to put into practice one of the major ideals of Unitarianism, the Christian necessity of charitable acts, by giving aid to his half-sister, Isabel, and likewise rescuing the ruined maid-servant, Delly, he does so at the cost of his mother's love, his future prosperity, the respect of the community—and his life. Needless to say, Pierre has no counterpart in Longfellow's book. As if to point up the knife-sharp difference, Melville first houses Isabel and Delly in a rural cottage that approximates the house called home by Alice Archer and her maid, an architectural counterpointing that matches the connection between Kavanagh's steeple and Pinlimmon's tower—though, as I long ago pointed out, the cottage also evokes Hawthorne's little red house in Lenox.

Isabel's place is set against an isolated lake, with "long, mysterious mountain masses" in the background, "shaggy with pines and hemlocks, mystical with dread and gloom," a rather Usher-like place well suited to incestuous passions. The signposts of the moss-encrusted farmhouse are "three straight gigantic lindens" that "stand guardians of this verdant spot," much as in *Kavanagh,* Alice Archer's dark old dwelling is shaded by "four sickly Lombardy poplars" that suggest "gloomy and mournful thoughts" in keeping with her temper and fate. Here she is visited by her happy friend, Cecilia, who brings "sunshine" into the "dark mansion," and here they share their secrets, "a rehearsal in girlhood of the great drama of woman's life," including Cecilia's budding romance with Kavanagh, tidings of which are torture to the miserable Alice.

For her part, Cecilia lives in the village, in a house clearly modeled after Major Melville's, as described in Longfellow's journal: a "large, square building, with a portico in front, whose door in Summer time stood open from morning until night. A pleasing stillness reigned about it, and soft gusts of pine-embalmed air, and distant cawings from the crow-haunted mountains, filled its airy and simple halls." It is in this nature-filled space that Cecilia has grown up, in the shadow of Greylock, described as "the mysterious mountain, whose coolness was a perpetual invitation to her, and whose silence [was] a perpetual fear," a somewhat patriarchal (and Wordsworthian) presence that has nourished her "dreamy and poetic temperament." In effect, Cecilia has grown up in Pierre's house, with the aristocratic furniture removed, and like Pierre she is half an orphan (having lost her mother) and a child of privilege. Notably, it is to this house that the Reverend Kavanagh comes on his first errand of love, not to Alice's gloomy home. For all of his stated interest in doing good, the Reverend Kavanagh (like the Reverend Falsgrave) is attracted not to beauty in want but to its opposite number, beauty amply provided with a dowry.

Although the leading characters in *Kavanagh* are champions of charity, the favors are mostly done by the wealthy and privileged for one another. It is in Melville's novel that a child of wealth impulsively sets out to do good for someone who is poor and a social outcast—yet someone also beautiful, as Melville wryly notes—an idealistic young man who hurls himself from the center of the social register to the most marginal of margins, and who perishes as a result. Sentimental literature, by and large, struggles to pull marginal elements of society toward the domestic center and thereby redeem them— "Father, dear father, come home with me now." But Melville was not a sentimental writer. His sympathies are always with outcasts and renegades permanently beyond the pale of reform. Therefore, he reverses the sentimental pattern in *Pierre* and in so doing refutes it, along with the ideology of Unitarianism, that sentimental sect and its evangelical mission of doing good that is central to so much domestic literature of the mid–nineteenth century, including (and most especially) *Uncle Tom's Cabin*, published the same year as *Pierre*. As the work of an author who was the child of one of New England's most prominent Calvinists, Stowe's protest novel is also somewhat subversive in its Unitarian aspect, but it was hardly Subversive in Reynolds's sense of the term, that is, not in its Unitarian dimension. Longfellow reveals in his journal that he read Stowe's novel with enthusiasm (the Domestic, reform dimension) mixed with anguish (the Subversive, violent dimension), perhaps recognizing in it his own little novel raised to a much higher power. There is no mention of his having read *Pierre*.

None of Melville's books, it can be said, were written to do good—with the exception perhaps of *White-Jacket,* and that after the fact of naval reform. Quite to the contrary, his greatest works of fiction were written about the futility of any intentional act in a world ruled over by Fate and Chance, and even his poems celebrating Union victories in the Civil War worry aloud about the long-range effects of that conflict. *Moby-Dick, Pierre, The Confidence-Man* all do battle with equivalents to Unitarianism's well-intentioned faith in the power of positive action. Even *Billy Budd,* so late in the century as to be anachronistic, drags goodness personified to the masthead and finds him guilty of being innocent. "To where it belongs with your charity," snarls the superannuated custom house officer in *The Confidence-Man,* another echo of Melville's Hawthorne not much different from the lesson of Plinlimmon's pamphlet, both expressions of cynicism toward confusing heaven with earth. Nor was Hawthorne's Hawthorne much in sympathy with Unitarian cheeriness—having married into it—despite his praises of *Kavanagh* as "a most precious and rare book; as fragrant as a bunch of flowers, and as simple as one flower," a floral tribute confined to his correspondence with Longfellow and of a similar kind to Emerson's feelings of safety.

Hawthorne's pastoral figure brings us to the final dimension distinguishing *Pierre* from *Kavanagh* in terms of definitive characteristics. Though subversive in the eyes of the master of the Dickinson home, Longfellow's novel does not belong in Reynolds's house of Subversive fiction if only for the simple fact that none of the action takes place in the city, where much of *Pierre* does. The eponymous hero and his bride spend their honeymoon (offstage) in Europe, there taking on a larger (universal) perspective, and return to find Fairmeadow "completely transformed" by the coming of a railroad: "The simple village had become a very precocious town." But the touch is as gratuitous as the renovations taking place in the Old Manse as Hawthorne and his wife departed, a sign of modern times that occurs too late to affect the story. *Kavanagh* is entirely cast in a rural mode. "The country is lyric," muses Mr. Churchill, "—the town is dramatic. When mingled, they make the most perfect musical drama." This celebration of suburban life is one of a number of meditations he scrawls on the panels of his writing desk, a pulpit salvaged from the renovation of the old village church in anticipation of Kavanagh's arrival. But, like the coming of the railroad, it has nothing to do with the meaning of the story, though it may serve as an ironic commentary on *Pierre*, which mingles town and country with dissonant results.

The irrelevance of Churchill's motto is easily explained: Like the pulpit on which it is written, the sentiment—along with all the others—is salvage, having been cut from the manuscript of Hyperion and used for padding in the subsequent book. They are in harmony with Longfellow's other autobiographical story, a highly Europeanized romance conceived in the spirit of Jean Paul Richter and Goethe, but are gratuitous additions to his American tale. They do serve as a convenient antithesis to the maxim that decorated Melville's chimney at Arrowhead and may likewise be contrasted with the bitter scrawls that litter the floor of Pierre's study in New York City. Again, no sweet music emerges from the mingling of town and country in Melville's book. Nor is "mingling" the right word, for Melville characteristically dichotomizes the two regions, and though the country may be lyric, it is a specious lyricism, and his urban drama darkens into the tragedy of grand opera. At the start, the busily intrusive narrator ruminates fruitily on Pierre's good fortune to have been born in the country, but the country proves insufficient for the hero's subsequent occasion, and he must leave for the city, a necessity dictated as much by genre considerations as his falling out with his imperious mother. Much as Longfellow abstained from involving his characters in city matters, obeying the rural call of the Domestic, regionalist muse, so Melville was caught (as his hero is trapped) in the romantic, Subversive necessity, moving a cast of characters similar to Longfellow's into Manhattan, where his intended rural bowl of milk becomes a kind of chowder.

We should note here that Pierre first goes to the city because it is a place where he expects to find a home. He plans to take up his cousin's long-standing offer of a cottage, complete with a servant, and the house, though located in New York City, is something of an anomaly, being "very charming, little," and old, rather a rusticated retreat located in a quiet and secluded part of the city, just the place "for the retired billings and cooings of a honeymoon." It is the other place in which Pierre and his entourage finally find quarters—his cousin having refused him the use of the cozy cottage—the old church building known as the Apostles, that is truly integral to the urban world, having been cut up into offices for the conduct of business. It is here that Pierre sets up shop as a writer, but in such a way as to offend the proprieties of his publishers, writing the kind of book that could never make a profit, dashing his hopes of prosperity and inspiring the desperation that results in the death of Glen Stanly. It is a sensationalist climax that perfectly fits Reynolds's definition of Subversiveness in fiction, as does the double suicide with which the miseries of Pierre and Isabel end.

Pierre must go to the city and there he must die, an action that confirms the traditional American ambivalence about cities in general, that Jeffersonian sentiment that bred the artistic convention that cities are bad places in which bad things happen, even though writers as different as Longfellow and Melville both knew how essential the urban context was to the vitality of literature, in terms both of publishing and the cultural matrix that sustained it. Ironically, as a bad place the city also gave life to the "mysteries" romance: *Pierre* the novel is sustained by the very forces that destroy Pierre the idealistic champion of Truth. Curiously enough, *Pierre* is an anomaly in that regard. Where both Dickens and Thackeray in England repeatedly made use of the urban scene, there is no major novelist in America before the Civil War who chose the city as a setting, nor does Reynolds, for all his enthusiasm for Lippard's works, claim that writer as yet another neglected genius. Lippard belongs to that interesting lower layer of American writers, which includes advocates of reform like T. S. Arthur, for whom the city was a profitable mine of material, but artists of Melville's stature avoided the city like the plague, even as in the case of Hawthorne's *Blithedale Romance,* carrying an urban cast of characters into the country to act out their fated romance.

We must go back to the late eighteenth century in American literature to find a time when the city figures in major works of fictions, back to *Charlotte Temple,* or, even better for our purposes, that tangled, revised-in-progressed tale that in so many ways prefigures Melville's *Pierre,* Charles Brockden Brown's *Arthur Mervyn.* For, like Melville's, Brown's is a novel that began with one genre in mind, the Jacobin novel as written by William Godwin, and in the midst of composition (and the French Revolution) took another turn, becoming an increasingly gothicized and even reactionary fiction set against the yellow fever epidemics of the period (here the city was literally the plague), which serve to demonstrate the callously selfish passions of mankind. Starting out with the apparent intention of returning his hero to the country—having shown him the horrors of urban life—and to marriage with a worthy rural maid, Brown instead brought Mervyn yet again into the city, where at the last we leave him contemplating marriage with a wealthy blue-stocking, a "happy" but rather cynical ending, the hero escaping Pierre's fate by marrying up out of it.

Reynolds regards *Arthur Mervyn* as an important precursor of the "city mysteries" Subversive genre and traces the influence of the Jacobin novel down through the eccentric fictions of John Neal. He does not, however, go quite far enough; because although we may doubt that Melville ever read *Arthur Mervyn*—never mind the novels of Neal—*Pierre* belongs to that same class of fiction, rather more closely than to Lippard's Subversive mode, being like so much that Melville wrote, rather much anachronistic, even atavistic. *Pierre* is a modified version of the Jacobin novel, with the same bifurcation of town and country as we find in *Arthur Mervyn* but with a tragic, not a positively recon-structed, resolution. The Jacobin novel is not really "Jacobin," having been called such by conservative critics objecting to its reformational aims. *Caleb Godwin* was not written to overthrow society, merely to reform it, and like all of Brown's anti-Jacobin novels, it ends happily, with the hero rescued from the clutches of the villain. I have elsewhere diagrammed Brown's complex love-hate relationship with the genre, which was put by him to a conservative, even federalist, use; nor is Melville's own adaptation of the Jacobin novel in the spirit of Godwin.

What Pierre shares with the genre is that characteristic move of the action from a rural to an urban setting and the use of the city as the "bad place" where human viciousness, like the population, seems more compact than in rural areas. Enemies appear suddenly and without warning or sufficient mo-tivation. An atmosphere of peril and threat prevails. Misery thrives, as does eccentricity and madness. The city is a concentration camp of woe and depri-vation for those who have no means to protect themselves, who have, in sum, no money. But where for Brown and, let me add, for Charles Dickens the city is a demonstration of human degradation, it is not a fatal trap, only a danger-ous place, and one may emerge a wiser if not necessarily a better person. After all, the Jacobin novel and the Bildungsroman are closely related genres, and if *Pierre* does not belong to that family of hopeful texts, its plot does bend to the same necessity, that the hero must go from the country to the city in order to taste the bitterness that lies at the bottom of the well. It is, wrote Richard Henry Dana, Jr., in a book Melville read and admired, below decks, down in the fo'csle that Truth resides, not up with the elites on the quarterdeck. But then *Two Years Before the Mast* is a landmark of reform literature in America, written in the spirit of Unitarianism, where *Pierre,* once again, is not. Melville's ideology was inimical to the kind of optimism that inspires reform. Pierre must go to the city and he must die, victim of his own privileged impulse to do good.

Written against a contemporary novel of Convention like *Kavanagh,* with its solicitous regard for the sufferings of the middle-class set in the New England countryside, *Pierre* plunges a similar cast of characters into New York City, where their earlier sufferings take a much more serious turn. At the point that Isabel unites herself with Pierre, she is living in genteel poverty, but after he takes charge, she experiences the real thing, near-starvation and bitter want. And Pierre, who has been raised with the greatest expectations, like a Dickens hero, finds them greatly reversed; there is no happy, middle-class resolution, no Dickensian rescue, no opportunity to settle for the bliss of domesticity on a modest income, no love in a cottage. Pierre becomes caught up in the gears of a relentless machine that pushes him toward destruction.

We do not know what Melville had in mind when he promised Sophia Hawthorne that bowl of milk, perhaps some sort of country pudding like *Kavanagh.* But like his own hero, he was driven by a power larger than his conscious intention, creating a story that not only reverses the implications of Longfellow's novel but calls its ideological basis into question. *Kavanagh* is certainly worth the short time it takes to read it, being a novel that correctly reflects ("a reflection of a reflection," Hawthorne called it) the Unitarian/transcendental mood of such happy suburban sites as Concord and Cambridge. Moreover, it lay the foundation for the genteelism of a later generation of writers whose personal lives were identified with urban scenes but who never quite relinquished rural values, where *Pierre* did not.

NOTE

This essay is the most recent addition to a sequence that amounts to an invisible monograph entitled "Melville-Hawthorne-Emerson-Longfellow-Emerson-Hawthorne-Melville; or, The Lesson of Queequeg's Quilt," in which I meld four quite different authors into a corporate, if not always happy, unit. The reader interested in piecing together the whole is referred to my articles: "The Structure of Encounter: Melville's Review of Hawthorne's *Mosses," Melville and Hawthorne in the Berkshires, a Symposium,* ed. Howard P. Vincent (Kent, Ohio: Kent State UP, 1968), 63–69; "Ungraspable Phantom: Reflections of Hawthorne in *Pierre* and *The Confidence-Man," Studies in the Novel* 1 (1969): 436–43; "The Contemporary 'Bartleby,'" *American Transcendental Quarterly* 7 (1970): 12–18; and "Attic Shape: Dusting off *Evangeline," Virginia Quarterly Review* 60 (1984): 21–44.

My reflections on C. B. Brown's use of the Jacobin novel may be found in "Charles Brockden Brown and Early American Fiction," *Columbia Literary History of the United States,* ed. Emory Elliott (New York: Columbia UP, 1988), 168–86.

WORKS CITED

Buell, Lawrence. *New England Literary Culture: From Revolution through Renaissance.* Cambridge: Cambridge UP, 1986.

Kelley, Mary. *Private Woman, Public Stage: Literary Domesticity in Nineteenth-Century America.* New York: Oxford UP, 1984.

Murray, Henry A. Introduction. *Pierre; or, The Ambiguities.* Vol. 7: *Complete Works of Herman Melville.* Ed. Howard P. Vincent. Chicago: Hendricks House, 1949.

Reynolds, David. *Beneath the American Renaissance: The Subversive Imagination in the Age of Emerson and Melville.* New York: Knopf, 1988.

Spengemann, William. *The Adventurous Muse.* New Haven: Yale UP, 1977.

Tompkins, Jane. *Sensational Designs: The Cultural Work of American Fiction, 1790–1860.* New York: Oxford UP, 1985.

20

Pierre in a Labyrinth:
The Mysteries and Miseries of New York

WYN KELLEY

Yes, here I had come to seek my fortune: a mere boy, friendless, unprotected, innocent of the ways of the world—without wealth, favor, or wisdom—here I stood at the entrance of the mighty labyrinth, and with hardly any consciousness of the temptations, doubts, and dangers that awaited me there.

—Walt Whitman, *Franklin Evans*

Ah, thou rash boy! Are there no couriers in the air to warn thee away from these emperilings, and point thee to those Cretan labyrinths, to which thy life's cord is leading thee?

—*Pierre*

Since the beginnings of its burst of growth in the early nineteenth century, New York often appeared in its own culture—ranging from guidebooks, moral and religious tracts, periodicals, and popular fiction in the literary arts to prints, panoramas, and dioramas in the graphic arts—as a labyrinth of unprecedented physical and social complexity. The idea of the city as a labyrinth, of course, was not new to a culture saturated in classical literature and popular European writers. Melville's Pierre is only one among the many young men and women of nineteenth-century fiction who venture into an urban maze that tests their intelligence, nerve, moral strength, and heroism. As a metaphor for urban complexity, danger, and temptation, as well as literary intricacy, the labyrinth adapts itself to a number of plots and intentions and would seem to be a familiar tool in any writer's workshop. Melville's insistence, however, on Pierre's entering a *Cretan* labyrinth draws attention to his distinct construction of the literary labyrinth; and although I cannot do more than outline the literary and cultural context for his use of the theme, or allude to the historical changes in New York that made it a compelling idea, I do expect to show how radically Melville revised this cultural trope. By emphasizing that Pierre's labyrinth is a Cretan, rather than a Christian, construction of the idea, Melville turns much of popular contemporary labyrinth literature—the literature of mystery and misery—on its head.[1]

In a recent example of what I am going to call the labyrinth literature of New York, Tom Wolfe's *The Bonfire of the Vanities* (1987), a Wall Street broker takes one wrong turn in the urban labyrinth and precipitates himself into a racial and legal labyrinth from which he can never truly escape. His story takes its place in the familiar tradition of novels of youthful indiscretion and ruin in the big city, starting with temperance novels like Whitman's *Franklin Evans* or T. S. Arthur's *Ten Nights in a Bar-Room,* the sensational urban crime stories and police catalogs, and the popular fictions of George Lippard *(The Empire City, New York: Its Upper Ten and Lower Million),* Joseph Holt Ingraham *The Miseries of New York, The Beautiful Cigar Girl, or the Mysteries of Broadway),* Harrison G. Buchanan *(Asmodeus),* James Rees *(The Mysteries of City Life),* and E. Z. C. Judson or Ned Buntline *(The Mysteries and Miseries of New York).* Mystery-and-misery novels claimed to reveal to provincial outsiders the secret crimes, vices, and woes of the city. Much of the popular nineteenth-century urban fiction, in fact, might be viewed as attempts to provide reliable guides to the growing urban labyrinth of New York. Melville's *Pierre* seems to fall into this tradition too: a young man leaves his safe provincial home, enters a mysterious and frightening city in search of knowledge and success, loses himself in a labyrinth of moral and metaphysical complexity, and ends in poverty, crime, imprisonment, and death. But Pierre is the first of Melville's characters, and, I suspect, one of the first American urban characters, to discover that the urban labyrinth he has been trying to penetrate in search of truth is actually a construction of his own mind, imagination, and will.[2] The labyrinth is not just out there in the physical and social structure of the city, but it originates in him, with his own choices and decisions. Rather than judge his protagonist in conventional moral terms, however, as the writers of much mystery-and-misery fiction tended to do, relying on a broadly Christian construction of the labyrinth and its erring hero, Melville's narrator takes a more Daedalian perspective: having created a wondrously intricate labyrinth, he watches Pierre's progress through it with the detached and at times cruel irony of the artist genius. In this sense, the novel *Pierre* broke with nineteenth-century conventions of urban literature and has also proved alien and offensive to its readers.

Although I am distinguishing between two constructions of the urban labyrinth, a Christian and a Cretan notion of the idea, I do not want to suggest that these terms existed within the culture as neat categories or even that Melville had a clear or totalizing sense of what the labyrinth meant. Rather, I see Melville drawing on what had become a universally available symbol for his growing city, but using it in an adversarial way to pursue literary and metaphysical interests of his own. Whitman's description of Franklin Evans pausing to contemplate New York before entering "the mighty labyrinth" is a good example of typical uses of the term. Temperance novels relied heavily on a notion of the city as a labyrinth in which the erring youth loses his or her way among a wealth of dangerous temptations.[3] In part these and other popular accounts responded to concrete physical changes in urban topography as the older parts of the city became more dense and complex. In a series of articles in *Putnam's* glorifying New York's expansion and change, one author, comparing the shape of lower Manhattan to a boot, affirmed that "though you may with some assurance navigate the instep, and are not wholly beyond hope in the heel, yet none but an old-fashioned New-York pig or policeman can ever be perfectly at home in the sole of the metropolitan foot" (124). The part of town near where Pierre and Isabel live was described by Joel Ross as riddled with "narrow zigzagging cow-path streets" (14), by George Lippard as a "subterranean world" (*New York* 116), by George Foster as "the very type and physical semblance, in fact, of hell itself" (*Gas-Light* 120), and by Charles Dickens, the great outsider and tourist who helped define New York for itself, as a place of "narrow ways diverging to the right and left, and reeking everywhere of dirt and filth" (87). Guidebooks spoke of the labyrinth of utility pipes—bringing gas and water into the city and carrying waste out—as a source of urban pride, but the *Putnam's* article also described the "confusion into which the wholesale repairs and alterations going on in this street have plunged it" (128). With the indiscriminate traffic of horses, vehicles, and humans, the mountains of rotting waste and dust, and the social complexity of urban crowds displaying newly visible varieties of class and ethnicity, New York in the 1840s and 1850s looked more and more like a physical and social labyrinth.[4]

But Whitman was drawing on a moral culture as well which saw the city as a labyrinth of sin. In this construction of the ancient myth, the hero is essentially "innocent of the ways of the world," as Franklin Evans is, until exposed to the dangers of liquor, gambling, sex, and crime. These influences, however, exert an almost irresistible pressure on the unwary provincial to lose himself in what George Foster called the "misery, destitution, filth, and crime, in the dark labyrinths of this metropolis" (*New York Naked* 17). The urban labyrinth, then, may be seen as a trap, or as another author described it, like the "mighty cataract" that rushes the insentient youth to ruin: "on, on, down, down; the brink is gained; one wild *hurrah* rises above the torrent's voice, and the young voyager makes the final, fatal, returnless plunge" (*Life in New York* 13). In the pattern established by Lippard, Judson, Foster, Whitman, and numerous writers of moral and reform literature, the hero's venture into the urban labyrinth leads him inevitably to disaster. Religious, family, or female influences may counterbalance the temptations of the city, bringing wisdom and reform, but not until the protagonist has suffered and experienced the worst in this "dark sea of licentiousness and dissipation" (*Gas-Light* 124).

Two particular aspects of this paradigm are important for a discussion of *Pierre*. This first is that this notion of the urban labyrinth serves the Christian and moral intentions of much reform literature, the literature that David S. Reynolds has called Conventional. Drawing on a medieval tradition that used the labyrinth typologically to represent the Christian journey toward salvation, it stresses the hero's vulnerability and proneness to error in a landscape created by a larger moral force, God or the devil, to test his faith. The labyrinth stands as an image either of man's fall or of man's progress toward salvation, but in either case its intricacy and difficulty serve the larger spiritual purposes of its divine creator. Furthermore, the hero has only limited power to choose his path or control the journey once it has started. The labyrinth works to fulfill the logic of his initial choice for redemption or error and bring him to the logical consequences of that choice. The hero may choose, then, whether to enter the labyrinth or not, but once inside he finds all paths leading to the inevitable conclusion. If he is good, he will succeed and triumph; if sinful, he will fall.[5]

The other implication of this construction of the labyrinth lies in its physical structure. In general, the Christian labyrinth has what Penelope Reed Doob defines as a unicursal design. That is, the labyrinth, though intricate, winding, and lengthy, does not offer the traveler significant choices: "Its structural basis is a single path, twisting and turning to the point of desperation but entailing no dead ends or choices between paths" (48). After making the initial choice to enter the labyrinth, the wanderer faces a landscape of circuitous paths and walls that block his vision and will undoubtedly cause confusion, but there are no wrong turns; the path leads inevitably to the center of the maze. Such a structure works perfectly to emphasize the consequences of a single choice, to place the burden for that choice on the individual but leave the design of its outcome to an ultimate force.

It should be clear how a unicursal design would support the moral intentions of reform literature, the mystery-and-misery novels, and other forms of urban labyrinth literature by offering a graphic display of the inevitable results of the provincial's bad decisions. By warning young readers away from the city's temptations, by stressing the miseries following upon youthful errors, moral reform literature might hope to influence the initial choice from which all others proceeded. A second model, however, the multicursal design, offered a more complex structure, one that "incorporates an extended series of *bivia,* an array of choices" (Doob 46). This structure would be useful in a Christian or moral framework too, but would add to the unicursal elements of confusion and error a wider range of possibilities. The traveler could move along a wrong path for quite awhile before discovering his error and having to retrace his steps; or he could experience the sweet triumph of having made a right turn after a series of wrong choices. Whereas the unicursal design leads the wanderer inevitably to the center or heart of the labyrinth, the multicursal structure might leave him perpetually trapped and lost, never knowing where the center is or if it exists. This model emphasizes the dubiousness and uncertainty of the whole enterprise, but it also offers opportunities for a different kind of heroism. The traveler of the unicursal maze need only hold firm to the original faith that brought him into the labyrinth to begin with, and he will arrive at his destination. The multicursal maze, however, rewards an ingenious mind, one that seeks a solution to the puzzle, that weighs choices and makes decisions, that persists in the face of continual challenges to faith. If used to test a Christian hero, it offers a chance for active, rather than passive, Christianity.

But such a model might challenge Christian virtue and faith to a dangerous degree. By offering more room for individual choice and action, it risks losing the hero to unwitting error. And a wily hero may subvert the moral purposes of the labyrinth altogether by finding his own way through it, by circumventing the intended spiritual journey entirely, as Theseus did by relying on Ariadne's ball of thread. By rewarding ingenuity, skill, and creative thinking, the multicursal labyrinth may breed just the traits that challenge passive faith, giving the individual faith in himself rather than in divine will. In any case, the added complexity of the multicursal structure will necessarily complicate the task, possibly obscuring its spiritual meaning or exhausting the traveler before he reaches his goal.

The two passages that head this essay represent young men on the verge of entering the perilous urban labyrinth of New York, but Whitman and Melville construe the labyrinth very differently. For Franklin Evans, as well as for may other provincial heroes of New York labyrinth novels by writers like Ned Buntline or George Lippard, the city is a unicursal, Christian labyrinth of temptation and sin where with one false step the unwary youth falls into an abyss. The hero may choose to resist temptation or not, but once he enters the Christian labyrinth, few further choices present themselves; everything develops from the moral logic of his initial step. Pierre too makes one false step, his decision to enter a pretended marriage with his supposed sister Isabel; he goes to New York to escape the worst consequences of this bold design. But Melville does not present Pierre as a passive innocent caught unwittingly in a Christian labyrinth of sin and temptation. Rather, he places Pierre in a position where he weighs his choices at every juncture. And because Pierre is given endless opportunities to make disastrous choices, the labyrinth grows logically out of his own decisions. Melville calls Pierre's labyrinth a Cretan, not a Christian, labyrinth. And, as we shall see, the Cretan labyrinth was built by human hands with mixed human motives. It is not the morally unambiguous landscape of Christian virtue and faith, but the dangerous, ambiguous, pre-Christian environment of deadly choice. The hero bears enormous responsibility for his own choices; he may be said, in fact, to play a role in the creation of the labyrinth itself by choosing his own path. In emphasizing Pierre's agency in creating his own labyrinth, Melville chronicles Pierre's chosen complicity in his ruin.

That process begins in the Melville passage that heads this essay, one of the most puzzling in the novel, when Pierre is making his fateful decision to marry Isabel. The narrator tells us that because of his youth Pierre lacks the calm resolve that would foresee the dangers of what he is doing. Instead he rushes recklessly into his new life, ignoring, "the thousand ulterior intricacies and emperilings to which it must conduct" (NN *Pierre* 175). With supreme confidence in the rightness of his choice, "this hapless youth [is] all eager to involve himself in such an inextricable twist of Fate, that the three dextrous maids themselves could hardly disentangle him, if once he tie the complicating knots about him and Isabel" (175). Certainly the narrator's tone warns of the dire consequences of Pierre's entering the labyrinth of an assumed marriage with his assumed sister. But in the next sentence the narrator implies that there are other labyrinths toward which Pierre could or ought to move: "Ah, thou rash boy! are there no couriers in the air to warn thee away from these emperilings, and point thee to those Cretan labyrinths, to which thy life's cord is leading thee? Where now are the high beneficences? Whither fled the sweet angels that are alledged guardians to man?" (176). This passage implies that Pierre's guardian angels, in directing him away from the intricacies and "emperilings" of his fateful decision, would lead him toward another labyrinth, the Cretan labyrinth to which his life's cord is leading him. Whatever Pierre chooses, then, he will find himself in a labyrinth. But the Cretan labyrinth calls for an especially high degree of choice.

The emphasis on choice, even a choice attended and aided by fates and angels, suggests what for Melville defines the experience of traveling through a labyrinth. The Cretan labyrinth tested a hero's skill and nerve by offering a structure of winding and roundabout paths called, in the works of Ovid and other classical writers, ambages, from *ambo,* meaning "two" or "both"; the ambage always offers the traveler a choice between two possible paths. The *Oxford Latin Dictionary* defines *ambages* as a technical term for a labyrinthine structure and also as a metaphor for labyrinthine forms of speech or experience: ". . . A roundabout or circuitous path, course, etc., meanderings, twists and turns. . . . Long-winded, obscure or evasive speech, a circumlocution, digression, evasion. . . . Mental confusion or uncertainty" (Doob 53). As this definition of the Latin term makes clear, the English *ambiguity* bears a direct linguistic relationship with the structure, experience, and language of the labyrinth. Ambiguity in this context means doubleness, causing doubt or uncertainty because of that doubleness. Calling his novel *Pierre, or the Ambiguities,* Melville suggests that Pierre is a man in a labyrinth: wandering, uncertain, and forced to choose between two paths. And *Pierre*'s language, often long-winded and obscure, full of circumlocution and evasion, appears to be the language of the labyrinth as well.

But Melville also makes it clear that Pierre's labyrinth, the one to which his life's cord is leading him, is a Cretan labyrinth and hence invokes the myth of Daedalus, Minos, Theseus, Ariadne, Pasiphäe, and her son the Minotaur. This myth reminds us that humans built the labyrinth, that it did not, as the antebellum New York authors of literary and Christian labyrinths often implied, simply appear. This human agency in the building of the labyrinth is important for our understanding of Pierre's agency in building his, and so I will review the myth.

In the story as told by Ovid, Pasiphäe, wife of Minos, fell in love with a bull. Daedalus constructed for her a wooden cow so that she could receive the bull's advances, and she bore a son, the Minotaur. Minos, enraged by this violation of marriage and nature, ordered Daedalus to build a labyrinth for the Minotaur; he then arranged to feed the monster tributary youths and maids from Athens. The Athenian hero Theseus, however, managed to kill the Minotaur with the help of Minos's daughter, Ariadne. Acting probably according to Daedalus's advice, she gave Theseus a ball of thread that allowed him to mark his path through the labyrinth. Although Theseus, Ariadne, and Daedalus had their difficulties after this successful outcome, the labyrinth remained a cultural monument and an enduring symbol of their triumph and skill.

The primary difficulty, however, in locating human agency in the creation of the labyrinth is identifying the builder and his motives. Daedalus, of course, designed the labyrinth; but Minos commissioned it, and if it had not been for Pasiphäe's love for a bull, Minos would not have wanted one in the first place. The labyrinth Minos had in mind served as a prison, foremost, for the dangerous Minotaur; but Minos also sought to hide the Minotaur, evidence of his cuckoldry and shame, from public view. Later, when he devised the idea of feeding his enemies to the Minotaur, the labyrinth became a slaughterhouse as well. Its intricacy, then, served several political purposes: to protect the Minotaur from intruders, to protect the public from the Minotaur, and eventually to create a grisly game or ritual out of the Minotaur's meals. That is the labyrinth that Minos commissioned, a construction to demonstrate and bolster his own power. But the labyrinth Daedalus built attests to his creative genius in designing a structure of wondrous intricacy and beauty. Daedalus created the labyrinth as a test of heroic ingenuity; the hero who can find his way deserves a kingdom. But finally, Daedalus made the labyrinth an artifact of desire—or what the temperance and reform writers might call temptation. It housed the offspring of Pasiphäe's desire for a bull, and it brought the passionate Ariadne and Theseus together in their successful conquest of the Minotaur. Thus, at the heart of Minos's labyrinth is power and death, at the heart of Daedalus's creativity and desire. Both forces are morally ambiguous, however, and in that sense most un-Christian. Minos represents the patriarchal power of the state oppressing young men and maids; but on the other hand he upholds marriage and family by punishing Pasiphäe and her son, and he strengthens Crete by subjugating Athens. Daedalus represents heroic ingenuity and unfettered desire, but at the same time he is powerless to prevent the human sacrifice and the disasters that threaten Theseus and Ariadne's love. The labyrinth, then, is doubly double in its ambiguous origins and its structure. There is no doubt, however, that it grows out of the mixed motives and failings of human beings, rather than from some divine intention, as in the Christian labyrinth.

Without referring again specifically to the Cretan labyrinth, Melville nevertheless implies that Pierre has in fact chosen a Cretan labyrinth, a succession of critical junctures and ambages, rather than the Christianized moral labyrinth, a single path moving inevitably from the initial false step toward the hero's ruin. In *Pierre* the labyrinth—the labyrinth of New York, but also Pierre's labyrinthine quest for truth—grows out of ambiguous human desires, as a creation of the imagination and an expression of human will. It is not something natural but something chosen, something created. By choosing Isabel, Pierre creates a moral, legal, and sexual labyrinth for himself; by attempting a novel that will explode moral and literary conventions, Pierre constructs a literary labyrinth that he can never penetrate or extricate himself from; and in entering enthusiastically into a condition of ambiguity, Pierre becomes mystified by his own creations. In its outlines, at least, Pierre's story does not seem that different from other urban tales of youthful ruin. But Melville makes one crucial distinction: his New York is not a *moral* labyrinth. Pierre fails in the city; Pierre is certainly wrong, but not for any moral reason that he acknowledges; nor does the narrator adopt the standard Christian moral tone toward his hero. Rather, Pierre learns that he was *mistaken*. He took the wrong path, not out of immoral motives—he considers his motives heroic and noble—but because at different critical ambages he could not see the right path.

An example of such an ambage appears in Book 14 when Pierre, traveling toward the city and clutching the pages of the as-yet-unread pamphlet by Plotinus Plinlimmon, contemplates his actions anew. Melville's narrator compares Pierre to a priest tempted by the Evil One who "propounded the possibility of the mere moonshine of all his self-renouncing Enthusiasm" (205). Pierre, however, lacks the priest's certain faith:

But Pierre—where could *he* find the Church, the monument, the Bible, which unequivocally said to him—"Go on; thou art in the Right; I endorse thee all over; go on"—So the difference between Priest and Pierre was herein:—with the priest it was a matter, whether certain bodiless thoughts of his were true or not true; but with Pierre it was a question whether certain vital acts of his were right or wrong. (205)

Pierre is certainly not amoral. He can weigh the moral choices and agonize over his decision: "'Lo! I leave corpses wherever I go!' groaned Pierre to himself—'Can then my conduct be right?'" (206) But no clear answer presents itself. At that point he reads the pamphlet, which tells him that "the only great original moral doctrine of Christianity (*i.e.* the chronometrical gratuitous return of good for evil, as distinguished from the horological forgiveness of injuries taught by some Pagan philosophers), has been found (horologically) a false one; because after 1800 years' inculcation from tens of thousands of pulpits, it has proved entirely impracticable" (215). Pierre believes this practical philosophy is wrong and that he is morally right to persist in his course. He has made a moral choice, informed by Scriptural considerations. But he learns later that he has taken the wrong path after all. Clearly, then, as this and other choices show, he has entered a multicursal labyrinth where one can take a path that looks promising only to find it a dead end.

Melville's narrator views Pierre's predicament with a mixture of compassion and sarcastic contempt that suggests Daedalus's ambiguous moral position. For Daedalus, the labyrinth is an aesthetic triumph of engineering skill. Presumably he admires his own creation and would be unwilling to see someone succeed in penetrating its mysteries. In fact, legend suggests that Daedalus did not himself know how to find his way through the labyrinth and could watch people losing their way with only helpless regret. The solution he proposed to Ariadne (unless she thought of it herself) had a certain horological efficacy, a "virtuous expediency" (*Pierre* 214), but it cheated not only Minos and the Minotaur but also Daedalus's design. The narrator's mockery of Pierre's motives and efforts to succeed, particularly at writing a great novel but also in attaining his metaphysical goals, shows the creator's critical eye. He vents on Pierre, whom he scathingly calls the Fool of Virtue, Civilization's victim, much the same jealousy that Daedalus exhibited toward his nephew Talus, another ingenious designer who threatened to compete with Daedalus's own skill. Daedalus killed Talus, and Melville kills Pierre, an image of his own metaphysical and literary strivings.[6] Although Melville's narrator periodically shows considerable sympathy for his protagonist, identifying with his creative struggles, he also regards him with a detachment and irony that seem to come from an aesthetic rather than a moral point of view.

That irony appears most strikingly in the way he frames Pierre's fall. For in an ingenious twist, Pierre is undone by his own Daedalian skill in creating and penetrating mystery. Like the protagonist of the conventional urban novel, Pierre is led astray in the bewildering city. But what led him astray? Paradoxically, Pierre is led astray by the literature of mystery and misery, by the very labyrinth literature of which the novel *Pierre* might seem to be an example.

In his youth, we learn early in the novel, Pierre read widely in the literature of mystery and misery, beginning with somewhat elite forms of the genre: "the sublime Italian, Dante, . . . had first opened to his shuddering eyes the infinite cliffs and gulfs of human mystery and misery" (54). But he also soaked up more popular works; in fact, he has "read more novels than most people of his years" (141). These have convinced him that life is full of "enigmas that the stars themselves, and perhaps the highest seraphim can not resolve" (139); and when he meets Isabel, the very personification of Mystery and Misery herself, his extensive reading has prepared him to enter enthusiastically into her "unraveled plot" (141). She teaches him to reject the labyrinths of popular literature, however, for "the countless tribes of common novels laboriously spin vails of mystery, only to complacently clear them up at last" (141). Pierre wants to move beyond such common labyrinths into a labyrinth of the "profounder emanations of the human mind . . . [that] never unravel their own intricacies, and have no proper endings" (141). Such a quest requires, however, that he enter the ambiguous labyrinth of New York, for in the country his actions will be judged simply as immoral. In the city he hopes to find success, not only in carrying out his unconventional scheme of marrying Isabel but in creating a literary labyrinth of his own, a novel that will tell the truth that others have obscured.

Instead he fails. His novel attracts only disgust, and eventually his fiancee Lucy and all her relatives catch up with him and expose his actions as immoral. But never does Pierre acknowledge that he has done anything wrong, nor does he undergo the customary moral collapse of the unwary provincial trapped in an urban labyrinth. On the contrary, he avoids the usual temptations of gambling, seduction, and drinking, because he has enthusiastically adopted his own higher, metaphysical versions of these urban sins. Instead of gambling in dens of infamy, he gambles his soul and the welfare of three women on his own metaphysical quest for truth; instead of submitting to the seductions of prostitutes, he submits to the seductions of Isabel's mysteries; and instead of the more typical intoxications of the tavern, he allows himself to be intoxicated by his own philosophical speculations. But always he assumes himself to be in the right because he has undertaken these questionable actions heroically. He consistently asserts the power and rightness of his choice, and the narrator, though mocking him for his foolishness, does not judge him morally any more than Pierre does himself.

When Pierre discovers he may be wrong, however, at that critical moment when a coincidental resemblance between Isabel and a portrait of a gentleman causes him to ask, "How did he know that Isabel was his sister?" (353), he questions his choices. He begins to see that his conviction of her identity came from a "nebulous legend," "his own dim reminiscences of his wandering father's death-bed," and most damaging of all, "his own manifold and interenfolding mystic and transcendental persuasions—originally born, as he now seemed to feel, purely of an intense procreative enthusiasm—an enthusiasm no longer so all-potential with him as of yore" (353). Tom Wolfe's Sherman McCoy comes to a similar discovery: he is *not* the Master of the Universe. Now Pierre begins to see his own complicity in the creation of Isabel's mysteries and miseries. But even more than that, he recognizes her art in mystery-making because he has acquired it himself. In developing his own skill in creating literary mysteries, he learns to penetrate the labyrinth he wandered in with her; now he is suspicious of her mysteries: ". . . especially since he had got so deep into the inventional mysteries of his book. For . . . he who professionally deals in mysticisms and mysteries himself; often that man, more than any body else, is disposed to regard such things in others as very deceptively bejuggling" (353–54). Somewhat like Plotinus Plinlimmon, then, Pierre has become a professional in the creation of mystery and misery; his own skill exposes Isabel's fiction-making as amateur. A true Theseus, he learns Daedalus's secret and can leave the labyrinth.

At this ambage in his progress, however, Pierre chooses the path to annihilation, again not because he has finally succumbed to the sins of the city, as the Christian narrator would stress, but because he wants to. The murder of his enemies Glen Stanly and Frederic Tartan seals his doom but also releases him from the false situation in which he has been living with Isabel and Lucy. This act, paradoxically, brings him to the heart of the labyrinth, the prison, but he finds that New York is not the labyrinth Daedalus created, the sanctuary of creativity and desire, but rather the labyrinth Minos envisioned, the world of law and death. He has decided the outcome, however, and at each point of the journey made the choice that brought him to the labyrinth's heart. There is no sense, as in the conventional urban fictions, that the labyrinth drew him in. He marched.

Melville's novel then, deliberately challenges the Christian framework of conventional urban fiction. Instead of using Pierre's drastic fate in the urban labyrinth as a moral warning against the city's temptations, he shows someone who chooses disaster as the solution to his personal and metaphysical crisis. Like Theseus, Pierre undergoes a quest that exposes the moral ambiguity at the heart of the labyrinth. Pierre perishes in a bonfire of vanities, but not for lack of skill in threading the paths of New York's labyrinth. In fact, it is his skill in penetrating the city's mysteries and miseries that brings him to his sensational demise. Primarily for that reason, for its mockery of the moral urban quest, Melville's novel has escaped the labyrinth of popularity.

NOTES

1. For discussion of the literature of mystery and misery, see Giamo; Reynolds; Siegel; and Stout. I have adapted much of what follows from my chapter "Provincial in a Labyrinth" in *Melville's City*.

2. I emphasize that Pierre is the first of Melville's characters to make this discovery about the urban labyrinth because I consider Redburn and White-Jacket earlier urban explorers, Redburn in the cities of New York, Liverpool, and London and White-Jacket on a ship that Melville identifies with New York and other cities. Both may be said to wander in labyrinths, but neither penetrates the meaning of the labyrinth in the way that Pierre does.

3. Although I have used the male pronoun throughout this essay, in deliberate reference to the Thesean model of labyrinth-hero, women did have an important place in the literature of mystery and misery, temperance, urban reform, and sensational fiction. For discussions of the role of women in urban culture in New York, see Rosenberg; Ryan; Stansell; and Wilson.

4. See Belden; Jones; Kouwenhoven; Spann; and Stokes.

5. I am indebted to Penelope Reed Doob for this summary of the medieval tradition of labyrinth literature and for the discussion of unicursal and multicursal labyrinths.

6. Talus, of course, reappears in "The Bell Tower" as the Bannadonna's "iron slave" (NN *PT* 184). In this story, however, "the creator was killed by the creature" (NN *PT* 187).

WORKS CITED

Belden, E. Porter. *New York: Past, Present, and Future.* New York: George Putnam, 1849.

Dickens, Charles. *American Notes and Pictures from Italy.* New York: Dutton, 1970.

Doob, Penelope Reed. *The Idea of the Labyrinth from Classical Antiquity through the Middle Ages.* Ithaca: Cornell UP, 1990.

Foster, George. *New York by Gas-Light.* Ed. Stuart M. Blumin. Berkeley: U of California P, 1990.

———. *New York Naked.* New York: Robert M. DeWitt, 1854.

Giamo, Benedict. *On the Bowery: Confronting Homelessness in American Society.* Iowa City: U of Iowa P, 1989.

Jones, Pamela. *Under the City Streets.* New York: Holt, Rinehart, and Winston, 1978.

Judson, E. Z. C. *The Mysteries and Miseries of New York.* New York: Berford, 1848.

Kelley, Wyn. *Melville's City: Literary and Urban Form in Nineteenth-Century New York.* New York: Cambridge UP, 1996.

Kouwenhoven, John. *The Columbia Historical Portrait of New York: An Essay in Graphic History.* New York: Doubleday, 1953.

Life in New York. New York: Robert Carter, 1847.

Lippard, George. *The Empire City: or, New York by Night and Day. Its Aristocracy and Its Dollars.* Freeport, NY: Books for Libraries Press, 1969.

———. *New York: Its Upper Ten and Lower Million.* Upper Saddle River, NJ: Literature House/Gregg Press, 1970.

"New York Daguerreotyped." *Putnam's Monthly Magazine* 1 (February 1853).

Reynolds, David S. *Beneath the American Renaissance: The Subversive Imagination in the Age of Emerson and Melville.* Cambridge: Harvard UP, 1989.

Rosenberg, Carroll Smith. *Religion and the Rise of the American City.* Ithaca: Cornell UP, 1971.

Ross, Joel. *What I Saw in New York: or, A Bird's Eye View of City Life.* Auburn, NY: Derby and Miller, 1851.

Ryan, Mary. *Women in Public: Between Banners and Ballots, 1825–1880.* Baltimore: Johns Hopkins UP, 1990.

Siegel, Adrienne. *The Image of the American City in Popular Literature, 1820–1870.* Port Washington, NY: Kennikat Press, 1981.

Spann, Edward K. *The New Metropolis: New York City, 1840–1857.* New York: Columbia UP, 1981.

Stansell, Christine. *City of Women: Sex and Class in New York, 1789–1850.* New York: Knopf, 1986.

Stokes, Isaac Newton Phelps. *The Iconography of Manhattan Island, 1498–1909.* New York: R. H. Dodd, 1915.

Stout, Janis. *Sodoms in Eden: The City in American Fiction before 1860.* Westport, CT: Greenwood, 1976.

Whitman, Walt. *Franklin Evans, or The Inebriate: A Tale of the Times.* Ed. Jean Downey. New Haven: Collegiate Press, 1978.

Wilson, Elizabeth. *The Sphinx in the City: Urban Life, the Control of Disorder, and Women.* Berkeley: U of California P, 1991.

Wolfe, Tom. *The Bonfire of the Vanities.* New York: Farrar Strauss Giroux, 1987.

Contributors

JEAN ASHTON is director of the Rare Book and Manuscript Library of Columbia University. Since receiving her Ph.D. in 1971, she has held a variety of jobs in research libraries, including the Library of The New-York Historical Society, where she was librarian from 1991 to 1993. She has written on Stowe, James, Melville, and P. T. Barnum.

WALTER E. BEZANSON has been a leading scholar-critic of Melville for more than fifty years. Professor Emeritus of American Studies and English at Rutgers University, he edited the Hendricks House *Clarel* in 1960, rescuing the poem from long oblivion, and authored the Historical Note in the Northwestern-Newberry *Israel Potter* (1982) and the Historical and Critical Note and Supplementary Discussions in the Northwestern-Newberry *Clarel* (1991). Among his many essays and articles on Melville is the landmark "*Moby-Dick:* Work of Art" (1951).

DAVID BRADLEY received a B.A. in creative writing from the University of Pennsylvania in 1972 and an M.A. in U.S. studies from the University of London in 1974. He is the author of two novels, *South Street* (1975) and *The Chaneysville Incident* (1981), which was awarded the 1982 PEN/Faulkner Prize.

RICHARD BRODHEAD is A. Bartlett Giamatti Professor of English at Yale University and dean of Yale College. His previous writings on Melville include *Hawthorne, Melville, and the Novel* (1976) and *The School of Hawthorne* (1985).

JOHN BRYANT, professor of English at Hofstra University an editor of *Melville Society Extracts*, is the author of *Melville and Repose: The Rhetoric of Humor in the American Renaissance* (1993) and of articles on Melville in *American Literature, Nineteeth-Century Fiction, Philological Quarterly*, and other journals and is the editor of a collection of scholarly, critical, and bibliographical essays on Melville, *A Companion to Melville Studies* (1986).

LAWRENCE BUELL is John P. Marquand Professor of English at Harvard University. He has published extensively on nineteenth-century American literature and is the author of *Literary Transcendentalism* (1973), *New England Literary Culture* (1986), and *The Environmental Imagination* (1995).

SHIRLEY M. DETTLAFF, who received her doctorate from the University of Southern California, has taught English at Glendale High School in California since 1963. Her publications on Melville include "Ionian Form and Esau's Waste: Melville's View of Art in *Clarel*" (*American Literature* 1982) and "Melville's Aesthetics" in Bryant, ed., *A Companion to Melville Studies.*

WAI CHEE DIMOCK, professor of English at Yale University, is the author of *Empire for Liberty: Melville and the Politics of Individualism* (1989) and *Residues of Justice: Literature, Law, Philosophy* (1994), along with a wide range of essays on American literature and culture.

H. BRUCE FRANKLIN, John Cotton Dana Professor of English and American Studies at Rutgers University, Newark, is the author or editor of seventeen books on culture and history. A past president of the Melville Society, he has been publishing on Melville since 1961.

STANTON GARNER is visiting professor of American literature at Southwest Texas State University in San Marcos, Texas, having previously taught at Brown University, at the United States Naval Academy, and in the University of Texas system. Author of *Harold Frederic* and general editor of the Harold Frederic Edition, he has written widely on Melville and is a former secretary and president of the Melville Society. His book *The Civil War World of Herman Melville* appeared in 1993.

LYNN HORTH is assistant professor of English at Principia College in Elsah, Illinois, and is editor of the Northwestern-Newberry edition of Melville's *Correspondence* (1993).

WYN KELLEY, who teaches in the Department of Literature at the Massachusetts Institute of Technology, has published essays in *American Literature, Resources for American Literary Studies, Partisan Review,* and *Melville Society Extracts*, of which she is assistant editor. She is the author of *Melville's City: Literary and Urban Form in Nineteenth-Century New York* (1996) and is also a contributor to the forthcoming *Cambridge Companion to Melville.* She is currently working on a study of the Melville family correspondence.

ROBERT MILDER is professor of English at Washington University in St. Louis. His writings on Melville include "Herman Melville" in *The Columbia Literary History of the United States* and *Critical Essays on Herman Melville's "Billy Budd, Sailor"* (1989) and articles on *Moby-Dick, Pierre, Battle-Pieces,* and *Billy Budd.* He is also the author of *Reimagining Thoreau* (1995).

SAMUEL OTTER, associate professor of English at the University of California, Berkeley, has published on Melville in *American Literature* and other journals. His book *Melville's Anatomics* is forthcoming from the University of California Press.

HERSHEL PARKER is H. Fletcher Brown Professor at the University of Delaware and associate general editor of the Northwestern-Newberry *Writings of Herman Melville.* He is the author of *Flawed Texts and Verbal Icons* (1984) and *Reading "Billy Budd"* (1990) and an editor of *The Norton Anthology of American Literature* (1994). The first volume of his biography *Herman Melville: 1819–1851* appeared in 1996, and he is at work on *Herman Melville: 1851–1891* and on *The New Melville Log.* His edition of *Pierre,* illustrated by Maurice Sendak, was published in 1995.

ARNOLD RAMPERSAD is professor of English at Princeton University, where he has served as director of American Studies and of Afro-American Studies. He is the author or editor of several volumes, including the two-volume *The Life of Langston Hughes.*

ROBERT C. RYAN is a former associate professor of English at Boston University. A scholar of Melville's poetry, he joins Frank Goodman and Charlie Noble in expressing confidence that the Northwestern-Newberry edition of the *Published Poems,* which he is editing, will appear in his lifetime.

MERTON M. SEALTS, JR., Henry A. Pochmann Professor of English, Emeritus, at the University of Wisconsin-Madison, is a preeminent scholar-critic and editor of Melville and Emerson. His publications include the important University of Chicago Edition of *Billy Budd, Sailor* (with Harrison Hayford, 1962), *Melville's Reading* (1966; rev. ed. 1988), *The Early Lives of Melville* (1974), *Pursuing Melville, 1940–1980* (1982), the Historical Note to the Northwestern-Newberry Edition of *The Piazza Tales and Other Prose Pieces* (1987), and *Beyond the Classroom: Essays on American Authors* (1996).

JOHN SEELYE, novelist and professor of English at the University of Florida, is the author of, among other works, *Melville: The Ironic Diagram* (1970), *Prophetic Waters* (1977), and *Beautiful Machine: Rivers and the Republican Plan, 1775–1825* (1991).

G. THOMAS TANSELLE, vice president of the John Simon Guggenheim Memorial Foundation and adjunct professor of English at Columbia University, is one of the three co-editors of the Northwestern-Newberry Edition of Melville. Among his writings on textual matters are *A Rationale of Textual Criticism* and *Textual Criticism and Scholarly Editing.*

DONALD YANNELLA, former editor of *Melville Society Extracts* and Distinguished Professor of English at Barat College, is the author of *Ralph Waldo Emerson* (1982) and, with Hennig Cohen, of *Herman Melville's Malcolm Letter* (1992).

Index

Melville's Evermoving Dawn

was designed by Will Underwood;

composed in 10/13 Adobe Minion

on a Macintosh Power PC system with PostScript output

by The Book Page, Inc.;

printed by sheet-fed offset lithography

on 50-pound Glatfelter Natural Hi Bulk acid-free stock,

notch bound over 88-point binder's boards

in ICG Arrestox B-grade cloth,

and wrapped with dust jackets printed in two colors

on 100-pound enamel stock finished with matte film lamination

by Braun-Brumfield, Inc.;

and published by

The Kent State University Press

KENT OHIO 44242